Reading African American Literature

Reading African American Literature

JOSH DICKINSON, SBCTC, AND LUMEN LEARNING

Cover Image credit: Abstract blue geometric shapes by Starline. This cover has been designed using resources from Freepik.com.

Published by State University of New York Press, Albany

Printed in the United States of America

Contents

About This Book i
How to Use This Book ii
Reading African American Literature iii

1. Reading and Interpreting Literary Texts

Academic Writing Review 2
Not Taking Sides is Like the Beetlejuice Waiting Room Scene. . . 4
Tragedy and Comedy 6
When Interpreting, Avoid Relativism (Because I Think So) 9
Literary Terms: A Guide 10
How to Avoid Plagiarizing 18
How to Analyze a Short Story 20
Literary Criticism 23
A Short History of the Early American Novel 31
Connecting Reading & Writing: The Voice You Hear Response 34
Approaching Poetry 36
Proper Source Use in Paragraphs 56
Annotation: Why Mark Up Your Texts? 59
With Analysis, Focus Upon Functions or Effects 60
Paragraph Menu Settings Use No Extra Vertical Spaces 61
Analysis is the Breaking Down of a Whole into its Parts 62
Binary Patterns: A Western Obsession 64
Video: The American Enlightenment 66
Irony 67
Free Verse 69
Critical Approaches to Literature Chart 70

2. Tricksters, Humor, Myths, and Folktales

Papa Legba 74
Tips for Reading Mythology 75
Same Old Story?: Propp Fairy Tale Analysis 76
Schooly D, Signifying Rapper 78
African Myths and Folktales 79
YG FTP 80

YG - Blood Walk feat. Lil Wayne & D3szn 81
Shaking up the World: Trickster Tales, by Terri Windling 82
Dave Chappelle, When Keepin' it Real can go Very Wrong 83
Dick Gregory: Race, Comedy, & Justice 84

3. Slave Narratives & Voices of Resistance

History of American Literature 86
Resistance and Abolition 90
The Interesting Narrative of the Life of Olaudah Equiano 91
Harriet Jacobs, Incidents in the Life of a Slave Girl 92
The Narrative of Sojourner Truth 93
Video: Frederick Douglass 94
Narrative of the Life of Frederick Douglass, an American Slave 95
American Slave Narratives: An Online Anthology 142

4. Literary Nonfiction

The 1619 Project 144
Booker T. Washington, Up From Slavery 145
W. E. B. Du Bois, The Souls of Black Folk 146
Zora Neale Hurston, Mules and Men 147
Zora Neale Hurston, "Origin of Hoodoo" 148
James Baldwin, Letter from a Region in My Mind 152
Amirah Mercer, 5 Times James Baldwin Read America 153
David Walker, An Appeal to the Coloured Citizens of the World, Article IV 154
Richard Wright, I Choose Exile 170
Ida B. Wells-Barnett, The Red Record, 1. The Case Stated 171
George S. Schuyler, Black No More 176
Ralph Ellison, Hidden Name and Complex Fate 177
Malcolm X, How I Learned to Read 178
Martin Luther King Jr., Three Ways of Meeting Oppression 179
Toni Morrison Interview (1977) 180
Toni Morrison, Nobel Prize for Literature Lecture 181
Alice Walker, Beauty: When the Other Dancer is the Self 182
Gloria Naylor, The Meanings of a Word 183
Ta-Nehisi Coates, The Case for Reparations 184

5. Poetry Readings

Paul Laurence Dunbar Poems 186
Countee Cullen Poems 191

Angelina Weld Grimké, The Black Finger 192
Sterling Brown Poems 193
Jean Toomer Poems 194
Jessie Redmon Fauset Poems 195
Langston Hughes Poems 196
Lucille Clifton Poems 197
Amiri Baraka Poems 198
Maya Angelou Poems 199
Ishmael Reed Poems 200
Rita Dove Poems 201

6. Fiction

Alice Dunbar-Nelson, A Carnival Jangle 204
Paul Laurence Dunbar, The Scapegoat 207
Charles W. Chesnutt, The Goophered Grapevine & Po' Sandy 215
Jean Toomer, Cane 228
Alice Walker, Everyday Use 301
Toni Cade Bambara, Gorilla, My Love 302

7. Drama

Angelina Weld Grimké, Rachel: A Play in Three Acts 304
Amiri Baraka, Dutchman 305

8. Criticism and Literary Theory

Slavery to Liberation: The African-American Experience 308
Langston Hughes, The Negro Artist and the Racial Mountain 309
Zora Neale Hurston, What White Publishers Won't Print 310
Ambrose Olumuyiwa Faturoti, Renaissance Collage 311
Zora Neale Hurston, Characteristics of Negro Expression 312
bell hooks, Postmodern Blackness 313
Paul Fry, African-American Criticism 314
Henry Wiencek, The Dark Side of Thomas Jefferson 315
Norman W. Powell, Concepts of Beauty: Black and White Connotations 316

9. Student Resources

Six Tips for Being a Better Literature Student 318
Defining Literature 319
Self-Diagnosis of One's Writing Ailments can be Fun! 321

Experiencing Literature 322
Here are Some Dos and Don'ts Graders Think Through 324
Signal Phrases 326
Reader-Response Criticism 327

10. Writing About Literature

Introduction to Writing About Literature 334
Finding Literary Criticism 335
Using Modern Language Association (MLA) Style 337
Works Cited Entries: What to Include 343
How not to Write the Introduction and Conclusion 344
Using Sources: Blending Source Material with Your Own Work 345
The Paragraph Body: Supporting Your Ideas 346
How Might I Avoid Letting Source Use Take Over? 352
Checklist: Using Quotations Effectively 354

About the Author 355

Welcome!

Prior to my adaptation, this course was created from materials originally developed by the State Board of Community Technical Colleges (SBCTC) of Washington State. *American Literature 1* is a modified version of the Lumen *American Literature I* text. The original version of this book was released under a CC-BY license and is copyright by Lumen Learning. Only a few parts of the original Lumen text are included, as all the primary sources and most of the lecture material (unless otherwise noted) is from me.

The changes to this book listed are released under a CC-BY-SA license and are copyright by Joshua Dickinson of Jefferson Community College in Watertown, NY. I also adapted a *Writer's Handbook* resource for the College that goes into far more depth in coverage of the writing process and MLA style. This and the other dozen OER texts I created are available at: https://sunyjefferson.libguides.com/JCCOERtextbooks

List of Changes

- Added several student resources, including every part *except* Reader-Response Criticism.
- Added the following lectures to the Reading and Responding to Literary Texts part: Academic Writing Review; Troubleshoot Your Reading; Not Taking Sides is Like That Beetlejuice Waiting Room Scene. . . ; Tragedy and Comedy; How to Avoid Plagiarizing; When Interpreting, Avoid Relativism (Because I Think So); Proper Source Use in Paragraphs; Connecting Reading & Writing: The Voice You Hear Response; With Analysis, Focus Upon Functions or Effects; Analysis is a Breaking Down of a Whole into its Parts; Paragraph Menu Settings Use No Extra Spaces; and Annotation: Why Mark Up Your Texts?; and Irony.
- In the Writing About Literature section, added Works Cited Entries: What to Include; Checklist: Using Quotations Effectively; How not to Write the Introduction and Conclusion; Using Sources: Blending Source Material With Your Own Work; The Paragraph Body: Supporting Your Ideas; and How Might I Avoid Letting Sources Take Over?
- Updated the About the Author section to End Matter.

Where possible, I listed URLs as well as hyperlinking so that users of print copies of the text could locate the source.

You are free to use, modify or adapt any of this material providing the terms of the Creative Commons licenses are adhered to, acknowledging that those parts which are by me.

How to Use This Book

How to Use This Text

Reading African American Literature is meant to accompany book length explorations of Black literature. In my community-college course, I would pair this OER resource with drama, as well as a novel such as William Attaway's *Blood on the Forge*, an account of the Great Migration and Pittsburgh steel strikes. The text's aim is not to cover every major voice, but to present enough genres and figures that the arc of African-American literary history could be covered sufficiently well. For example, early in a course, I might focus heavily on mythology from Africa, the origins of rap and hip hop, and how openly political art can compromise its quality. This in turn would bring up discussions of quality, Western literary standards, and binaries. The OER has only slight coverage of those matters, but enough with which to begin a course. Different instructors can use the readings as a sort of skeletal structure on which to build their own approaches. There are numerous Creative Commons images in the book which may be useful for discussion or classroom activities.

Inclusion of Jean Toomer's book *Cane* works well for students, since it includes poetry and explicit use of the blues. Other works are linked. If any of the links fails to function, users can search for the work on the web, often by adding "PDF" to a query. There are several chapters focused on the conventions of academic writing and literary analysis.

I adopt *The New York Times* editorial convention of capitalizing *Black*. Following recent convention, I use *African American* without the hyphen unless the words are part of a compound adjective.

Genre chapters could be broken up into a theme-based course, as there are many obvious thematic connections among them. Alternately, a historical organization could be fashioned from them. The more thorough slave narrative selection brings up questions of authorship, identity, and representation that can be applied to any of the later readings. This OER is being created for a recently-approved class at Jefferson Community College, so it is going to reflect the strengths and weak points of that newness.

Users of Open Educational Resources often find navigation of the books to be difficult, especially if the OER is included in a learning management system like Blackboard. Electronic use of the book as a PDF allows for easy navigation using CNTRL F (find command) searches. Instructors should be aware that page numbering can differ among texts due to text sizing. Most OERs are also available in both print or EPUB formats. The latter can be used easily on tablets.

Since the goals of OER include making quality materials accessible to more students and encouraging adaptation, I would welcome any feedback on the text, its blind spots, or usability issues. Contact me at jdickinson@sunyjefferson.edu or by calling (315) 786-2221. Thanks!

Reading African American Literature

1. READING AND INTERPRETING LITERARY TEXTS

Academic Writing Review

Remember these items as you edit your essay. They can make a big difference. I hope this sort of things helps. It's incomplete, but it's a start.

Think of the purpose of your paper, and of how each paragraph helps you fulfill it. As I mentioned elsewhere, the essays in the book aren't pure models for the academic writing we will be doing. What we write should look more solid, even if it is less flashy. You'll need to cite details and quickly follow up on their meanings through strong interpretation of the cited material. Topic sentences and transitions are key elements as well.

Thesis/Introduction

- Set up your thesis; it's best to place it near/at the end of the introduction.
- Two-part introductions or other types of unconventional introductions tend not to work. Why? The writer tends not to do the jobs of the introduction. These include previewing the rest of the essay, setting up the thesis (and showing other sides to the point you're trying to prove).
- Make sure your introduction promises what you'll do. (Don't say "In this essay I'll. . ." or "First, I'll discuss," though. Just go ahead and start previewing the paper.)
- Avoid using "I" as much as possible.
- "Don't use don't." Avoid contractions–as I haven't in this posting!
- "Oh, I almost forgot." Be careful of the formal writing voice you need to use. Don't sound chatty. I want you to write more formally than you are in your postings.

Thesis Checklist

With the thesis statement, keep the following questions in mind. They might work for most academic writing. Get good at asking follow-up questions of your own so that you can edit your work.

- Is it a statement?
- Is it a complex sentence? (Most good thesis statements provide an overview of what you'll go into. Therefore, most good thesis statements need to be complex sentences.)
- Does it take into account your 2-3 main reasons? (These are usually your body paragraph topics, right?)
- Does it take different sides into account? You want to appear fair, and the thesis is a great place for you to frame the merits and weak points of contending sides.
- Where will you locate this statement? Usually, though not always, we put the thesis either at the end of the introduction, or near the end. This allows us to set up the thesis carefully. Your introduction should take care to preview what you'll get into in the body paragraphs, just as the conclusion reviews what you did.

Paragraphing

- Starting/ending paragraphs with quotes is often a warning sign. Why is that?
    - When editing, check for strong topic sentences. Are they there? (Go a step further: did your major topics make it into the introduction as preview material, and into the conclusion as review?)
    - Citing properly matters. If readers are wondering where a source begins or ends, they are not attending to the content you chose to cite. Their job of appreciating what you brought to the essay is made impossible by citing problems.
    - Do interpret between quotes. Avoid stacking two or three quotes. I'm more interested in what you have to write about the quotes than what's in the quotes.

- Fix the problems with Smart Quotes. (See that mini-lecture in Module 1.)
- Are your paragraphs connected directly to the thesis? How? (Is the connection clear enough?)
- End paragraphs well. (Consider **transitions** as well as restatement of topic sentence.)

Interpretation

Perhaps the biggest frustration is that many of you include great quotes. They're promising, they're useful, they're. . . sitting there! Use the words in the quote. Get readers to see their meaning. If you aren't doing some work at this level, then you aren't interpreting. Good readers are waiting for you to prove your points through close reading of the text. (Sell us on what the words mean. That takes some time.)

Conclusion

- Lack of a conclusion will seriously affect your readers' reactions to the essay (and thus, your grade).
- I value strong conclusions that restate your points and remind readers about *how* you proved your claim(s).
- Do not add new information to the conclusion.
- Restate your thesis at a strategic point. Otherwise, readers will not remember your work soon afterwards–or a week from now.
- Be detailed: this is where you remind us of what you did.
- Don't write two or three sentences and "be done with it."

Not Taking Sides is Like the Beetlejuice Waiting Room Scene. . .

It is important that we recognize the benefits and limitations of methodology. Likely, you know your major discipline's approaches well. There are ways of being recognized or not. For instance, in *Jeopardy* contests, one has to phrase the answer in the form of a question. In discussion postings, many instructors require the post subject to be in sentence form. In *Fast Times at Ridgemont High*, Jeff Spicoli, the surfer doesn't recognize his little brother: "Curtis, you know I don't hear you unless you knock. . . " (Heckerling). In science, hypotheses have to be provable. In academic writing, thesis claims must be both provable and arguable.

I'm reminded of the notion of Purgatory, an invention of Dante in his *La Divina Commedia* (*Divine Comedy*). This gets played up famously in *Beetlejuice* and its waiting room scene:

A YouTube element has been excluded from this version of the text. You can view it online here: https://africanamericanlit.pressbooks.sunycreate.cloud/?p=26

What's interesting is that this echoes Dante, who puts people who failed to distinguish themselves into Hell. For Dante's Italians, not choosing was worse than choosing an opposite side to one's preferred side. Strangely enough, we are often more knowledgeable of our opponents–more tolerant of them, even–than of those who never choose. He even puts the neutral angels into Hell. In that era (1300 Florence), he even put living people into Hell, claiming that these people were so bad that demons inhabited their bodies and they were already in hell.

So these ideas can receive dogmatic answers. They get recognized or not, but over time they accrete meaning, slow down, and become concrete. (No *Dogma* references necessary. . .)

What I find interesting is that we're often struggling with the abstract rules of MLA style in the same way.

As with science, though, we can essentialize this a bit: We are always already entering ongoing conversations. We do have to be for or against something. Likely ways of being against something are going to lead to tone issues and assumptions about audience agreement.

As the *Beetlejuice* move states, “Take a number!” and “It’s showtime!” (Burton).

Tragedy and Comedy

Tragedy isn't Accidental

"That was such a tragic accident." Huh?

Tragedy is a balloon word, like "culture" or "freedom." It has been used in so many ways that its exact meaning is lost. I'll expect you to be more precise with it. Know its roots. Tragedy and comedy are complementary forms. Stemming from early drama (with its rituals), a tragic protagonist makes a choice which leads to their eventual, inevitable destruction. Conversely, comedy's choices are about marriage and sex. There is usually a marriage at the end of a comedy—they are life-affirming in a positive way.

Typically, tragic protagonists fall from on high and we enjoy watching this inevitable, choice-driven event while noticing the characteristic within them that led to it. In this way, tragedy is much like blues music, where we might feel joy at hearing that someone is "diggin' my potatoes" (cheating on the singer with "his" woman). The Greeks called this *catharsis*, a ritual purging (out both ends, grossly enough, but we politely think of the upper one).

What Tragedies Accomplish

Tragedies are life-affirming in a negative sense. The "body count" at the end usually evokes "pity" and "terror." Aristotle used these terms, and we still do today. And why do we feel good after a tragedy? Why, it didn't happen to us! That's one reason. Another is that we shared in someone's suffering, and this causes us to reflect on things. Are there many ways in which Americans communally share anything? How much more individualized are we now than we were 100 years ago?

Genres and categories like tragedy and comedy are artificially applied to much modern literature, and to all NA literature. When a Mohawk writer is intentionally using tragedy, they are also using their Mohawk culture and mixing in elements from white culture, too. How are readers going to separate these threads? Is it even possible? Do you see what an interesting mess this provides for us as readers? It's not necessarily a bad thing that we can't get easy answers.

Problems Using Terms like Tragedy

Not only is tragedy a misused term, then, but when applied to another world literature–like Native American literature–it becomes problematic. If we can test some of these, we won't have to rely on problem terms like "tragedy" that much.

I'd like you to leave this lecture as a seeker for the tragic and the non-tragic in their properly literary senses, and not merely the pop culture idea of good/bad, which is oversimplified.

What of Comedy, Then?

Well, comedy is easy. . . it's about union, with most comedies featuring sexual union occurring offstage while the wedding guests joke about how long it will take till the wife starts cheating on the husband. It's a strange genre, really, with old people trying to create matches for the young, often involving their older friends marrying to maintain wealth and control. Critic Northrop Frye on comedy: "A comedy is not a play which ends happily: it is a play in which a certain structure is present and works through to its own logical end [. . .]"

Frye's Use of Mythical Cycles–and I'm not talking Harleys!

Frye continues, connecting comedy and tragedy with the workings of the four seasons.

> The mythical backbone of all literature is the cycle of nature, which rolls from birth to death and back again to rebirth. The first half of this cycle, the movement from birth to death, spring to winter, dawn to dark, is the basis of the great alliance of nature and reason, the sense of nature as a rational order in which all movement is toward the increasingly predictable . . . [T]ragedy [and] the history play (always very close to tragedy) . . . are always close to this first half. There may be surprises in the last act of a Shakespearean tragedy, but the pervading feeling is of something inevitable working itself out . . . Comedy, however, is based on the second half of the great cycle, moving from death to rebirth, decadence to renewal, winter to spring, darkness to a new dawn . . . This movement from sterility to renewed life is as natural as the tragic movement, because it happens. But though natural it is somehow irrational: the sense of the alliance of nature with reason and predictable order is no longer present. We can see that death is the inevitable result of birth, but new life is not the inevitable result of death. It is hoped for, even expected, but at its core is something unpredictable and mysterious, something that belongs to the imaginative equivalents of faith, hope, and love, not to the rational virtues (119-22).

So we're often partly correct about these genres while perhaps missing the key workings of each. There! You are cursed to correct any newscaster who utters "That was a tragic accident!"

And if all this isn't strangely contingent enough, do some web searches to see how the original festivals of Dionysus worked out (with their Maenads) prior to the Greeks settling down and merely watching plays! See the connections?

"Dionysus Mosaic" by miriam.mollerus is licensed under CC BY 2.0

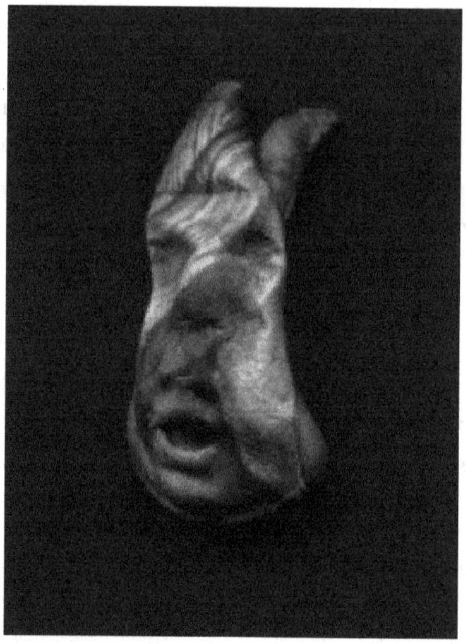

“Dionysus” by TheoJunior is licensed under CC BY 2.0

When Interpreting, Avoid Relativism (Because I Think So)

Get the title?

So that we avoid the major problem of relativism, heed the following warnings:

- If you don't happen to resemble an author's audience, don't attack the audience that writer appealed to
- What I often see in essays based on model reading assignments is reactive rather than flexible reading. For instance, I often teach skeptic Michael Shermer's book *The Science of Good and Evil*. In online discussion posts, I'll see people react with "Well, he is sarcastic but people already agreeing with him would find that funny. I just find it offensive." Then the student writer proceeds to do that Samuel L. Jackson "Allow me to retort" move from *Pulp Fiction* (Tarantino), trying to match snarkiness with Shermer or to refute him. When they get really desperate, they go to the web and find attack sites. "Allow me to retort!" is not our purpose in most academic writing. Later in the course, though, we will cover refutals, which are appropriately-handled counterarguments.
- "It's true for me" doesn't work here. I see this happen a lot in definition or rhetorical analysis essays that often start courses. If the writing is rhetorical analysis, cut out one's views from this process . . . it is supposed to be about form, not content, so if you start getting too much into content, you're not doing a formal analysis. In fact, to the extent that you go off (or gush in support) at the writer, you're not doing your job of analyzing. And definitions—while they may not seem arguable—actually contain areas of genuine, ongoing disagreement that we would do well to recognize.
- Academic writing is public, not private. Don't overuse *I* or *you*. Filtering this through the self is a bad idea. As Charlton Heston says of the mystery food in the movie *Soylent Green* "It's people!" (Fleischer). Don't serve us yourself . . . your friend Willie Wonka says "But that is called cannibalism, my dear children, and is in fact frowned upon in most societies" (Burton). I'm having fun with this, but the idea remains: The chapter is the source, not the self. Subjectivism pushes discussion only through our limited selves.

> I realize I am only going against the whole of American culture by stating this. . .

In interpreting literature, you may be right. . . just not only because you think so!

Literary Terms: A Guide

Metre

Metre refers to the rhythmic structure of lines of verse. The majority of English verse since Chaucer is in**accentual-syllabic metre**, which consists of alternating stressed and unstressed syllables within a fixed total number of syllables in each line. The metrical rhythm is thus the pattern of stressed and unstressed syllables in each line. Groups of syllables are known as metrical **feet**; each line of verse is made up of a set number of feet. Thus:

Monometer: one foot per line
Dimeter: two feet per line
Trimeter: three feet per line
Tetrameter: four feet per line
Pentameter: five feet per line
Hexameter: six feet per line
Heptameter: seven feet per line
Octameter: eight feet per line

Each foot usually consists of a single stressed syllable—though there are some important variations—therefore these patterns correspond to the number of stressed syllables in a line; thus tetrameter has four, pentameter five, etc.

There are two types of metrical feet in English accentual-syllabic metre: **duple metre**, consisting of disyllabic (2-syllable) feet, in which stressed syllables (**x**) and unstressed syllables (**o**) alternate in pairs; and **triple metre**, consisting of trisyllabic (3-syllable) feet, in which single stressed syllables are grouped with a pair of unstressed syllables. Duple metre is the metre most commonly found in English verse.

The following metrical feet make up the most common rhythmical patterns:

Duple metre:

Iamb (iambic foot): **o x**
Trochee (trochaic foot): **x o**
Spondee (spondaic foot): **x x**
Pyrrhus / dibrach (pyrrhic foot): **o o**

Triple metre:

Dactyl (dactylic foot): **x o o**
Anapaest (anapaestic foot): **o o x**
Amphibrach: **o x o**
Molossus: **x x x**

Note that the spondee, pyrrhus and molossus do not usually form the basis for whole lines of verse, but are considered forms of **substitution**: that is, when a foot required by the metrical pattern being used is replaced by a different sort of foot. A frequently-found example of substitution is the replacement of the initial iamb in an iambic line by a trochee, e.g. (underlined syllables represent stressed syllables):

In me thou seest the twilight of such day
As after sunset fadeth in the west,
Which by and by black night doth take away,
Death's second self, that seals up all in rest.

—Shakespeare, Sonnet 73

(The first three lines of this quatrain are perfectly iambic; the initial foot of the fourth line is an example of trochaic substitution, also known as **inversion**.)

Other variations in metrical rhythm include **acephalexis**, in which the first syllable of a line that would be expected according to the regular metre of the line, is lacking; and **catalexis**, in which a line lacks the final syllable expected by its metrical pattern. A**masculine ending** is a line that ends on a stressed syllable, while a **feminine ending** is a line that ends on an unstressed syllable.

Free verse is poetry that does not conform to any regular metre.

Examples of different meters and metrical substitutions:

Iambic pentameter:

We few, we happy few, we band of brothers.
For he today that sheds his blood with me
Shall be my brother; be he ne'er so vile,
This day shall gentle his condition.
Shall think themselves accursed they were not here,
And hold their manhoods cheap whiles any speaks
That fought with us upon Saint Crispin's day.

—Shakespeare, *Henry V*, IV.iii

An example of perfect iambic pentameter. Note the feminine ending in l.1 (in iambic metre a feminine ending adds an extra syllable to the line), and how the stresses follow the sense of the lines.

Trochaic tetrameter:

In what distant deeps or skies
Burnt the fire of thine eyes?
On what wings dare he aspire?
What the hand dare seize the fire?

—Blake, "The Tyger"

The first two lines exhibit masculine endings, and thus are catalectic according to the regular pattern of trochaic metre; that is, they lack their final syllable. Arguably, the second foot in l.4 could be read as a spondaic substitution (if *dare* is stressed).

Spondaic substitution in iambic pentameter (l.3):

Or if thy mistress some rich anger shows,
Em prison her soft hand, and let her rave,
And feed deep, deep upon her peerless eyes.

—Keats, "Ode on Melancholy"

Pyrrhic substitution in iambic tetrameter (l.2):

The woods are lovely, dark and deep.
But I have promises to keep,
And miles to go before I sleep,
And miles to go before I sleep.

—Frost, "Stopping by Woods on a Snowy Evening"

Dactylic dimeter:

Theirs not to make reply,
Theirs not to reason why,
Theirs but to do and die

—Tennyson, "The Charge of the Light Brigade"

Anapaestic metre:

There was an Old Lady of Chertsey,
Who made a remarkable curtsey;
She twirled round and round,
Till she sunk underground,
Which distressed all the people of Chertsey.

—Edward Lear, "There Was an Old Lady of Chertsey"

As is common in limericks, this example includes multiple iambic substitutions, here in the initial syllables of lines 1-3.

Amphibrach:

And now comes an act of enormous enormance!
No former performer's performed this performance!

—Dr. Seuss, *If I Ran the Circus*

Molossus:

Break, break, break,
On thy cold gray stones, O Sea!
And I would that my tongue could utter
The thoughts that arise in me.

—Tennyson, "Break, Break, Break"

The first line is an example of a molossus; it is also an example of epizeuxis (see below).

Stanzas

When a poem is divided into sections, each section is known as a stanza. Stanzas usually share the same structure as the other stanzas within the poem.

Tercet: a unit or stanza of three verse lines
Quatrain: a unit or stanza of four verse lines
Quintain: a stanza of five verse lines

Sestet: a unit or stanza of six verse lines
Septet or **heptastich**: a stanza of seven lines
Octave: a unit or stanza of eight verse lines
Decastich: a stanza or poem of ten lines

Note that many of these terms refer to a unit of this number of lines within a larger stanza or within a poem not divided into stanzas (e.g. a Shakespearean sonnet, which consists of three quatrains followed by a couplet).

Refrain: a line or lines regularly repeated throughout a poem, traditionally at the end of each stanza. Very often found in ballads; it was also used to great effect by Yeats (see for example 'The Withering of the Boughs' or 'The Black Tower'). Usually nowadays printed in *italic* to distinguish it from the main body of the poem.

Enjambment: when the sense of a verse line runs over into the next line with no punctuated pause. The opposite is known as an **end-stopped** line. An example of enjambment in iambic pentameter:

A dungeon horrible, on all sides round

As one great furnace flamed, yet from those flames

No light, but rather darkness visible

Served only to discover sights of woe

—Milton, *Paradise Lost*, I

Rhyme

End rhyme: rhyme occurring on stressed syllables at the ends of verse lines. The most common form of rhyme. Couplet: a pair of end-rhyming verse lines, usually of the same length. E.g.:

Had we but World enough, and Time,

This coyness Lady were no crime.

We would sit down, and think which way

To walk, and pass our long Loves Day.

—Marvell, "To his Coy Mistress"

Internal rhyme: rhyme occurring within a single verse line.

Crossed rhyme: the rhyming of one word in the middle of a verse line with a word in the middle of the following line.

Half rhyme: also known as **slant rhyme**; an incomplete form of rhyme in which final consonants match but vowel sounds do not. E.g.:

I have heard that hysterical women say

They are sick of the palette and fiddle-bow.

Of poets that are always gay,

For everybody knows or else should know

That if nothing drastic is done

Aeroplane and Zeppelin will come out.

Pitch like King Billy bomb-balls in

Until the town lie beaten flat.

—Yeats, "Lapis Lazuli"

The first quatrain is an example of full end rhyme; the second quatrain an example of half rhyme.

Para-rhyme: a form of half rhymel; when all the consonants of the relevant words match, not just the final consonants. E.g.:

It seemed that out of battle I escaped
Down some profound dull tunnel, long since scooped
Through granites which titanic wars had groined.
Yet also there encumbered sleepers groaned,
Too fast in thought or death to be bestirred.
Then, as I probed them, one sprang up, and stared
With piteous recognition in fixed eyes,
Lifting distressful hands, as if to bless.
And by his smile, I knew that sullen hall, –
By his dead smile I knew we stood in Hell.

—Wilfred Owen, "Strange Meeting"

Eye rhyme: a visual-only rhyme; i.e. when spellings match but in pronunciation there is no rhyme, e.g. want/pant, five/give.

Double rhyme: a rhyme on two syllables, the first stressed, the second unstressed. E.g.

I want a hero: —an uncommon want,

When every year and month sends forth a new one,

Till, after cloying the gazettes with can't,

The age discovers he is not the true one

—Byron, *Don Juan*, I.i

The second and fourth lines are double rhymes; the first and third lines are examples of half rhyme/eye rhyme.

Assonance: the recurrence of similar vowel sounds in neighbouring words where the consonants do not match. E.g.:

For the r**a**re and r**a**diant m**ai**den whom the **a**ngels n**a**me Lenore—
N**a**meless here for evermore.

—Poe, "The Raven"

Consonance: the recurrence of similar consonants in neighbouring words where the vowel sounds do not match. The most commonly found forms of consonance, other than half rhyme and para-rhyme, are alliteration and sibilance.

Alliteration: the repetition of initial consonants in a sequence of neighbouring words. E.g.:

Hear the loud alarum bells—

Brazen **B**ells!

What a **t**ale of **t**error, now, their **t**urbulency **t**ells!

—Poe, "The Bells"

Sibilance: the repetition of sibilants, i.e. consonants producing a hissing sound. E.g.:

Ships that pass in the night, and speak each other in passing;

Only a signal shown and a distant voice in the darkness

—Longfellow, *Tales of a Wayside Inn*

Blank verse: metrical verse that does not rhyme. Milton's *Paradise Lost* is an example; the majority of Shakespeare is also in blank verse.

Figurative, rhetorical, and structural devices

Metaphor: when one thing is said to be another thing, or is described in terms normally connected to another thing, in order to suggest a quality shared by both. E.g.:

Love, fame, ambition, avarice—'tis the same,

Each idle, and all ill, and none the worst—

For all are meteors with a different name,

And Death the sable smoke where vanishes the flame.

—Byron, *Childe Harold's Pilgrimage*, IV

Simile: when one thing is directly compared with another thing; indicated by use of the words "as" or "like." E.g.:

I wandered lonely as a cloud

—Wordsworth, "Daffodils"

Metonymy: when something is referred to by an aspect or attribute of it, or by something associated with it. E.g.:

Now is the winter of our discontent

Made glorious summer by this son of York . . .

—Shakespeare, *Richard III*, I.i

Here "winter" and "summer" are examples of metaphor; "son of York" is an example of metonymy, being an attribute of Richard's brother, Edward IV, here the person being referred to.

Synecdoche: a form of metonymy in which something is referred to by a specific part of its whole. "All hands on deck" is an example, in which the crew are being referred to by one specific part—their hands. E.g.:

Take thy face hence.

—Shakespeare, *Macbeth*, V.iii

Personification or **prosopopoeia**: when inanimate objects, animals or ideas are referred to as if they were human. Similar terms are anthropomorphism, when human form is ascribed to something not human, e.g., a deity; and the pathetic fallacy, when natural phenomena are described as if they could feel as humans do. Shelley's 'Invocation to Misery' is an example.

Onomatopoeia: a word that imitates the sound to which it refers. E.g. "clang," "crackle," "bang," etc.

Synaesthesia: the application of terms relating to one sense to a different one, e.g., "a warm sound." For example:

> Odours there are . . . green as meadow grass
>
> —Baudelaire, "Correspondences"

Oxymoron: the combination of two contradictory terms. E.g.:

> Feather of lead, bright smoke, cold fire, sick health,
>
> Still-waking sleep that is not what it is!
>
> —Shakespeare, *Romeo and Juliet*, I.i

Hendiadys: when a single idea is expressed by two nouns, used in conjunction. E.g. "house and home" or Hamlet's "Angels and ministers of grace" (*Hamlet*, I.iv).

Anaphora: the repetition of the same word or group of words at the beginnings of successive lines or clauses. E.g.:

> Is **this** the region, **this** the soil, the clime,
>
> Said then the lost archangel, **this** the seat
>
> That we must change for heaven . . .
>
> —Milton, *Paradise Lost*, I

Epistrophe: the repetition of the same word or group of words at the ends of successive lines or clauses. E.g.:

> I know **thee**, I have found **thee**, & I will not let **thee** go
>
> —Blake, "America—a Prophecy"

Epizeuxis: the repetition of a word with no intervening words. E.g., Tennyson's "Break, break, break," quoted above.

Polysyndeton: use of more than the required amount of conjunctions. E.g.:

> Havoc and spoil and ruin are my gain.
>
> —Milton, *Paradise Lost*, II

The opposite of asyndeton, which refers to the deliberate omission of conjunctions.

Anachronism: when an object, custom or idea is misplaced outside of its proper historical time. A famous example is the clock in Shakespeare's *Julius Caesar*.

Apostrophe: an address to an inanimate object, abstraction, or a dead or absent person. E.g.:

> Busie old foole, unruly Sunne,
>
> Why dost thou thus,

Through windowes, and through curtaines call on us?

—Donne, “The Sunne Rising”

Hyperbole: extreme exaggeration, not intended literally. E.g.:

Since Hero’s time hath half the world been black.

—Marlowe, *Hero and Leander*

Adynaton: a form of hyperbole—a figure of speech that stresses the inexpressibility of something, usually by stating that words cannot describe it. H. P. Lovecraft’s short story “The Unnamable” is essentially a riff on this figure of speech, satirizing Lovecraft’s own regular use of it in his work.

Meiosis: an intentional understatement in which something is described as less significant than it really is. A well-known example is found in *Romeo and Juliet* when Mercutio describes his death-wound as ‘a scratch’ (III.iii).

Litotes: a form of meiosis; the affirmation of something by the denial of its opposite, e.g. “not uncommon,” “not bad.” Erotesis (rhetorical question): asking a question without requiring an answer, in order to assert or deny a statement. E.g.:

What though the field be lost? All is not lost . . .

—*Paradise Lost*, I

In medias res: the technique of beginning a narrative in the middle of the action, before relating preceding events at a later point. *Paradise Lost* is an example (following the convention of epic poetry).

Leitmotif: a phrase, image or situation frequently repeated throughout a work, supporting a central theme. An example is the personification of the mine shaft lift as a devouring creature in Zola’s
Germinal, repeated throughout the novel. Remember! Simply being able to identify the devices and knowing the terms is not enough. They are only a means to an end. You must always consider: why they are being used, what effect they have, and how they affect meaning(s).

Further reading

Baldick, C., *Oxford Dictionary of Literary Terms*, Oxford: Oxford University Press, 2008.

Preminger, A., Brogan, T. and Warnke, F. (eds), *The New Princeton Encyclopedia of Poetry and Poetics*, Princeton, NJ: Princeton University Press, 1993.

Hollander, J., *Rhyme’s Reason: A Guide to English Verse*, New Haven, CT: Yale University Press, 2001.

Attridge, D., *Poetic Rhythm: An Introduction*, Cambridge: Cambridge University Press, 1995.

Strand, M., *The Making of a Poem: A Norton Anthology of Poetic Forms*, New York: W. W. Norton & Co., 2001.

How to Avoid Plagiarizing

Tip #1: Make Sure You Are Very Certain about What Is and is Not Plagiarism

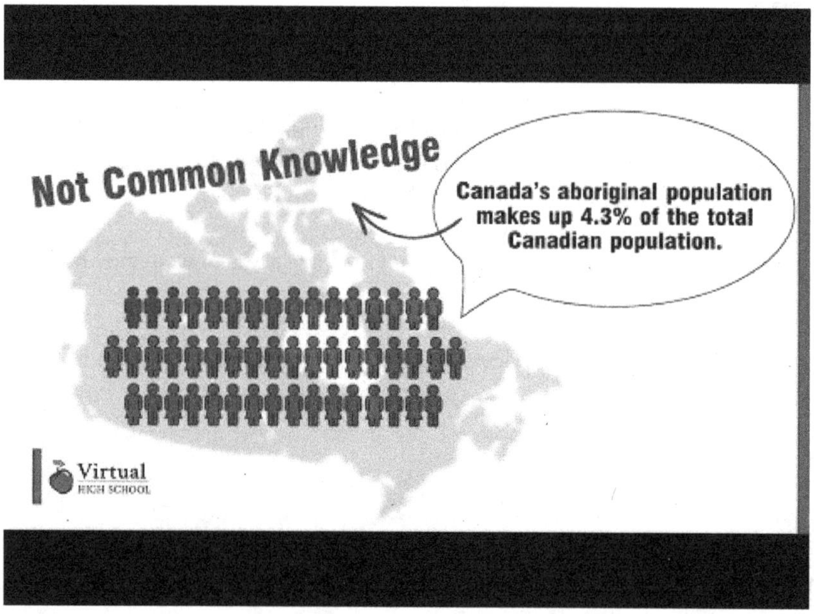

A YouTube element has been excluded from this version of the text. You can view it online here: https://africanamericanlit.pressbooks.sunycreate.cloud/?p=30

Tip #2: Give Yourself Plenty of Time to Complete an Assignment

Running out of time on an assignment is a main cause of plagiarism. Rushing to meet a deadline can result in carelessness (leading to unintentional plagiarism – see the next tip) and the desire to find a quick, easy solution such as copying someone else's work. Don't give in to that temptation! Plagiarism is a serious academic offense, and the chance of being caught (which is likely) is not worth it.

Avoid this situation entirely by starting your assignment far ahead of time and planning out when you will complete each phase of the writing process. Even if your teacher does not require you to turn in materials for each stage of the writing process (i.e. brainstorming, creating a thesis statement, outlining, drafting, revising, etc.), set your own personal deadlines for each step along the way and make sure to give yourself more than enough time to finish everything.

Tip #3: Document Everything

Plagiarism isn't always a conscious choice. Sometimes it can be unintentional, typically resulting from poor documentation of one's sources during the research phase. For example, sometimes students will write down an idea from a source using words identical to or very close to those in the original, but then when they go to write their paper forget that the material was not already in their own words. Adopting good research habits can prevent this type of plagiarism.

Print, photocopy, or scan the relevant pages of every source you are using (including the title and copyright pages, since they have the information you need for a bibliographic citation). When taking notes by hand (or typed into a file), list the bibliographic information for each source you use. Make sure to put quotation marks around any wordings taken directly from the source (and note the page where you found it), and remember to put everything else into your own words right away, so there is no danger of forgetting something is a quote. Documenting where all of your ideas, information, quotations, and so on come from is an important step in avoiding plagiarism.

Tip #4: Don't Include Too Much Material Taken from Other Sources

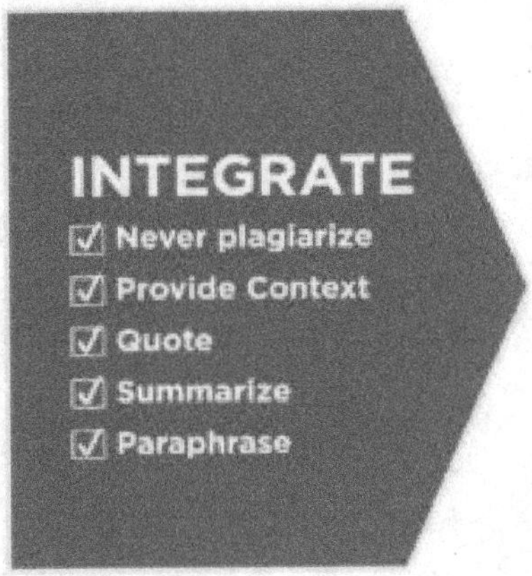

Tips for integrating sources into your research.

Writing assignments are about your ideas, your interpretations, and your ability to synthesize information. You should use relevant sources to support your ideas using evidence such as quotes, paraphrases, and summaries, as well as statistics and other data. But don't lose sight of the fact that your argument is central! Including too much material from other sources can result in a paper that feels like it has been pasted together from a variety of authors, rather than a cohesive essay. Such papers also run a much higher risk of setting off plagiarism warnings in SafeAssign or other plagiarism-detecting software. Try to find a balance: use enough evidence from credible sources to prove your points but don't let the ideas of others take the place of your own thoughts.

Tip #5: When in Doubt, Give a Citation

There are certain types of information – typically referred to as common knowledge – that don't require a citation when you include them in your writing. These are facts that are widely known and can be easily found in a number of sources. They are not ideas that originated with one particular source. Examples include scientific facts (for example, that solid, liquid, and gas are three states of matter), general historical information (for example, that George Washington was the first US president), or even information commonly known to certain groups of people but not others (for example, most musicians know that a C major triad includes the notes C, E, and G, even though many non-musicians would have no idea what a C major triad is).

For everything else, you need to include a citation, regardless of whether you are quoting directly from the source, paraphrasing it, or giving a summary. If you are at all unsure whether something qualifies as common knowledge or not, give a citation. You can also consult a more experienced figure in your field, such as your instructor, to find out if something counts as common knowledge or not.

In academic writing, the **"Quote Sandwich" approach** is useful for incorporating other writers' voices into your essays. It gives meaning and context to a quote, and helps you avoid plagiarism. This 3-step approach offers your readers a deeper understanding of what the quote is and how it relates to your essay's goals.

1. **Step 1***:* Provide context for the source. If you haven't used it yet in the essay, tell us the source's title and author (if known), and any other information that's relevant, like the purpose of the organization that published it, for instance.
2. **Step 2***:* Provide the quote itself. Be sure to format correctly and use quotation marks around exact language.
3. **Step 3***:* Provide a summary and/or analysis of what the quote says, and how it relates to the subject matter of your essay and your thesis.

How to Analyze a Short Story

What Is a Short Story?

Old Fence. A short story has a structure and a message. Can you analyze this picture in much the same way as a short story?

A short story is a work of short, narrative prose that is usually centered around one single event. It is limited in scope and has an introduction, body and conclusion. Although a short story has much in common with a novel (See How to Analyze a Novel), it is written with much greater precision. You will often be asked to write a literary analysis. An analysis of a short story requires basic knowledge of literary elements. The following guide and questions may help you:

Setting

Setting is a description of where and when the story takes place. In a short story there are fewer settings compared to a novel. The time is more limited. Ask yourself the following questions:

- How is the setting created? Consider geography, weather, time of day, social conditions, etc.
- What role does setting play in the story? Is it an important part of the plot or theme? Or is it just a backdrop against which the action takes place?

Study the time period, which is also part of the setting, and ask yourself the following:

- When was the story written?
- Does it take place in the present, the past, or the future?
- How does the time period affect the language, atmosphere or social circumstances of the short story?

Characterization

Characterization deals with how the characters in the story are described. In short stories there are usually fewer characters compared to a novel. They usually focus on one central character or protagonist. Ask yourself the following:

- Who is the main character?
- Are the main character and other characters described through dialogue – by the way they speak (dialect or slang for instance)?
- Has the author described the characters by physical appearance, thoughts and feelings, and interaction (the way they act towards others)?
- Are they static/flat characters who do not change?
- Are they dynamic/round characters who DO change?
- What type of characters are they? What qualities stand out? Are they stereotypes?
- Are the characters believable?

Plot and structure

The plot is the main sequence of events that make up the story. In short stories the plot is usually centered around one experience or significant moment. Consider the following questions:

- What is the most important event?
- How is the plot structured? Is it linear, chronological or does it move around?
- Is the plot believable?

Narrator and Point of view

The narrator is the person telling the story. Consider this question: Are the narrator and the main character the same?

By point of view we mean from whose eyes the story is being told. Short stories tend to be told through one character's point of view. The following are important questions to consider:

- Who is the narrator or speaker in the story?
- Does the author speak through the main character?
- Is the story written in the first person "I" point of view?
- Is the story written in a detached third person "he/she" point of view?
- Is there an "all-knowing" third person who can reveal what all the characters are thinking and doing at all times and in all places?

Conflict

Conflict or tension is usually the heart of the short story and is related to the main character. In a short story there is usually one main struggle.

- How would you describe the main conflict?
- Is it an internal conflict within the character?
- Is it an external conflict caused by the surroundings or environment the main character finds himself/herself in?

Climax

The climax is the point of greatest tension or intensity in the short story. It can also be the point where events take a major turn as the story races towards its conclusion. Ask yourself:

- Is there a turning point in the story?
- When does the climax take place?

Theme

The theme is the main idea, lesson, or message in the short story. It may be an abstract idea about the human condition, society, or life. Ask yourself:

- How is the theme expressed?
- Are any elements repeated and therefore suggest a theme?

- Is there more than one theme?

Style

The author's style has to do with the his or her vocabulary, use of imagery, tone, or the feeling of the story. It has to do with the author's attitude toward the subject. In some short stories the tone can be ironic, humorous, cold, or dramatic.

- Is the author's language full of figurative language?
- What images are used?
- Does the author use a lot of symbolism? Metaphors (comparisons that do not use "as" or "like") or similes (comparisons that use "as" or "like")?

Your literary analysis of a short story will often be in the form of an essay where you may be asked to give your opinions of the short story at the end. Choose the elements that made the greatest impression on you. Point out which character/characters you liked best or least and always support your arguments.

Literary Criticism

By reading and discussing literature, we expand our imagination, our sense of what is possible, and our ability to empathize with others. Improve your ability to read critically and interpret texts while gaining appreciation for different literary genres and theories of interpretation. Read samples of literary interpretation. Write a critique of a literary work.

Texts that interpret literary works are usually persuasive texts. Literary critics may conduct a close reading of a literary work, critique a literary work from the stance of a particular literary theory, or debate the soundness of other critics' interpretations. The work of literary critics is similar to the work of authors writing evaluative texts. For example, the skills required to critique films, interpret laws, or evaluate artistic trends are similar to those skills required by literary critics.

A YouTube element has been excluded from this version of the text. You can view it online here: https://africanamericanlit.pressbooks.sunycreate.cloud/?p=32

Why Write Literary Criticism?

People have been telling stories and sharing responses to stories since the beginning of time. By reading and discussing literature, we expand our imagination, our sense of what is possible, and our ability to empathize with others. Reading and discussing literature can enhance our ability to write. It can sharpen our critical faculties, enabling us to assess works and better understand why literature can have such a powerful effect on our lives.

"Literary texts" include works of fiction and poetry. In school, English instructors ask students to critique literary texts, or works. Literary criticism refers to a genre of writing whereby an author critiques a literary text, either a work of fiction, a play, or poetry. Alternatively, some works of literary criticism address how a particular theory of interpretation informs a reading of a work or refutes some other critics' reading of a work.

Diverse Rhetorical Situations

The genre of literary interpretation is more specialized than most of the other genres addressed in this section, as suggested by the table below. People may discuss their reactions to literary works informally (at coffee houses, book clubs, or the gym) but the lion's share of literary criticism takes place more formally: in college classrooms, professional journals, academic magazines, and Web sites.

Students interpret literary works for English instructors or for students enrolled in English classes. In their interpretations, students may argue for a particular interpretation or they may dispute other critics' interpretations. Alternatively, students may read a text with a particular literary theory in mind, using the theory to explicate a particular point of view. For example, writers could critique The Story of an Hour by Kate Chopin from a feminist theoretical perspective. Thanks to the Internet, some English classes are now publishing students' interpretations on Web sites. In turn, some students and English faculty publish their work in academic literary criticism journals.

Over the years, literary critics have argued about the best ways to interpret literature. Accordingly, many "schools" or "theories of criticism" have emerged. As you can imagine–given that they were developed by sophisticated specialists–some of these theoretical approaches are quite sophisticated and abstract.

Below is a summary of some of the more popular literary theories. Because it is a summary, the following tends to oversimplify the theories. In any case, unless you are enrolled in a literary criticism course, you won't need to learn the particulars of all of these approaches. Instead, your teacher may ask you to take an eclectic approach, pulling interpretative questions from multiple literary theories.

Note: If you are interested in learning more about these theories, review either Skylar Hamilton Burris' Literary Criticism: An Overview of Approaches or Dino F. Felluga's Undergraduate Guide to Critical Theory

- Schools of Literary Criticism
- New Criticism: Focuses on "objectively" evaluating the text, identifying its underlying form. May study, for example, a text's use of imagery, metaphor, or symbolism. Isn't concerned with matters outside the text, such as biographical or contextual information. Online Examples: A Formalist Reading of Sandra Cisneros's "Woman Hollering Creek" , Sound in William Shakespeare's The Tempest by Skylar Hamilton Burris
- Reader-Respons: Criticism Focuses on each reader's personal reactions to a text, assuming meaning is created by a reader's or interpretive community's personal interaction with a text. Assumes no single, correct, universal meaning exists because meaning resides in the minds of readers. Online Examples:Theodore Roethke's "My Papa's Waltz": A Reader's Response (PDF)
- Feminism: Criticism Focuses on understanding ways gender roles are reflected or contradicted by texts, how dominance and submission play out in texts, and how gender roles evolve in texts. Online Example: "The Yellow Wall-Paper": A Twist on Conventional Symbols, Subverting the French Androcentric Influence by Jane Le Marquand
- New Historicism Focuses on understanding texts by viewing texts in the context of other texts. Seeks to understand economic, social, and political influences on texts. Tend to broadly define the term "text," so, for example, the Catholic Church could be defined as a "text." May adopt the perspectives of other interpretive communities–particularly reader-response criticism, feminist criticism, and Marxist approaches–to interpret texts. Online Example Monstrous Acts by Jonathan Lethem
- Media Criticism Focuses on writers' use of multimedia and hypertexts. Online Examples The Electronic Labyrinth by Christopher Keep, Tim McLaughlin, and Robin Parmar
- Psychoanalytical Criticism Focuses on psychological dimensions of the work. Online Examples: A Freudian Approach to Erin McGraw's "A Thief" by Skylar Hamilton Burris
- Marxist Criticism Focuses on ways texts reflect, reinforce, or challenge the effects of class, power relations, and social roles. Online Example: A Reading of Shirley Jackson's "The Lottery" by Peter Kosenko

- Archetypal Criticism Focuses on identifying the underlying myths in stories and archetypes, which reflect what the psychologist Carl Jung called the "collective unconsciousness." Online Example: A Catalogue of Symbols in The Awakening by Kate Chopin by Skylar Hamilton Burris
- Postcolonial Criticism Focuses on how Western culture's (mis)representation of third-world countries and peoples in stories, myths, and stereotypical images encourages repression and domination. Online Example: Other Voices
- Structuralism/Semiotics Focuses on literature as a system of signs where meaning is constructed in a context, where words are inscribed with meaning by being compared to other words and structures. Online Example: Applied Semiotics [Online journal with many samples]
- Post-Structuralism/Deconstruction Focuses, along with Structuralism, on viewing literature as a system of signs, yet rejects the Structuralist view that a critic can identify the inherent meaning of a text, suggesting, instead that literature has no center, no single interpretation, that literary language is inherently ambiguous

Powerful works of literature invoke multiple readings. In other words, we can all read the same story or poem (or watch the same movie or listen to the same song) and come up with different, even conflicting, interpretations about what the work means. Who we are reflects how we read texts. Our experiences inspire us to relate to and sympathize with characters and difficult situations. Have we read similar stories? Have we actually faced some of the same challenges the characters in the story face?

In addition, literary theories have unique ways to develop and substantiate arguments. Some theories draw extensively on the work of other critics, while others concentrate on the reader's thoughts and feelings. Some theories analyze a work from an historical perspective, while others focus solely on a close reading of a text.

Accordingly, as with other genres, the following key features need to be read as points of departure as opposed to a comprehensive blueprint:

Focus

Examine a subject from a rhetorical perspective. Identify the intended audience, purpose, context, media, voice, tone, and persona.Distinguish between summarizing the literary work and presenting your argument. Many students fall into the trap of spending too much time summarizing the literature being analyzed as opposed to critiquing it. As a result, it would be wise to check with your teacher regarding how much plot summary is expected. As you approach this project, remember to keep your eye on the ball: What, exactly (in one sentence) is the gist of your interpretation?

Development

You can develop your ideas by researching the work of other literary critics. How do other critics evaluate an author's work? What literary theories do literary critics use to interpret texts or particular moments in history? Reading sample proposals can help you find and adopt an appropriate voice and persona. By reading samples, you can learn how others have prioritized particular criteria.

Below are some of the questions invoked by popular literary theories. Consider these questions as you read a work, perhaps taking notes on your thoughts as you reread. You may focus on using one theory to "read and interpret" text or, more commonly, you may compare the critical concerns of different theories.

New Criticism/Formalism

- Character: How does the character evolve during the story? What is unique or interesting about a character? Is the character a stereotypical action hero, a patriarchal father figure, or Madonna? How does a character interact with other characters?

- Setting: How does the setting enhance tension within the work? Do any elements in the setting foreshadow the conclusion of the piece?
- Plot:What is the conflict? How do scenes lead to a suspenseful resolution? What scenes make the plot unusual, unexpected, suspenseful?
- Point of View: Who is telling the story? Is the narrator omniscient (all knowing) or does the narrator have limited understanding?

Reader-Response Criticism

How does the text make you feel? What memories or experiences come to mind when you read? If you were the central protagonist, would you have behaved differently? Why? What values or ethics do you believe are suggested by the story? As your reading of a text progresses, what surprises you, inspires you?

Feminist Criticism

How does the story re-inscribe or contradict traditional gender roles? For example, are the male characters in "power positions" while the women are "dominated"? Are the men prone to action, decisiveness, and leadership while the female characters are passive, subordinate? Do gender roles create tension within the story? Do characters' gender roles evolve over the course of the narrative?

New Historicism Cristicism

How does the story reflect the aspirations and conditions of the lower classes or upper classes? Is tension created by juxtaposing privileged, powerful positions to subordinated, dominated positions? What information about the historical context of the story helps explain the character's motivations? Who benefits from the outcome of the story or from a given character's motivation?

Media Criticism

How does the medium alter readers' interactions with the text? Has the reader employed multimedia or hypertext? What traditions from print and page design have shaped the structure of the text? In what ways has the author deviated from traditional, deductively organized linear texts?

Cite from the Work

Literary criticism involves close reading of a literary work, regardless of whether you are arguing about a particular interpretation, comparing stories or poems, or using a theory to interpret literature.Do not summarize the story. The purpose of the document is not to inform the readers, but to argue a particular interpretation. You only need to cite parts of the work that support or relate to your argument and follow the citation format required by your instructor (see Using and Citing Sources).

Below is an example from Sample Essays for English 103: Introduction to Fiction, Professor Matthew Hurt. Note how the writer uses block quotes to highlight key elements and paraphrase and summarizes the original works, using quotation marks where necessary.

> ...Twain offers a long descriptive passage of Huck and Jim's life on the raft that seems, at first glance, to celebrate the idyllic freedom symbolized by the river and nature. . . A close reading of this passage, however, shows that the river is not a privileged natural space outside of and uncontaminated by society, but is inextricably linked to the social world on the shore, which itself has positive value for Huck. Instead of seeking to escape society, Huck wants to escape the dull routines of life.

The passage abounds with lyrical descriptions of the river's natural beauty. For example, Huck's long description of the sunrise over the river captures the peaceful stillness and the visual beauty of the scene:

> The first thing to see, looking away over the water, was a kind of dull line — that was the woods on t'other side — you couldn't make nothing else out; then a pale place in the sky; then more paleness, spreading around; then the river softened up, away off, and warn't black any more, but gray; . . . sometimes you could hear a sweep screaking; or jumbled up voices, it was so still, and sounds come so far; and by-and-by you could see a streak on the water which you know by the look of the streak that there's a snag there in the swift current which breaks on it and makes the streak look that way; and you see the mist curl up off of the water, and the east reddens up, and the river, and you make out a log cabin in the edge of the woods, away on the bank on t'other side of the river, . . . then the nice breeze springs up, and comes fanning you from over there, so cool and fresh, and sweet to smell, on account of the woods and the flowers; . . . and next you've got the full day, and everything smiling in the sun, and the song-birds just going at it! (129-130)

Here Huck celebrates the beauty of the natural world coming to life at the beginning of a new day. The "paleness" gradually spreading across the sky makes new objects visible which he describes in loving detail for the reader. The "nice breeze" is "cool and fresh" and "sweet to smell," and the world seems to be "smiling in the sun" as the song-birds welcome the new day.

However, Huck includes a number of details within this passage that would seem to work against the language of natural beauty. After describing the gradually brightening sky, Huck notes that "you could see little dark spots drifting along, ever so far away — trading scows, and such things; and long black streaks — rafts." The sun rise reveals not only natural objects (the brightening sky, the "snag," the "mist"), but also brings into view man-made objects ("trading scows" and "rafts") that signify human society's presence in this natural environment. Similarly, Huck speculates that the picturesque "log cabin" on the distant shore is a "woodyard, likely, and piled by them cheats so you can throw a dog through it anywheres." Here the marker of human society takes on a sinister tone of corruption as Huck describes how unscrupulous wood sellers stack wood loosely to cheat their customers. Finally, although the breeze is "sweet to smell," Huck assures the reader that this isn't always the case: "but sometimes not that way, because they've left dead fish laying around, gars, and such, and they do get pretty rank."

These signs of society's presence on the river are largely negative. The woodyard is "piled by cheats" and the stacked fish pollute the "sweet" smell of the breeze. At this point, the opposition between "good nature" and "bad society" remains intact. The signs of human presence suggest a corruption of nature's beauty. In the paragraphs that follow, however, this opposition is subtly reversed. After Huck's account of the sunrise over the river, he describes how he and Jim watch the steamboats "coughing along up stream." But when there are no steamboats or rafts to watch, he describes the scene as "solid lonesomeness" (130). No songbirds, no sweet breezes. Without human activities to watch, the scene suddenly becomes empty and "lonesome," and nothing captures Huck's attention until more rafts and boats pass by and he can watch them chopping wood or listen to them beating pans in the fog.

Cite Other Critics' Interpretations of the Work

Criticism written by advanced English majors, graduate students, and literary critics may be more about what other critics have said than about the actual text. Indeed, many critics spend more time reading criticism and arguing about critical approaches than actually reading original works. However, unless you are enrolled in a literary theory course, your instructor probably wants you to focus more on interpreting the work than discussing other critical interpretations. This does not mean, however, that you should write about a literary work "blindly." Instead, you are wise to find out what other students and critics have said about the work.

Below is a sample passage that illustrates how other critics' works can inspire an author and guide him or her in constructing a counter argument, support an author's interpretation, and provide helpful biographical information.

> In her critical biography of Shirley Jackson, Lenemaja Friedman notes that when Shirley Jackson's story "The Lottery" was published in the June 28, 1948 issue of the New Yorker it received a response that "no New Yorker story had ever received": hundreds of letters poured in that were characterized by "bewilderment, speculation, and old-fashioned abuse."1 It is not hard to account for this response: Jackson's story portrays an "average" New England village with "average" citizens engaged in a deadly rite, the annual selection of a sacrificial victim by means of a public lottery, and does so quite deviously: not until well along in the story do we suspect that the "winner" will be stoned to death by the rest of the villagers.

Organization

The format for literary critiques is fairly standard:

- State your claim(s).
- Forecast your organization.
- Marshal evidence for your claim.
- Reiterate argument and elaborate on its significance.

In English classes, you may be able to assume that your readers are familiar with the work you are critiquing. Perhaps, for example, the entire class is responding to one particular work after some class discussions about it. However, if your instructor asks you to address a broader audience, you may need to provide bibliographical information for the work. In other words, you may need to cite the title, publisher, date, and pages of the work (see Citing Sources).

Literary critiques are arguments. As such, your instructors expect you to state a claim in your introduction and then provide quotes and paraphrased statements from the text to serve as evidence for your claim. Ideally, your critique will be insightful and interesting. You'll want to come up with an interpretation that isn't immediately obvious. Below are some examples of "thesis statements" or "claims" from literary critiques:

- In "The Yellow Wallpaper," by Charlotte Perkins Gilman, the protagonist is oppressed and represents the effect of the oppression of women in society. This effect is created by the use of complex symbols such as the house, the window, and the wall-paper which facilitate her oppression as well as her self expression. ["'The Yellow Wall-Paper': A Twist on Conventional Symbols" by Liselle Sant]
- "The Yellow Wallpaper" by Charlotte Gilman is a sad story of the repression that women face in the days of the late 1800's as well as being representative of the turmoil that women face today. [Critique of "The Yellow Wallpaper" by Brandi Mahon]
- "The Yellow Wallpaper," written by Charlotte Perkins Gilman, is a story of a woman, her psychological difficulties and her husband's so called therapeutic treatment of her aliments during the late 1800s. . . Gilman does well throughout the story to show with descriptive phrases just how easily and effectively the man "seemingly" wields his "maleness" to control the woman. But, with further interpretation and insight I believe Gilman succeeds in nothing more than showing the weakness of women, of the day, as active persons in their own as well as society's decision making processes instead of the strength of men as women dominating machines. "The View from the Inside" by Timothy J. Decker
- In *Adventures of Huckleberry Finn*, Mark Twain creates a strong opposition between the freedom of Huck and Jim's life on the raft drifting down the Mississippi River, which represents "nature," and the confining and restrictive life on the shore, which represents "society." ["'All I wanted was a change': Positive Images of Nature and Society in Chapter 19 of Adventures of Huckleberry Finn" from Professor Matthew Hurt's "Sample Essays for English 103: Introduction to Fiction"]
- In Gabriel Garcia Marquez's short story, "A Very Old Man with Enormous Wings," an unexpected visitor comes down from the sky, and seems to test the faith of a community. The villagers have a difficult time figuring out just how the very old man with enormous wings fits into their lives. Because this character does not agree with their conception of what an angel should look like, they try to determine if the aged man could actually be an angel. In trying to prove the origin of their visitor, the villagers lose faith in the possibility of him being an angel because he does not adhere to their ordered world. Marquez keeps the identity of the very old man with enormous wings ambiguous to critique the villagers and, more generally, organized religion for having a lack of faith to believe in miracles that do not comply with their master narrative. ["Prove It: A Critique of the Villagers' Faith in 'A Very Old Man with Enormous Wings'" from Sample Essays for English 103: Introduction to Fiction, Professor Matthew Hurt]

Style

Literary criticism is a fairly specialized kind of writing. Instead of writing to a general lay audience, you are writing to members of a literary community who have read a work and who developed opinions about the work–as well as a vocabulary of interpretation.

Following are some common words used by literary critics. More specialized terms can be learned by reading criticism or by referring to a good encyclopedia for criticism or writing, including the *Writer's Encyclopedia*:

- Protagonist: The protagonist is the major character of the story; typically the character must overcome significant challenges.

- Antagonist: The protagonist's chief nemesis; in other words, the character whom the protagonist must overcome.
- Symbols: Metaphoric language; see A Catalogue of Symbols in The Awakening by Kate Chopin
- Viewpoint: Stories are told either in the first person or third person point of view. The first person is limited to a single character, although dialog can let you guess at other characters' intentions. The third person allows readers inside the character's mind so you know what the character feels and thinks.Viewpoint can be "limited," where the character knows less than the reader, or "omniscient," where the reader can hear the thoughts and feelings of all characters. Occasionally writers will use multiple character viewpoint, which takes you from one character's perspective to another.
- Plot: Plots are a series of scenes, typically moving from a conflict situation to a resolution. To surprise readers, authors will foreshadow "false plants," which lead readers to anticipate other resolutions. The term "denouement" refers to the unraveling of the plot in the conclusion.

A Short History of the Early American Novel

While most historians of the modern novel trace its beginnings to Cervantes's *Don Quixote* (1605, 1616) and its English-language origins are often located in Daniel Defoe's *Robinson Crusoe* (1719), the novel did not truly emerge in the United States until the end of the eighteenth century. Critics and historians have offered several reasons for this delay, citing a continuing Puritan distrust of fictional representations, a relative lack of leisure time, and, relatedly, the lack of a large, concentrated group of middle-class readers with substantial enough wealth and time to pursue the genre. Most accounts of the development of the novel, such as Ian Watt's *The Rise of the Novel*, Michael McKeon's *The Origins of the English Novel* (on England), M. M. Bakhtin's various writings, and Georg Lukács's *Theory of the Novel* (focusing more on the European continent), describe the genre as arising with a number of socioeconomic, religious, cultural, and philosophical factors. In particular, they point to the birth of the middle-class, with its emphasis on social fluidity and individual self-determination; the Protestant Reformation and its appeal to individual interpretation of texts; and the development of scientific and philosophical empiricism with its focus on specific sensual details of life as the ultimate source of knowledge.

From these different factors emerge the novel's distinctive break from earlier long narrative forms such as the epic—its emphasis on everyday people, living their lives in familiar places according to a realistic time frame; its narratives of personal psychological, economic, and social struggle and development; and its close attention to the details of everyday life, including the objects purveyed through the rising commodity culture of which the novel itself was a part. Among other things that set the novel apart from preceding literary forms—perhaps most important, unlike poetry and drama, it was never an oral or performative form—was the fact that from its inception it was a commodity, a work produced for a literary marketplace. In the American context, we can see these connections through Benjamin Franklin's relationship to the novel. While Franklin never wrote a novel and sometimes derided the fine arts, he was the first American printer to publish a novel (Samuel Richardson's *Pamela* in 1742), and he offered one of the most succinct accounts of the novel's attraction in his *Autobiography* in commenting on John Bunyan's *Pilgrim's Progress*, a Protestant allegory often seen as anticipating many elements of the novel:

> Honest John was the first that I know of who mix'd Narration and Dialogue, a Method of Writing very engaging to the Reader, who in the most interesting Parts finds himself as it were brought into the Company, and present at the Discourse. Defoe in his *Crusoe*, his *Moll Flanders* . . . has imitated it with Success. And Richardson has done the same in his *Pamela*, etc. (24).

While many readers now identify "literature" with the novel (most bookstores' "literature" sections are comprised mainly of novels), most critics in the eighteenth and early-nineteenth centuries viewed the novel as sub-literary, as merely popular dross. This disdain towards the genre lingered longer, perhaps, in the United States than in most of Western Europe. Especially in the first years of the United States, a variety of critics registered significant concerns about the immoral (or, at best, amoral) nature of the novel. These critics were particularly concerned about what Franklin identified as its chief attraction, its ability to draw readers into the fictive world and make them feel like participants in the action. Samuel Miller, for example, in his *Brief Retrospect of the Eighteenth Century*, abjured that he "has no hesitation in saying, that, if it were possible, he would wholly prohibit the reading of novels . . . . For it may, with confidence, be pronounced that no one was ever an extensive and especially an habitual reader of novels, even supposing them to be all well selected, without suffering both intellectual and moral injury" (2:179). During a period when social and political hierarchies were in transition in the wake of the Revolution, the novel's emphasis on individual happiness, on an individual reader's sentiments, and on an individual reader's identification were seen as endangering the future of the young nation.

In response, many early American novels actively positioned themselves against other, less morally upright novels. For example, William Hill Brown's *The Power of Sympathy* (1789), a work often taken to be the first American novel, offers a contrast in his preface to those "novels which expose no particular Vice, and which *recommend* no particular Virtue," before moving into its epistolary seduction tale in which the moral characters often comment on the detrimental effects of novel-reading (7). Brown's *Power of Sympathy* exemplifies one of the major trends within the development of the early American novel—the use of seduction plots to elicit readers' sympathy and warn them of the dangers of straying even the least bit from moral propriety. Perhaps the most popular novel of the era was Susanna Rowson's *Charlotte Temple* (1791). Although first published in England (when Rowson resided there), the novel was immediately popular in the United States (where Rowson soon moved). Through the text, the reader follows the title character from being ensconced in a girls' school in England to being seduced by a soldier on his way to fight against the American revolutionaries to her pregnancy and death in New York. Republished repeatedly throughout the nineteenth century, *Charlotte Temple* exemplified the appeal the novel made specifically to women readers, an appeal that male critics often attacked or derided.

While sentimental works such as *Charlotte Temple* were perhaps the most popular fare among early American novel-readers, the most prominent novelist of the early period in the critical tradition is Charles Brockden Brown. Brockden Brown produced a series of four gothic novels between 1798 and 1800 (and two more sentimental ones in 1800–1801) before giving up novel-writing altogether. In these works, which would be read avidly by some British romantics and picked up by early-nineteenth-century American critics as a first glimmer of a national literature, Brown explores the dark side of the American nation and the human psyche. In his first novel, *Wieland* (1798), for example, he tells the story of an apparently model family that is destroyed through madness and murder when a stranger employing his ventriloquism skills throws their assumptions about one another and the world into turmoil. Often seen as prefiguring later themes explored by later American writers, Brown's attention to the psychological, political, and economic influence of American society and nature on his characters marked a new development.

Only somewhere around one hundred American novels were published before 1820, but in the decade that followed, nearly that many again would be published, with the 1830s, 40s, and 50s seeing an explosion in the number of American novels. Even as elite critics continued to express concerns about the morality of the novel, readers would make the novel the most popular genre of the antebellum period. In fact, the novel would come not just to dominate but also, in many ways, to define the literary marketplace. The exponential growth in the production of novels paralleled that of the American literary marketplace, and both depended on the same socio-economic factors—increasing literacy rates due to the expansion of public education; improvements in printing technology, including the steam-powered press and the use of stereotype plates; and what has been called the transportation revolution, with roads, canals, and eventually railroads, tying far-flung urban publishing centers to the outskirts of the nation. The 1820s saw the emergence of the United States' first critically and economically successful novelist with James Fenimore Cooper. After writing an Austen-esque novel of manners, Cooper turned to historical fiction, following in the footsteps of Sir Walter Scott, whose *Waverly* novels had become incredibly popular in both Europe and the United States in the 1810s (and whose novels would remain quite popular in the U.S. through the Civil War). After writing *The Spy* (1821), a novel set during the American Revolution, Cooper penned the first of the Leatherstocking Tales, *The Pioneers* (1823), beginning one of the most successful novel series in American literary history and introducing his most famous character, Natty Bumppo. In *The Pioneers* and *The Last of the Mohicans* (along with several other works), Cooper would depict the decline and disappearance of Native Americans from the nation. Often taking an elegiac tone, these works depicted some Native Americans as noble savages, nearly as role models for the Euro-American characters attempting to make their way in the new world. At the same time, however, they embraced the idea of the Native Americans' inexorable, if regrettable, withdrawal from the nation.

While Cooper's accounts are most famous, the theme of the "vanishing" Native American appeared widely in American literature of the 1820s and 1830s (and later), across numerous genres, from long epic poems (Eastburn and Sands, *Yamoyden* [1820]); drama (Stone, *Metamora* [1829]); and autobiography (*Black Hawk* [1833]). It was the novel that gave the fullest shape to this narrative. In recent years, critics and historians have begun to explore a broader range of texts that develop this theme, including sentimental texts such as Lydia Maria Child's *Hobomok* (1824) and Catharine Sedgwick's *Hope Leslie* (1827) and gothic ones such as John Neal's *Logan* (1822). While these different works offer alternative conceptions of the relationship between gender and race and sometimes more equivocal visions of the future of the U. S., they tend to share the idea that Native Americans have already all but disappeared from the American landscape. The great irony, of course, was that this period saw the election of Andrew Jackson (1828), with his program of Native American removal. While novels portrayed the Native American's disappearance as a *fait accompli*, Jackson and other politicians worked to make sure it actually happened.

The antebellum decades (1830s–1850s) saw not only the immense expansion of the market for novels in the United States but also the further development of specific genres. Critics throughout most of the twentieth century focused on the artistic achievement of a few novelists during this period, especially Nathaniel Hawthorne and Herman Melville. Variously read in terms of their interest in the romance (with its greater imaginative range) as opposed to the novel or their darker romanticism (as opposed to the transcendentalist optimism of Emerson and Thoreau), or their deep exploration of human psychology, Hawthorne and Melville seemed to anticipate the modernist emphasis on symbolic layering, linguistic complexity, and ambiguous truths that would dominate critical thought for most of the twentieth century. However, in recent decades, American literary historians have increasingly attended to the vast variety amongst the novels produced during this period. In particular, they have investigated more popular genres, including domestic sentimental literature and sensational gothic and urban fictions. Even more recently, scholars have begun to distinguish the work and popularity of religious novels, reform novels, and regional fictions that deployed sentimental, sensational, and symbolic modes to differing extents. At the time of the Civil War, the novel was still seen by most American critics as inferior to poetry, as a less significant artistic form.

–The remainder of the lecture was cut for space concerns. (JD)

Connecting Reading & Writing: The Voice You Hear Response

Too often, reading is viewed as a passive act where the information is poured into static readers' minds. To succeed at the college level, a reworking of the way one reads may be necessary. Read the following passage from reading researcher Katherine McCormick and jot down your interpretation of its meaning:

Tony slowly got up from the mat, planning his escape. He hesitated a moment and thought. Things were not going well. What bothered him the most was being held, especially since the charge against him had been weak. He considered his present situation. The lock that held him was strong but he thought he could break it . . . . He was being ridden unmercifully . . . . He felt that he was ready to make his move.

From the two possible interpretations here, it seems clear that 1) readers use their previous experiences to make meaning out of a text, and 2) context influences meaning. After all, if we knew we were reading a short story on wrestling, our understanding of the passage would differ. Reading needs to be recognized as an active process. **Read the following poem by Thomas Lux and answer all of the questions below in complete sentences. The questions appear after the poem.**

The Voice You Hear When You Read Silently

is not silent, it is a speaking-out-loud voice in your head;

it is *spoken*,a voice is *saying* it as you read.

It's the writer's words, of course, in a literary sense his or her "voice"

but the sound of that voice is the sound of *your* voice.

Not the sound your friends know or the sound of a tape played back

but your voice

caught in the dark cathedral of your skull, your voice heard by an internal

ear informed by internal abstracts

and what you know by feeling, having felt.

It is your voice saying, for example, the word "barn" that the writer wrote

but the "barn" you say is a barn you know or knew.

The voice in your head, speaking as you read, never says anything

neutrally–some people hated the barn they knew,

some people love the barn they know

so you hear the word loaded and a sensory constellation is lit:

horse-gnawed stalls, hayloft, black heat tape wrapping a water pipe,

a slippery spilled *chirr* of oats from a split sack,

the bony, filthy haunches of cows . . .

And "barn" is only a noun–no verb or subject has entered into the sentence yet!

The voice you hear when you read to yourself is the clearest voice: you speak its speaking to you.

1. When you hear the word *barn*, what barn or barns from your own life do you first see? What feelings and associations do you have with this word? How do you think the barn in your head is different from the barns in your classmates' heads?
2. When you hear the word *cathedral*, what images and associations from your own life come into your head? Once again, how might your classmates' internal images and associations with the word *cathedral* differ from yours?
3. Now reread the poem and consider the lines "Not the sound your friends know or the sound of a tape played back / but your voice / caught in the dark cathedral of your skull." What do you think Lux means by the metaphor "dark cathedral of your skull"? What seems important about his choice of the word *cathedral* (rather than, say, *house* or *cave* or *gymnasium* or *mansion*)? How does *skull* work (rather than *mind* or *brain* or *head*)? Freewriting for several minutes, create your interpretation of "dark cathedral of the skull."
4. Finally, reflect for a moment about your thinking processes in trying to interpret "cathedral of the skull." Did you go back and reread the poem, looking for how this line fits other lines of the poem? Did you explore further your own ideas about cathedrals and skull? See if you can catch yourself in the act of interacting with the text—or actively constructing meaning.

Approaching Poetry

Introduction

This reading is designed to develop the analytical skills you need for a more in-depth study of literary texts. You will learn about rhythm, alliteration, rhyme, poetic inversion, voice and line lengths and endings. You will examine poems that do not rhyme and learn how to compare and contrast poetry.

By the end of this reading you should be able to:

- have an awareness of the role of analysis to inform appreciation and understanding of poetry;
- be able to identify and discuss the main analytical concepts used in analyzing poetry.

What is the point of analyzing poetry? One simple answer is that the more we know about anything the more interesting it becomes: listening to music or looking at paintings with someone who can tell us a little about what we hear or see – or what we're reading – is one way of increasing our understanding and pleasure. That may mean learning something about the people who produced the writing, music, painting that we are interested in, and why they produced it. But it may also mean understanding why one particular form was chosen rather than another: why, for example, did the poet choose to write a sonnet rather than an ode, a ballad, or a villanelle? To appreciate the appropriateness of one form, we need to be aware of a range of options available to that particular writer at that particular time. In the same way, we also need to pay attention to word choice. Why was this particular word chosen from a whole range of words that might have said much the same? Looking at manuscript drafts can be really enlightening, showing how much effort was expended in order to find the most appropriate or most evocative expression.

ACTIVITY 1

Click on William Blake's "Tyger" to read and compare the two versions of the poem. The one on the left is a draft; the other is the final published version. (http://www.open.edu/openlearn/ocw/mod/oucontent/olink.php?id=1713&targetdoc=William+Blake%27s+%E2%80%98Tyger%E2%80%99)

Discussion

The most obvious difference between the two is that stanza 4 of the draft does not survive in the published version, and an entirely new stanza, "When the stars threw down their spears," appears in the finished poem. Significantly, this introduces the idea of "the Lamb," a dramatic contrast to the tiger, as well as the idea of a "he" who made the lamb. One similarity between the draft and final version is that each is made up entirely of unanswered questions. But if you look at the manuscript stanza 5, you can see revisions from "What" to "Where," and the struggle with the third line, where Blake eventually decided that the idea of an arm was redundant, subsumed in the notions of grasping and clasping. The two rhyme words are decided—grasp/clasp—but in which order should they come? 'Clasp' is a less aggressive word than 'grasp'; 'clasp' is not quite as gentle as an embrace, but it is closer to embracing than 'grasp' is – so it must be for deliberate effect that we end up with 'What dread grasp/Dare its deadly terrors clasp?

It is rare to have manuscript drafts to examine in this way, but I hope that this convinces you of the kind of attention writers pay to word choice. Let us take one more example. Think about this first stanza of Thomas Hardy's 'Neutral Tones' (1867):

> We stood by a pond that winter day,
>
> And the sun was white, as though chidden of God,
>
> And a few leaves lay on the starving sod;
>
> —They had fallen from an ash, and were gray. (Gibson, 1976, p. 12)

Notice that, in the last line, 'oak' or 'elm' would work just as well as far as the rhythm or music of the line is concerned, but 'ash' has extra connotations of grayness, of something burnt out, dead, finished ('ashes to ashes', too, perhaps?), all of which contribute to the mood that Hardy conveys in a way that 'oak' or 'elm' wouldn't.

To return to my original question then, 'what is the point of analyzing poetry?', one answer is that only an analytical approach can help us arrive at an informed appreciation and understanding of the poem. Whether we like a poem or not, we should be able to recognize the craftsmanship that has gone into making it, the ways in which stylistic techniques and devices have worked to create meaning. General readers may be entirely happy to find a poem pleasing, or unsatisfactory, without stopping to ask why. But *studying* poetry is a different matter and requires some background understanding of what those stylistic techniques might be, as well as an awareness of constraints and conventions within which poets have written throughout different periods of history.

You may write poetry yourself. If so, you probably know only too well how difficult it is to produce something you feel really expresses what you want to convey. Writing an essay presents enough problems – a poem is a different matter, but certainly no easier. Thinking of poetry as a discipline and a craft which, to some extent, can be learned, is another useful way of approaching analysis. After all, how successful are emotional outpourings on paper? Words one might scribble down in the heat of an intense moment may have some validity in conveying that intensity, but in general might they not be more satisfactory if they were later revised? My own feeling is that a remark Wordsworth made 200 years ago has become responsible for a number of misconceptions about what poetry should do. In the Preface to a volume of poems called *Lyrical Ballads* (1802) he wrote that 'all good poetry is the spontaneous overflow of powerful feelings' (Owens and Johnson, 1998, p.85,11.105–6). The second time he uses the same phrase he says something that I think is often forgotten today: 'poetry is the spontaneous overflow of powerful feelings; it takes its origin from emotion *recollected in tranquillity'* (my italics) (ibid., p. 95, ll.557–8). Notice the significant time lapse implied there – the idea that, however powerful or spontaneous the emotion, it needs to be carefully considered before you start writing. He goes on:

> The emotion is contemplated till, by a species of reaction, the tranquillity gradually disappears, and an emotion kindred to that which was before the subject of contemplation is gradually reproduced, and does itself actually exist in the mind. In this mood successful composition generally begins.

You don't have to agree with Wordsworth about what poetry is or how best to achieve it. (Would you always want a poem to express powerful emotion, for example? I referred to Hardy's 'Neutral Tones' above, where the whole point is that neither of the two characters described feels anything much at all.) But the idea of contemplation is a useful and important one: it implies distance, perhaps detachment, but above all re-creation, not the thing itself. And if we try to re-create something, we must choose our methods and our words carefully in order to convey what we experienced as closely as possible. A word of warning though: writers do not always aim to express personal experiences; often a persona is created.

The poet Ezra Pound offered this advice to other poets in an essay written in 1913: 'Use no superfluous word, no adjective, which does not reveal something' (Gray, 1990, p. 56). And in the 1950s William Carlos Williams advised, 'cut and cut again whatever you write'. In his opinion, the 'test of the artist is to be able to revise without showing a seam' (loc. cit.). That sewing image he uses appeals to me particularly because it stresses the notion of skilled craftsmanship. Pound and Williams were American, writing long after Wordsworth, but, as you can see, like countless other poets they too reflected very seriously on their own poetic practice. I hope this helps convince you that as students we owe it to the poems we read to give them close analytical attention.

Note About Organization

In what follows, section headings like 'Rhyme', 'Rhythm', 'Line lengths and line endings', 'Alliteration', and so on, are intended to act as signposts to help you (if terms are unfamiliar, look them up in the glossary at the end). But these headings indicate only the *main* technique being discussed. While it is something we need to attempt, it is very difficult to try to isolate devices in this way – to separate out, for example, the effects of rhythm from rhyme. This doesn't mean that we shouldn't look for particular techniques at work in a poem, but we need to be aware that they will be interdependent and the end product effective or not because of the way such elements work together.

As you work through this reading, don't be discouraged if your response to exercises differs from mine. Remember that I had the advantage of choosing my own examples and that I've long been familiar with the poems I've used. On a daily basis, we probably read much less poetry than we do prose. This is perhaps one reason why many people say they find poetry difficult – unfamiliarity and lack of practice. But, like anything else, the more effort we put in, the wider the range of experiences we have to draw on. I hope that when you come across an unfamiliar extract in the discussions that follow you might decide to look up the whole poem on your own account, widening your own experience and enjoying it too.

Remember that language changes over the years. I've deliberately chosen to discuss poems from different periods, and given dates of first publication. Do keep this in mind, especially as you may find some examples more accessible than others. The idiom and register of a poem written in the eighteenth century will usually be quite different from one written in the twentieth. Different verse forms are popular at different times: while sonnets have been written for centuries, they were especially fashionable in Elizabethan times, for example. Don't expect to find free verse written much before the twentieth century.

If you are working on a poem, it can be a good idea to print it, maybe even enlarge it, and then write anything you find particularly striking in the margins. Use highlighters or colored pens to underline repetitions and link rhyme words. Patterns may well emerge that will help you understand the way the poem develops. Make the poems your own in this way, and then, if you are the kind of person who doesn't mind writing in books, you can insert notes in a more restrained way in the margins of your book.

If you prefer to work on your computer, you can do a similar thing by using an annotation tool on your word processor.

Whatever you do, always ask yourself what the effect of a particular technique that you identify is. Noticing an unusual choice of words, a particular rhyme scheme or use of alliteration is an important first step, but you need to take another one. Unless you go on to say why what you have noticed is effective, what it contributes to the rest of the poem, how it endorses or changes things, then you are doing less than half the job. Get into the habit of asking yourself questions, even if you can't always answer them satisfactorily.

Rhythm

All speech has rhythm because we naturally stress some words or syllables more than others. The rhythm can sometimes be very regular and pronounced, as in a children's nursery rhyme – 'JACK and JILL went UP the HILL' – but even in the most ordinary sentence the important words are given more stress. In poetry, rhythm is extremely important: patterns are deliberately created and repeated for varying effects. The rhythmical pattern of a poem is called its meter, and we can analyze, or 'scan' lines of poetry to identify stressed and unstressed syllables. In marking the text to show this, the mark '/' is used to indicate a stressed syllable, and 'x' to indicate an unstressed syllable. Each complete unit of stressed and unstressed syllables is called a 'foot', which usually has one stressed and one or two unstressed syllables.

The most common foot in English is known as the iamb, which is an unstressed syllable followed by a stressed one (x /). Many words in English are iambic: a simple example is the word 'forgot'. When we say this, the stresses naturally fall in the sequence:

x /
'forgot'.

Iambic rhythm is in fact the basic sound pattern in ordinary English speech. If you say the following line aloud you will hear what I mean:

x / x / x / x / x / x /
I went across the road and bought a pair of shoes.

The next most common foot is the trochee, a stressed syllable (or 'beat', if you like) followed by an unstressed one (/x), as in the word

/ x
'mountain'.

Both the iamb and the trochee have two syllables, the iamb being a 'rising' rhythm and the trochee a 'falling' rhythm. Another two-syllable foot known as the spondee has two equally stressed beats (/ /), as in

/ /
'blue spurt'.

Other important feet have three syllables. The most common are the anapest (x x /) and the dactyl (/ x x), which are triple rhythms, rising and falling respectively, as in the words

x x /   / x x
'unimpressed' and 'probably'.

Here are some fairly regular examples of the four main kinds of meter used in poetry. (I have separated the feet by using a vertical slash.) You should say the lines aloud, listening for the stress patterns and noting how the 'beats' fall on particular syllables or words.

Iambic meter

x / | x / | x / | x / | x /
The cur- | few tolls | the knell | of part- | ing day

Trochaic meter

/ x | / x | / x | /
Tiger | tiger | burning | bright

Anapestic meter

x x / | x x / | x x / | x x /
She is far | from the land | where her young | hero sleeps

Dactylic meter

/ x x | / x x | / x x | / x x
Woman much | missed how you | call to me, | call to me

The other technical point that you need to know about is the way the lengths of lines of verse are described. This is done according to the number of feet they contain, and the names given to different lengths of lines are as follows:

monometer	a line of one foot
dimeter	a line of two feet
trimeter	a line of three feet
tetrameter	a line of four feet
pentameter	a line of five feet
hexameter	a line of six feet
heptameter	a line of seven feet
octameter	a line of eight feet.

By far the most widely used of these are the tetrameter and the pentameter. If you look back at the four lines of poetry given as examples above, you can count the feet. You will see that the first one has five feet, so it is an iambic pentameter line; the second one has four feet, so it is a trochaic tetrameter line; the fourth and fifth also have four feet, so are anapestic and dactylic tetrameter lines respectively. Lines do not always have exactly the 'right' number of beats. Sometimes a pentameter line will have an extra 'beat', as in the famous line from *Hamlet*, 'To be or not to be: that is the question', where the 'tion' of question is an eleventh, unstressed beat. (It is worth asking yourself why Shakespeare wrote the line like this. Why did he not write what would have been a perfectly regular ten-syllable line, such as 'The question is, to be or not to be'?)

Having outlined some of the basic meters of English poetry, it is important to say at once that very few poems would ever conform to a perfectly regular metrical pattern. The effect of that would be very boring indeed: imagine being restricted to using only iambic words, or trying to keep up a regular trochaic rhythm. Poets therefore often include trochaic or anapestic or dactylic words or phrases within what are basically iambic lines, in order to make them more interesting and suggestive, and to retain normal pronunciation. Here is a brief example from Shakespeare to show you what I mean. I have chosen a couple of lines spoken by Rosalind in
As You Like It, Act 1, scene 2, and have marked this first version to show you the basic iambic meter:

x / x / x / x / x /
My fa- | ther loved | Sir Row- | land as | his soul,
x / x / x / x / x /
And all | the world | was of | my fa | ther's mind.

If you say the lines out loud in this regular way you can hear that the effect is very unnatural. Here is one way the lines might be scanned to show how the stresses would fall in speech (though there are other ways of scanning them):

/ / x / x x x x x /
My father loved Sir Rowland as his soul,
x / x / x x x / x /
And all the world was of my father's mind.

It must be emphasized that there is no need to feel that you must try to remember all the technical terms I have been introducing here. The purpose has been to help you to become aware of the importance of rhythmic effects in poetry, and it can be just as effective to try to describe these in your own words. The thing to hang on to when writing about the rhythm of a poem is that, as Ezra Pound put it, 'Rhythm MUST have meaning': 'It can't be merely a careless dash off with no grip and no real hold to the words and sense, a tumty tum tumpty tum tum ta' (quoted in Gray, 1990,, p. 56). There are occasions, of course, when a tum-ty-ty-tum rhythm may be appropriate, and 'have meaning'. When Tennyson wrote 'The Charge of the Light Brigade', he recreated the sound, pace, and movement of horses thundering along with the emphatic dactyls of 'Half a league, half a league, half a league onward / Into the valley of death rode the six hundred'. But for a very different example we might take a short two-line poem by Pound himself. This time there is no fixed meter: like much twentieth-century poetry, this poem is in 'free verse'. Its title is 'In a Station of the Metro' (the Metro being the Paris underground railway), and it was written in 1916:

x x xx x x / / x x /
The apparition of these faces in the crowd;
/ x x x / / /
Petals on a wet, black bough.

Here you can see that the rhythm plays a subtle part in conveying the meaning. The poem is comparing the faces of people in a crowded underground to petals that have fallen on to a wet bough. The rhythm not only highlights the key words in each line, but produces much of the emotional feeling of the poem by slowing down the middle words of the first line and the final three words of the second.

For our final example of rhythm I've chosen a passage from Alexander Pope's *An Essay on Criticism* (1711).

ACTIVITY 2

Take a look at this excerpt from An Essay on Criticism. Read it aloud if you can. Listen to the rhythm, and identify why the rhythm is appropriate to the meaning. (http://www.open.edu/openlearn/ocw/mod/oucontent/olink.php?id=1713&targetdoc=Criticism)

Discussion

Pope here uses a basic structure of iambic pentameters with variations, so that the lines sound as if they have a different pace, faster or slower, depending on what is being described. It is not just rhythm that contributes to the effect here: rhyme and alliteration (successive words beginning with the same sound) recreate smooth, rough, slow and swift movement. Rhythm is entirely dependent on word choice, but is also influenced by other interdependent stylistic devices. Pope's lines enact what they describe simply because of the care that has gone into choosing the right words. It doesn't matter if you don't recognise the classical allusions: from the descriptions it is clear that Ajax is a strong man and Camilla is quick and light. If you count the beats of each line, you'll notice that, in spite of the variety of sound and effect, all have five stresses, except the last, which has six. Strangely enough it is the last and longest line that creates an impression of speed. How is this achieved? Try to hear the lines by reading them again out loud.

There is really only one way, and that is through the words chosen to represent movement: the repeated 's' sounds associated with Camilla trip swiftly off the tip of the tongue, whereas Ajax's lines demand real physical effort from mouth, lips, and tongue. You will get a much stronger sense of this if you form the words in this way, even if you are unable to say them out loud. In an exam, for instance, silent articulation of a poem will help you grasp many poetic techniques and effects that may otherwise be missed.

This extract from Pope's *An Essay on Criticism*, like the whole poem, is written in rhyming couplets (lines rhyming in pairs). They confer a formal, regular quality to the verse. The punctuation helps to control the way in which we read: notice that there is a pause at the end of each line, either a comma, a semi-colon, or a full stop. This use of the end-stopped line is characteristic of eighteenth-century heroic couplets (iambic pentameter lines rhyming in pairs), where the aim was to reproduce classical qualities of balance, harmony, and proportion.

Get into the habit of looking at rhyme words. Are any of Pope's rhymes particularly interesting here? One thing I noticed was what is known as poetic inversion. The rhyme 'shore'/'roar'is clearly important to the sound sense of the verse, but the more natural word order (were this ordinary speech) would be 'The hoarse rough verse should roar like the torrent'. Had he written this, Pope would have lost the sound qualities of the rhyme 'shore'/'roar'. He would have had to find a word such as 'abhorrent' to rhyme with 'torrent' and the couplet would have had a very different meaning. He would also have lost the rhythm of the line, in spite of the fact that the words are exactly the same.

Before we leave *An Essay on Criticism*, did you notice that Pope's subject in this poem is really poetry itself? Like Wordsworth, Pound, and William Carlos Williams, all of whom I've quoted earlier, Pope too was concerned with poetry as a craft.

Alliteration

Alliteration is the term used to describe successive words beginning with the same sound – usually, then, with the same letter.

To illustrate this I would like to use a stanza from Arthur Hugh Clough's poem, 'Natura naturans'. There is not enough space to quote the whole poem, but to give you some idea of the context of this stanza so that you can more fully appreciate what

Clough is doing, it is worth explaining that 'Natura naturans' describes the sexual tension between a young man and woman who sit next to each other in a railway carriage. They have not been introduced, and they neither speak nor exchange so much as a glance. The subject matter and its treatment is unusual and also extraordinarily frank for the time of writing (about 1849), but you need to know what is being described in order to appreciate the physicality of the lines I quote.

ACTIVITY 3

Read the attached stanza from Arthur Hugh Clough's poem "Natura Naturans" and consider the following questions: (http://www.open.edu/openlearn/ocw/mod/oucontent/olink.php?id=1713&targetdoc=Natura+naturans%E2%80%99)

1. What is the single most striking technique used, and what are the effects?
2. How would you describe the imagery, and what does it contribute to the overall effect?

Discussion

1. Visually the use of alliteration is striking, particularly in the first line and almost equally so in the second. If you took the advice above about paying attention to the physical business of articulating the words too, you should be in a good position to discriminate between the rapidity of the flies and the heavier movement of the bees, and to notice how tactile the language is. The effect is actually to create sensuality in the stanza.
2. Notice that though we begin with flies, bees and rooks, all of which are fairly common flying creatures, we move to the more romantic lark with its 'wild' song, and then to the positively exotic gazelle, leopard, and dolphin. From the rather homely English air (flies, bees, birds), we move to foreign locations 'Libyan dell' and 'Indian glade', and from there to 'tropic seas'. (Cod in the North Sea would have very different connotations from dolphins in the tropics.) Air, earth, and sea are all invoked to help express the variety of changing highly charged erotic feelings that the speaker remembers. The images are playful and preposterous, joyfully expressing the familiar poetic subject of sexual attraction and arousal in a way that makes it strange and new. Notice that in each case the image is more effective because the alliteration emphasizes it.

Rhyme

If a poem rhymes, then considering how the rhyme works is always important.

Rhyme schemes can be simple or highly intricate and complex; it will always be worth considering why a particular rhyme pattern was chosen and trying to assess its effects.

ACTIVITY 4

Read "Love from the North" (1862) by Christina Rossetti. What is the poem about, and how does the rhyme contribute to the meaning and overall effect? (http://www.open.edu/openlearn/ocw/mod/oucontent/olink.php?id=1713&targetdoc=%E2%80%98Love+From+the+North%E2%80%99)

Discussion

'Love From the North' tells a simple story. A woman about to marry one man is whisked away by another, just as she is about to exchange vows. The form of the poem is very simple: the second and fourth lines of each of the eight 4-line stanzas rhyme. More significantly, because the last word of each stanza is 'nay', there is only one rhyme sound throughout. There are more internal rhymes relying on the same repeated sound, however, aren't there? Look at the last lines of stanzas 1, 2, 6, 7 and 8 where 'say' 'nay'; 'nay' 'nay'; 'say' 'nay'; 'yea' 'nay'; and 'say' 'nay' appear. In the second stanza, 'gay' occurs twice in line 2; stanza five and six both have 'yea' in line 3. What is the effect of this?

Do you think the effect might be to help over-simplify the story? Clearly the woman has doubts about the man from the south's devotion: he 'never dared' to say no to her. He seems to have no will of his own: he 'saddens' when she does, is 'gay' when she is, wants only what she does. On her wedding day she thinks: 'It's quite too late to think of nay'. But is she any happier with the strong man from the north? Who is he? Has he carried her off against her will? And what exactly do you make of the last stanza? Do the 'links of love' imply a chain? This strong-minded woman who imposed her will on the man from the south has 'neither heart nor power/Nor will nor wish' to say no to the man from the north. Is that good, or bad? And what do you make of the 'book and bell' with which she's made to stay? Certainly they imply something different from the conventional Christian marriage she was about to embark on in the middle of the poem – witchcraft, perhaps, or magic? And are the words 'Till now' particularly significant at the beginning of line 3 in the last stanza? Might they suggest a new resolve to break free?

How important is it to resolve such questions? It is very useful to ask them, but not at all easy to find answers. In fact, that is one of the reasons I like the poem so much. The language is very simple and so is the form – eight quatrains (or four-line stanzas) – and yet the more I think about the poem, the more interesting and ambiguous it seems. In my opinion, that is its strength. After all, do we always know exactly what we want or how we feel about relationships? Even if we do, is it always possible to put such feelings into words? Aren't feelings often ambivalent rather than straightforward?

It is also worth bearing in mind the fact that the poem is written in ballad form. A ballad tells a story, but it does only recount events – part of the convention is that ballads don't go into psychological complexities. It is likely that Rossetti chose this ancient oral verse form because she was interested in raising ambiguities. But perhaps the point of the word 'nay' chiming throughout 'Love From the North' is to indicate the female speaker saying no to both men – the compliant lover and his opposite, the demon lover, alike? After all, 'nay' is the sound which gives the poem striking unity and coherence.

Keats's 'Eve of St Agnes' (1820) also tells a tale of lovers, but it isn't a ballad, even though the rhyme scheme of the first four lines is the same as Rossetti's quatrains. The stanzas are longer, and the form more complex and sophisticated. The rhyme pattern is the same throughout all 42 stanzas, the first two of which are reproduced for the following activity:

ACTIVITY 5

Read the first two stanzas of Keats's "Eve of St Agnes." How would you describe the rhyme scheme, and does it seem appropriate for the subject matter? (http://www.open.edu/openlearn/ocw/mod/oucontent/olink.php?id=1713&targetdoc=Keats%27s+%E2%80%98Eve+of+St+Agnes.)

Discussion

In comparison to the Rossetti poem the rhyme sounds form complex patterns, don't they? While 'was'/'grass' in the first stanza and 'man'/'wan' in the second do not quite produce a full rhyme (depending on your accent), the first and third lines do rhyme in subsequent stanzas. Using a letter of the alphabet to describe each new rhyme sound, we could describe the pattern like this: a b a b b c b c c (imagine sustaining that intricate patterning for 42 stanzas). This kind of formula is useful up to a point for showing how often the same sounds recur, and it does show how complicated the interweaving of echoing sounds is. But it says nothing about how the sounds relate to what is being said – and, as I have been arguing all along, it is the relationship between meaning and word choice that is of particular interest. To give a full answer to my own question, I'd really need to consider the function of rhyme throughout the poem. It would not be necessary to describe what happens in each stanza, but picking out particular pertinent examples would help me argue a case. With only the first two stanzas to work with, I could say that, if nothing else, the intricate rhyme pattern seems appropriate not only for the detailed descriptions but also for the medieval, slightly gothic setting of the chapel where the holy man prays.

ACTIVITY 6

Read the extract from Tennyson's "Mariana" (1830). Again, this comes from a longer poem, so it would be useful to look it up and read the rest if you have the opportunity. (http://www.open.edu/openlearn/ocw/mod/oucontent/olink.php?id=1713&targetdoc=Tennyson%27s+%E2%80%98Mariana)

Read the extract and consider the following questions:

1. Describe the rhyme in the stanza from Tennyson's 'Mariana'.
2. What is the first stanza about?

Discussion

1. As with the Keats poem, the rhyme scheme here is quite complicated. Using the same diagrammatic formula of a letter for each new rhyme sound, we could describe this as 'a b a b c d d c e f e f. You might notice too that indentations at the beginning of each line emphasise lines that rhyme with each other: usually the indentations are alternate, except for lines 6 and 7, which form a couplet in the middle of the stanza. It is worth telling you too that each of the stanzas ends with a variation of the line 'I would that I were dead' (this is known as a refrain) so – as in Christina Rossetti's 'Love From the North' – a dominant sound or series of sounds throughout helps to control the mood of the poem.
2. We may not know who Mariana is, or why she is in the lonely, crumbling grange, but she is obviously waiting for a man who is slow in arriving. The 'dreary'/'aweary' and 'dead'/'said' rhymes, which, if you read the rest of the poem, you will see are repeated in each stanza, convey her dejection and express the boredom of endless waiting. As with the stanzas from Keats's 'Eve of St Agnes', there is plenty of carefully observed detail – black moss on the flower-plots, rusty nails, a clinking latch on a gate or door – all of which description contributes to the desolation of the scene and Mariana's mood. Were the moated grange a lively, sociable household, the poem would be very different. Either Mariana would be cheerful, or her suicidal misery would be in sharp contrast to her surroundings. It is always worth considering what settings contribute to the overall mood of a poem.

Poetic Inversion

Poetic inversion, or changing the usual word order of speech, is often linked to the need to maintain a rhythm or to find a rhyme. We noticed Pope's poetic inversion in *An Essay on Criticism* and saw how the rhyme was intimately linked to the rhythm of the verse. The song 'Dancing in the Street', first recorded by Martha and the Vandellas in the 1960s, does violence to word order in the interests of rhyme – 'There'll be dancing in the street/ A chance new folk to meet' – but, because the words are sung to a driving rhythm, we are unlikely to notice how awkward they are. There's a convention that we recognise, however unconsciously, that prevents us from mentally re-writing the line as 'a chance to meet new people'. ('People' rather than 'folk' would be more usual usage for me, but, as with the Pope example, this would mean that the rhythm too would be lost.)

Poems That Don't Rhyme

Are poems that don't rhyme prose? Not necessarily. Virginia Woolf (1882–1941), a novelist rather than a poet, and T.S. Eliot (1888–1965), known particularly for his poetry, both wrote descriptive pieces best described as 'prose poems'. These look like short prose passages since there is no attention to line lengths or layout on the page, as there was, for example, in 'Mariana'. When you study Shakespeare you will come across blank verse. 'Blank' here means 'not rhyming', but the term 'blank verse' is used specifically to describe verse in unrhyming iambic pentameters.

Although iambic pentameters resemble our normal speech patterns, in ordinary life we speak in prose. You'll notice if you look through Shakespeare's plays that blank verse is reserved for kings, nobles, heroes and heroines. They may *also* speak in prose, as lesser characters do, but commoners don't ever have speeches in blank verse. Shakespeare – and other playwrights like him – used the form to indicate status. It is important to recognise this convention, which would have been understood by his contemporaries – writers, readers, and audiences alike. So choosing to write a poem in blank verse is an important decision: it will elevate the subject. One such example is Milton's epic *Paradise Lost*(1667), a long poem in twelve Books describing Creation, Adam and Eve's temptation, disobedience and expulsion from Paradise. It sets out to justify the ways of God to man, so blank verse is entirely appropriate. This great epic was in Wordsworth's mind when he chose the same form for his autobiographical poem, *The Prelude*.

ACTIVITY 7

Read and compare these extracts. One is from Book XIII of *The Prelude*, where Wordsworth is walking up Mount Snowdon; the other is from "The Idiot Boy," one of his *Lyrical Ballads*. What effects are achieved by the different forms? (http://www.open.edu/openlearn/ocw/mod/oucontent/olink.php?id=1713&targetdoc=%E2%80%98The+Idiot+Boy%E2%80%99)

Discussion

Both poems use iambic meter – an unstressed followed by a stressed syllable. The extract from *The Prelude* uses iambic pentameters, five metrical feet in each line, whereas 'The Idiot Boy' (like the ballad, 'Love From the North') is in tetrameters, only four, establishing a more sing-song rhythm. Other stylistic techniques contribute to the difference in tone too: the language of *The Prelude* is formal (Wordsworth's 'Ascending' rather than 'going up'), whereas 'The Idiot Boy' uses deliberately homely diction, and rhyme. Three simple rhyme words ring out throughout the 92 stanzas of the latter: 'Foy', 'boy' and 'joy' stand at the heart of the poem, expressing the mother's pride in her son. The moon features in each extract. In *The Prelude*, as Wordsworth climbs, the ground lightens, as it does in The Old Testament before a prophet appears. Far from being a meaningless syllable to fill the rhythm of a line, 'lo' heightens the religious parallel, recalling the biblical 'Lo, I bring you tidings of great joy': this episode from *The Prelude* describes a moment of spiritual illumination. Wordsworth's intentions in these two poems were quite different, and the techniques reflect that.

Other poems that don't use rhyme are discussed later ('Wherever I Hang'; 'Mona Lisa'; 'Poem'). Notice that they use a variety of rhythms, and because of that none can be described as blank verse.

Voice

Is the speaker in a poem one and the same as the writer? Stop and consider this for a few moments. Can you think of any poems you have read where a writer has created a character, or persona, whose voice we hear when we read?

Wordsworth's *The Prelude* was written as an autobiographical poem, but there are many instances where it is obvious that poet and persona are different. Charlotte Mew's poem, 'The Farmer's Bride' (1916) begins like this:

Three summers since I chose a maid,
Too young maybe – but more's to do
At harvest-time than bide and woo.
When us was wed she turned afraid
Of love and me and all things human;

(Warner, 1981, pp. 1–2)

Mew invents a male character here, and clearly separates herself as a writer from the voice in her poem. Some of the most well-known created characters – or personae – in poetry are Browning's dramatic monologues.

ACTIVITY 8

Consider the opening lines from three Robert Browning poems. Who do you think is speaking? (http://www.open.edu/openlearn/ocw/mod/oucontent/olink.php?id=1713&targetdoc=Robert+Browning+poems)

Discussion

Well, the first speaker isn't named, but we can infer that, like Brother Lawrence whom he hates, he's a monk. The second must be a Duke since he refers to his 'last Duchess' and, if we read to the end of the third poem, we discover that the speaker is a man consumed with such jealousy that he strangles his beloved Porphyria with her own hair. Each of the poems is written in the first person ('
my heart's abhorrence'; 'That's *my* last Duchess'; *I* listened with heart fit to break'). None of the characters Browning created in these poems bears any resemblance to him: the whole point of a dramatic monologue is the creation of a character who is most definitely not the poet. Charlotte Mew's poem can be described in the same way.

Line Lengths and Line Endings

Read the following prose extract taken from Walter Pater's discussion of the *Mona Lisa*, written in 1893, and then complete the activity:

> “
>
> She is older than the rocks among which she sits; like the vampire, she has been dead many times, and learned the secrets of the grave; and has been a diver in deep seas, and keeps their fallen day about her; and trafficked for strange webs with Eastern merchants: and, as Leda, was the mother of Helen of Troy, and, as Saint Anne, the mother of Mary; and all this has been to her but as the sound of lyres and flutes, and lives only in the delicacy with which it has moulded the changing lineaments, and tinged the eyelids and the hands.

ACTIVITY 9

When W.B. Yeats was asked to edit *The Oxford Book of Modern Verse 1892–1935* (1936), he chose to begin with this passage from Pater, but he set it out quite differently on the page. Before you read his version, write out the extract as a poem yourself. The exercise is designed to make you think about line lengths, where to start a new line and where to end it when there is no rhyme to give you a clue. There is no *regular* rhythm either, though I'm sure you will discover rhythms in the words, as well as repeated patterns. How can you best bring out these poetic features?

Discussion

Of course, there is no right answer to this exercise, but you should compare your version to Yeats's, printed below, to see if you made similar decisions.

She is older than the rocks among which she sits;
Like the Vampire,
She has been dead many times,
And learned the secrets of the grave;
And has been a diver in deep seas,
And keeps their fallen day about her;
And trafficked for strange webs with Eastern merchants;
And, as Leda,
Was the mother of Helen of Troy,
And, as St Anne,
Was the mother of Mary;
And all this has been to her but as the sound of lyres and flutes,
And lives
Only in the delicacy
With which it has moulded the changing lineaments,
And tinged the eyelids and the hands.

View the document as a PDF.

I wonder whether you used upper case letters for the first word of each line, as Yeats did? You may have changed the punctuation, or perhaps have left it out altogether. Like Yeats, you may have used 'And' at the beginnings of lines to draw attention to the repetitions: nine of the lines begin in this way, emphasising the way the clauses pile up, defining and redefining the mysterious Mona Lisa. Two lines begin with 'She': while there was no choice about the first, beginning the third in the same way focuses attention on her right at the start of the poem. Yeats has used Pater's punctuation to guide his line endings in all but two places: lines 13 and 14 run on – a stylistic device known as enjambment. The effect is an interesting interaction between eyes and ears. While we may be tempted to read on without pausing to find the sense, the line endings and white space of the page impose pauses on our reading, less than the commas and semi-colons that mark off the other lines, but significant nevertheless.

Yeats's arrangement of the words makes the structure and movement of Pater's long sentence clearer than it appears when written as prose. The poem begins with age – she is 'older than the rocks' – and refers to 'Vampire', death, and 'grave' in the first lines. The decision to single out the two words 'And lives' in a line by themselves towards the end of the poem sets them in direct opposition to the opening; we have moved from great age and living death to life. The arrangement of lines 8–11 highlights her links with both pagan and Christian religions: the Mona Lisa was the mother of Helen of Troy and the Virgin Mary. The wisdom and knowledge she has acquired is worn lightly, nothing more than 'the sound of lyres and flutes', apparent only in the 'delicacy' of colour on 'eyelids and hands'.

The aim of the preceding exercise was to encourage you to think about form and structure even when a poem does not appear to follow a conventional pattern. Because you have now 'written' a poem and had the opportunity to compare it with someone else's version of the same words, you should begin to realise the importance of decisions about where exactly to place a word for maximum effect, and how patterns can emerge which will control our reading when, for example, successive lines begin with repetitions. It should have made you think about the importance of the beginnings of lines, as well as line endings. What has been achieved by using a short line here, a longer one there? How do these decisions relate to what is being said? These are questions that can usefully be asked of any poem.

Earlier, discussing the extract from Pope's *An Essay on Criticism*, I asked you to concentrate on the sound qualities of the poetry. Here, I want you to consider the visual impact of the poem on the page. It is a good thing to be aware of what a complex task reading is, and to be alive to the visual as well as the aural qualities of the verse.

ACTIVITY 10

When W.B. Yeats was asked to edit *The Oxford Book of Modern Verse 1892–1935* (1936), he chose to begin with this passage from Pater, but he set it out quite differently on the page. Before you read his version, write out the extract as a poem yourself. The exercise is designed to make you think about line lengths, where to start a new line and where to end it when there is no rhyme to give you a clue. There is no *regular* rhythm either, though I'm sure you will discover rhythms in the words, as well as repeated patterns. How can you best bring out these poetic features?

Further exercise: taking Grace Nichols's 'Wherever I Hang', discussed in Activity 10, you could reverse the process carried out in the previous exercise by writing out the poem as prose. Then, covering up the original, you could rewrite it as verse and compare your version with the original.

Comparing and Contrasting

Often you will find that an assignment asks you to 'compare and contrast' poems. There's a very good reason for this, for often it is only by considering different treatments of similar subjects that we become aware of a range of possibilities, and begin to understand why particular choices have been made. You will have realised that often in the previous discussions I've used a similar strategy, showing, for example, how we can describe the rhyme scheme of 'Love From the North' as simple once we have looked at the more intricate patterning of Keats's 'The Eve of St Agnes' or Tennyson's 'Mariana'. Anne Brontë's 'Home' and Grace Nichols's 'Wherever I Hang' treat the subject of exile in quite different ways, and looking at one can sharpen our understanding of what the other does.

ACTIVITY 11

Read the opening lines from these two poems commemorating deaths. What can you explain why they sound so very different? (http://www.open.edu/openlearn/ocw/mod/oucontent/olink.php?id=1713&targetdoc=poems+commemorating+deaths.)

Discussion

If I had to identify one thing, I would say that the first begins more elaborately and with a more formal tone than the second. 'Felix Randal' tends to use language in an unusual way, but you would probably agree that the first sentence is quite straightforward and sounds colloquial (or informal), as if the speaker has just overheard someone talking about Randal's death and wants to confirm his impression. 'Lycidas' opens quite differently. It is not immediately apparent what evergreens have to do with anything (in fact they work to establish an appropriately melancholy atmosphere or tone), and it isn't until line 8 that we learn of a death. The word 'dead' is repeated, and the following line tells us that Lycidas was a young man. While 'Felix Randal' has an immediacy, the speaker of 'Lycidas' seems to find it hard to get going.

Both poems are elegies – poems written to commemorate death – and both poets are aware of writing within this convention, although they treat it differently.

ACTIVITY 12

What do the titles of the poems used in Activity 13 tell us about each poem, and how might they help us understand the different uses of the elegiac convention? (http://www.open.edu/openlearn/history-the-arts/culture/literature-and-creative-writing/literature/approaching-poetry/content-section-12#act013/?printable=1)

Discussion

I think it would be apparent to most readers that 'Felix Randall' is simply a man's name, while 'Lycidas' is more mysterious. In fact Lycidas is a traditional pastoral name, but unless you know something about the classical pastoral tradition it might mean very little to you. The young man whose death Milton was commemorating was actually called Edward King, but, at the time he was writing, elegies were formal, public and impersonal poems rather than private expressions of grief. 'Lycidas' commemorates a member of a prominent family rather than a close friend of the poet's. Over two hundred years later, Hopkins, while working loosely within the same elegiac convention, adapts it. Felix Randal is an ordinary working man, not a public figure. In the seventeenth century it would have been unlikely that he would have been considered worthy of a poem like this.

If you were making a special study of elegies, there would be a great deal more to say. That's not the idea here, though. The point is that by comparing and contrasting the tone of the opening lines and the titles, and considering when the poems were written, we have come up with a number of significant differences.

ACTIVITY 13

Read this poem by Robert Browning carefully. Who is speaking, and who is being addressed? (http://www.open.edu/openlearn/ocw/mod/oucontent/olink.php?id=1713&targetdoc=Robert+Browning+poem)

Discussion

From the evidence of the poem we know that the speaker once walked across a moor, found an eagle's feather, and has a high regard for the poet Shelley (1792–1822). The person being addressed is not named, but we discover that he (or she) once met Shelley, and this alone confers status by association. The word 'you' ('your' in one instance) is repeated in 6 out of the first 8 lines. 'You' becomes a rhyme word at the end of the second line, so when we reach the word 'new' in line four – one of the two lines in the first stanzas that doesn't contain 'you' – the echo supplies the deficiency. 'You' clearly represents an important focus in the first half of the poem, but who exactly is 'you' ?

Thinking about this apparently straightforward question of who is being addressed takes us into an important area of critical debate: for each one of us who has just read the poem has, in one sense, become a person who not only knows who Shelley is (which may not necessarily be the case) but lived when he did, met him, listened to him, and indeed exchanged at least a couple of words with him. Each of us reads the poem as an individual, but the poem itself constructs a reader who is not identical to any of us. We are so used to adopting 'reading' roles dictated by texts like this that often we don't even notice the way in which the text has manipulated us.

ACTIVITY 14

Now read the Robert Browning poem again, this time asking yourself if the speaking voice changes in the last two stanzas, and if the person who is being addressed remains the same. (http://www.open.edu/openlearn/ocw/mod/oucontent/olink.php?id=1713&targetdoc=Robert+Browning+poem)

Discussion

If the first half of the poem is characterised by the repetition of 'you' and the sense of an audience that pronoun creates, then the second half seems quite different in content and tone. The speaker is trying to find a parallel in his experience to make sense of and explain his feeling of awe; the change of tone is subtle. Whereas someone is undoubtedly being addressed directly in the first stanza, in the third and fourth, readers overhear – as if the speaker is talking to himself.

At first the connection between the man who met Shelley and the memory of finding an eagle's feather may not be obvious, but there is a point of comparison. As stanza 2 explains, part of the speaker's sense of wonder stems from the fact that time did not stand still: 'you were living before that, / And also you are living after'. The moor in stanza 3, like the listener, is anonymous – it has 'a name of its own ... no doubt' – but where it is or what it is called is unimportant: only one 'hand's-breadth' is memorable, the spot that 'shines alone' where the feather was found. The poem is about moments that stand out in our memories while the ordinary daily stuff of life fades. It also acknowledges that we don't all value the same things.

ACTIVITY 15

Take another look at the poem. How would you describe its form? (http://www.open.edu/openlearn/ocw/mod/oucontent/olink.php?id=1713&targetdoc=Robert+Browning+poem)

Discussion

The structure of the poem is perfectly balanced: of the four quatrains, two deal with each memory, so, although the nature of each seems quite different, implicitly the form invites us to compare them. Think about the way in which Browning introduces the eagle feather. How does he convince us that this is a rare find?

To begin with, the third and fourth stanzas make up one complete sentence, with a colon at the end of the third announcing the fourth; this helps to achieve a sense of building up to something important. Then we move from the visual image of a large space of moor to the very circumscribed place where the feather is found, but the reason why this 'hand's-breadth' shines out is delayed for the next two lines 'For there I picked up on the heather' – yes? what? – 'And there I put inside my breast' – well? – 'A moulted feather', ah (and notice the internal rhyme there of 'feather' with 'heather' which draws attention to and emphasises the harmony of the moment), and then the word 'feather' is repeated and expanded: 'an eagle-feather' Clearly the feather of no other bird would do, for ultimately the comparison is of eagle to the poet; Browning knows Shelley through his poetry as he knows the eagle through its feather, and that feather presents a striking visual image.

There is an immediacy about the conversational opening of the poem which, I have suggested, deliberately moves into a more contemplative tone, possibly in the second stanza (think about it), but certainly by the third. We have considered some of the poetic techniques that Browning employs to convince us of the rarity of his find in the third and fourth stanzas. You might like to think more analytically about the word sounds, not just the rhyme but, for example, the repeated 'ae' sound in 'breadth' 'heather' 'breast' and 'feather'. What, however, do you make of the tone of the last line? Try saying the last lines of each stanza out loud. Whether you can identify the meter with technical language or not is beside the point. The important thing is that 'Well, I forget the rest' sounds deliberately lame. After the intensity of two extraordinary memories, everything else pales into insignificance and, to reiterate this, the rhythm tails off. While the tone throughout is informal, the last remark is deliberately casual.

Glossary

Alliteration	repetition of sounds, usually the first letters of successive words, or words that are close together. Alliteration usually applies only to consonants.
Anapest	*see under* foot.
Assonance	repetition of identical or similar vowel sounds.
Ballad	originally a song which tells a story, often involving dialogue. Characteristically, the storyteller's own feelings are not expressed.
Caesura	strong pause in a line of verse, usually appearing in the middle of a line and marked with a comma, semi-colon, or a full stop.
Couplet	pair of rhymed lines, often used as a way of rounding off a sonnet; hence the term 'closing couplet'.
Dactyl	*see under* foot.
Dialogue	spoken exchange between characters, usually in drama and fiction but also sometimes in poetry.
Diction	writer's choice of words. Poetic diction might be described, for instance, as formal or informal, elevated or colloquial.
Elegy	poem of loss, usually mourning the death of a public figure, or someone close to the poet.
Ellipsis	omission of words from a sentence to achieve brevity and compression.
Enjambment	the use of run-on lines in poetry. Instead of stopping or pausing at the end of a line of poetry, we have to carry on reading until we complete the meaning in a later line. The term comes from the French for 'striding'.
Epic	a long narrative poem dealing with events on a grand scale, often with a hero above average in qualities and exploits.
Epigram	witty, condensed expression. The closing couplet in some of Shakepeare's sonnets is often described as an epigram.
Foot	a unit of meter with a pattern of stressed and unstressed syllables. In the examples that follow, a stressed syllable is indicated by '/', and an unstressed syllable by 'x': anapest: xx/; dactyl: /xx; iamb: x/; spondee: //; trochee: /x
Heroic couplet	iambic pentameter lines rhyming in pairs, most commonly used for satiric or didactic poetry, and particularly favoured in the eighteenth century.
Iamb	*see under* foot.
Iambic pentameter	a line consisting of five iambs.
Imagery	special use of language in a way that evokes sense impressions (usually visual). Many poetic images function as mental pictures that give shape and appeal to something otherwise vague and abstract; for example, 'yonder before us lie/ Deserts of vast Eternity'. Simile and metaphor are two types of imagery.
Metaphor	image in which one thing is substituted for another, or the quality of one object is identified with another. The sun, for Shakespeare, becomes 'the eye of heaven'.
Meter	(from the Greek *metron*, 'measure') measurement of a line of poetry, including its length and its pattern of stressed and unstressed syllables. There are different meter in poetry. Most sonnets, for example, written in English are divided into lines of ten syllables with five stresses – a measure known as pentameter (from the Greek *pente* for 'five'). The sonnet also tends to use a line (known as the iambic line) in which an unstressed syllable is followed by a stressed one, as in this line: 'If I should die, think only this of me'. Most sonnets, then are written in iambic pentameters.
Narrative	the telling of a series of events (either true or fictitious). The person relating these events is the narrator. However, it is often more usual in poetry to refer to 'the speaker'.
Octave	group of eight lines of poetry, often forming the first part of a sonnet.
Ode	a poem on a serious subject, usually written in an elevated formal style; often written to commemorate public events.

Onomatopoeia	a word that seems to imitate the sound or sounds associated with the object or action, for example, 'cuckoo'.
Ottava rima	a poem in eight-line stanzas, rhyming a b a b a b c c.
Personification	writing about something not human as if it were a person, for example 'Busy old fool, unruly Sun,/Why dost thou thus,/Through windows and through curtains call onus?'.
Poetic inversion	reversing the order of normal speech in order to make the words fit a particular rhythm, or rhyme, or both.
Pun	double meaning or ambiguity in a word, often employed in a witty way. Puns are often associated with wordplay.
Quatrain	group of four lines of poetry, usually rhymed.
Refrain	a line or phrase repeated throughout a poem, sometimes with variations, often at the end of each stanza.
Rhyme	echo of a similar sound, usually at the end of a line of poetry. Occasionally, internal rhymes can be found, as in: 'Sister, my sister, O *fleet, sweet* swallow'.
Rhyme scheme	pattern of rhymes established in a poem. The pattern of rhymes in a quatrain, for instance, might be 'a b a b' or 'a b b a'.
Rhythm	the pattern of beats or stresses in a line creating a sense of movement. Sestet: group of six lines of poetry, often forming the second part of a sonnet.
Simile	image in which one thing is likened to another. The similarity is usually pointed out with the word 'like' or 'as': 'My love is like a red, red rose'.
Sonnet	fourteen iambic pentameter lines with varying rhyme schemes.
Spondee	*see under* foot.
Syllable	single unit of pronunciation. 'Sun' is one syllable; 'sunshine' is two syllables.
Tercet	group of three lines in poetry, sometimes referred to as a triplet. Trochee: *see under* foot.
Turn	distinctive movement of change in mood or thought or feeling. In the sonnet, the turn usually occurs between the octave and the sestet, though the closing couplet in Shakespeare's sonnets often constitutes the turn.
Villanelle	an intricate French verse form with some lines repeated, and only two rhyme sounds throughout the five three-line stanzas and the final four-line stanza.

References

Abrams, M.H. (1971) *A Glossary of Literary Terms*, Holt, Rinehart and Winston.

Barker, J.R.V. (ed.) (1985) *The Brontes: Selected Poems*, Dent.

Bush, D. (ed.) (1966) *Milton: Poetical Works*, Oxford University Press.

Bygrave, S. (ed.) (1998) *Romantic Writings*, The Open University.

Clough, A.H. (1890) *Poems*, Macmillan.

Gardner, W.H. (1953) *Poems and Prose of Gerard Manley Hopkins*, Penguin.

Gibson, J. (ed.) (1976) *The Complete Poems of Thomas Hardy*, Macmillan.

Goodman, L. (1996) *Literature and Gender*, The Open University.

Gray, R. (1990) *American Poetry of the Twentieth Century*, Longman.

Hutchinson, T. (ed.) (1936) (revised 1969 by E. De Selincourt) *Wordsworth: Poetical Works*, Oxford University Press.

Jack, I. and Fowler, R. (eds) (1988) *The Poetical Works of Robert Browning*, vol. III *Bells and Pomegranates*, Clarendon Press.

Matterson, S. and Jones, D. (2000) *Studying Poetry*, Arnold. O'Hara, F. (1964) *Lunch Poems*, City Lights Books.

Owens, W.R. and Johnson, H. (eds) (1998) *Romantic Writings: An Anthology*, The Open University.

Pater, W. (1893) (1998) *The Renaissance: Studies in Art and Poetry*, ed. Adam Phillips, Oxford University Press.

Regan, S. (1997) 'Form and Meaning in Poetry: The Sonnet', in *A103 An Introduction to the Humanities*, Block 1 'Form and Reading', The Open University.

Sisson, C.H. (1984) *Christina Rossetti: Selected Poems*, Carcanet.

Trilling, T. and Bloom, H. (1973) *Victorian Prose and Poetry*, Oxford University Press.

Wain, J. (ed.) (1990) *The Oxford Library of English Poetry*, vol.II, Oxford University Press / Guild Publishing.

Warner, V. (ed.) (1981)

Charlotte Mew: Collected Poems and Prose, Virago Press. Yeats, W.B. (1936) *The Oxford Book of Modern Verse 1892–1935*, Clarendon Press.

Proper Source Use in Paragraphs

Function of Source Use

You use sources as a form of backup for what you write. They support your claims. This means that you own your paper

Consequences of the String of Pearls Effect

Using a single source several times in a row and then moving on as if some writing occurred is a common writing problem. How great a percentage of an average body paragraph should come from the source? Answers vary, of course, depending on your purpose and the sophistication of your topic. However, if you consistently let the sources take over more than one-third of your body paragraphs, you will not be a successful arguer, thinker, or writer.

If you consistently string together a bunch of quotes, then readers are left with unused material. If you have two or three quotes in a row, that means you did not interpret them. For some reason, many writers think that the quotation marks are magic, as if the quotes speak–or mean something–for themselves. They don't. If you think of the quotes as excuses for you to discuss their meaning, you will be much better off.

We call the stringing together of paraphrases or quotes "the string of pearls effect." What is the effect on readers of such lists?

I usually tell students that readers need lots of prompts and reminders. Say things again, even if you think the quote did a good job of making meaning. Tell readers what something means–just don't use "I" or "you" as you follow up on the quote. The ends of paragraphs are where things tend to fall apart, I think. Succeed in synthesizing your source, in using it and proving the meaning of source information.

With cited material, follow up by

1. linking the paraphrase/quote to the paragraph's topic sentence,
2. linking the cited information to the thesis
3. restating the relevance, credibility, or context of the source material
4. setting up a transition to the upcoming paragraph(s)
5. using a signal phrase like "In other words, . . ." and launching into a direct interpretation of the cited bit

Use your options. Take an active approach so papers–especially the research essay–actually use the sources actively.

A Typical Paragraph Pattern

(Remember, though, that this is not a formula. Vary your paragraphs, sentences, details, appeals, etc.)

Topic sentence. This is your own. **Avoid** starting w/quote (Why is this so?)
setup for source use (1-3 sentences)
source use (quote then cite, **or paraphrase one sentence** then cite)
direct interpretation of the quote's words or the paraphrase's meaning(s) (1-4 sentences, right?)
paragraph closing/transition/restated topic sentence/link to thesis

End the paragraph on your own with emphasis and power.

In large part, how well you do from here on out depends on how well you learn MLA citing and the standards of writing academic arguments. If we're stuck with poorly-written paragraphs, the papers will only reach a certain level of quality.

Function of Source Use

You use sources as a form of backup for what you write. They support your claims. This means that you own your paper

Consequences of the String of Pearls Effect

Using a single source several times in a row and then moving on as if some writing occurred is a common writing problem. How great a percentage of an average body paragraph should come from the source? Answers vary, of course, depending on your purpose and the sophistication of your topic. However, if you consistently let the sources take over more than one-third of your body paragraphs, you will not be a successful arguer, thinker, or writer.

If you consistently string together a bunch of quotes, then readers are left with unused material. If you have two or three quotes in a row, that means you did not interpret them. For some reason, many writers think that the quotation marks are magic, as if the quotes speak–or mean something–for themselves. They don't. If you think of the quotes as excuses for you to discuss their meaning, you will be much better off.

We call the stringing together of paraphrases or quotes "the string of pearls effect." What is the effect on readers of such lists?

I usually tell students that readers need lots of prompts and reminders. Say things again, even if you think the quote did a good job of making meaning. Tell readers what something means–just don't use "I" or "you" as you follow up on the quote. The ends of paragraphs are where things tend to fall apart, I think. Succeed in synthesizing your source, in using it and proving the meaning of source information.

With cited material, follow up by

1. linking the paraphrase/quote to the paragraph's topic sentence,
2. linking the cited information to the thesis
3. restating the relevance, credibility, or context of the source material
4. setting up a transition to the upcoming paragraph(s)
5. using a signal phrase like "In other words, . . ." and launching into a direct interpretation of the cited bit

Use your options. Take an active approach so papers–especially the research essay–actually use the sources actively.

A Typical Paragraph Pattern

(Remember, though, that this is not a formula. Vary your paragraphs, sentences, details, appeals, etc.)

Topic sentence. This is your own. **Avoid** starting w/quote (Why is this so?)
setup for source use (1-3 sentences)
source use (quote then cite, **or paraphrase one sentence** then cite)

direct interpretation of the quote's words or the paraphrase's meaning(s) (1-4 sentences, right?)
paragraph closing/transition/restated topic sentence/link to thesis
End the paragraph on your own with emphasis and power.

In large part, how well you do from here on out depends on how well you learn MLA citing and the standards of writing academic arguments. If we're stuck with poorly-written paragraphs, the papers will only reach a certain level of quality.

Annotation: Why Mark Up Your Texts?

Marking up your book properly is a survival skill in college literature classes. Most instructors expect you to develop your own system for noting "significant stuff" when reading. Marking up your book will allow you to locate information while testing.

Even if you are renting a text or reading it on a Kindle or other device, there are annotation tools. In fact, some of the electronic tools can allow you collection your annotations.

How to Mark Up Your Book

There is no set way to mark up a text, but active readers tend to do several of the following things:

- Underline important passages. As an alternative, you could put vertical lines in the margin next to important areas.
- Put ?, ! or questions of your own in the margins next to confusing or surprising passages. This way, you won't have to stop your reading for too long in order to look up words, phrases, etc.
- Draw lines and arrows between connected ideas. Try and find your own level of connections so that these become more meaningful.
- List concepts, themes, or the names of other authors in the margins. These indicate connections.
- List the page number or beginning of a quote similar to the one you're annotating. Connect one quote with another. Quotes can be linked based on similarity, difference, emphasis, subtlety, etc. It's up to you.
- Doubt the author. Be skeptical this in the margins! Insults work, too. . .
- Use literary terms like irony, ambiguity, symbolism, tone to indicate where the author is making these moves.
- Create your own shorthand for marking the book. This could be as simple as using the triangle (delta), the mathematical symbol for change. I have a bunch of these. Seriously, this works.

With Analysis, Focus Upon Functions or Effects

At the college level, putting in the right-sounding quotes in the right-looking spots of a body paragraph is insufficient. Writers are expected to use the quotes as excuses to argue their points. Close reading is a crucial skill which helps the writer make sense of how something makes sense. Humanities courses largely aim to enhance or bring about readers' abilities to handle complex, indirect texts that demand multiple responses.

Close reading is an analytical activity where the writer picks parts of larger whole and discusses how they function. This can be done while annotating or deciding what to say about an annotated chunk of text. Because your audience often knows the text and has ideas about how it works, it is up to you to do more than simply point out the existence of an important line, phrase, or word. Within the line, the critic must move from pointing out an idea to arguing how it functions. What effect is created by that phrase? How does this word affect readers? These questions get proved after careful setup and cited quotation work.

Once you have dissected a speech, description, or dialogue, remember that you have committed a fairly aggressive, destructive act. You yanked a part from the whole. Remember to use the late portions of paragraphs to put the pieces back together. ("Pick up your toys when you are done with them!")

What You Might Look for in a Text

Focus on an author's use of complexity by discussing the effects of any of the following:

word choice (diction) word order (syntax)

connotation denotation

irony (dramatic, situational, verbal) symbolism

mood tone

paradox (seeming contradiction) how words fit/bring about character

rhetorical appeals (logos, ethos, pathos) logical patterns (valid or not)

Rhetorical modes (description, narration, definition, process, illustration, comparison/contrast, classification/division, cause/effect, argument)

> Basically, looking for moves of any sort is a good starting point with analysis.

Paragraph Menu Settings Use No Extra Vertical Spaces

MLA calls for double-spacing with no extra spaces (around titles, heading, between paragraphs). Avoid getting a significant penalty for multiple MLA errors.

Here's a screen shot of the proper Paragraph menu settings in Word:

When managing the works cited page, use the Paragraph menu to create the hanging indent that indent the second or third lines of a given works cited entry.

Analysis is the Breaking Down of a Whole into its Parts

Analysis is the Breaking Down of a Whole into its Parts

Part-to-whole relationships and breaking those down into their functions is what we do when we analyze. We argue about how the parts function.

For practice, look at the following image. It is Edward Hicks's *The Cornell Farm*. The image has a fascinating composition, so watch the way one's eyes are directed from area to area in the painting. Are there any symbols? Signs? (Do you know the difference between a sign and a symbol? [https://en.wikipedia.org/wiki/Sign_%28semiotics%29])

When we write, we analyze most of the time. Whether we are reading a student post or model essay, we look over each text and think about how we are looking. It's a composition, so some of the vocabulary we use in its analysis is shared with other humanities courses like art appreciation or music appreciation.

Consider how the whole is broken down. If its artful, then there's a guiding of one's eyes as well as a frustration of easy expectations. See what you see and share that! Again, italicize the artworks' titles.

Edward Hicks, *The Cornell Farm* (1848).

Clearly, we can argue the parts and how they function. Analysis is all about functions in the structure and effects upon the viewer/reader. It's worth remembering that the act is destructive (*lysis* meaning just that), sort of like taking apart a watch and seeing if it will function without this or that gear. And, no, don't use the creationist blind watchmaker argument here just because I mentioned watches. Their idea that something as sophisticated as an eye could not have evolved is easily-enough refuted. (http://darwiniana.org/eyes.htm)

Binary Patterns: A Western Obsession

This or that? Me or you? I or thou? Subject or object?

"child-binary" by TLC-kios is marked with CC0 1.0

Along with these basic either/or questions, Western thought is built on other key binaries.

A binary is an either/or choice like the zeroes and ones making up DVDs or other digital codes. While some things lend themselves to "this or that" choices, we know that the world is often much more complicated. The answer "Pepsi or Coke?" might define a person privately, but whether you like one or the other may not carry much public meaning. Ironically, it did carry meaning in the 80s during the Cola Wars.

These either/or choices often have strange histories. For instance, the tragedy/comedy binary informs genres on television and in literature. It is based on a thinker, Aristotle, who was not even approving of literature. Dig into the history of tragedy and comedy and you will find some strangeness. For instance, tragedy was supposed by Aristotle to feature someone making a choice which leads inevitably to their downfall, which we witness and feel *catharsis*, a sense of purging out of both ends. . .! Weird enough for you? It makes a certain amount of sense, just as listening to a blues song makes us feel happy, but it's what we'd call *contingent*: based on a quirky, particular set of happenings that did not have to occur. So binaries are contingent. (Call this the non-tragic theory of approaching binaries.) And comedy was supposed to involve a mating and joining offstage in early Greek comedies—which were held at the festival of the god Dionysus, at which, originally, his devotees called Maenads were said to mate with willing victims on mountainsides, after which they would rend apart the sacrificial victim. And this is what informs our genres—and has done so for 2,500 years. So I'd add necessary vs. contingent as a binary that can be useful.

For more on the strangeness of binaries, you might do a search for *humor theory* or look at the history of academia (gowns, gavels, graduations. . .). Or if you're talking good or evil, one might look at how evil always comes back (Sauron, Voldemort). Weirdly enough, this even contributes to a type of cannibalism whereby an enemy's body is eaten so that his soul can be erased–for a time–from the eternal battlefield. As the cliche goes, "The truth is stranger than fiction." In fields like literary analysis, there is no "capital-T Truth." That idea of there being one would go back to Plato and his theory of Forms.

So these issues have histories of which we should become aware. As a critical reader, it is important for you to take note of binaries and gauge their effects. Though they may exclude other choices, it is the case that humans notice contrasts and oppositions.

Binaries are crutches, tools. They can work but can put blinders on what we notice. Early in stages of the writing or critical thinking processes, they can be useful.

> Which side of a binary does the author notice or value more?
>
> Which views are portrayed as negative?
>
> What is undervalued or missing from a given text?

In a writing course, then, you might create a persuasive essay that argues one side against another. We contribute to these ongoing debates most thoughtfully if we realize that they arguments will continue, however well we write about them! Just don't fall into the trap of thinking that the world is either/or, comforting as that notion may be.

Video: The American Enlightenment

Featuring discussions of John Bunyan's Pilgrim's Progress; perfectionism; Deism; Benjamin Franklin; errata; Thomas Jefferson; syllogisms; John Locke; and the Declaration of Independence.

A YouTube element has been excluded from this version of the text. You can view it online here: https://africanamericanlit.pressbooks.sunycreate.cloud/?p=42

Irony

Defining Irony

Irony is all about noticing contrast. No noticing by you = inaccurate interpretations.

Verbal irony occurs when the intended meaning and the stated meaning are different—and usually opposite. Huh? Let me clarify. Irony is when the connotation is the opposite of the denotation. Connotations are the contexts, the situations and feelings around a word. Denotations are the dictionary definitions surrounding a word.

When these don't match up, a space is created. You see that space, and you react to it by giving that situation meaning.

Exemplifying Verbal Irony

Irony is like sarcasm. For example, if I said "That's a **Great** tie" to someone with an extremely ugly tie, you would hear the tone in which I said it, right? You could look up "Great" in the dictionary and find that it means good, admirable, wonderful, etc. But "good" is opposite of the usage, right? I mean, I said it so he'd see it was **ugly and bad**. Some critics dispute this connection between sarcasm and irony.

How to Approach Irony

Ask questions about irony. Use the term in your discussions and your papers.

Do you think you'll see irony in the works we'll read? Will it be used in the same ways?

If irony is the difference between the stated meaning and the intended meaning, then is it used by all cultures?

Dramatic and Situation Irony: The Sidekick Types

Dramatic irony arises when an audience knows more about a situation than the character(s). The characters say or do something whose significance they don't know. For example, you go to *Oedipus the King* knowing that he has married his mom. You know this, he doesn't. So, as he discovers this, you watch and appreciate it.

Situational irony would result from a gapping—a difference—between what readers expect and what actually occurs. This is not to be confused with the popular misconception that irony occurs when something surprising or coincidental occurs. (Think of that 90s song by Alanis Morrissette, "Isn't it Ironic?" which actually featured nonexamples of irony. Now *that's* ironic!)

The Irony" by Jack Sirichumsaeng is licensed under CC BY 2.0

"Irony" by EyeMindSoul is licensed under CC BY 2.0

Free Verse

Free verse refers to poetry that does not follow standard or regularized meter (the organization of stressed and unstressed syllables) or rhyme scheme. As opposed to more traditional poetry, which tends to use recurring line lengths, metrical patterns, and rhyme to unify individual lines of verse and tie them to other lines within the same poem, free verse can, at times, seem to be random, having no pattern or organization at all. Yet in the hands of many poets, free verse enables a different kind of organization, as they balance free verse's openness, its ability to provide elements of the poem with a different amount of emphasis, with the use of repeated imagery or syntactic patterns (parallel organization of grammatical elements) to maintain coherence and create a sense of connection among lines. Even as it eschews regular meter and rhyme schemes, free verse does, at times, draw on metrical patterns and occasional rhyme to tie lines together. What distinguishes free verse from other traditional forms of verse is that it only uses these elements occasionally—for a few lines here and there in a longer poem—and does not use them to structure the poem as a whole. A poem in free verse, then, does not lack structure—or, in many cases, some instances of metrical organization or rhyme—it simply does not maintain or use a regular pattern of meter or rhyme to structure the poem as a whole. Instead, free verse relies more on thematic, syntactic, or semantic repetition and development to create coherence.

Walt Whitman's *Leaves of Grass* is often credited as introducing free verse into English-language poetry. While not quite true (other experiments and uses preceded his), Whitman's poetry helped to establish free verse's potential for exploring a broad range of topics and its ability to embrace an extensive number of ways of organizing verse lines. Later-nineteenth-century poets, such as Matthew Arnold in England, further explored the use of free verse, but it was the French symbolists (Jules Laforgue, Gustave Kahn, and Arthur Rimbaud) who practiced what they called vers libre most fully during this period. In the twentieth century, free verse came to dominate much poetic production in English, beginning with the modernists (such as T. S. Eliot, Ezra Pound, and William Carlos Williams) who saw the open form as allowing for the more nimble representation of a modern fragmented and accelerated world.

Critical Approaches to Literature Chart

Critical Approaches to Literature Chart

Use the critical approaches discussed in the chart below to help you find an interesting angle from which to approach a text. Each approach is given a brief description **(Beliefs)**, some guidelines for studying a text **(Practices)** and prompts to inspire your discussion **(Questions)**.

Do not simply list and answer the questions for a particular critical approach. Instead, use the questions as a starting place for your actual analysis. The questions are intended to be thought-provoking, not a list to be completed.

Approach	Beliefs	Practices	Questions
Deconstructive Criticism	• Meaning is made by binary oppositions (happy/sad, man/woman, black/white); in every binary relationship, one item is favored over the other one • This favoring of one concept in the binary relationship can be questioned and reversed to open up new ideas and meanings	• Identify the binary oppositions in the text, and determine which items are favored	1. What are the binary oppositions that govern the text? 2. What ideas, concepts, and values are being established by these binaries? 3. Cite three different interpretations for the text by flipping a series of three major binaries.
Feminist Criticism	• Any interpretation of the text is influenced by the reader's own status, which includes gender and attitudes towards gender • Men and women are different: they write differently, read differently, and write about their reading differently	• Identify the gender of the author and narrator/main character of the text • Observe how sexual stereotypes might be reinforced or undermined in the text–specifically, how the text reflects, distorts, or supports the place of women (and men) in society	1. What types of roles do men/women have in the text? Do any stereotypical characterizations of men/women appear? 2. What are the attitudes toward women held by the male characters? 3. What is the author's attitude toward women in society? Explain your reasoning using detailed examples from the text.
Reader-Oriented Criticism	• The reader's response is what counts. We can't know for sure what an author intended, and the text is meaningless unless a reader responds • Responding to a text is a process. Descriptions of the process are valuable because one person's response may enrich another reader's response	• Focus on how particular details shape readers' expectations and responses	1. What did the author intend for you to feel while reading this work, and how did he or she make you feel it? 2. What kind of reader is implied by this text? For example, does it address you as if you are intelligent and well-informed, or as if you are inexperienced and innocent? 3. How is your response shaped by the text? For example, do the actions of a certain character bring you pleasure or displeasure? Why?
Historical Criticism	• Interpretation of a text should be based on an understanding of its context • The context includes information about the author; when the text was written; where the text was written	• Research the author's life and relate that information to the text • Research the author's time and location (the political history, economic history, etc.) and relate that information to the text	1. How can you connect the author's life to his or her text? Are there common issues, events, concerns? 2. Is the author part of a dominant culture, and how does that status affect the work?

			3. What events occurred surrounding the original production of the text? How may these events be relevant to the text under investigation?

2. TRICKSTERS, HUMOR, MYTHS, AND FOLKTALES

Papa Legba

Papa Legba

We can use a current page typical of the coverage of African and African-American trickster figures to situate the transition from Africa to America. These trickster figures remain vivid and instructive. As readers of literature, we can analyze them critically to understand what remains vibrant culturally from this centuries-long removal of people from Africa.

https://papalegba.weebly.com/tricksters.html

Do sites like this represent the complexity of the trickster accurately? What distortions may appear on a blog, website, or other popular web-based medium?

Tips for Reading Mythology

Tips for Reading Mythology

Reading mythology can be difficult. Here are several suggestions to help you read them.

1. Take time to make time: account for the frequent gaps in chronology and timeline continuity. Give weight to time, thinking about how myths figure the passage of time.
2. Try different lenses: Myth often reveals psychological states or changes. Also read the way a scientist would, using hypotheses and tests. Be an anthropologist, studying the structure and function of a story or hero or monster. Read as a literary critic, adopting approaches, using literary terms like motivation, conflict, irony.
3. Have cognitive complexity, the ability to hold two or more disagreeing points of view at once.
4. Look it up: If a word or name doesn't make sense, find its origin.
5. Read flexibly: As with reading Shakespeare, readings of myth run into dead end words, reordered phrases, and stilted, archaic language. Try and do a running translation of the work as you see it. Boil down long phrases: It may take forty lines to say that a hero was angry. Conversely, it may take six lines to discuss the creation of the world and man! Clearly, dealing with time flexibly is a must for a reader of myth.
6. Cognitive Dissonance-Struggle with It! The notion of cognitive dissonance states that we'll attempt to "gel" two or more contradictory ideas, reaching a state where we're comfortable. This is often impossible with mythology, so you should try and read against the tendency to explain away contradictions. (This is sort of like attempts to keep metaphors-which are dissonant identifications of two unlike things-in our minds for a while.)
7. Use binaries/get past binaries: Pairs of choices (binaries) can be useful tools in analysis. We can look at a hero in terms of what they are and are not, just as we can contrast a protagonist with an antagonist. We can contrast Eastern and Western mythological systems. Still, don't get stuck in the either/or logic of binaries. For example, many heroes go beyond fear and desire, achieving something transcendent of both (i.e., Buddha, Jesus).
8. E.M. Forster, the English novelist, said "Only connect." Making thematic, symbolic or other connections helps. Heroes and myths have many similarities. By marking your book with care, you can draw upon the obvious connections and discover implicit ones.
9. Keep asking "How does the action reflect psychological awareness and changes in awareness?" Tie your answers to specific textual details.
10. Reading these myths aloud creates an experience of them that goes beyond reading silently. Reread, too. Adopt a voice as you do this. Take a stance with your tone.
11. Appreciate what's lost in translation. Read names, think of alternate syntax (word order), and focus on alternate verbs that'd do better at conveying the action of what you're reading.
12. Remembering audience and purpose, we know that most myths are limited in usefulness as scientific or even narrative pieces. For example, the labors of Herakles isn't primarily an account of the constellation Sagittarius and its founding. What is it for, then?
13. Figure out what your favorite lenses are: anthropological, psychological-of which there are many, mythological, literary, historical, feminist, Marxist, structuralist, reader response. Usually, you're using at least two of these approaches when you read.
14. Setting and conflict are good lenses for understanding difficult myths. There's almost always an emphasis on how the landscape affects the plot, or how conflict relates to the audience.

Same Old Story?: Propp Fairy Tale Analysis

Same Old Story?: Propp Fairy Tale Analysis

Directions: Are all folk stories composed of a set of common elements? If we counted them, how many would we see? Use the classification of fairy tales sheet on the back, from Russian critic Vladimir Propp, to break down the parts of the

First, break the tale into its component parts. It has probably eight to ten of those breaks between one part of the story and another. Tell what happens in each part. List the plot events and prove they fit specific schema—elements—from Propp.

Propp's Schema—The 31 Elements into Which any Fairy Tale can be Broken

1. A member of a family leaves home (the hero is introduced);
2. An interdiction is addressed to the hero ('don't go there', 'go to this place');
3. The interdiction is violated (villain enters the tale);
4. The villain makes an attempt at reconnaissance (either villain tries to find the children/jewels etc; or intended victim questions the villain);
5. The villain gains information about the victim;
6. The villain attempts to deceive the victim to take possession of victim or victim's belongings (trickery; villain disguised, tries to win confidence of victim);
7. Victim taken in by deception, unwittingly helping the enemy;
8. Villain causes harm/injury to family member (by abduction, theft of magical agent, spoiling crops, plunders in other forms, causes a disappearance, expels someone, casts spell on someone, substitutes child etc, commits murder, imprisons/ detains someone, threatens forced marriage, provides nightly torments); Alternatively, a member of family lacks something or desires something (magical potion etc);
9. Misfortune or lack is made known, (hero is dispatched, hears call for help etc/ alternative is that victimized hero is sent away, freed from imprisonment);
10. Seeker agrees to, or decides upon counter-action;
11. Hero leaves home;
12. Hero is tested, interrogated, attacked etc, preparing the way for his/her receiving magical agent or helper (donor);
13. Hero reacts to actions of future donor (withstands/fails the test, frees captive, reconciles disputants, performs service, uses adversary's powers against them);
14. Hero acquires use of a magical agent (directly transferred, located, purchased, prepared, spontaneously appears, eaten/ drunk, help offered by other characters);
15. Hero is transferred, delivered or led to whereabouts of an object of the search;
16. Hero and villain join in direct combat;
17. Hero is branded (wounded/marked, receives ring or scarf);
18. Villain is defeated (killed in combat, defeated in contest, killed while asleep, banished);
19. Initial misfortune or lack is resolved (object of search distributed, spell broken, slain person revived, captive freed);
20. Hero returns;
21. Hero is pursued (pursuer tries to kill, eat, undermine the hero);
22. Hero is rescued from pursuit (obstacles delay pursuer, hero hides or is hidden, hero transforms unrecognizably, hero saved from attempt on his/her life);
23. Hero unrecognized, arrives home or in another country;
24. False hero presents unfounded claims;
25. Difficult task proposed to the hero (trial by ordeal, riddles, test of strength/endurance, other tasks);
26. Task is resolved;
27. Hero is recognized (by mark, brand, or thing given to him/her);
28. False hero or villain is exposed;

29. Hero is given a new appearance (is made whole, handsome, new garments etc);
30. Villain is punished;
31. Hero marries and ascends the throne (is rewarded/promoted).

THE LION, THE JACKAL, AND THE MAN

It so happened one day that Lion and Jackal came together to converse on affairs of land and state. Jackal, let me say, was the most important adviser to the king of the forest, and after they had spoken about these matters for quite a while, the conversation took a more personal turn.

Lion began to boast and talk big about his strength. Jackal had, perhaps, given him cause for it, because by nature he was a flatterer. But now that Lion began to assume so many airs, said he, "See here, Lion, I will show you an animal that is still more powerful than you are."

They walked along, Jackal leading the way, and met first a little boy.

"Is this the strong man?" asked Lion.

"No," answered Jackal, "he must still become a man, O king."

After a while they found an old man walking[26] with bowed head and supporting his bent figure with a stick.

"Is this the wonderful strong man?" asked Lion.

"Not yet, O king," was Jackal's answer, "he has been a man."

Continuing their walk a short distance farther, they came across a young hunter, in the prime of youth, and accompanied by some of his dogs.

"There you have him now, O king," said Jackal. "Pit your strength against his, and if you win, then truly you are the strength of the earth."

Then Jackal made tracks to one side toward a little rocky kopje from which he would be able to see the meeting.

Growling, growling, Lion strode forward to meet the man, but when he came close the dogs beset him. He, however, paid but little attention to the dogs, pushed and separated them on all sides with a few sweeps of his front paws. They howled aloud, beating a hasty retreat toward the man.

Thereupon the man fired a charge of shot, hitting him behind the shoulder, but even to this Lion paid but little attention. Thereupon the hunter pulled out his steel knife, and gave him a few good jabs. Lion retreated, followed by the flying bullets of the hunter.

"Well, are you strongest now?" was Jackal's first question when Lion arrived at his side.

"No, Jackal," answered Lion, "let that fellow there keep the name and welcome. Such as he I have never before seen. In the first place he had about ten of his bodyguard storm me. I really did not bother myself much about them, but when I attempted to turn him to chaff, he spat and blew fire at me, mostly into my face, that burned just a little but not very badly. And when I again endeavored to pull him to the ground he jerked out from his body one of his ribs with which he gave me some very ugly wounds, so bad that I had to make chips fly, and as a parting he sent some warm bullets after me. No, Jackal, give him the name."

Schooly D, Signifying Rapper

Schooly D, Signifying Rapper

A YouTube element has been excluded from this version of the text. You can view it online here: https://africanamericanlit.pressbooks.sunycreate.cloud/?p=50

"File:Schooly D and Chuck D at the House of Blues in Chicago.jpg" by swimfinfan is licensed under CC BY-SA 2.0

African Myths and Folktales

African Myths and Folktales

http://www.mythfolklore.net/andrewlang/indexbib.htm#African

Andrew Lang's *Fairy Book* archives some African tales and myths. His use also brings up problematic translation and adaptation challenges we will take up with the slave narratives.

"Pink Fairy Book 66" by thecmn is marked with CC PDM 1.0

YG FTP

YG FTP

https://www.youtube.com/watch?v=ramteyfi9bE

"File:Rapper YG 2015.jpg" by The Come Up Show is licensed under CC BY 2.0

YG - Blood Walk feat. Lil Wayne & D3szn

YG - Blood Walk feat. Lil Wayne & D3szn

A YouTube element has been excluded from this version of the text. You can view it online here:
https://africanamericanlit.pressbooks.sunycreate.cloud/?p=53

Shaking up the World: Trickster Tales, by Terri Windling

Shaking up the World: Trickster Tales

https://www.terriwindling.com/folklore/tricksters.html

Read this linked essay and comment on it in the current discussion. Consider the artworks accompanying Windling's essay, as well as the examples she uses.

Dave Chappelle, When Keepin' it Real can go Very Wrong

https://www.youtube.com/watch?v=D3U55usfJK8

We will use this video to examine the purpose of satire, which involves making fun of something with a serious social purpose behind it. What are the social issues Chappelle is satirizing here? Since the video's making, have they worsened? Why or why not?

"TIFF 2018 Dave Chappelle" by JiBs. is licensed under CC BY 2.0

Dick Gregory: Race, Comedy, & Justice

Books by influential comedian and activist Dick Gregory were a common presence in my household growing up, as my father was a big fan of his work. The following address is from the Chicago Humanities Festival:

https://www.youtube.com/watch?v=aD9wJoEfHvE

"Dick Gregory for President Campaign Button Peace and Freedom Party 1968" by Mpls55408 is licensed under CC BY-NC 2.0

3. SLAVE NARRATIVES & VOICES OF RESISTANCE

History of American Literature

New England Transcendentalism was a late and local manifestation of that great movement for the liberation of humanity which, invading practically every sphere of civilized activity, swept over Europe at the end of the eighteenth and the beginning of the nineteenth century.

With the fading of the Renaissance, Europe had passed into an age of criticism, during which all it had inherited and achieved in the preceding era was subjected to the test of reason. Throughout the eighteenth century especially, the existing structure of society was subtly undermined, and when, at the end of that century, it finally collapsed, the revolution which in reality had long been in preparation took on an abrupt and miraculous appearance.

"Heaven smiles, and faiths and empires gleam / Like wrecks of a dissolving dream," cried Shelley, attempting to describe this remarkable period, and his lines are scarcely an exaggeration. Smiles and wrecks, these were the characteristic products of the time, blasted institutions and blossoming ideals.

What those ideals were—some of them soon to be realized, others destined to remain distant visions—is tolerably clear. Socially this revolution meant democracy, the assertion of the brotherhood and potential equality of men. Politically and religiously it meant the overthrow of feudal and ecclesiastical tyrannies and customs, and the setting up of liberal forms of government and belief as instruments for testing the new social doctrine. Philosophically it meant the contention, in the face of existing rationalisms and skepticisms, that man's practical and imaginative faculties play a part in his apprehension of the truth. In the realm of art and literature it meant the shattering of pseudo-classic rules and forms in favor of a spirit of freedom, the creation of works filled with the new passion for nature and common humanity and incarnating a fresh sense of the wonder, promise, and romance of life. In the scientific and industrial worlds it meant those fundamental and far-reaching changes which came with the constantly fuller recognition and adoption of the scientific method.

To the special student, each of these revolutionary movements has its separate history. But life, in spite of the student, is not a matter of watertight compartments, and a first fact to be seized and held fast in any discussion of New England transcendentalism is that the new spirit which appeared in Europe a century and more ago was neither social, nor political, nor industrial, nor economic, nor literary, nor scientific, nor religious. It was all of them at once. It transcended every phase of life—though it is true, of course, that in this particular locality or at that particular time, in this individual or in that social atmosphere, it did take on this or that predominant emphasis or color.

On this side of the Atlantic, for instance, it assumed at the outset a preeminently political character, and America, in her own Revolution and in the events which followed it, made an early and memorable contribution to that greater revolution of the human spirit of which the source and center was in Europe. But America, save in the case here and there of an exceptional mind, remained largely unconscious, even as a matter of political theory, of the general significance for the world of what she had accomplished. Still less had she distilled from her democratic practice any fresh philosophy or faith. When, then, voices from abroad of those who were seeking a religion for the new order of things penetrated to a community which, religious to the core, had long been religiously starved, those voices were bound to be heard and answered. That is precisely what began happening near Boston shortly before the year 1830. The result was similar to what occurs, under like conditions, in the case of an individual.

Whoever has seen a young man of high mental and spiritual endowment lifted out of a provincial environment and placed suddenly in contact with the central intellectual and religious forces of his time, has a key to much of the transcendental movement in New England. The unsettling of traditional foundations, the ferment of thought and emotion, the aspirations, the excesses, the unleashing of dormant and unsuspected powers, all the effects, in fact, which attend such an experience in the case of the individual were reproduced on a wider scale when the spirit of revolutionary Europe descended upon a group of the finest minds of early nineteenth-century New England. The spirit of the eighteenth century had survived in the neighborhood of Boston long after the eighteenth century was dead. And suddenly—so at least it seemed—this group of young men and women became intensely aware of that fact. The new ideas and ideals found their way to them through a score of channels and affected as many phases of New England life. But because of the predominant part which religion still played in that life and its traditions, it was within the religious world that the influence of the new spirit was immediate and marked. Transcendentalism was the religious conversion of early nineteenth-century New England. And because of the relative cultural eminence of New England, it became indirectly, in some measure, the religious conversion of America. Emerson's address, The American scholar, is called our intellectual Declaration of Independence. With far more fundamental truth his little volume, Nature, might be called our religious Declaration of Independence.

New England transcendentalism, then, was the product of European forces brought to bear on New England character and conditions. To analyze the movement further it will be necessary to look somewhat more closely at the nature of those conditions and that character and to study in a little more detail the outside forces which were brought in contact with them.

The religious evolution of New England from the period of the Puritan theocracy to the beginning of the nineteenth century is on the whole, with a certain change of scale and retardation of movement, strikingly similar to the religious development during the same period abroad, a fact which, at the outset, renders futile any hope to estimate with exactness how far the two movements were parallel, how far the one was influenced by the other.

New England took no plunge, as England did, from the moral heights of Puritanism into the abyss of Restoration licentiousness. But there was a descent, which, if more gradual, was not on that account less real. Seventeenth-century Puritanism held within itself the germ of its own disintegration.[1] Already, by the second generation, under the law of psychological reaction and the exacting material demands of a pioneer community, "the decay of godliness in the land" had become conspicuous, and it seems difficult not to regard Salem witchcraft as the *reductio ad absurdum* of the extreme religious spirit. The revulsion of feeling that followed that outburst of superstition, the increasing interest in commercial and political questions, the gradual introduction of English rationalistic doctrines, the growing influence of the philosophy of Locke and of the literature of the "classical" school, all these causes, and many others, combined to accelerate the change in spiritual atmosphere, and it was not long before there was prevalent, especially in the neighborhood of Boston, much of that temper of prose and reason which we habitually associate with the eighteenth century. With this changing mood, "heresies" began to creep into the religious world: Arminianism, Arianism, and other dissolvents of Calvinism. Interest in "morality" began to infringe on interest in theology. A line of increasingly "liberal" ministers occupied prominent Boston pulpits.

The career of Jonathan Edwards serves, by contrast, to tell the story of what was happening. He, if anyone, was fitted to stem the tide of encroaching secular interests. The Great Awakening, that transitory religious revival of the second generation of the eighteenth century which is in many ways the American counterpart of the Methodist movement, was designed to remedy the spiritual deadness of the time. But it merely widened the opening gulf in the religious world. The New Calvinists, as the followers of Edwards were called, went on to develop a theology of their own, while the liberals, constantly in closer touch with English thinking, grew more and more radical, until, as the two schools diverged, the term Unitarian was finally applied to them. Though 1785, the year in which King's Chapel in the revision of its liturgy tacitly denied the doctrine of the Trinity, is often selected as the beginning of the Unitarian movement, and though the actual schism between the Unitarian and the Trinitarian churches did not come till 1815, it is convenient, if not strictly accurate, to speak of the whole evolution of American liberalism in the eighteenth century as the Unitarian movement.

Throughout that century the position of the New England liberal had been an increasingly strong one, the typical Unitarian of the time being a man of tolerance, of intellect, of cultured tastes, of unexceptionable private morality and notable civic virtue. Emotional or spiritual in temperament, however, he was not. When, therefore, the intense fervor and the new ideals of revolutionary Europe began to make their way to New England, the Unitarian (like the orthodox Calvinist of a century before) began to find himself in an untenable position, transformed by the altered spirit of the age from a radical into a conservative. A number of Unitarian clergymen, notably the Rev. Joseph Stevens Buckminster (1784–1812), seem to have had an inkling of new things, but Buckminster died at the age of twenty-eight, and it was left to William Ellery Channing to be the first Unitarian to show something like a full appreciation of the significance for religion of the changing spirit of the time. Channing is the bridge between Unitarianism and transcendentalism.

Channing was born in Newport, Rhode Island, in 1780. His early religious environment was Calvinistic but not illiberal, his parents being orthodox in belief but tolerant in spirit. The stern Calvinism of Dr. Samuel Hopkins, Edwards's pupil, the minister to whose preaching Channing listened as a boy, shocked his delicately sensitive nature, and was doubtless one of the influences that by reaction led to his liberal religious views. During his college days at Harvard Channing's early tendency toward revolt was strengthened and his seeking for intellectual independence encouraged. Contact in his reading with radical English writers of the eighteenth century gave a direction to his thinking which, in spite of marked mental growth in later years, was never fundamentally altered.

On leaving Harvard he acted for nearly two years as tutor in a Virginia family, imbibing in the course of this experience an intense hatred of slavery. During this period, too, he became acquainted with the works of Rousseau, Godwin, and Mary Wollstonecraft, and from that time the kinship of many of his ideas with those of French Revolutionary origin can be clearly traced, though in passing through his serene and profoundly Christian mind those ideas often became scarcely recognizable.

On returning north Channing studied theology, becoming in 1803 minister of the Federal Street Society, Boston, a pulpit from which, until his death in 1842, he preached, in a spirit of singularly mingled benignity and power, sermons of constantly increasing influence that emphasized consistently the spiritual and practical as opposed to the doctrinal aspects of Christianity. Ultimately his fame even crossed the ocean, a number of his essays and reviews being translated and widely read, especially in France. The eminence he attained was due fundamentally to the gracious, almost saintly, character behind both his written and his spoken words; and it is worth remembering that all he did was accomplished in the face of a physical condition that made him essentially an invalid.

Although Channing is usually spoken of as the greatest Unitarian of his time, his sermon on Unitarian Christianity, preached at the ordination of Jared Sparks at Baltimore in 1819, being often called the creed of that denomination, he was, if we are to give him that name, a Unitarian of an entirely new type, and his works are full of indictments of what Emerson later called "the pale negations of Boston Unitarianism."

"Unitarianism," we find him writing, for instance, "has suffered from union with a heart- withering philosophy. . . . I fear that we must look to other schools for the thoughts which thrill us, which touch the most inward springs, and disclose to us the depths of our own souls."

Or again:

> Now, religion ought to be dispensed in accommodation to this spirit and character of our age. Men desire excitement, and religion must be communicated in a more exciting form. . . . Men will not now be trifled with . . . . They want a religion which will take a strong hold upon them.

"And they desire the same quality in their literature," he says elsewhere, "a poetry which pierces beneath the exterior of life to the depths of the soul."

Manifestly, as these references to changing standards in philosophy, religion, and literature make clear, a new spirit was abroad in the land, and though Channing himself had caught much of it from other and earlier sources, it is certain that German philosophy and literature, some of it directly, much more of it indirectly, was, by the third decade of the century, becoming a chief influence in its dissemination.

Resistance and Abolition

Resistance to slavery came in many forms, all of which contributed to the abolition of slavery as an institution in the Americas in the second half of the nineteenth century. There were two main arms of resistance: that of slaves themselves and that of abolitionists, whose calls for the end of slavery became louder and more forceful beginning in the last two decades of the eighteenth century.

Africans resisted slavery in several ways. First, they adopted defensive measures in their own villages to elude capture by slavers. Second, they launched attacks on the crews aboard slave ships. Slavers' reports document more than four hundred such attacks, but scholars believe there were many more. Third, once ashore, Africans ran away, sometimes establishing Maroon communities. Maroon communities, such as those in Suriname and Jamaica, and the Republic of Palmares in Brazil, warred with white settlers throughout the seventeenth and eighteenth centuries. Fourth, African slaves revolted on the very lands on which they were enslaved. The first slave revolt in the Americas we know of occurred in 1522 on the island of Hispaniola. This revolt, like most that would follow in the next two hundred fifty years, was quickly put down. During the late eighteenth century, however, the Americas saw an increase in slave revolts, especially in the French Caribbean. The French and Haitian Revolutions, which began in 1789 and 1791 respectively, largely inspired these revolts. Both revolutions were fought in the name of natural rights and the equality of men, ideas not lost on those who remained enslaved in the French colonial world. The French revolutionary government even abolished slavery in its colonies, although this did not last for very long, as slavery was soon reinstated during the reign of Napoleon. Slave revolts continued into the nineteenth century in British and Spanish Caribbean colonies. A revolt on the British-controlled island of Barbados in 1816 involved twenty thousand slaves from more than seventy plantations.

In 1831, a slave revolt in Virginia led by Nat Turner, although small in comparison with other slave revolts of the same period, became a symbol for American slaveholders of the danger posed by abolition. For others, however, two decades of increased slave unrest supported calls for the end of slavery. These were the individuals involved in antislavery movements, which began gaining substantial ground with public opinion beginning in the 1780s. The antislavery movement was perhaps strongest in Britain, where member of Parliament William Wilberforce led antislavery campaigns from the 1780s onwards. Evangelical Protestant Christians joined him. These campaigns led to thousands of petitions to end slavery between the 1780s and 1830s. The slave trade was antislavery's first target, and in 1787 the Society for the Abolition of the Slave Trade was established in Britain. Wilberforce and evangelical Protestants saw slavery and slaveholders as evil. So, too, did the Quakers (or the Society of Friends). On both sides of the Atlantic, Quakers attacked slavery as immoral and prohibited their members from owning slaves or being involved in any part of the slave trade.

In addition to these moral attacks on slavery, Enlightenment thinkers attacked slavery on philosophical grounds. French Enlightenment philosophers such as Montesquieu argued that slavery went against the natural rights of man. During the French Revolution, members of the Society of the Friends of Blacks, which originated among Enlightenment thinkers, joined with free blacks from the Caribbean colonies living in France, who organized the Society of Colored Citizens, to advocate for equal rights for free people of color and the end of slavery. The antislavery movement scored a victory in 1807 when the United States and then Britain signed bills to end their nations' involvement in the slave trade. Many in the antislavery movement believed this was the first step to abolishing slavery as an institution.

The Interesting Narrative of the Life of Olaudah Equiano

The Interesting Narrative of the Life of Olaudah Equiano

https://www.gutenberg.org/files/15399/15399-h/15399-h.htm

Olaudah Equiano
or
GUSTAVUS VASSA,
the African

Harriet Jacobs, Incidents in the Life of a Slave Girl

Harriet Jacobs, Incidents in the Life of a Slave Girl

http://xroads.virginia.edu/~Hyper/JACOBS/hj-site-index.htm

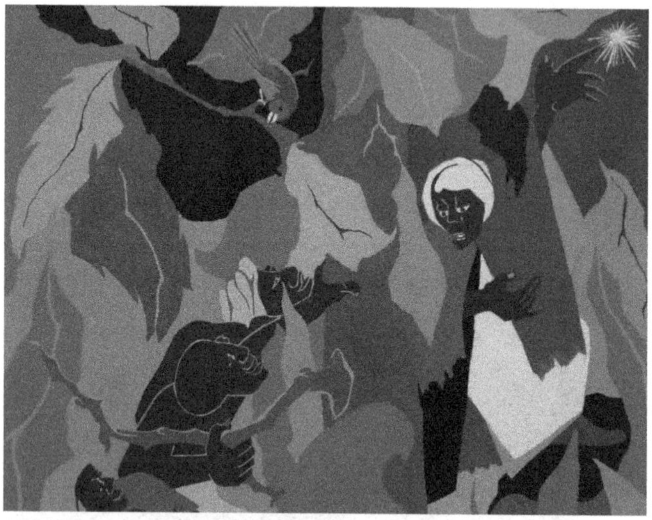

"MASTERWORKS OF COLOR: African-American Art from the Greenville Collection (2017) – at the Greenville County Museum of Art until August 27, 2017" by UGArdener is licensed under CC BY-NC 2.0

The Narrative of Sojourner Truth

The Narrative of Sojourner Truth

http://xroads.virginia.edu/~Hyper/TRUTH/toc.html

"Sojourner Truth" by edenpictures is licensed under CC BY 2.0

Video: Frederick Douglass

"Frederick Douglass in winter" by theothermonalisa slowed down with the new is licensed under CC BY 2.0

Featuring discussions of Frederick Douglass's 1845 Narrative as well as John Locke's Second Treatises of Government (1690); ontological individualism and possessive individualism ; Orlando Patterson and the idea of social death.

A YouTube element has been excluded from this version of the text. You can view it online here: https://africanamericanlit.pressbooks.sunycreate.cloud/?p=63

Narrative of the Life of Frederick Douglass, an American Slave

Narrative of the Life of Frederick Douglass is an 1845 memoir and treatise on abolition written by famous orator and former slave Frederick Douglass. It is generally held to be the most famous of a number of narratives written by former slaves during the same period. In factual detail, the text describes the events of his life and is considered to be one of the most influential pieces of literature to fuel the abolitionist movement of the early 19th century in the United States.

Narrative of the Life of Frederick Douglass encompasses eleven chapters that recount Douglass' life as a slave and his ambition to become a free man.

Preface

In the month of August, 1841, I attended an anti-slavery convention in Nantucket, at which it was my happiness to become acquainted with *Frederick Douglass*, the writer of the following Narrative. He was a stranger to nearly every member of that body; but, having recently made his escape from the southern prison-house of bondage, and feeling his curiosity excited to ascertain the principles and measures of the abolitionists,—of whom he had heard a somewhat vague description while he was a slave,—he was induced to give his attendance, on the occasion alluded to, though at that time a resident in New Bedford.

Fortunate, most fortunate occurrence!—fortunate for the millions of his manacled brethren, yet panting for deliverance from their awful thraldom!—fortunate for the cause of negro emancipation, and of universal liberty!—fortunate for the land of his birth, which he has already done so much to save and bless!—fortunate for a large circle of friends and acquaintances, whose sympathy and affection he has strongly secured by the many sufferings he has endured, by his virtuous traits of character, by his ever-abiding remembrance of those who are in bonds, as being bound with them!—fortunate for the multitudes, in various parts of our republic, whose minds he has enlightened on the subject of slavery, and who have been melted to tears by his pathos, or roused to virtuous indignation by his stirring eloquence against the enslavers of men!—fortunate for himself, as it at once brought him into the field of public usefulness, "gave the world assurance of a MAN," quickened the slumbering energies of his soul, and consecrated him to the great work of breaking the rod of the oppressor, and letting the oppressed go free!

I shall never forget his first speech at the convention—the extraordinary emotion it excited in my own mind—the powerful impression it created upon a crowded auditory, completely taken by surprise—the applause which followed from the beginning to the end of his felicitous remarks. I think I never hated slavery so intensely as at that moment; certainly, my perception of the enormous outrage which is inflicted by it, on the godlike nature of its victims, was rendered far more clear than ever. There stood one, in physical proportion and stature commanding and exact—in intellect richly endowed—in natural eloquence a prodigy—in soul manifestly "created but a little lower than the angels"—yet a slave, ay, a fugitive slave,—trembling for his safety, hardly daring to believe that on the American soil, a single white person could be found who would befriend him at all hazards, for the love of God and humanity! Capable of high attainments as an intellectual and moral being—needing nothing but a comparatively small amount of cultivation to make him an ornament to society and a blessing to his race—by the law of the land, by the voice of the people, by the terms of the slave code, he was only a piece of property, a beast of burden, a chattel personal, nevertheless!

A beloved friend from New Bedford prevailed on *Mr. Douglass* to address the convention: He came forward to the platform with a hesitancy and embarrassment, necessarily the attendants of a sensitive mind in such a novel position. After apologizing for his ignorance, and reminding the audience that slavery was a poor school for the human intellect and heart, he proceeded to narrate some of the facts in his own history as a slave, and in the course of his speech gave utterance to many noble thoughts and thrilling reflections. As soon as he had taken his seat, filled with hope and admiration, I rose, and declared that *Patrick Henry*, of revolutionary fame, never made a speech more eloquent in the cause of liberty, than the one we had just listened to from the lips of that hunted fugitive. So I believed at that time—such is my belief now. I reminded the audience of the peril which surrounded this self-emancipated young man at the North,—even in Massachusetts, on the soil of the Pilgrim Fathers, among the descendants of revolutionary sires; and I appealed to them, whether they would ever allow him to be carried back into slavery,—law or no law, constitution or no constitution. The response was unanimous and in thunder-tones—"NO!" "Will you succor and protect him as a brother-man—a resident of the old Bay State?" "YES!" shouted the whole mass, with an energy so startling, that the ruthless tyrants south of Mason and Dixon's line might almost have heard the mighty burst of feeling, and recognized it as the pledge of an invincible determination, on the part of those who gave it, never to betray him that wanders, but to hide the outcast, and firmly to abide the consequences.

It was at once deeply impressed upon my mind, that, if *Mr. Douglass* could be persuaded to consecrate his time and talents to the promotion of the anti-slavery enterprise, a powerful impetus would be given to it, and a stunning blow at the same time inflicted on northern prejudice against a colored complexion. I therefore endeavored to instil hope and courage into his mind, in order that he might dare to engage in a vocation so anomalous and responsible for a person in his situation; and I was seconded in this effort by warm-hearted friends, especially by the late General Agent of the Massachusetts Anti-Slavery Society, *Mr. John A. Collins*, whose judgment in this instance entirely coincided with my own. At first, he could give no encouragement; with unfeigned diffidence, he expressed his conviction that he was not adequate to the performance of so great a task; the path marked out was wholly an untrodden one; he was sincerely apprehensive that he should do more harm than good. After much deliberation, however, he consented to make a trial; and ever since that period, he has acted as a lecturing agent, under the auspices either of the American or the Massachusetts Anti-Slavery Society. In labors he has been most abundant; and his success in combating prejudice, in gaining proselytes, in agitating the public mind, has far surpassed the most sanguine expectations that were raised at the commencement of his brilliant career. He has borne himself with gentleness and meekness, yet with true manliness of character. As a public speaker, he excels in pathos, wit, comparison, imitation, strength of reasoning, and fluency of language. There is in him that union of head and heart, which is indispensable to an enlightenment of the heads and a winning of the hearts of others. May his strength continue to be equal to his day! May he continue to "grow in grace, and in the knowledge of God," that he may be increasingly serviceable in the cause of bleeding humanity, whether at home or abroad!

It is certainly a very remarkable fact, that one of the most efficient advocates of the slave population, now before the public, is a fugitive slave, in the person of *Frederick Douglass*; and that the free colored population of the United States are as ably represented by one of their own number, in the person of *Charles Lenox Remond*, whose eloquent appeals have extorted the highest applause of multitudes on both sides of the Atlantic. Let the calumniators of the colored race despise themselves for their baseness and illiberality of spirit, and henceforth cease to talk of the natural inferiority of those who require nothing but time and opportunity to attain to the highest point of human excellence.

It may, perhaps, be fairly questioned, whether any other portion of the population of the earth could have endured the privations, sufferings and horrors of slavery, without having become more degraded in the scale of humanity than the slaves of African descent. Nothing has been left undone to cripple their intellects, darken their minds, debase their moral nature, obliterate all traces of their relationship to mankind; and yet how wonderfully they have sustained the mighty load of a most frightful bondage, under which they have been groaning for centuries! To illustrate the effect of slavery on the white man,—to show that he has no powers of endurance, in such a condition, superior to those of his black brother,—*Daniel O'connell*, the distinguished advocate of universal emancipation, and the mightiest champion of prostrate but not conquered Ireland, relates the following anecdote in a speech delivered by him in the Conciliation Hall, Dublin, before the Loyal National Repeal Association, March 31, 1845. "No matter," said *Mr. O'connell*, "under what specious term it may disguise itself, slavery is still hideous. *It has a natural, an inevitable tendency to brutalize every noble faculty of man.* An American sailor, who was cast away on the shore of Africa, where he was kept in slavery for three years, was, at the expiration of that period, found to be imbruted and stultified—he had lost all reasoning power; and having forgotten his native language, could only utter some savage gibberish between Arabic and English, which nobody could understand, and which even he himself found difficulty in pronouncing. So much for the humanizing influence of *The Domestic Institution*!" Admitting this to have been an extraordinary case of mental deterioration, it proves at least that the white slave can sink as low in the scale of humanity as the black one.

Mr. Douglass has very properly chosen to write his own Narrative, in his own style, and according to the best of his ability, rather than to employ some one else. It is, therefore, entirely his own production; and, considering how long and dark was the career he had to run as a slave,—how few have been his opportunities to improve his mind since he broke his iron fetters,—it is, in my judgment, highly creditable to his head and heart. He who can peruse it without a tearful eye, a heaving breast, an afflicted spirit,—without being filled with an unutterable abhorrence of slavery and all its abettors, and animated with a determination to seek the immediate overthrow of that execrable system,—without trembling for the fate of this country in the hands of a righteous God, who is ever on the side of the oppressed, and whose arm is not shortened that it cannot save,—must have a flinty heart, and be qualified to act the part of a trafficker "in slaves and the souls of men." I am confident that it is essentially true in all its statements; that nothing has been set down in malice, nothing exaggerated, nothing drawn from the imagination; that it comes short of the reality, rather than overstates a single fact in regard to *slavery as it is*. The experience of *Frederick Douglass*, as a slave, was not a peculiar one; his lot was not especially a hard one; his case may be regarded as a very fair specimen of the treatment of slaves in Maryland, in which State it is conceded that they are better fed and less cruelly treated than in Georgia, Alabama, or Louisiana. Many have suffered incomparably more, while very few on the plantations have suffered less, than himself. Yet how deplorable was his situation! what terrible chastisements were inflicted upon his person! what still more shocking outrages were perpetrated upon his mind! with all his noble powers and sublime aspirations, how like a brute was he treated, even by those professing to have the same mind in them that was in Christ Jesus! to what dreadful liabilities was he continually subjected! how destitute of friendly counsel and aid, even in his greatest extremities! how heavy was the midnight of woe which shrouded in blackness the last ray of hope, and filled the future with terror and gloom! what longings after freedom took possession of his breast, and how his misery augmented, in proportion as he grew reflective and intelligent,—thus demonstrating that a happy slave is an extinct man! how he thought, reasoned, felt, under the lash of the driver, with the chains upon his limbs! what perils he encountered in his endeavors to escape from his horrible doom! and how signal have been his deliverance and preservation in the midst of a nation of pitiless enemies!

This Narrative contains many affecting incidents, many passages of great eloquence and power; but I think the most thrilling one of them all is the description *Douglass* gives of his feelings, as he stood soliloquizing respecting his fate, and the chances of his one day being a freeman, on the banks of the Chesapeake Bay—viewing the receding vessels as they flew with their white wings before the breeze, and apostrophizing them as animated by the living spirit of freedom. Who can read that passage, and be insensible to its pathos and sublimity? Compressed into it is a whole Alexandrian library of thought, feeling, and sentiment—all that can, all that need be urged, in the form of expostulation, entreaty, rebuke, against that crime of crimes,—making man the property of his fellow-man! O, how accursed is that system, which entombs the godlike mind of man, defaces the divine image, reduces those who by creation were crowned with glory and honor to a level with four-footed beasts, and exalts the dealer in human flesh above all that is called God! Why should its existence be prolonged one hour? Is it not evil, only evil, and that continually? What does its presence imply but the absence of all fear of God, all regard for man, on the part of the people of the United States? Heaven speed its eternal overthrow!

So profoundly ignorant of the nature of slavery are many persons, that they are stubbornly incredulous whenever they read or listen to any recital of the cruelties which are daily inflicted on its victims. They do not deny that the slaves are held as property; but that terrible fact seems to convey to their minds no idea of injustice, exposure to outrage, or savage barbarity. Tell them of cruel scourgings, of mutilations and brandings, of scenes of pollution and blood, of the banishment of all light and knowledge, and they affect to be greatly indignant at such enormous exaggerations, such wholesale misstatements, such abominable libels on the character of the southern planters! As if all these direful outrages were not the natural results of slavery! As if it were less cruel to reduce a human being to the condition of a thing, than to give him a severe flagellation, or to deprive him of necessary food and clothing! As if whips, chains, thumb-screws, paddles, blood-hounds, overseers, drivers, patrols, were not all indispensable to keep the slaves down, and to give protection to their ruthless oppressors! As if, when the marriage institution is abolished, concubinage, adultery, and incest, must not necessarily abound; when all the rights of humanity are annihilated, any barrier remains to protect the victim from the fury of the spoiler; when absolute power is assumed over life and liberty, it will not be wielded with destructive sway! Skeptics of this character abound in society. In some few instances, their incredulity arises from a want of reflection; but, generally, it indicates a hatred of the light, a desire to shield slavery from the assaults of its foes, a contempt of the colored race, whether bond or free. Such will try to discredit the shocking tales of slaveholding cruelty which are recorded in this truthful Narrative; but they will labor in vain. *Mr. Douglass* has frankly disclosed the place of his birth, the names of those who claimed ownership in his body and soul, and the names also of those who committed the crimes which he has alleged against them. His statements, therefore, may easily be disproved, if they are untrue.

In the course of his Narrative, he relates two instances of murderous cruelty,—in one of which a planter deliberately shot a slave belonging to a neighboring plantation, who had unintentionally gotten within his lordly domain in quest of fish; and in the other, an overseer blew out the brains of a slave who had fled to a stream of water to escape a bloody scourging. *Mr. Douglass* states that in neither of these instances was any thing done by way of legal arrest or judicial investigation. The Baltimore American, of March 17, 1845, relates a similar case of atrocity, perpetrated with similar impunity—as follows:—"*Shooting a slave.*—We learn, upon the authority of a letter from Charles county, Maryland, received by a gentleman of this city, that a young man, named Matthews, a nephew of General Matthews, and whose father, it is believed, holds an office at Washington, killed one of the slaves upon his father's farm by shooting him. The letter states that young Matthews had been left in charge of the farm; that he gave an order to the servant, which was disobeyed, when he proceeded to the house, *obtained a gun, and, returning, shot the servant.*He immediately, the letter continues, fled to his father's residence, where he still remains unmolested."—Let it never be forgotten, that no slaveholder or overseer can be convicted of any outrage perpetrated on the person of a slave, however diabolical it may be, on the testimony of colored witnesses, whether bond or free. By the slave code, they are adjudged to be as incompetent to testify against a white man, as though they were indeed a part of the brute creation. Hence, there is no legal protection in fact, whatever there may be in form, for the slave population; and any amount of cruelty may be inflicted on them with impunity. Is it possible for the human mind to conceive of a more horrible state of society?

The effect of a religious profession on the conduct of southern masters is vividly described in the following Narrative, and shown to be any thing but salutary. In the nature of the case, it must be in the highest degree pernicious. The testimony of *Mr. Douglass*, on this point, is sustained by a cloud of witnesses, whose veracity is unimpeachable. "A slaveholder's profession of Christianity is a palpable imposture. He is a felon of the highest grade. He is a man-stealer. It is of no importance what you put in the other scale."

Reader! are you with the man-stealers in sympathy and purpose, or on the side of their down-trodden victims? If with the former, then are you the foe of God and man. If with the latter, what are you prepared to do and dare in their behalf? Be faithful, be vigilant, be untiring in your efforts to break every yoke, and let the oppressed go free. Come what may—cost what it may—inscribe on the banner which you unfurl to the breeze, as your religious and political motto—"NO COMPROMISE WITH SLAVERY! NO UNION WITH SLAVEHOLDERS!"

Wm. Lloyd Garrison Boston,
May 1, 1845.

Letter from Wendell Phillips, Esq.

Boston, April 22, 1845.

My Dear Friend:

You remember the old fable of "The Man and the Lion," where the lion complained that he should not be so misrepresented "when the lions wrote history."

I am glad the time has come when the "lions write history." We have been left long enough to gather the character of slavery from the involuntary evidence of the masters. One might, indeed, rest sufficiently satisfied with what, it is evident, must be, in general, the results of such a relation, without seeking farther to find whether they have followed in every instance. Indeed, those who stare at the half-peck of corn a week, and love to count the lashes on the slave's back, are seldom the "stuff" out of which reformers and abolitionists are to be made. I remember that, in 1838, many were waiting for the results of the West India experiment, before they could come into our ranks. Those "results" have come long ago; but, alas! few of that number have come with them, as converts. A man must be disposed to judge of emancipation by other tests than whether it has increased the produce of sugar,—and to hate slavery for other reasons than because it starves men and whips women,—before he is ready to lay the first stone of his anti-slavery life.

I was glad to learn, in your story, how early the most neglected of God's children waken to a sense of their rights, and of the injustice done them. Experience is a keen teacher; and long before you had mastered your A B C, or knew where the "white sails" of the Chesapeake were bound, you began, I see, to gauge the wretchedness of the slave, not by his hunger and want, not by his lashes and toil, but by the cruel and blighting death which gathers over his soul.

In connection with this, there is one circumstance which makes your recollections peculiarly valuable, and renders your early insight the more remarkable. You come from that part of the country where we are told slavery appears with its fairest features. Let us hear, then, what it is at its best estate—gaze on its bright side, if it has one; and then imagination may task her powers to add dark lines to the picture, as she travels southward to that (for the colored man) Valley of the Shadow of Death, where the Mississippi sweeps along.

Again, we have known you long, and can put the most entire confidence in your truth, candor, and sincerity. Every one who has heard you speak has felt, and, I am confident, every one who reads your book will feel, persuaded that you give them a fair specimen of the whole truth. No one-sided portrait,—no wholesale complaints,—but strict justice done, whenever individual kindliness has neutralized, for a moment, the deadly system with which it was strangely allied. You have been with us, too, some years, and can fairly compare the twilight of rights, which your race enjoy at the North, with that "noon of night" under which they labor south of Mason and Dixon's line. Tell us whether, after all, the half-free colored man of Massachusetts is worse off than the pampered slave of the rice swamps!

In reading your life, no one can say that we have unfairly picked out some rare specimens of cruelty. We know that the bitter drops, which even you have drained from the cup, are no incidental aggravations, no individual ills, but such as must mingle always and necessarily in the lot of every slave. They are the essential ingredients, not the occasional results, of the system.

After all, I shall read your book with trembling for you. Some years ago, when you were beginning to tell me your real name and birthplace, you may remember I stopped you, and preferred to remain ignorant of all. With the exception of a vague description, so I continued, till the other day, when you read me your memoirs. I hardly knew, at the time, whether to thank you or not for the sight of them, when I reflected that it was still dangerous, in Massachusetts, for honest men to tell their names! They say the fathers, in 1776, signed the Declaration of Independence with the halter about their necks. You, too, publish your declaration of freedom with danger compassing you around. In all the broad lands which the Constitution of the United States overshadows, there is no single spot,—however narrow or desolate,—where a fugitive slave can plant himself and say, "I am safe." The whole armory of Northern Law has no shield for you. I am free to say that, in your place, I should throw the MS. into the fire.

You, perhaps, may tell your story in safety, endeared as you are to so many warm hearts by rare gifts, and a still rarer devotion of them to the service of others. But it will be owing only to your labors, and the fearless efforts of those who, trampling the laws and Constitution of the country under their feet, are determined that they will "hide the outcast," and that their hearths shall be, spite of the law, an asylum for the oppressed, if, some time or other, the humblest may stand in our streets, and bear witness in safety against the cruelties of which he has been the victim.

Yet it is sad to think, that these very throbbing hearts which welcome your story, and form your best safeguard in telling it, are all beating contrary to the "statute in such case made and provided." Go on, my dear friend, till you, and those who, like you, have been saved, so as by fire, from the dark prison-house, shall stereotype these free, illegal pulses into statutes; and New England, cutting loose from a blood-stained Union, shall glory in being the house of refuge for the oppressed,—till we no longer merely "
hide the outcast," or make a merit of standing idly by while he is hunted in our midst; but, consecrating anew the soil of the Pilgrims as an asylum for the oppressed, proclaim our *welcome* to the slave so loudly, that the tones shall reach every hut in the Carolinas, and make the broken-hearted bondman leap up at the thought of old Massachusetts.

God speed the day!

Till then, and ever,
Yours truly,

Wendell Phillips

Frederick Douglass

Frederick Douglass was born in slavery as Frederick Augustus Washington Bailey near Easton in Talbot County, Maryland. He was not sure of the exact year of his birth, but he knew that it was 1817 or 1818. As a young boy he was sent to Baltimore, to be a house servant, where he learned to read and write, with the assistance of his master's wife. In 1838 he escaped from slavery and went to New York City, where he married Anna Murray, a free colored woman whom he had met in Baltimore. Soon thereafter he changed his name to Frederick Douglass. In 1841 he addressed a convention of the Massachusetts Anti-Slavery Society in Nantucket and so greatly impressed the group that they immediately employed him as an agent. He was such an impressive orator that numerous persons doubted if he had ever been a slave, so he wrote
Narrative Of The Life Of Frederick Douglass. During the Civil War he assisted in the recruiting of colored men for the 54th and 55th Massachusetts Regiments and consistently argued for the emancipation of slaves. After the war he was active in securing and protecting the rights of the freemen. In his later years, at different times, he was secretary of the Santo Domingo Commission, marshall and recorder of deeds of the District of Columbia, and United States Minister to Haiti. His other autobiographical works are *My Bondage And My Freedom* and *Life And Times Of Frederick Douglass*, published in 1855 and 1881 respectively. He died in 1895.

Chapter 1

I was born in Tuckahoe, near Hillsborough, and about twelve miles from Easton, in Talbot county, Maryland. I have no accurate knowledge of my age, never having seen any authentic record containing it. By far the larger part of the slaves know as little of their ages as horses know of theirs, and it is the wish of most masters within my knowledge to keep their slaves thus ignorant. I do not remember to have ever met a slave who could tell of his birthday. They seldom come nearer to it than planting-time, harvest-time, cherry-time, spring-time, or fall-time. A want of information concerning my own was a source of unhappiness to me even during childhood. The white children could tell their ages. I could not tell why I ought to be deprived of the same privilege. I was not allowed to make any inquiries of my master concerning it. He deemed all such inquiries on the part of a slave improper and impertinent, and evidence of a restless spirit. The nearest estimate I can give makes me now between twenty-seven and twenty-eight years of age. I come to this, from hearing my master say, some time during 1835, I was about seventeen years old.

My mother was named Harriet Bailey. She was the daughter of Isaac and Betsey Bailey, both colored, and quite dark. My mother was of a darker complexion than either my grandmother or grandfather.

My father was a white man. He was admitted to be such by all I ever heard speak of my parentage. The opinion was also whispered that my master was my father; but of the correctness of this opinion, I know nothing; the means of knowing was withheld from me. My mother and I were separated when I was but an infant—before I knew her as my mother. It is a common custom, in the part of Maryland from which I ran away, to part children from their mothers at a very early age. Frequently, before the child has reached its twelfth month, its mother is taken from it, and hired out on some farm a considerable distance off, and the child is placed under the care of an old woman, too old for field labor. For what this separation is done, I do not know, unless it be to hinder the development of the child's affection toward its mother, and to blunt and destroy the natural affection of the mother for the child. This is the inevitable result.

I never saw my mother, to know her as such, more than four or five times in my life; and each of these times was very short in duration, and at night. She was hired by a Mr. Stewart, who lived about twelve miles from my home. She made her journeys to see me in the night, travelling the whole distance on foot, after the performance of her day's work. She was a field hand, and a whipping is the penalty of not being in the field at sunrise, unless a slave has special permission from his or her master to the contrary—a permission which they seldom get, and one that gives to him that gives it the proud name of being a kind master. I do not recollect of ever seeing my mother by the light of day. She was with me in the night. She would lie down with me, and get me to sleep, but long before I waked she was gone. Very little communication ever took place between us. Death soon ended what little we could have while she lived, and with it her hardships and suffering. She died when I was about seven years old, on one of my master's farms, near Lee's Mill. I was not allowed to be present during her illness, at her death, or burial. She was gone long before I knew any thing about it. Never having enjoyed, to any considerable extent, her soothing presence, her tender and watchful care, I received the tidings of her death with much the same emotions I should have probably felt at the death of a stranger.

Called thus suddenly away, she left me without the slightest intimation of who my father was. The whisper that my master was my father, may or may not be true; and, true or false, it is of but little consequence to my purpose whilst the fact remains, in all its glaring odiousness, that slaveholders have ordained, and by law established, that the children of slave women shall in all cases follow the condition of their mothers; and this is done too obviously to administer to their own lusts, and make a gratification of their wicked desires profitable as well as pleasurable; for by this cunning arrangement, the slaveholder, in cases not a few, sustains to his slaves the double relation of master and father.

I know of such cases; and it is worthy of remark that such slaves invariably suffer greater hardships, and have more to contend with, than others. They are, in the first place, a constant offence to their mistress. She is ever disposed to find fault with them; they can seldom do any thing to please her; she is never better pleased than when she sees them under the lash, especially when she suspects her husband of showing to his mulatto children favors which he withholds from his black slaves. The master is frequently compelled to sell this class of his slaves, out of deference to the feelings of his white wife; and, cruel as the deed may strike any one to be, for a man to sell his own children to human flesh-mongers, it is often the dictate of humanity for him to do so; for, unless he does this, he must not only whip them himself, but must stand by and see one white son tie up his brother, of but few shades darker complexion than himself, and ply the gory lash to his naked back; and if he lisp one word of disapproval, it is set down to his parental partiality, and only makes a bad matter worse, both for himself and the slave whom he would protect and defend.

Every year brings with it multitudes of this class of slaves. It was doubtless in consequence of a knowledge of this fact, that one great statesman of the south predicted the downfall of slavery by the inevitable laws of population. Whether this prophecy is ever fulfilled or not, it is nevertheless plain that a very different-looking class of people are springing up at the south, and are now held in slavery, from those originally brought to this country from Africa; and if their increase do no other good, it will do away the force of the argument, that God cursed Ham, and therefore American slavery is right. If the lineal descendants of Ham are alone to be scripturally enslaved, it is certain that slavery at the south must soon become unscriptural; for thousands are ushered into the world, annually, who, like myself, owe their existence to white fathers, and those fathers most frequently their own masters.

I have had two masters. My first master's name was Anthony. I do not remember his first name. He was generally called Captain Anthony—a title which, I presume, he acquired by sailing a craft on the Chesapeake Bay. He was not considered a rich slaveholder. He owned two or three farms, and about thirty slaves. His farms and slaves were under the care of an overseer. The overseer's name was Plummer. Mr. Plummer was a miserable drunkard, a profane swearer, and a savage monster. He always went armed with a cowskin and a heavy cudgel. I have known him to cut and slash the women's heads so horribly, that even master would be enraged at his cruelty, and would threaten to whip him if he did not mind himself. Master, however, was not a humane slaveholder. It required extraordinary barbarity on the part of an overseer to affect him. He was a cruel man, hardened by a long life of slaveholding. He would at times seem to take great pleasure in whipping a slave. I have often been awakened at the dawn of day by the most heart-rending shrieks of an own aunt of mine, whom he used to tie up to a joist, and whip upon her naked back till she was literally covered with blood. No words, no tears, no prayers, from his gory victim, seemed to move his iron heart from its bloody purpose. The louder she screamed, the harder he whipped; and where the blood ran fastest, there he whipped longest. He would whip her to make her scream, and whip her to make her hush; and not until overcome by fatigue, would he cease to swing the blood-clotted cowskin. I remember the first time I ever witnessed this horrible exhibition. I was quite a child, but I well remember it. I never shall forget it whilst I remember any thing. It was the first of a long series of such outrages, of which I was doomed to be a witness and a participant. It struck me with awful force. It was the blood-stained gate, the entrance to the hell of slavery, through which I was about to pass. It was a most terrible spectacle. I wish I could commit to paper the feelings with which I beheld it.

This occurrence took place very soon after I went to live with my old master, and under the following circumstances. Aunt Hester went out one night,—where or for what I do not know,—and happened to be absent when my master desired her presence. He had ordered her not to go out evenings, and warned her that she must never let him catch her in company with a young man, who was paying attention to her belonging to Colonel Lloyd. The young man's name was Ned Roberts, generally called Lloyd's Ned. Why master was so careful of her, may be safely left to conjecture. She was a woman of noble form, and of graceful proportions, having very few equals, and fewer superiors, in personal appearance, among the colored or white women of our neighborhood.

Aunt Hester had not only disobeyed his orders in going out, but had been found in company with Lloyd's Ned; which circumstance, I found, from what he said while whipping her, was the chief offence. Had he been a man of pure morals himself, he might have been thought interested in protecting the innocence of my aunt; but those who knew him will not suspect him of any such virtue. Before he commenced whipping Aunt Hester, he took her into the kitchen, and stripped her from neck to waist, leaving her neck, shoulders, and back, entirely naked. He then told her to cross her hands, calling her at the same time a d——d b—-h. After crossing her hands, he tied them with a strong rope, and led her to a stool under a large hook in the joist, put in for the purpose. He made her get upon the stool, and tied her hands to the hook. She now stood fair for his infernal purpose. Her arms were stretched up at their full length, so that she stood upon the ends of her toes. He then said to her, "Now, you d——d b—-h, I'll learn you how to disobey my orders!" and after rolling up his sleeves, he commenced to lay on the heavy cowskin, and soon the warm, red blood (amid heart-rending shrieks from her, and horrid oaths from him) came dripping to the floor. I was so terrified and horror-stricken at the sight, that I hid myself in a closet, and dared not venture out till long after the bloody transaction was over. I expected it would be my turn next. It was all new to me. I had never seen any thing like it before. I had always lived with my grandmother on the outskirts of the plantation, where she was put to raise the children of the younger women. I had therefore been, until now, out of the way of the bloody scenes that often occurred on the plantation.

Chapter 2

My master's family consisted of two sons, Andrew and Richard; one daughter, Lucretia, and her husband, Captain Thomas Auld. They lived in one house, upon the home plantation of Colonel Edward Lloyd. My master was Colonel Lloyd's clerk and superintendent. He was what might be called the overseer of the overseers. I spent two years of childhood on this plantation in my old master's family. It was here that I witnessed the bloody transaction recorded in the first chapter; and as I received my first impressions of slavery on this plantation, I will give some description of it, and of slavery as it there existed. The plantation is about twelve miles north of Easton, in Talbot county, and is situated on the border of Miles River. The principal products raised upon it were tobacco, corn, and wheat. These were raised in great abundance; so that, with the products of this and the other farms belonging to him, he was able to keep in almost constant employment a large sloop, in carrying them to market at

Baltimore. This sloop was named Sally Lloyd, in honor of one of the colonel's daughters. My master's son-in-law, Captain Auld, was master of the vessel; she was otherwise manned by the colonel's own slaves. Their names were Peter, Isaac, Rich, and Jake. These were esteemed very highly by the other slaves, and looked upon as the privileged ones of the plantation; for it was no small affair, in the eyes of the slaves, to be allowed to see Baltimore.

Colonel Lloyd kept from three to four hundred slaves on his home plantation, and owned a large number more on the neighboring farms belonging to him. The names of the farms nearest to the home plantation were Wye Town and New Design. "Wye Town" was under the overseership of a man named Noah Willis. New Design was under the overseership of a Mr. Townsend. The overseers of these, and all the rest of the farms, numbering over twenty, received advice and direction from the managers of the home plantation. This was the great business place. It was the seat of government for the whole twenty farms. All disputes among the overseers were settled here. If a slave was convicted of any high misdemeanor, became unmanageable, or evinced a determination to run away, he was brought immediately here, severely whipped, put on board the sloop, carried to Baltimore, and sold to Austin Woolfolk, or some other slave-trader, as a warning to the slaves remaining.

Here, too, the slaves of all the other farms received their monthly allowance of food, and their yearly clothing. The men and women slaves received, as their monthly allowance of food, eight pounds of pork, or its equivalent in fish, and one bushel of corn meal. Their yearly clothing consisted of two coarse linen shirts, one pair of linen trousers, like the shirts, one jacket, one pair of trousers for winter, made of coarse negro cloth, one pair of stockings, and one pair of shoes; the whole of which could not have cost more than seven dollars. The allowance of the slave children was given to their mothers, or the old women having the care of them. The children unable to work in the field had neither shoes, stockings, jackets, nor trousers, given to them; their clothing consisted of two coarse linen shirts per year. When these failed them, they went naked until the next allowance-day. Children from seven to ten years old, of both sexes, almost naked, might be seen at all seasons of the year.

There were no beds given the slaves, unless one coarse blanket be considered such, and none but the men and women had these. This, however, is not considered a very great privation. They find less difficulty from the want of beds, than from the want of time to sleep; for when their day's work in the field is done, the most of them having their washing, mending, and cooking to do, and having few or none of the ordinary facilities for doing either of these, very many of their sleeping hours are consumed in preparing for the field the coming day; and when this is done, old and young, male and female, married and single, drop down side by side, on one common bed,—the cold, damp floor,—each covering himself or herself with their miserable blankets; and here they sleep till they are summoned to the field by the driver's horn. At the sound of this, all must rise, and be off to the field. There must be no halting; every one must be at his or her post; and woe betides them who hear not this morning summons to the field; for if they are not awakened by the sense of hearing, they are by the sense of feeling: no age nor sex finds any favor. Mr. Severe, the overseer, used to stand by the door of the quarter, armed with a large hickory stick and heavy cowskin, ready to whip any one who was so unfortunate as not to hear, or, from any other cause, was prevented from being ready to start for the field at the sound of the horn.

Mr. Severe was rightly named: he was a cruel man. I have seen him whip a woman, causing the blood to run half an hour at the time; and this, too, in the midst of her crying children, pleading for their mother's release. He seemed to take pleasure in manifesting his fiendish barbarity. Added to his cruelty, he was a profane swearer. It was enough to chill the blood and stiffen the hair of an ordinary man to hear him talk. Scarce a sentence escaped him but that was commenced or concluded by some horrid oath. The field was the place to witness his cruelty and profanity. His presence made it both the field of blood and of blasphemy. From the rising till the going down of the sun, he was cursing, raving, cutting, and slashing among the slaves of the field, in the most frightful manner. His career was short. He died very soon after I went to Colonel Lloyd's; and he died as he lived, uttering, with his dying groans, bitter curses and horrid oaths. His death was regarded by the slaves as the result of a merciful providence.

Mr. Severe's place was filled by a Mr. Hopkins. He was a very different man. He was less cruel, less profane, and made less noise, than Mr. Severe. His course was characterized by no extraordinary demonstrations of cruelty. He whipped, but seemed to take no pleasure in it. He was called by the slaves a good overseer.

The home plantation of Colonel Lloyd wore the appearance of a country village. All the mechanical operations for all the farms were performed here. The shoemaking and mending, the blacksmithing, cartwrighting, coopering, weaving, and grain-grinding, were all performed by the slaves on the home plantation. The whole place wore a business-like aspect very unlike the neighboring farms. The number of houses, too, conspired to give it advantage over the neighboring farms. It was called by the slaves the

Great House Farm. Few privileges were esteemed higher, by the slaves of the out-farms, than that of being selected to do errands at the Great House Farm. It was associated in their minds with greatness. A representative could not be prouder of his election to a seat in the American Congress, than a slave on one of the out-farms would be of his election to do errands at the Great House Farm. They regarded it as evidence of great confidence reposed in them by their overseers; and it was on this account, as well as a constant desire to be out of the field from under the driver's lash, that they esteemed it a high privilege, one worth careful living for. He was called the smartest and most trusty fellow, who had this honor conferred upon him the most frequently. The competitors for this office sought as diligently to please their overseers, as the office-seekers in the political parties seek to please and deceive the people. The same traits of character might be seen in Colonel Lloyd's slaves, as are seen in the slaves of the political parties.

The slaves selected to go to the Great House Farm, for the monthly allowance for themselves and their fellow-slaves, were peculiarly enthusiastic. While on their way, they would make the dense old woods, for miles around, reverberate with their wild songs, revealing at once the highest joy and the deepest sadness. They would compose and sing as they went along, consulting neither time nor tune. The thought that came up, came out—if not in the word, in the sound;—and as frequently in the one as in the other. They would sometimes sing the most pathetic sentiment in the most rapturous tone, and the most rapturous sentiment in the most pathetic tone. Into all of their songs they would manage to weave something of the Great House Farm. Especially would they do this, when leaving home. They would then sing most exultingly the following words:—

> "I am going away to the Great House Farm! O, yea! O, yea! O!"

This they would sing, as a chorus, to words which to many would seem unmeaning jargon, but which, nevertheless, were full of meaning to themselves. I have sometimes thought that the mere hearing of those songs would do more to impress some minds with the horrible character of slavery, than the reading of whole volumes of philosophy on the subject could do.

I did not, when a slave, understand the deep meaning of those rude and apparently incoherent songs. I was myself within the circle; so that I neither saw nor heard as those without might see and hear. They told a tale of woe which was then altogether beyond my feeble comprehension; they were tones loud, long, and deep; they breathed the prayer and complaint of souls boiling over with the bitterest anguish. Every tone was a testimony against slavery, and a prayer to God for deliverance from chains. The hearing of those wild notes always depressed my spirit, and filled me with ineffable sadness. I have frequently found myself in tears while hearing them. The mere recurrence to those songs, even now, afflicts me; and while I am writing these lines, an expression of feeling has already found its way down my cheek. To those songs I trace my first glimmering conception of the dehumanizing character of slavery. I can never get rid of that conception. Those songs still follow me, to deepen my hatred of slavery, and quicken my sympathies for my brethren in bonds. If any one wishes to be impressed with the soul-killing effects of slavery, let him go to Colonel Lloyd's plantation, and, on allowance-day, place himself in the deep pine woods, and there let him, in silence, analyze the sounds that shall pass through the chambers of his soul,—and if he is not thus impressed, it will only be because "there is no flesh in his obdurate heart."

I have often been utterly astonished, since I came to the north, to find persons who could speak of the singing, among slaves, as evidence of their contentment and happiness. It is impossible to conceive of a greater mistake. Slaves sing most when they are most unhappy. The songs of the slave represent the sorrows of his heart; and he is relieved by them, only as an aching heart is relieved by its tears. At least, such is my experience. I have often sung to drown my sorrow, but seldom to express my happiness. Crying for joy, and singing for joy, were alike uncommon to me while in the jaws of slavery. The singing of a man cast away upon a desolate island might be as appropriately considered as evidence of contentment and happiness, as the singing of a slave; the songs of the one and of the other are prompted by the same emotion.

Chapter 3

Colonel Lloyd kept a large and finely cultivated garden, which afforded almost constant employment for four men, besides the chief gardener, (Mr. M'Durmond.) This garden was probably the greatest attraction of the place. During the summer months, people came from far and near—from Baltimore, Easton, and Annapolis—to see it. It abounded in fruits of almost every description, from the hardy apple of the north to the delicate orange of the south. This garden was not the least source of trouble on the plantation. Its excellent fruit was quite a temptation to the hungry swarms of boys, as well as the older slaves, belonging to the colonel, few of whom had the virtue or the vice to resist it. Scarcely a day passed, during the summer, but that some slave had to take the lash for stealing fruit. The colonel had to resort to all kinds of stratagems to keep his slaves out of the garden. The last and most successful one was that of tarring his fence all around; after which, if a slave was caught with any tar upon his person, it was deemed sufficient proof that he had either been into the garden, or had tried to get in. In either case, he was severely whipped by the chief gardener. This plan worked well; the slaves became as fearful of tar as of the lash. They seemed to realize the impossibility of touching *tar* without being defiled.

The colonel also kept a splendid riding equipage. His stable and carriage-house presented the appearance of some of our large city livery establishments. His horses were of the finest form and noblest blood. His carriage-house contained three splendid coaches, three or four gigs, besides dearborns and barouches of the most fashionable style.

This establishment was under the care of two slaves—old Barney and young Barney—father and son. To attend to this establishment was their sole work. But it was by no means an easy employment; for in nothing was Colonel Lloyd more particular than in the management of his horses. The slightest inattention to these was unpardonable, and was visited upon those, under whose care they were placed, with the severest punishment; no excuse could shield them, if the colonel only suspected any want of attention to his horses—a supposition which he frequently indulged, and one which, of course, made the office of old and young Barney a very trying one. They never knew when they were safe from punishment. They were frequently whipped when least deserving, and escaped whipping when most deserving it. Every thing depended upon the looks of the horses, and the state of Colonel Lloyd's own mind when his horses were brought to him for use. If a horse did not move fast enough, or hold his head high enough, it was owing to some fault of his keepers. It was painful to stand near the stable-door, and hear the various complaints against the keepers when a horse was taken out for use. "This horse has not had proper attention. He has not been sufficiently rubbed and curried, or he has not been properly fed; his food was too wet or too dry; he got it too soon or too late; he was too hot or too cold; he had too much hay, and not enough of grain; or he had too much grain, and not enough of hay; instead of old Barney's attending to the horse, he had very improperly left it to his son." To all these complaints, no matter how unjust, the slave must answer never a word. Colonel Lloyd could not brook any contradiction from a slave. When he spoke, a slave must stand, listen, and tremble; and such was literally the case. I have seen Colonel Lloyd make old Barney, a man between fifty and sixty years of age, uncover his bald head, kneel down upon the cold, damp ground, and receive upon his naked and toil-worn shoulders more than thirty lashes at the time. Colonel Lloyd had three sons—Edward, Murray, and Daniel,—and three sons-in-law, Mr. Winder, Mr. Nicholson, and Mr. Lowndes. All of these lived at the Great House Farm, and enjoyed the luxury of whipping the servants when they pleased, from old Barney down to William Wilkes, the coach-driver. I have seen Winder make one of the house-servants stand off from him a suitable distance to be touched with the end of his whip, and at every stroke raise great ridges upon his back.

To describe the wealth of Colonel Lloyd would be almost equal to describing the riches of Job. He kept from ten to fifteen house-servants. He was said to own a thousand slaves, and I think this estimate quite within the truth. Colonel Lloyd owned so many that he did not know them when he saw them; nor did all the slaves of the out-farms know him. It is reported of him, that, while riding along the road one day, he met a colored man, and addressed him in the usual manner of speaking to colored people on the public highways of the south: "Well, boy, whom do you belong to?" "To Colonel Lloyd," replied the slave. "Well, does the colonel treat you well?" "No, sir," was the ready reply. "What, does he work you too hard?" "Yes, sir." "Well, don't he give you enough to eat?" "Yes, sir, he gives me enough, such as it is."

The colonel, after ascertaining where the slave belonged, rode on; the man also went on about his business, not dreaming that he had been conversing with his master. He thought, said, and heard nothing more of the matter, until two or three weeks afterwards. The poor man was then informed by his overseer that, for having found fault with his master, he was now to be sold to a Georgia trader. He was immediately chained and handcuffed; and thus, without a moment's warning, he was snatched away, and forever sundered, from his family and friends, by a hand more unrelenting than death. This is the penalty of telling the truth, of telling the simple truth, in answer to a series of plain questions.

It is partly in consequence of such facts, that slaves, when inquired of as to their condition and the character of their masters, almost universally say they are contented, and that their masters are kind. The slaveholders have been known to send in spies among their slaves, to ascertain their views and feelings in regard to their condition. The frequency of this has had the effect to establish among the slaves the maxim, that a still tongue makes a wise head. They suppress the truth rather than take the consequences of telling it, and in so doing prove themselves a part of the human family. If they have any thing to say of their masters, it is generally in their masters' favor, especially when speaking to an untried man. I have been frequently asked, when a slave, if I had a kind master, and do not remember ever to have given a negative answer; nor did I, in pursuing this course, consider myself as uttering what was absolutely false; for I always measured the kindness of my master by the standard of kindness set up among slaveholders around us. Moreover, slaves are like other people, and imbibe prejudices quite common to others. They think their own better than that of others. Many, under the influence of this prejudice, think their own masters are better than the masters of other slaves; and this, too, in some cases, when the very reverse is true. Indeed, it is not uncommon for slaves even to fall out and quarrel among themselves about the relative goodness of their masters, each contending for the superior goodness of his own over that of the others. At the very same time, they mutually execrate their masters when viewed separately. It was so on our plantation. When Colonel Lloyd's slaves met the slaves of Jacob Jepson, they seldom parted without a quarrel about their masters; Colonel Lloyd's slaves contending that he was the richest, and Mr. Jepson's slaves that he was the smartest, and most of a man. Colonel Lloyd's slaves would boast his ability to buy and sell Jacob Jepson. Mr. Jepson's slaves would boast his ability to whip Colonel Lloyd. These quarrels would almost always end in a fight between the parties, and those that whipped were supposed to have gained the point at issue. They seemed to think that the greatness of their masters was transferable to themselves. It was considered as being bad enough to be a slave; but to be a poor man's slave was deemed a disgrace indeed!

Chapter 4

Mr. Hopkins remained but a short time in the office of overseer. Why his career was so short, I do not know, but suppose he lacked the necessary severity to suit Colonel Lloyd. Mr. Hopkins was succeeded by Mr. Austin Gore, a man possessing, in an eminent degree, all those traits of character indispensable to what is called a first-rate overseer. Mr. Gore had served Colonel Lloyd, in the capacity of overseer, upon one of the out-farms, and had shown himself worthy of the high station of overseer upon the home or Great House Farm.

Mr. Gore was proud, ambitious, and persevering. He was artful, cruel, and obdurate. He was just the man for such a place, and it was just the place for such a man. It afforded scope for the full exercise of all his powers, and he seemed to be perfectly at home in it. He was one of those who could torture the slightest look, word, or gesture, on the part of the slave, into impudence, and would treat it accordingly. There must be no answering back to him; no explanation was allowed a slave, showing himself to have been wrongfully accused. Mr. Gore acted fully up to the maxim laid down by slaveholders,—"It is better that a dozen slaves should suffer under the lash, than that the overseer should be convicted, in the presence of the slaves, of having been at fault." No matter how innocent a slave might be—it availed him nothing, when accused by Mr. Gore of any misdemeanor. To be accused was to be convicted, and to be convicted was to be punished; the one always following the other with immutable certainty. To escape punishment was to escape accusation; and few slaves had the fortune to do either, under the overseership of Mr. Gore. He was just proud enough to demand the most debasing homage of the slave, and quite servile enough to crouch, himself, at the feet of the master. He was ambitious enough to be contented with nothing short of the highest rank of overseers, and persevering enough to reach the height of his ambition. He was cruel enough to inflict the severest punishment, artful enough to descend to the lowest trickery, and obdurate enough to be insensible to the voice of a reproving conscience. He was, of all the overseers, the most dreaded by the slaves. His presence was painful; his eye flashed confusion; and seldom was his sharp, shrill voice heard, without producing horror and trembling in their ranks.

Mr. Gore was a grave man, and, though a young man, he indulged in no jokes, said no funny words, seldom smiled. His words were in perfect keeping with his looks, and his looks were in perfect keeping with his words. Overseers will sometimes indulge in a witty word, even with the slaves; not so with Mr. Gore. He spoke but to command, and commanded but to be obeyed; he dealt sparingly with his words, and bountifully with his whip, never using the former where the latter would answer as well. When he whipped, he seemed to do so from a sense of duty, and feared no consequences. He did nothing reluctantly, no matter how disagreeable; always at his post, never inconsistent. He never promised but to fulfil. He was, in a word, a man of the most inflexible firmness and stone-like coolness.

His savage barbarity was equalled only by the consummate coolness with which he committed the grossest and most savage deeds upon the slaves under his charge. Mr. Gore once undertook to whip one of Colonel Lloyd's slaves, by the name of Demby. He had given Demby but few stripes, when, to get rid of the scourging, he ran and plunged himself into a creek, and stood there at the depth of his shoulders, refusing to come out. Mr. Gore told him that he would give him three calls, and that, if he did not come out at the third call, he would shoot him. The first call was given. Demby made no response, but stood his ground. The second and third calls were given with the same result. Mr. Gore then, without consultation or deliberation with any one, not even giving Demby an additional call, raised his musket to his face, taking deadly aim at his standing victim, and in an instant poor Demby was no more. His mangled body sank out of sight, and blood and brains marked the water where he had stood.

A thrill of horror flashed through every soul upon the plantation, excepting Mr. Gore. He alone seemed cool and collected. He was asked by Colonel Lloyd and my old master, why he resorted to this extraordinary expedient. His reply was, (as well as I can remember,) that Demby had become unmanageable. He was setting a dangerous example to the other slaves,—one which, if suffered to pass without some such demonstration on his part, would finally lead to the total subversion of all rule and order upon the plantation. He argued that if one slave refused to be corrected, and escaped with his life, the other slaves would soon copy the example; the result of which would be, the freedom of the slaves, and the enslavement of the whites. Mr. Gore's defence was satisfactory. He was continued in his station as overseer upon the home plantation. His fame as an overseer went abroad. His horrid crime was not even submitted to judicial investigation. It was committed in the presence of slaves, and they of course could neither institute a suit, nor testify against him; and thus the guilty perpetrator of one of the bloodiest and most foul murders goes unwhipped of justice, and uncensured by the community in which he lives. Mr. Gore lived in St. Michael's, Talbot county, Maryland, when I left there; and if he is still alive, he very probably lives there now; and if so, he is now, as he was then, as highly esteemed and as much respected as though his guilty soul had not been stained with his brother's blood.

I speak advisedly when I say this,—that killing a slave, or any colored person, in Talbot county, Maryland, is not treated as a crime, either by the courts or the community. Mr. Thomas Lanman, of St. Michael's, killed two slaves, one of whom he killed with a hatchet, by knocking his brains out. He used to boast of the commission of the awful and bloody deed. I have heard him do so laughingly, saying, among other things, that he was the only benefactor of his country in the company, and that when others would do as much as he had done, we should be relieved of "the d——d niggers."

The wife of Mr. Giles Hicks, living but a short distance from where I used to live, murdered my wife's cousin, a young girl between fifteen and sixteen years of age, mangling her person in the most horrible manner, breaking her nose and breastbone with a stick, so that the poor girl expired in a few hours afterward. She was immediately buried, but had not been in her untimely grave but a few hours before she was taken up and examined by the coroner, who decided that she had come to her death by severe beating. The offence for which this girl was thus murdered was this:—She had been set that night to mind Mrs. Hicks's baby, and during the night she fell asleep, and the baby cried. She, having lost her rest for several nights previous, did not hear the crying. They were both in the room with Mrs. Hicks. Mrs. Hicks, finding the girl slow to move, jumped from her bed, seized an oak stick of wood by the fireplace, and with it broke the girl's nose and breastbone, and thus ended her life. I will not say that this most horrid murder produced no sensation in the community. It did produce sensation, but not enough to bring the murderess to punishment. There was a warrant issued for her arrest, but it was never served. Thus she escaped not only punishment, but even the pain of being arraigned before a court for her horrid crime.

Whilst I am detailing bloody deeds which took place during my stay on Colonel Lloyd's plantation, I will briefly narrate another, which occurred about the same time as the murder of Demby by Mr. Gore.

Colonel Lloyd's slaves were in the habit of spending a part of their nights and Sundays in fishing for oysters, and in this way made up the deficiency of their scanty allowance. An old man belonging to Colonel Lloyd, while thus engaged, happened to get beyond the limits of Colonel Lloyd's, and on the premises of Mr. Beal Bondly. At this trespass, Mr. Bondly took offence, and with his musket came down to the shore, and blew its deadly contents into the poor old man.

Mr. Bondly came over to see Colonel Lloyd the next day, whether to pay him for his property, or to justify himself in what he had done, I know not. At any rate, this whole fiendish transaction was soon hushed up. There was very little said about it at all, and nothing done. It was a common saying, even among little white boys, that it was worth a half-cent to kill a "nigger," and a half-cent to bury one.

Chapter 5

As to my own treatment while I lived on Colonel Lloyd's plantation, it was very similar to that of the other slave children. I was not old enough to work in the field, and there being little else than field work to do, I had a great deal of leisure time. The most I had to do was to drive up the cows at evening, keep the fowls out of the garden, keep the front yard clean, and run of errands for my old master's daughter, Mrs. Lucretia Auld. The most of my leisure time I spent in helping Master Daniel Lloyd in finding his birds, after he had shot them. My connection with Master Daniel was of some advantage to me. He became quite attached to me, and was a sort of protector of me. He would not allow the older boys to impose upon me, and would divide his cakes with me.

I was seldom whipped by my old master, and suffered little from any thing else than hunger and cold. I suffered much from hunger, but much more from cold. In hottest summer and coldest winter, I was kept almost naked—no shoes, no stockings, no jacket, no trousers, nothing on but a coarse tow linen shirt, reaching only to my knees. I had no bed. I must have perished with cold, but that, the coldest nights, I used to steal a bag which was used for carrying corn to the mill. I would crawl into this bag, and there sleep on the cold, damp, clay floor, with my head in and feet out. My feet have been so cracked with the frost, that the pen with which I am writing might be laid in the gashes.

We were not regularly allowanced. Our food was coarse corn meal boiled. This was called *mush*. It was put into a large wooden tray or trough, and set down upon the ground. The children were then called, like so many pigs, and like so many pigs they would come and devour the mush; some with oyster-shells, others with pieces of shingle, some with naked hands, and none with spoons. He that ate fastest got most; he that was strongest secured the best place; and few left the trough satisfied.

I was probably between seven and eight years old when I left Colonel Lloyd's plantation. I left it with joy. I shall never forget the ecstasy with which I received the intelligence that my old master (Anthony) had determined to let me go to Baltimore, to live with Mr. Hugh Auld, brother to my old master's son-in-law, Captain Thomas Auld. I received this information about three days before my departure. They were three of the happiest days I ever enjoyed. I spent the most part of all these three days in the creek, washing off the plantation scurf, and preparing myself for my departure.

The pride of appearance which this would indicate was not my own. I spent the time in washing, not so much because I wished to, but because Mrs. Lucretia had told me I must get all the dead skin off my feet and knees before I could go to Baltimore; for the people in Baltimore were very cleanly, and would laugh at me if I looked dirty. Besides, she was going to give me a pair of trousers, which I should not put on unless I got all the dirt off me. The thought of owning a pair of trousers was great indeed! It was almost a sufficient motive, not only to make me take off what would be called by pig-drovers the mange, but the skin itself. I went at it in good earnest, working for the first time with the hope of reward.

The ties that ordinarily bind children to their homes were all suspended in my case. I found no severe trial in my departure. My home was charmless; it was not home to me; on parting from it, I could not feel that I was leaving any thing which I could have enjoyed by staying. My mother was dead, my grandmother lived far off, so that I seldom saw her. I had two sisters and one brother, that lived in the same house with me; but the early separation of us from our mother had well nigh blotted the fact of our relationship from our memories. I looked for home elsewhere, and was confident of finding none which I should relish less than the one which I was leaving. If, however, I found in my new home hardship, hunger, whipping, and nakedness, I had the consolation that I should not have escaped any one of them by staying. Having already had more than a taste of them in the house of my old master, and having endured them there, I very naturally inferred my ability to endure them elsewhere, and especially at Baltimore; for I had something of the feeling about Baltimore that is expressed in the proverb, that "being hanged in England is preferable to dying a natural death in Ireland." I had the strongest desire to see Baltimore. Cousin Tom, though not fluent in speech, had inspired me with that desire by his eloquent description of the place. I could never point out any thing at the Great House, no matter how beautiful or powerful, but that he had seen something at Baltimore far exceeding, both in beauty and strength, the object which I pointed out to him. Even the Great House itself, with all its pictures, was far inferior to many buildings in Baltimore. So strong was my desire, that I thought a gratification of it would fully compensate for whatever loss of comforts I should sustain by the exchange. I left without a regret, and with the highest hopes of future happiness.

We sailed out of Miles River for Baltimore on a Saturday morning. I remember only the day of the week, for at that time I had no knowledge of the days of the month, nor the months of the year. On setting sail, I walked aft, and gave to Colonel Lloyd's plantation what I hoped would be the last look. I then placed myself in the bows of the sloop, and there spent the remainder of the day in looking ahead, interesting myself in what was in the distance rather than in things near by or behind.

In the afternoon of that day, we reached Annapolis, the capital of the State. We stopped but a few moments, so that I had no time to go on shore. It was the first large town that I had ever seen, and though it would look small compared with some of our New England factory villages, I thought it a wonderful place for its size—more imposing even than the Great House Farm!

We arrived at Baltimore early on Sunday morning, landing at Smith's Wharf, not far from Bowley's Wharf. We had on board the sloop a large flock of sheep; and after aiding in driving them to the slaughterhouse of Mr. Curtis on Louden Slater's Hill, I was conducted by Rich, one of the hands belonging on board of the sloop, to my new home in Alliciana Street, near Mr. Gardner's ship-yard, on Fells Point.

Mr. and Mrs. Auld were both at home, and met me at the door with their little son Thomas, to take care of whom I had been given. And here I saw what I had never seen before; it was a white face beaming with the most kindly emotions; it was the face of my new mistress, Sophia Auld. I wish I could describe the rapture that flashed through my soul as I beheld it. It was a new and strange sight to me, brightening up my pathway with the light of happiness. Little Thomas was told, there was his Freddy,—and I was told to take care of little Thomas; and thus I entered upon the duties of my new home with the most cheering prospect ahead.

I look upon my departure from Colonel Lloyd's plantation as one of the most interesting events of my life. It is possible, and even quite probable, that but for the mere circumstance of being removed from that plantation to Baltimore, I should have to-day, instead of being here seated by my own table, in the enjoyment of freedom and the happiness of home, writing this Narrative, been confined in the galling chains of slavery. Going to live at Baltimore laid the foundation, and opened the gateway, to all my subsequent prosperity. I have ever regarded it as the first plain manifestation of that kind providence which has ever since attended me, and marked my life with so many favors. I regarded the selection of myself as being somewhat remarkable. There were a number of slave children that might have been sent from the plantation to Baltimore. There were those younger, those older, and those of the same age. I was chosen from among them all, and was the first, last, and only choice.

I may be deemed superstitious, and even egotistical, in regarding this event as a special interposition of divine Providence in my favor. But I should be false to the earliest sentiments of my soul, if I suppressed the opinion. I prefer to be true to myself, even at the hazard of incurring the ridicule of others, rather than to be false, and incur my own abhorrence. From my earliest recollection, I date the entertainment of a deep conviction that slavery would not always be able to hold me within its foul embrace; and in the darkest hours of my career in slavery, this living word of faith and spirit of hope departed not from me, but remained like ministering angels to cheer me through the gloom. This good spirit was from God, and to him I offer thanksgiving and praise.

Chapter 6

My new mistress proved to be all she appeared when I first met her at the door,—a woman of the kindest heart and finest feelings. She had never had a slave under her control previously to myself, and prior to her marriage she had been dependent upon her own industry for a living. She was by trade a weaver; and by constant application to her business, she had been in a good degree preserved from the blighting and dehumanizing effects of slavery. I was utterly astonished at her goodness. I scarcely knew how to behave towards her. She was entirely unlike any other white woman I had ever seen. I could not approach her as I was accustomed to approach other white ladies. My early instruction was all out of place. The crouching servility, usually so acceptable a quality in a slave, did not answer when manifested toward her. Her favor was not gained by it; she seemed to be disturbed by it. She did not deem it impudent or unmannerly for a slave to look her in the face. The meanest slave was put fully at ease in her presence, and none left without feeling better for having seen her. Her face was made of heavenly smiles, and her voice of tranquil music.

But, alas! this kind heart had but a short time to remain such. The fatal poison of irresponsible power was already in her hands, and soon commenced its infernal work. That cheerful eye, under the influence of slavery, soon became red with rage; that voice, made all of sweet accord, changed to one of harsh and horrid discord; and that angelic face gave place to that of a demon.

Very soon after I went to live with Mr. and Mrs. Auld, she very kindly commenced to teach me the A, B, C. After I had learned this, she assisted me in learning to spell words of three or four letters. Just at this point of my progress, Mr. Auld found out what was going on, and at once forbade Mrs. Auld to instruct me further, telling her, among other things, that it was unlawful, as well as unsafe, to teach a slave to read. To use his own words, further, he said, "If you give a nigger an inch, he will take an ell. A nigger should know nothing but to obey his master—to do as he is told to do. Learning would *spoil* the best nigger in the world. Now," said he, "if you teach that nigger (speaking of myself) how to read, there would be no keeping him. It would forever unfit him to be a slave. He would at once become unmanageable, and of no value to his master. As to himself, it could do him no good, but a great deal of harm. It would make him discontented and unhappy." These words sank deep into my heart, stirred up sentiments within that lay slumbering, and called into existence an entirely new train of thought. It was a new and special revelation, explaining dark and mysterious things, with which my youthful understanding had struggled, but struggled in vain. I now understood what had been to me a most perplexing difficulty—to wit, the white man's power to enslave the black man. It was a grand achievement, and I prized it highly. From that moment, I understood the pathway from slavery to freedom. It was just what I wanted, and I got it at a time when I the least expected it. Whilst I was saddened by the thought of losing the aid of my kind mistress, I was gladdened by the invaluable instruction which, by the merest accident, I had gained from my master. Though conscious of the difficulty of learning without a teacher, I set out with high hope, and a fixed purpose, at whatever cost of trouble, to learn how to read. The very decided manner with which he spoke, and strove to impress his wife with the evil consequences of giving me instruction, served to convince me that he was deeply sensible of the truths he was uttering. It gave me the best assurance that I might rely with the utmost confidence on the results which, he said, would flow from teaching me to read. What he most dreaded, that I most desired. What he most loved, that I most hated. That which to him was a great evil, to be carefully shunned, was to me a great good, to be diligently sought; and the argument which he so warmly urged, against my learning to read, only served to inspire me with a desire and determination to learn. In learning to read, I owe almost as much to the bitter opposition of my master, as to the kindly aid of my mistress. I acknowledge the benefit of both.

I had resided but a short time in Baltimore before I observed a marked difference, in the treatment of slaves, from that which I had witnessed in the country. A city slave is almost a freeman, compared with a slave on the plantation. He is much better fed and clothed, and enjoys privileges altogether unknown to the slave on the plantation. There is a vestige of decency, a sense of shame, that does much to curb and check those outbreaks of atrocious cruelty so commonly enacted upon the plantation. He is a desperate slaveholder, who will shock the humanity of his non-slaveholding neighbors with the cries of his lacerated slave. Few are willing to incur the odium attaching to the reputation of being a cruel master; and above all things, they would not be known as not giving a slave enough to eat. Every city slaveholder is anxious to have it known of him, that he feeds his slaves well; and it is due to them to say, that most of them do give their slaves enough to eat. There are, however, some painful exceptions to this rule. Directly opposite to us, on Philpot Street, lived Mr. Thomas Hamilton. He owned two slaves. Their names were Henrietta and Mary. Henrietta was about twenty-two years of age, Mary was about fourteen; and of all the mangled and emaciated creatures I ever looked upon, these two were the most so. His heart must be harder than stone, that could look upon these unmoved. The head, neck, and shoulders of Mary were literally cut to pieces. I have frequently felt her head, and found it nearly covered with festering sores, caused by the lash of her cruel mistress. I do not know that her master ever whipped her, but I have been an eye-witness to the cruelty of Mrs. Hamilton. I used to be in Mr. Hamilton's house nearly every day. Mrs. Hamilton used to sit in a large chair in the middle of the room, with a heavy cowskin always by her side, and scarce an hour passed during the day but was marked by the blood of one of these slaves. The girls seldom passed her without her saying, "Move faster, you *black gip!*" at the same time giving them a blow with the cowskin over the head or shoulders, often drawing the blood. She would then say, "Take that, you *black gip!*" continuing, "If you don't move faster, I'll move you!" Added to the cruel lashings to which these slaves were subjected, they were kept nearly half-starved. They seldom knew what it was to eat a full meal. I have seen Mary contending with the pigs for the offal thrown into the street. So much was Mary kicked and cut to pieces, that she was oftener called "*pecked*" than by her name.

Chapter 7

I lived in Master Hugh's family about seven years. During this time, I succeeded in learning to read and write. In accomplishing this, I was compelled to resort to various stratagems. I had no regular teacher. My mistress, who had kindly commenced to instruct me, had, in compliance with the advice and direction of her husband, not only ceased to instruct, but had set her face against my being instructed by any one else. It is due, however, to my mistress to say of her, that she did not adopt this course of treatment immediately. She at first lacked the depravity indispensable to shutting me up in mental darkness. It was at least necessary for her to have some training in the exercise of irresponsible power, to make her equal to the task of treating me as though I were a brute.

My mistress was, as I have said, a kind and tender-hearted woman; and in the simplicity of her soul she commenced, when I first went to live with her, to treat me as she supposed one human being ought to treat another. In entering upon the duties of a slaveholder, she did not seem to perceive that I sustained to her the relation of a mere chattel, and that for her to treat me as a human being was not only wrong, but dangerously so. Slavery proved as injurious to her as it did to me. When I went there, she was a pious, warm, and tender-hearted woman. There was no sorrow or suffering for which she had not a tear. She had bread for the hungry, clothes for the naked, and comfort for every mourner that came within her reach. Slavery soon proved its ability to divest her of these heavenly qualities. Under its influence, the tender heart became stone, and the lamblike disposition gave way to one of tiger-like fierceness. The first step in her downward course was in her ceasing to instruct me. She now commenced to practise her husband's precepts. She finally became even more violent in her opposition than her husband himself. She was not satisfied with simply doing as well as he had commanded; she seemed anxious to do better. Nothing seemed to make her more angry than to see me with a newspaper. She seemed to think that here lay the danger. I have had her rush at me with a face made all up of fury, and snatch from me a newspaper, in a manner that fully revealed her apprehension. She was an apt woman; and a little experience soon demonstrated, to her satisfaction, that education and slavery were incompatible with each other.

From this time I was most narrowly watched. If I was in a separate room any considerable length of time, I was sure to be suspected of having a book, and was at once called to give an account of myself. All this, however, was too late. The first step had been taken. Mistress, in teaching me the alphabet, had given me the *inch,* and no precaution could prevent me from taking the *ell.*

The plan which I adopted, and the one by which I was most successful, was that of making friends of all the little white boys whom I met in the street. As many of these as I could, I converted into teachers. With their kindly aid, obtained at different times and in different places, I finally succeeded in learning to read. When I was sent of errands, I always took my book with me, and by going one part of my errand quickly, I found time to get a lesson before my return. I used also to carry bread with me, enough of which was always in the house, and to which I was always welcome; for I was much better off in this regard than many of the poor white children in our neighborhood. This bread I used to bestow upon the hungry little urchins, who, in return, would give me that more valuable bread of knowledge. I am strongly tempted to give the names of two or three of those little boys, as a testimonial of the gratitude and affection I bear them; but prudence forbids;—not that it would injure me, but it might embarrass them; for it is almost an unpardonable offence to teach slaves to read in this Christian country. It is enough to say of the dear little fellows, that they lived on Philpot Street, very near Durgin and Bailey's ship-yard. I used to talk this matter of slavery over with them. I would sometimes say to them, I wished I could be as free as they would be when they got to be men. "You will be free as soon as you are twenty-one, *but I am a slave for life!* Have not I as good a right to be free as you have?" These words used to trouble them; they would express for me the liveliest sympathy, and console me with the hope that something would occur by which I might be free.

I was now about twelve years old, and the thought of being *a slave for life* began to bear heavily upon my heart. Just about this time, I got hold of a book entitled "The Columbian Orator." Every opportunity I got, I used to read this book. Among much of other interesting matter, I found in it a dialogue between a master and his slave. The slave was represented as having run away from his master three times. The dialogue represented the conversation which took place between them, when the slave was retaken the third time. In this dialogue, the whole argument in behalf of slavery was brought forward by the master, all of which was disposed of by the slave. The slave was made to say some very smart as well as impressive things in reply to his master—things which had the desired though unexpected effect; for the conversation resulted in the voluntary emancipation of the slave on the part of the master.

In the same book, I met with one of Sheridan's mighty speeches on and in behalf of Catholic emancipation. These were choice documents to me. I read them over and over again with unabated interest. They gave tongue to interesting thoughts of my own soul, which had frequently flashed through my mind, and died away for want of utterance. The moral which I gained from the dialogue was the power of truth over the conscience of even a slaveholder. What I got from Sheridan was a bold denunciation of slavery, and a powerful vindication of human rights. The reading of these documents enabled me to utter my thoughts, and to meet the arguments brought forward to sustain slavery; but while they relieved me of one difficulty, they brought on another even more painful than the one of which I was relieved. The more I read, the more I was led to abhor and detest my enslavers. I could regard them in no other light than a band of successful robbers, who had left their homes, and gone to Africa, and stolen us from our homes, and in a strange land reduced us to slavery. I loathed them as being the meanest as well as the most wicked of men. As I read and contemplated the subject, behold! that very discontentment which Master Hugh had predicted would follow my learning to read had already come, to torment and sting my soul to unutterable anguish. As I writhed under it, I would at times feel that learning to read had been a curse rather than a blessing. It had given me a view of my wretched condition, without the remedy. It opened my eyes to the horrible pit, but to no ladder upon which to get out. In moments of agony, I envied my fellow-slaves for their stupidity. I have often wished myself a beast. I preferred the condition of the meanest reptile to my own. Any thing, no matter what, to get rid of thinking! It was this everlasting thinking of my condition that tormented me. There was no getting rid of it. It was pressed upon me by every object within sight or hearing, animate or inanimate. The silver trump of freedom had roused my soul to eternal wakefulness. Freedom now appeared, to disappear no more forever. It was heard in every sound, and seen in every thing. It was ever present to torment me with a sense of my wretched condition. I saw nothing without seeing it, I heard nothing without hearing it, and felt nothing without feeling it. It looked from every star, it smiled in every calm, breathed in every wind, and moved in every storm.

I often found myself regretting my own existence, and wishing myself dead; and but for the hope of being free, I have no doubt but that I should have killed myself, or done something for which I should have been killed. While in this state of mind, I was eager to hear any one speak of slavery. I was a ready listener. Every little while, I could hear something about the abolitionists. It was some time before I found what the word meant. It was always used in such connections as to make it an interesting word to me. If a slave ran away and succeeded in getting clear, or if a slave killed his master, set fire to a barn, or did any thing very wrong in the mind of a slaveholder, it was spoken of as the fruit of *abolition.* Hearing the word in this connection very often, I set about learning what it meant. The dictionary afforded me little or no help. I found it was "the act of abolishing;" but then I did not know what was to be abolished. Here I was perplexed. I did not dare to ask any one about its meaning, for I was satisfied that it was something they wanted me to know very little about. After a patient waiting, I got one of our city papers, containing an account of the number of petitions from the north, praying for the abolition of slavery in the District of Columbia, and of the slave trade between the States. From this time I understood the words *abolition* and *abolitionist,* and always drew near when that word was spoken, expecting to hear something of importance to myself and fellow-slaves. The light broke in upon me by degrees. I went one day down on the wharf of Mr. Waters; and seeing two Irishmen unloading a scow of stone, I went, unasked, and helped them. When we had finished, one of them came to me and asked me if I were a slave. I told him I was. He asked, "Are ye a slave for life?" I told him that I was. The good Irishman seemed to be deeply affected by the statement. He said to the other that it was a pity so fine a little fellow as myself should be a slave for life. He said it was a shame to hold me. They both advised me to run away to the north; that I should find friends there, and that I should be free. I pretended not to be interested in what they said, and treated them as if I did not understand them; for I feared they might be treacherous. White men have been known to encourage slaves to escape, and then, to get the reward, catch them and return them to their masters. I was afraid that these seemingly good men might use me so; but I nevertheless remembered their advice, and from that time I resolved to run away. I looked forward to a time at which it would be safe for me to escape. I was too young to think of doing so immediately; besides, I wished to learn how to write, as I might have occasion to write my own pass. I consoled myself with the hope that I should one day find a good chance. Meanwhile, I would learn to write.

The idea as to how I might learn to write was suggested to me by being in Durgin and Bailey's ship-yard, and frequently seeing the ship carpenters, after hewing, and getting a piece of timber ready for use, write on the timber the name of that part of the ship for which it was intended. When a piece of timber was intended for the larboard side, it would be marked thus—"L." When a piece was for the starboard side, it would be marked thus—"S." A piece for the larboard side forward, would be marked thus—"L. F." When a piece was for starboard side forward, it would be marked thus—"S. F." For larboard aft, it would be marked thus—"L. A." For starboard aft, it would be marked thus—"S. A." I soon learned the names of these letters, and for what they were intended when placed upon a piece of timber in the ship-yard. I immediately commenced copying them, and in a short time was able to make the four letters named. After that, when I met with any boy who I knew could write, I would tell him I could write as well as he. The next word would be, "I don't believe you. Let me see you try it." I would then make the letters which I had been so fortunate as to learn, and ask him to beat that. In this way I got a good many lessons in writing, which it is quite possible I should never have gotten in any other way. During this time, my copy-book was the board fence, brick wall, and pavement; my pen and ink was a lump of chalk. With these, I learned mainly how to write. I then commenced and continued copying the Italics in Webster's Spelling Book, until I could make them all without looking on the book. By this time, my little Master Thomas had gone to school, and learned how to write, and had written over a number of copy-books. These had been brought home, and shown to some of our near neighbors, and then laid aside. My mistress used to go to class meeting at the Wilk Street meetinghouse every Monday afternoon, and leave me to take care of the house. When left thus, I used to spend the time in writing in the spaces left in Master Thomas's copy-book, copying what he had written. I continued to do this until I could write a hand very similar to that of Master Thomas. Thus, after a long, tedious effort for years, I finally succeeded in learning how to write.

Chapter 8

In a very short time after I went to live at Baltimore, my old master's youngest son Richard died; and in about three years and six months after his death, my old master, Captain Anthony, died, leaving only his son, Andrew, and daughter, Lucretia, to share his estate. He died while on a visit to see his daughter at Hillsborough. Cut off thus unexpectedly, he left no will as to the disposal of his property. It was therefore necessary to have a valuation of the property, that it might be equally divided between Mrs. Lucretia and Master Andrew. I was immediately sent for, to be valued with the other property. Here again my feelings rose up in detestation of slavery. I had now a new conception of my degraded condition. Prior to this, I had become, if not insensible to my lot, at least partly so. I left Baltimore with a young heart overborne with sadness, and a soul full of apprehension. I took passage with Captain Rowe, in the schooner Wild Cat, and, after a sail of about twenty-four hours, I found myself near the place of my birth. I had now been absent from it almost, if not quite, five years. I, however, remembered the place very well. I was only about five years old when I left it, to go and live with my old master on Colonel Lloyd's plantation; so that I was now between ten and eleven years old.

We were all ranked together at the valuation. Men and women, old and young, married and single, were ranked with horses, sheep, and swine. There were horses and men, cattle and women, pigs and children, all holding the same rank in the scale of being, and were all subjected to the same narrow examination. Silvery-headed age and sprightly youth, maids and matrons, had to undergo the same indelicate inspection. At this moment, I saw more clearly than ever the brutalizing effects of slavery upon both slave and slaveholder.

After the valuation, then came the division. I have no language to express the high excitement and deep anxiety which were felt among us poor slaves during this time. Our fate for life was now to be decided. we had no more voice in that decision than the brutes among whom we were ranked. A single word from the white men was enough—against all our wishes, prayers, and entreaties—to sunder forever the dearest friends, dearest kindred, and strongest ties known to human beings. In addition to the pain of separation, there was the horrid dread of falling into the hands of Master Andrew. He was known to us all as being a most cruel wretch,—a common drunkard, who had, by his reckless mismanagement and profligate dissipation, already wasted a large portion of his father's property. We all felt that we might as well be sold at once to the Georgia traders, as to pass into his hands; for we knew that that would be our inevitable condition,—a condition held by us all in the utmost horror and dread.

I suffered more anxiety than most of my fellow-slaves. I had known what it was to be kindly treated; they had known nothing of the kind. They had seen little or nothing of the world. They were in very deed men and women of sorrow, and acquainted with grief. Their backs had been made familiar with the bloody lash, so that they had become callous; mine was yet tender; for while at Baltimore I got few whippings, and few slaves could boast of a kinder master and mistress than myself; and the thought of passing out of their hands into those of Master Andrew—a man who, but a few days before, to give me a sample of his bloody disposition, took my little brother by the throat, threw him on the ground, and with the heel of his boot stamped upon his head till the blood gushed from his nose and ears—was well calculated to make me anxious as to my fate. After he had committed this savage outrage upon my brother, he turned to me, and said that was the way he meant to serve me one of these days,—meaning, I suppose, when I came into his possession.

Thanks to a kind Providence, I fell to the portion of Mrs. Lucretia, and was sent immediately back to Baltimore, to live again in the family of Master Hugh. Their joy at my return equalled their sorrow at my departure. It was a glad day to me. I had escaped a worse than lion's jaws. I was absent from Baltimore, for the purpose of valuation and division, just about one month, and it seemed to have been six.

Very soon after my return to Baltimore, my mistress, Lucretia, died, leaving her husband and one child, Amanda; and in a very short time after her death, Master Andrew died. Now all the property of my old master, slaves included, was in the hands of strangers,—strangers who had had nothing to do with accumulating it. Not a slave was left free. All remained slaves, from the youngest to the oldest. If any one thing in my experience, more than another, served to deepen my conviction of the infernal character of slavery, and to fill me with unutterable loathing of slaveholders, it was their base ingratitude to my poor old grandmother. She had served my old master faithfully from youth to old age. She had been the source of all his wealth; she had peopled his plantation with slaves; she had become a great grandmother in his service. She had rocked him in infancy, attended him in childhood, served him through life, and at his death wiped from his icy brow the cold death-sweat, and closed his eyes forever. She was nevertheless left a slave—a slave for life—a slave in the hands of strangers; and in their hands she saw her children, her grandchildren, and her great-grandchildren, divided, like so many sheep, without being gratified with the small privilege of a single word, as to their or her own destiny. And, to cap the climax of their base ingratitude and fiendish barbarity, my grandmother, who was now very old, having outlived my old master and all his children, having seen the beginning and end of all of them, and her present owners finding she was of but little value, her frame already racked with the pains of old age, and complete helplessness fast stealing over her once active limbs, they took her to the woods, built her a little hut, put up a little mud-chimney, and then made her welcome to the privilege of supporting herself there in perfect loneliness; thus virtually turning her out to die! If my poor old grandmother now lives, she lives to suffer in utter loneliness; she lives to remember and mourn over the loss of children, the loss of grandchildren, and the loss of great-grandchildren. They are, in the language of the slave's poet, Whittier,—

> "Gone, gone, sold and gone
> To the rice swamp dank and lone,
> Where the slave-whip ceaseless swings,
> Where the noisome insect stings,
> Where the fever-demon strews
> Poison with the falling dews,
> Where the sickly sunbeams glare
> Through the hot and misty air:—
> Gone, gone, sold and gone
> To the rice swamp dank and lone,
> From Virginia hills and waters—
> Woe is me, my stolen daughters!"

The hearth is desolate. The children, the unconscious children, who once sang and danced in her presence, are gone. She gropes her way, in the darkness of age, for a drink of water. Instead of the voices of her children, she hears by day the moans of the dove, and by night the screams of the hideous owl. All is gloom. The grave is at the door. And now, when weighed down by the pains and aches of old age, when the head inclines to the feet, when the beginning and ending of human existence meet, and helpless infancy and painful old age combine together—at this time, this most needful time, the time for the exercise of that tenderness and affection which children only can exercise towards a declining parent—my poor old grandmother, the devoted mother of twelve children, is left all alone, in yonder little hut, before a few dim embers. She stands—she sits—she staggers—she falls—she groans—she dies—and there are none of her children or grandchildren present, to wipe from her wrinkled brow the cold sweat of death, or to place beneath the sod her fallen remains. Will not a righteous God visit for these things?

In about two years after the death of Mrs. Lucretia, Master Thomas married his second wife. Her name was Rowena Hamilton. She was the eldest daughter of Mr. William Hamilton. Master now lived in St. Michael's. Not long after his marriage, a misunderstanding took place between himself and Master Hugh; and as a means of punishing his brother, he took me from him to live with himself at St. Michael's. Here I underwent another most painful separation. It, however, was not so severe as the one I dreaded at the division of property; for, during this interval, a great change had taken place in Master Hugh and his once kind and affectionate wife. The influence of brandy upon him, and of slavery upon her, had effected a disastrous change in the characters of both; so that, as far as they were concerned, I thought I had little to lose by the change. But it was not to them that I was attached. It was to those little Baltimore boys that I felt the strongest attachment. I had received many good lessons from them, and was still receiving them, and the thought of leaving them was painful indeed. I was leaving, too, without the hope of ever being allowed to return. Master Thomas had said he would never let me return again. The barrier betwixt himself and brother he considered impassable.

I then had to regret that I did not at least make the attempt to carry out my resolution to run away; for the chances of success are tenfold greater from the city than from the country.

I sailed from Baltimore for St. Michael's in the sloop Amanda, Captain Edward Dodson. On my passage, I paid particular attention to the direction which the steamboats took to go to Philadelphia. I found, instead of going down, on reaching North Point they went up the bay, in a north-easterly direction. I deemed this knowledge of the utmost importance. My determination to run away was again revived. I resolved to wait only so long as the offering of a favorable opportunity. When that came, I was determined to be off.

Chapter 9

I have now reached a period of my life when I can give dates. I left Baltimore, and went to live with Master Thomas Auld, at St. Michael's, in March, 1832. It was now more than seven years since I lived with him in the family of my old master, on Colonel Lloyd's plantation. We of course were now almost entire strangers to each other. He was to me a new master, and I to him a new slave. I was ignorant of his temper and disposition; he was equally so of mine. A very short time, however, brought us into full acquaintance with each other. I was made acquainted with his wife not less than with himself. They were well matched, being equally mean and cruel. I was now, for the first time during a space of more than seven years, made to feel the painful gnawings of hunger—a something which I had not experienced before since I left Colonel Lloyd's plantation. It went hard enough with me then, when I could look back to no period at which I had enjoyed a sufficiency. It was tenfold harder after living in Master Hugh's family, where I had always had enough to eat, and of that which was good. I have said Master Thomas was a mean man. He was so. Not to give a slave enough to eat, is regarded as the most aggravated development of meanness even among slaveholders. The rule is, no matter how coarse the food, only let there be enough of it. This is the theory; and in the part of Maryland from which I came, it is the general practice,—though there are many exceptions. Master Thomas gave us enough of neither coarse nor fine food. There were four slaves of us in the kitchen—my sister Eliza, my aunt Priscilla, Henny, and myself; and we were allowed less than a half of a bushel of corn-meal per week, and very little else, either in the shape of meat or vegetables. It was not enough for us to subsist upon. We were therefore reduced to the wretched necessity of living at the expense of our neighbors. This we did by begging and stealing, whichever came handy in the time of need, the one being considered as legitimate as the other. A great many times have we poor creatures been nearly perishing with hunger, when food in abundance lay mouldering in the safe and smoke-house, and our pious mistress was aware of the fact; and yet that mistress and her husband would kneel every morning, and pray that God would bless them in basket and store!

Bad as all slaveholders are, we seldom meet one destitute of every element of character commanding respect. My master was one of this rare sort. I do not know of one single noble act ever performed by him. The leading trait in his character was meanness; and if there were any other element in his nature, it was made subject to this. He was mean; and, like most other mean men, he lacked the ability to conceal his meanness. Captain Auld was not born a slaveholder. He had been a poor man, master only of a Bay craft. He came into possession of all his slaves by marriage; and of all men, adopted slaveholders are the worst. He was cruel, but cowardly. He commanded without firmness. In the enforcement of his rules, he was at times rigid, and at times lax. At times, he spoke to his slaves with the firmness of Napoleon and the fury of a demon; at other times, he might well be mistaken for an inquirer who had lost his way. He did nothing of himself. He might have passed for a lion, but for his ears. In all things noble which he attempted, his own meanness shone most conspicuous. His airs, words, and actions, were the airs, words, and actions of born slaveholders, and, being assumed, were awkward enough. He was not even a good imitator. He possessed all the disposition to deceive, but wanted the power. Having no resources within himself, he was compelled to be the copyist of many, and being such, he was forever the victim of inconsistency; and of consequence he was an object of contempt, and was held as such even by his slaves. The luxury of having slaves of his own to wait upon him was something new and unprepared for. He was a slaveholder without the ability to hold slaves. He found himself incapable of managing his slaves either by force, fear, or fraud. We seldom called him "master;" we generally called him "Captain Auld," and were hardly disposed to title him at all. I doubt not that our conduct had much to do with making him appear awkward, and of consequence fretful. Our want of reverence for him must have perplexed him greatly. He wished to have us call him master, but lacked the firmness necessary to command us to do so. His wife used to insist upon our calling him so, but to no purpose. In August, 1832, my master attended a Methodist camp-meeting held in the Bay-side, Talbot county, and there experienced religion. I indulged a faint hope that his conversion would lead him to emancipate his slaves, and that, if he did not do this, it would, at any rate, make him more kind and humane. I was disappointed in both these respects. It neither made him to be humane to his slaves, nor to emancipate them. If it had any effect on his character, it made him more cruel and hateful in all his ways; for I believe him to have been a much worse man after his conversion than before. Prior to his conversion, he relied upon his own depravity to shield and sustain him in his savage barbarity; but after his conversion, he found religious sanction and support for his slaveholding cruelty. He made the greatest pretensions to piety. His house was the house of prayer. He prayed morning, noon, and night. He very soon distinguished himself among his brethren, and was soon made a class-leader and exhorter. His activity in revivals was great, and he proved himself an instrument in the hands of the church in converting many souls. His house was the preachers' home. They used to take great pleasure in coming there to put up; for while he starved us, he stuffed them. We have had three or four preachers there at a time. The names of those who used to come most frequently while I lived there, were Mr. Storks, Mr. Ewery, Mr. Humphry, and Mr. Hickey. I have also seen Mr. George Cookman at our house. We slaves loved Mr. Cookman. We believed him to be a good man. We thought him instrumental in getting Mr. Samuel Harrison, a very rich slaveholder, to emancipate his slaves; and by some means got the impression that he was laboring to effect the emancipation of all the slaves. When he was at our house, we were sure to be called in to prayers. When the others were there, we were sometimes called in and sometimes not. Mr. Cookman took more notice of us than either of the other ministers. He could not come among us without betraying his sympathy for us, and, stupid as we were, we had the sagacity to see it.

While I lived with my master in St. Michael's, there was a white young man, a Mr. Wilson, who proposed to keep a Sabbath school for the instruction of such slaves as might be disposed to learn to read the New Testament. We met but three times, when Mr. West and Mr. Fairbanks, both class-leaders, with many others, came upon us with sticks and other missiles, drove us off, and forbade us to meet again. Thus ended our little Sabbath school in the pious town of St. Michael's.

I have said my master found religious sanction for his cruelty. As an example, I will state one of many facts going to prove the charge. I have seen him tie up a lame young woman, and whip her with a heavy cowskin upon her naked shoulders, causing the warm red blood to drip; and, in justification of the bloody deed, he would quote this passage of Scripture—"He that knoweth his master's will, and doeth it not, shall be beaten with many stripes."

Master would keep this lacerated young woman tied up in this horrid situation four or five hours at a time. I have known him to tie her up early in the morning, and whip her before breakfast; leave her, go to his store, return at dinner, and whip her again, cutting her in the places already made raw with his cruel lash. The secret of master's cruelty toward "Henny" is found in the fact of her being almost helpless. When quite a child, she fell into the fire, and burned herself horribly. Her hands were so burnt that she never got the use of them. She could do very little but bear heavy burdens. She was to master a bill of expense; and as he was a mean man, she was a constant offence to him. He seemed desirous of getting the poor girl out of existence. He gave her away once to his sister; but, being a poor gift, she was not disposed to keep her. Finally, my benevolent master, to use his own words, "set her adrift to take care of herself." Here was a recently-converted man, holding on upon the mother, and at the same time turning out her helpless child, to starve and die! Master Thomas was one of the many pious slaveholders who hold slaves for the very charitable purpose of taking care of them.

My master and myself had quite a number of differences. He found me unsuitable to his purpose. My city life, he said, had had a very pernicious effect upon me. It had almost ruined me for every good purpose, and fitted me for every thing which was bad. One of my greatest faults was that of letting his horse run away, and go down to his father-inlaw's farm, which was about five miles from St. Michael's. I would then have to go after it. My reason for this kind of carelessness, or carefulness, was, that I could always get something to eat when I went there. Master William Hamilton, my master's father-in-law, always gave his slaves enough to eat. I never left there hungry, no matter how great the need of my speedy return. Master Thomas at length said he would stand it no longer. I had lived with him nine months, during which time he had given me a number of severe whippings, all to no good purpose. He resolved to put me out, as he said, to be broken; and, for this purpose, he let me for one year to a man named Edward Covey. Mr. Covey was a poor man, a farm-renter. He rented the place upon which he lived, as also the hands with which he tilled it. Mr. Covey had acquired a very high reputation for breaking young slaves, and this reputation was of immense value to him. It enabled him to get his farm tilled with much less expense to himself than he could have had it done without such a reputation. Some slaveholders thought it not much loss to allow Mr. Covey to have their slaves one year, for the sake of the training to which they were subjected, without any other compensation. He could hire young help with great ease, in consequence of this reputation. Added to the natural good qualities of Mr. Covey, he was a professor of religion—a pious soul—a member and a class-leader in the Methodist church. All of this added weight to his reputation as a "nigger-breaker." I was aware of all the facts, having been made acquainted with them by a young man who had lived there. I nevertheless made the change gladly; for I was sure of getting enough to eat, which is not the smallest consideration to a hungry man.

Chapter 10

I had left Master Thomas's house, and went to live with Mr. Covey, on the 1st of January, 1833. I was now, for the first time in my life, a field hand. In my new employment, I found myself even more awkward than a country boy appeared to be in a large city. I had been at my new home but one week before Mr. Covey gave me a very severe whipping, cutting my back, causing the blood to run, and raising ridges on my flesh as large as my little finger. The details of this affair are as follows: Mr. Covey sent me, very early in the morning of one of our coldest days in the month of January, to the woods, to get a load of wood. He gave me a team of unbroken oxen. He told me which was the in-hand ox, and which the off-hand one. He then tied the end of a large rope around the horns of the in-hand ox, and gave me the other end of it, and told me, if the oxen started to run, that I must hold on upon the rope. I had never driven oxen before, and of course I was very awkward. I, however, succeeded in getting to the edge of the woods with little difficulty; but I had got a very few rods into the woods, when the oxen took fright, and started full tilt, carrying the cart against trees, and over stumps, in the most frightful manner. I expected every moment that my brains would be dashed out against the trees. After running thus for a considerable distance, they finally upset the cart, dashing it with great force against a tree, and threw themselves into a dense thicket. How I escaped death, I do not know. There I was, entirely alone, in a thick wood, in a place new to me. My cart was upset and shattered, my oxen were entangled among the young trees, and there was none to help me. After a long spell of effort, I succeeded in getting my cart righted, my oxen disentangled, and again yoked to the cart. I now proceeded with my team to the place where I had, the day before, been chopping wood, and loaded my cart pretty heavily, thinking in this way to tame my oxen. I then proceeded on my way home. I had now consumed one half of the day. I got out of the woods safely, and now felt out of danger. I stopped my oxen to open the woods gate; and just as I did so, before I could get hold of my ox-rope, the oxen again started, rushed through the gate, catching it between the wheel and the body of the cart, tearing it to pieces, and coming within a few inches of crushing me against the gate-post. Thus twice, in one short day, I escaped death by the merest chance. On my return, I told Mr. Covey what had happened, and how it happened. He ordered me to return to the woods again immediately. I did so, and he followed on after me. Just as I got into the woods, he came up and told me to stop my cart, and that he would teach me how to trifle away my time, and break gates. He then went to a large gum-tree, and with his axe cut three large switches, and, after trimming them up neatly with his pocketknife, he ordered me to take off my clothes. I made him no answer, but stood with my clothes on. He repeated his order. I still made him no answer, nor did I move to strip myself. Upon this he rushed at me with the fierceness of a tiger, tore off my clothes, and lashed me till he had worn out his switches, cutting me so savagely as to leave the marks visible for a long time after. This whipping was the first of a number just like it, and for similar offences.

I lived with Mr. Covey one year. During the first six months, of that year, scarce a week passed without his whipping me. I was seldom free from a sore back. My awkwardness was almost always his excuse for whipping me. We were worked fully up to the point of endurance. Long before day we were up, our horses fed, and by the first approach of day we were off to the field with our hoes and ploughing teams. Mr. Covey gave us enough to eat, but scarce time to eat it. We were often less than five minutes taking our meals. We were often in the field from the first approach of day till its last lingering ray had left us; and at saving-fodder time, midnight often caught us in the field binding blades.

Covey would be out with us. The way he used to stand it, was this. He would spend the most of his afternoons in bed. He would then come out fresh in the evening, ready to urge us on with his words, example, and frequently with the whip. Mr. Covey was one of the few slaveholders who could and did work with his hands. He was a hard-working man. He knew by himself just what a man or a boy could do. There was no deceiving him. His work went on in his absence almost as well as in his presence; and he had the faculty of making us feel that he was ever present with us. This he did by surprising us. He seldom approached the spot where we were at work openly, if he could do it secretly. He always aimed at taking us by surprise. Such was his cunning, that we used to call him, among ourselves, "the snake." When we were at work in the cornfield, he would sometimes crawl on his hands and knees to avoid detection, and all at once he would rise nearly in our midst, and scream out, "Ha, ha! Come, come! Dash on, dash on!" This being his mode of attack, it was never safe to stop a single minute. His comings were like a thief in the night. He appeared to us as being ever at hand. He was under every tree, behind every stump, in every bush, and at every window, on the plantation. He would sometimes mount his horse, as if bound to St. Michael's, a distance of seven miles, and in half an hour afterwards you would see him coiled up in the corner of the wood-fence, watching every motion of the slaves. He would, for this purpose, leave his horse tied up in the woods. Again, he would sometimes walk up to us, and give us orders as though he was upon the point of starting on a long journey, turn his back upon us, and make as though he was going to the house to get ready; and, before he would get half way thither, he would turn short and crawl into a fence-corner, or behind some tree, and there watch us till the going down of the sun.

Mr. Covey's *forte* consisted in his power to deceive. His life was devoted to planning and perpetrating the grossest deceptions. Every thing he possessed in the shape of learning or religion, he made conform to his disposition to deceive. He seemed to think himself equal to deceiving the Almighty. He would make a short prayer in the morning, and a long prayer at night; and, strange as it may seem, few men would at times appear more devotional than he. The exercises of his family devotions were always commenced with singing; and, as he was a very poor singer himself, the duty of raising the hymn generally came upon me. He would read his hymn, and nod at me to commence. I would at times do so; at others, I would not. My non-compliance would almost always produce much confusion. To show himself independent of me, he would start and stagger through with his hymn in the most discordant manner. In this state of mind, he prayed with more than ordinary spirit. Poor man! such was his disposition, and success at deceiving, I do verily believe that he sometimes deceived himself into the solemn belief, that he was a sincere worshipper of the most high God; and this, too, at a time when he may be said to have been guilty of compelling his woman slave to commit the sin of adultery. The facts in the case are these: Mr. Covey was a poor man; he was just commencing in life; he was only able to buy one slave; and, shocking as is the fact, he bought her, as he said, for *a breeder*. This woman was named Caroline. Mr. Covey bought her from Mr. Thomas Lowe, about six miles from St. Michael's. She was a large, able-bodied woman, about twenty years old. She had already given birth to one child, which proved her to be just what he wanted. After buying her, he hired a married man of Mr. Samuel Harrison, to live with him one year; and him he used to fasten up with her every night! The result was, that, at the end of the year, the miserable woman gave birth to twins. At this result Mr. Covey seemed to be highly pleased, both with the man and the wretched woman. Such was his joy, and that of his wife, that nothing they could do for Caroline during her confinement was too good, or too hard, to be done. The children were regarded as being quite an addition to his wealth.

If at any one time of my life more than another, I was made to drink the bitterest dregs of slavery, that time was during the first six months of my stay with Mr. Covey. We were worked in all weathers. It was never too hot or too cold; it could never rain, blow, hail, or snow, too hard for us to work in the field. Work, work, work, was scarcely more the order of the day than of the night. The longest days were too short for him, and the shortest nights too long for him. I was somewhat unmanageable when I first went there, but a few months of this discipline tamed me. Mr. Covey succeeded in breaking me. I was broken in body, soul, and spirit. My natural elasticity was crushed, my intellect languished, the disposition to read departed, the cheerful spark that lingered about my eye died; the dark night of slavery closed in upon me; and behold a man transformed into a brute!

Sunday was my only leisure time. I spent this in a sort of beast-like stupor, between sleep and wake, under some large tree. At times I would rise up, a flash of energetic freedom would dart through my soul, accompanied with a faint beam of hope, that flickered for a moment, and then vanished. I sank down again, mourning over my wretched condition. I was sometimes prompted to take my life, and that of Covey, but was prevented by a combination of hope and fear. My sufferings on this plantation seem now like a dream rather than a stern reality.

Our house stood within a few rods of the Chesapeake Bay, whose broad bosom was ever white with sails from every quarter of the habitable globe. Those beautiful vessels, robed in purest white, so delightful to the eye of freemen, were to me so many shrouded ghosts, to terrify and torment me with thoughts of my wretched condition. I have often, in the deep stillness of a summer's Sabbath, stood all alone upon the lofty banks of that noble bay, and traced, with saddened heart and tearful eye, the countless number of sails moving off to the mighty ocean. The sight of these always affected me powerfully. My thoughts would compel utterance; and there, with no audience but the Almighty, I would pour out my soul's complaint, in my rude way, with an apostrophe to the moving multitude of ships:—

"You are loosed from your moorings, and are free; I am fast in my chains, and am a slave! You move merrily before the gentle gale, and I sadly before the bloody whip! You are freedom's swift-winged angels, that fly round the world; I am confined in bands of iron! O that I were free! O, that I were on one of your gallant decks, and under your protecting wing! Alas! betwixt me and you, the turbid waters roll. Go on, go on. O that I could also go! Could I but swim! If I could fly! O, why was I born a man, of whom to make a brute! The glad ship is gone; she hides in the dim distance. I am left in the hottest hell of unending slavery. O God, save me! God, deliver me! Let me be free! Is there any God? Why am I a slave? I will run away. I will not stand it. Get caught, or get clear, I'll try it. I had as well die with ague as the fever. I have only one life to lose. I had as well be killed running as die standing. Only think of it; one hundred miles straight north, and I am free! Try it? Yes! God helping me, I will. It cannot be that I shall live and die a slave. I will take to the water. This very bay shall yet bear me into freedom. The steamboats steered in a north-east course from North Point. I will do the same; and when I get to the head of the bay, I will turn my canoe adrift, and walk straight through Delaware into Pennsylvania. When I get there, I shall not be required to have a pass; I can travel without being disturbed. Let but the first opportunity offer, and, come what will, I am off. Meanwhile, I will try to bear up under the yoke. I am not the only slave in the world. Why should I fret? I can bear as much as any of them. Besides, I am but a boy, and all boys are bound to some one. It may be that my misery in slavery will only increase my happiness when I get free. There is a better day coming."

Thus I used to think, and thus I used to speak to myself; goaded almost to madness at one moment, and at the next reconciling myself to my wretched lot.

I have already intimated that my condition was much worse, during the first six months of my stay at Mr. Covey's, than in the last six. The circumstances leading to the change in Mr. Covey's course toward me form an epoch in my humble history. You have seen how a man was made a slave; you shall see how a slave was made a man. On one of the hottest days of the month of August, 1833, Bill Smith, William Hughes, a slave named Eli, and myself, were engaged in fanning wheat. Hughes was clearing the fanned wheat from before the fan. Eli was turning, Smith was feeding, and I was carrying wheat to the fan. The work was simple, requiring strength rather than intellect; yet, to one entirely unused to such work, it came very hard. About three o'clock of that day, I broke down; my strength failed me; I was seized with a violent aching of the head, attended with extreme dizziness; I trembled in every limb. Finding what was coming, I nerved myself up, feeling it would never do to stop work. I stood as long as I could stagger to the hopper with grain. When I could stand no longer, I fell, and felt as if held down by an immense weight. The fan of course stopped; every one had his own work to do; and no one could do the work of the other, and have his own go on at the same time.

Mr. Covey was at the house, about one hundred yards from the treading-yard where we were fanning. On hearing the fan stop, he left immediately, and came to the spot where we were. He hastily inquired what the matter was. Bill answered that I was sick, and there was no one to bring wheat to the fan. I had by this time crawled away under the side of the post and rail-fence by which the yard was enclosed, hoping to find relief by getting out of the sun. He then asked where I was. He was told by one of the hands. He came to the spot, and, after looking at me awhile, asked me what was the matter. I told him as well as I could, for I scarce had strength to speak. He then gave me a savage kick in the side, and told me to get up. I tried to do so, but fell back in the attempt. He gave me another kick, and again told me to rise. I again tried, and succeeded in gaining my feet; but, stooping to get the tub with which I was feeding the fan, I again staggered and fell. While down in this situation, Mr. Covey took up the hickory slat with which Hughes had been striking off the half-bushel measure, and with it gave me a heavy blow upon the head, making a large wound, and the blood ran freely; and with this again told me to get up. I made no effort to comply, having now made up my mind to let him do his worst. In a short time after receiving this blow, my head grew better. Mr. Covey had now left me to my fate. At this moment I resolved, for the first time, to go to my master, enter a complaint, and ask his protection. In order to do this, I must that afternoon walk seven miles; and this, under the circumstances, was truly a severe undertaking. I was exceedingly feeble; made so as much by the kicks and blows which I received, as by the severe fit of sickness to which I had been subjected. I, however, watched my chance, while Covey was looking in an opposite direction, and started for St. Michael's. I succeeded in getting a considerable distance on my way to the woods, when Covey discovered me, and called after me to come back, threatening what he would do if I did not come. I disregarded both his calls and his threats, and made my way to the woods as fast as my feeble state would allow; and thinking I might be overhauled by him if I kept the road, I walked through the woods, keeping far enough from the road to avoid detection, and near enough to prevent losing my way. I had not gone far before my little strength again failed me. I could go no farther. I fell down, and lay for a considerable time. The blood was yet oozing from the wound on my head. For a time I thought I should bleed to death; and think now that I should have done so, but that the blood so matted my hair as to stop the wound. After lying there about three quarters of an hour, I nerved myself up again, and started on my way, through bogs and briers, barefooted and bareheaded, tearing my feet sometimes at nearly every step; and after a journey of about seven miles, occupying some five hours to perform it, I arrived at master's store. I then presented an appearance enough to affect any but a heart of iron. From the crown of my head to my feet, I was covered with blood. My hair was all clotted with dust and blood; my shirt was stiff with blood. I suppose I looked like a man who had escaped a den of wild beasts, and barely escaped them. In this state I appeared before my master, humbly entreating him to interpose his authority for my protection. I told him all the circumstances as well as I could, and it seemed, as I spoke, at times to affect him. He would then walk the floor, and seek to justify Covey by saying he expected I deserved it. He asked me what I wanted. I told him, to let me get a new home; that as sure as I lived with Mr. Covey again, I should live with but to die with him; that Covey would surely kill me; he was in a fair way for it. Master Thomas ridiculed the idea that there was any danger of Mr. Covey's killing me, and said that he knew Mr. Covey; that he was a good man, and that he could not think of taking me from him; that, should he do so, he would lose the whole year's wages; that I belonged to Mr. Covey for one year, and that I must go back to him, come what might; and that I must not trouble him with any more stories, or that he would himself *get hold of me*. After threatening me thus, he gave me a very large dose of salts, telling me that I might remain in St. Michael's that night, (it being quite late,) but that I must be off back to Mr. Covey's early in the morning; and that if I did not, he would *get hold of me,* which meant that he would whip me. I remained all night, and, according to his orders, I started off to Covey's in the morning, (Saturday morning,) wearied in body and broken in spirit. I got no supper that night, or breakfast that morning. I reached Covey's about nine o'clock; and just as I was getting over the fence that divided Mrs. Kemp's fields from ours, out ran Covey with his cowskin, to give me another whipping. Before he could reach me, I succeeded in getting to the cornfield; and as the corn was very high, it afforded me the means of hiding. He seemed very angry, and searched for me a long time. My behavior was altogether unaccountable. He finally gave up the chase, thinking, I suppose, that I must come home for something to eat; he would give himself no further trouble in looking for me. I spent that day mostly in the woods, having the alternative before me,—to go home and be whipped to death, or stay in the woods and be starved to death. That night, I fell in with Sandy Jenkins, a slave with whom I was somewhat acquainted. Sandy had a free wife who lived about four miles from Mr. Covey's; and it being Saturday, he was on his way to see her. I told him my circumstances, and he very kindly invited me to go home with him. I went home with him, and talked this whole matter over, and got his advice as to what course it was best for me to pursue. I found Sandy an old adviser. He told me, with great solemnity, I must go back to Covey; but that before I went, I must go with him into another part of the woods, where there was a certain *root,* which, if I would take some of it with me, carrying it *always on my right side,* would render it impossible for Mr. Covey, or any other white man, to whip me. He said he had carried it for years; and since he had done so, he had never received a blow, and never expected to while he carried it. I at first rejected the idea, that the simple carrying of a root in my pocket would have any such effect as he had said, and was not disposed to take it; but Sandy impressed the necessity with much earnestness, telling me it could do no harm, if it did no good. To please him, I at length took the root, and, according to his direction, carried it upon my right side. This was Sunday morning. I immediately started for home; and upon entering the yard gate, out came Mr.

Covey on his way to meeting. He spoke to me very kindly, bade me drive the pigs from a lot near by, and passed on towards the church. Now, this singular conduct of Mr. Covey really made me begin to think that there was something in the *root* which Sandy had given me; and had it been on any other day than Sunday, I could have attributed the conduct to no other cause than the influence of that root; and as it was, I was half inclined to think the *root* to be something more than I at first had taken it to be. All went well till Monday morning. On this morning, the virtue of the *root* was fully tested. Long before daylight, I was called to go and rub, curry, and feed, the horses. I obeyed, and was glad to obey. But whilst thus engaged, whilst in the act of throwing down some blades from the loft, Mr. Covey entered the stable with a long rope; and just as I was half out of the loft, he caught hold of my legs, and was about tying me. As soon as I found what he was up to, I gave a sudden spring, and as I did so, he holding to my legs, I was brought sprawling on the stable floor. Mr. Covey seemed now to think he had me, and could do what he pleased; but at this moment—from whence came the spirit I don't know—I resolved to fight; and, suiting my action to the resolution, I seized Covey hard by the throat; and as I did so, I rose. He held on to me, and I to him. My resistance was so entirely unexpected that Covey seemed taken all aback. He trembled like a leaf. This gave me assurance, and I held him uneasy, causing the blood to run where I touched him with the ends of my fingers. Mr. Covey soon called out to Hughes for help. Hughes came, and, while Covey held me, attempted to tie my right hand. While he was in the act of doing so, I watched my chance, and gave him a heavy kick close under the ribs. This kick fairly sickened Hughes, so that he left me in the hands of Mr. Covey. This kick had the effect of not only weakening Hughes, but Covey also. When he saw Hughes bending over with pain, his courage quailed. He asked me if I meant to persist in my resistance. I told him I did, come what might; that he had used me like a brute for six months, and that I was determined to be used so no longer. With that, he strove to drag me to a stick that was lying just out of the stable door. He meant to knock me down. But just as he was leaning over to get the stick, I seized him with both hands by his collar, and brought him by a sudden snatch to the ground. By this time, Bill came. Covey called upon him for assistance. Bill wanted to know what he could do. Covey said, "Take hold of him, take hold of him!" Bill said his master hired him out to work, and not to help to whip me; so he left Covey and myself to fight our own battle out. We were at it for nearly two hours. Covey at length let me go, puffing and blowing at a great rate, saying that if I had not resisted, he would not have whipped me half so much. The truth was, that he had not whipped me at all. I considered him as getting entirely the worst end of the bargain; for he had drawn no blood from me, but I had from him. The whole six months afterwards, that I spent with Mr. Covey, he never laid the weight of his finger upon me in anger. He would occasionally say, he didn't want to get hold of me again. "No," thought I, "you need not; for you will come off worse than you did before."

This battle with Mr. Covey was the turning-point in my career as a slave. It rekindled the few expiring embers of freedom, and revived within me a sense of my own manhood. It recalled the departed self-confidence, and inspired me again with a determination to be free. The gratification afforded by the triumph was a full compensation for whatever else might follow, even death itself. He only can understand the deep satisfaction which I experienced, who has himself repelled by force the bloody arm of slavery. I felt as I never felt before. It was a glorious resurrection, from the tomb of slavery, to the heaven of freedom. My long-crushed spirit rose, cowardice departed, bold defiance took its place; and I now resolved that, however long I might remain a slave in form, the day had passed forever when I could be a slave in fact. I did not hesitate to let it be known of me, that the white man who expected to succeed in whipping, must also succeed in killing me.

From this time I was never again what might be called fairly whipped, though I remained a slave four years afterwards. I had several fights, but was never whipped.

It was for a long time a matter of surprise to me why Mr. Covey did not immediately have me taken by the constable to the whipping-post, and there regularly whipped for the crime of raising my hand against a white man in defence of myself. And the only explanation I can now think of does not entirely satisfy me; but such as it is, I will give it. Mr. Covey enjoyed the most unbounded reputation for being a first-rate overseer and negro-breaker. It was of considerable importance to him. That reputation was at stake; and had he sent me—a boy about sixteen years old—to the public whipping-post, his reputation would have been lost; so, to save his reputation, he suffered me to go unpunished.

My term of actual service to Mr. Edward Covey ended on Christmas day, 1833. The days between Christmas and New Year's day are allowed as holidays; and, accordingly, we were not required to perform any labor, more than to feed and take care of the stock. This time we regarded as our own, by the grace of our masters; and we therefore used or abused it nearly as we pleased. Those of us who had families at a distance, were generally allowed to spend the whole six days in their society. This time, however, was spent in various ways. The staid, sober, thinking and industrious ones of our number would employ themselves in making corn-brooms, mats, horse-collars, and baskets; and another class of us would spend the time in hunting opossums, hares, and coons. But by far the larger part engaged in such sports and merriments as playing ball, wrestling, running foot-races, fiddling, dancing, and drinking whisky; and this latter mode of spending the time was by far the most agreeable to the feelings of our masters. A slave who would work during the holidays was considered by our masters as scarcely deserving them. He was regarded as one who rejected the favor of his master. It was deemed a disgrace not to get drunk at Christmas; and he was regarded as lazy indeed, who had not provided himself with the necessary means, during the year, to get whisky enough to last him through Christmas.

From what I know of the effect of these holidays upon the slave, I believe them to be among the most effective means in the hands of the slaveholder in keeping down the spirit of insurrection. Were the slaveholders at once to abandon this practice, I have not the slightest doubt it would lead to an immediate insurrection among the slaves. These holidays serve as conductors, or safety-valves, to carry off the rebellious spirit of enslaved humanity. But for these, the slave would be forced up to the wildest desperation; and woe betide the slaveholder, the day he ventures to remove or hinder the operation of those conductors! I warn him that, in such an event, a spirit will go forth in their midst, more to be dreaded than the most appalling earthquake.

The holidays are part and parcel of the gross fraud, wrong, and inhumanity of slavery. They are professedly a custom established by the benevolence of the slaveholders; but I undertake to say, it is the result of selfishness, and one of the grossest frauds committed upon the down-trodden slave. They do not give the slaves this time because they would not like to have their work during its continuance, but because they know it would be unsafe to deprive them of it. This will be seen by the fact, that the slaveholders like to have their slaves spend those days just in such a manner as to make them as glad of their ending as of their beginning. Their object seems to be, to disgust their slaves with freedom, by plunging them into the lowest depths of dissipation. For instance, the slaveholders not only like to see the slave drink of his own accord, but will adopt various plans to make him drunk. One plan is, to make bets on their slaves, as to who can drink the most whisky without getting drunk; and in this way they succeed in getting whole multitudes to drink to excess. Thus, when the slave asks for virtuous freedom, the cunning slaveholder, knowing his ignorance, cheats him with a dose of vicious dissipation, artfully labelled with the name of liberty. The most of us used to drink it down, and the result was just what might be supposed; many of us were led to think that there was little to choose between liberty and slavery. We felt, and very properly too, that we had almost as well be slaves to man as to rum. So, when the holidays ended, we staggered up from the filth of our wallowing, took a long breath, and marched to the field,—feeling, upon the whole, rather glad to go, from what our master had deceived us into a belief was freedom, back to the arms of slavery.

I have said that this mode of treatment is a part of the whole system of fraud and inhumanity of slavery. It is so. The mode here adopted to disgust the slave with freedom, by allowing him to see only the abuse of it, is carried out in other things. For instance, a slave loves molasses; he steals some. His master, in many cases, goes off to town, and buys a large quantity; he returns, takes his whip, and commands the slave to eat the molasses, until the poor fellow is made sick at the very mention of it. The same mode is sometimes adopted to make the slaves refrain from asking for more food than their regular allowance. A slave runs through his allowance, and applies for more. His master is enraged at him; but, not willing to send him off without food, gives him more than is necessary, and compels him to eat it within a given time. Then, if he complains that he cannot eat it, he is said to be satisfied neither full nor fasting, and is whipped for being hard to please! I have an abundance of such illustrations of the same principle, drawn from my own observation, but think the cases I have cited sufficient. The practice is a very common one.

On the first of January, 1834, I left Mr. Covey, and went to live with Mr. William Freeland, who lived about three miles from St. Michael's. I soon found Mr. Freeland a very different man from Mr. Covey. Though not rich, he was what would be called an educated southern gentleman. Mr. Covey, as I have shown, was a well-trained negro-breaker and slave-driver. The former (slaveholder though he was) seemed to possess some regard for honor, some reverence for justice, and some respect for humanity. The latter seemed totally insensible to all such sentiments. Mr. Freeland had many of the faults peculiar to slaveholders, such as being very passionate and fretful; but I must do him the justice to say, that he was exceedingly free from those degrading vices to which Mr. Covey was constantly addicted. The one was open and frank, and we always knew where to find him. The other was a most artful deceiver, and could be understood only by such as were skilful enough to detect his cunningly-devised frauds. Another advantage I gained in my new master was, he made no pretensions to, or profession of, religion; and this, in my opinion, was truly a great advantage. I assert most unhesitatingly, that the religion of the south is a mere covering for the most horrid crimes,—a justifier of the most appalling barbarity,—a sanctifier of the most hateful frauds,—and a dark shelter under, which the darkest, foulest, grossest, and most infernal deeds of slaveholders find the strongest protection. Were I to be again reduced to the chains of slavery, next to that enslavement, I should regard being the slave of a religious master the greatest calamity that could befall me. For of all slaveholders with whom I have ever met, religious slaveholders are the worst. I have ever found them the meanest and basest, the most cruel and cowardly, of all others. It was my unhappy lot not only to belong to a religious slaveholder, but to live in a community of such religionists. Very near Mr. Freeland lived the Rev. Daniel Weeden, and in the same neighborhood lived the Rev. Rigby Hopkins. These were members and ministers in the Reformed Methodist Church. Mr. Weeden owned, among others, a woman slave, whose name I have forgotten. This woman's back, for weeks, was kept literally raw, made so by the lash of this merciless, *religious* wretch. He used to hire hands. His maxim was, Behave well or behave ill, it is the duty of a master occasionally to whip a slave, to remind him of his master's authority. Such was his theory, and such his practice.

Mr. Hopkins was even worse than Mr. Weeden. His chief boast was his ability to manage slaves. The peculiar feature of his government was that of whipping slaves in advance of deserving it. He always managed to have one or more of his slaves to whip every Monday morning. He did this to alarm their fears, and strike terror into those who escaped. His plan was to whip for the smallest offences, to prevent the commission of large ones. Mr. Hopkins could always find some excuse for whipping a slave. It would astonish one, unaccustomed to a slaveholding life, to see with what wonderful ease a slaveholder can find things, of which to make occasion to whip a slave. A mere look, word, or motion,—a mistake, accident, or want of power,—are all matters for which a slave may be whipped at any time. Does a slave look dissatisfied? It is said, he has the devil in him, and it must be whipped out. Does he speak loudly when spoken to by his master? Then he is getting high-minded, and should be taken down a button-hole lower. Does he forget to pull off his hat at the approach of a white person? Then he is wanting in reverence, and should be whipped for it. Does he ever venture to vindicate his conduct, when censured for it? Then he is guilty of impudence,—one of the greatest crimes of which a slave can be guilty. Does he ever venture to suggest a different mode of doing things from that pointed out by his master? He is indeed presumptuous, and getting above himself; and nothing less than a flogging will do for him. Does he, while ploughing, break a plough,—or, while hoeing, break a hoe? It is owing to his carelessness, and for it a slave must always be whipped. Mr. Hopkins could always find something of this sort to justify the use of the lash, and he seldom failed to embrace such opportunities. There was not a man in the whole county, with whom the slaves who had the getting their own home, would not prefer to live, rather than with this Rev. Mr. Hopkins. And yet there was not a man any where round, who made higher professions of religion, or was more active in revivals,—more attentive to the class, love-feast, prayer and preaching meetings, or more devotional in his family,—that prayed earlier, later, louder, and longer,—than this same reverend slave-driver, Rigby Hopkins.

But to return to Mr. Freeland, and to my experience while in his employment. He, like Mr. Covey, gave us enough to eat; but, unlike Mr. Covey, he also gave us sufficient time to take our meals. He worked us hard, but always between sunrise and sunset. He required a good deal of work to be done, but gave us good tools with which to work. His farm was large, but he employed hands enough to work it, and with ease, compared with many of his neighbors. My treatment, while in his employment, was heavenly, compared with what I experienced at the hands of Mr. Edward Covey.

Mr. Freeland was himself the owner of but two slaves. Their names were Henry Harris and John Harris. The rest of his hands he hired. These consisted of myself, Sandy Jenkins,* and Handy Caldwell.

**This is the same man who gave me the roots to prevent my being whipped by Mr. Covey. He was "a clever soul." We used frequently to talk about the fight with Covey, and as often as we did so, he would claim my success as the result of the roots which he gave me. This superstition is very common among the more ignorant slaves. A slave seldom dies but that his death is attributed to trickery.*

Henry and John were quite intelligent, and in a very little while after I went there, I succeeded in creating in them a strong desire to learn how to read. This desire soon sprang up in the others also. They very soon mustered up some old spelling-books, and nothing would do but that I must keep a Sabbath school. I agreed to do so, and accordingly devoted my Sundays to teaching these my loved fellow-slaves how to read. Neither of them knew his letters when I went there. Some of the slaves of the neighboring farms found what was going on, and also availed themselves of this little opportunity to learn to read. It was understood, among all who came, that there must be as little display about it as possible. It was necessary to keep our religious masters at St. Michael's unacquainted with the fact, that, instead of spending the Sabbath in wrestling, boxing, and drinking whisky, we were trying to learn how to read the will of God; for they had much rather see us engaged in those degrading sports, than to see us behaving like intellectual, moral, and accountable beings. My blood boils as I think of the bloody manner in which Messrs. Wright Fairbanks and Garrison West, both class-leaders, in connection with many others, rushed in upon us with sticks and stones, and broke up our virtuous little Sabbath school, at St. Michael's—all calling themselves Christians! humble followers of the Lord Jesus Christ! But I am again digressing.

I held my Sabbath school at the house of a free colored man, whose name I deem it imprudent to mention; for should it be known, it might embarrass him greatly, though the crime of holding the school was committed ten years ago. I had at one time over forty scholars, and those of the right sort, ardently desiring to learn. They were of all ages, though mostly men and women. I look back to those Sundays with an amount of pleasure not to be expressed. They were great days to my soul. The work of instructing my dear fellow-slaves was the sweetest engagement with which I was ever blessed. We loved each other, and to leave them at the close of the Sabbath was a severe cross indeed. When I think that these precious souls are to-day shut up in the prison-house of slavery, my feelings overcome me, and I am almost ready to ask, "Does a righteous God govern the universe? and for what does he hold the thunders in his right hand, if not to smite the oppressor, and deliver the spoiled out of the hand of the spoiler?" These dear souls came not to Sabbath school because it was popular to do so, nor did I teach them because it was reputable to be thus engaged. Every moment they spent in that school, they were liable to be taken up, and given thirty-nine lashes. They came because they wished to learn. Their minds had been starved by their cruel masters. They had been shut up in mental darkness. I taught them, because it was the delight of my soul to be doing something that looked like bettering the condition of my race. I kept up my school nearly the whole year I lived with Mr. Freeland; and, beside my Sabbath school, I devoted three evenings in the week, during the winter, to teaching the slaves at home. And I have the happiness to know, that several of those who came to Sabbath school learned how to read; and that one, at least, is now free through my agency.

The year passed off smoothly. It seemed only about half as long as the year which preceded it. I went through it without receiving a single blow. I will give Mr. Freeland the credit of being the best master I ever had, *till I became my own master.* For the ease with which I passed the year, I was, however, somewhat indebted to the society of my fellow-slaves. They were noble souls; they not only possessed loving hearts, but brave ones. We were linked and interlinked with each other. I loved them with a love stronger than any thing I have experienced since. It is sometimes said that we slaves do not love and confide in each other. In answer to this assertion, I can say, I never loved any or confided in any people more than my fellow-slaves, and especially those with whom I lived at Mr. Freeland's. I believe we would have died for each other. We never undertook to do any thing, of any importance, without a mutual consultation. We never moved separately. We were one; and as much so by our tempers and dispositions, as by the mutual hardships to which we were necessarily subjected by our condition as slaves.

At the close of the year 1834, Mr. Freeland again hired me of my master, for the year 1835. But, by this time, I began to want to live *upon free land* as well as *with Freeland;* and I was no longer content, therefore, to live with him or any other slaveholder. I began, with the commencement of the year, to prepare myself for a final struggle, which should decide my fate one way or the other. My tendency was upward. I was fast approaching manhood, and year after year had passed, and I was still a slave.

These thoughts roused me—I must do something. I therefore resolved that 1835 should not pass without witnessing an attempt, on my part, to secure my liberty. But I was not willing to cherish this determination alone. My fellow-slaves were dear to me. I was anxious to have them participate with me in this, my life-giving determination. I therefore, though with great prudence, commenced early to ascertain their views and feelings in regard to their condition, and to imbue their minds with thoughts of freedom. I bent myself to devising ways and means for our escape, and meanwhile strove, on all fitting occasions, to impress them with the gross fraud and inhumanity of slavery. I went first to Henry, next to John, then to the others. I found, in them all, warm hearts and noble spirits. They were ready to hear, and ready to act when a feasible plan should be proposed. This was what I wanted. I talked to them of our want of manhood, if we submitted to our enslavement without at least one noble effort to be free. We met often, and consulted frequently, and told our hopes and fears, recounted the difficulties, real and imagined, which we should be called on to meet. At times we were almost disposed to give up, and try to content ourselves with our wretched lot; at others, we were firm and unbending in our determination to go. Whenever we suggested any plan, there was shrinking—the odds were fearful. Our path was beset with the greatest obstacles; and if we succeeded in gaining the end of it, our right to be free was yet questionable—we were yet liable to be returned to bondage. We could see no spot, this side of the ocean, where we could be free. We knew nothing about Canada. Our knowledge of the north did not extend farther than New York; and to go there, and be forever harassed with the frightful liability of being returned to slavery—with the certainty of being treated tenfold worse than before—the thought was truly a horrible one, and one which it was not easy to overcome. The case sometimes stood thus: At every gate through which we were to pass, we saw a watchman—at every ferry a guard—on every bridge a sentinel—and in every wood a patrol. We were hemmed in upon every side. Here were the difficulties, real or imagined—the good to be sought, and the evil to be shunned. On the one hand, there stood slavery, a stern reality, glaring frightfully upon us,—its robes already crimsoned with the blood of millions, and even now feasting itself greedily upon our own flesh. On the other hand, away back in the dim distance, under the flickering light of the north star, behind some craggy hill or snow-covered mountain, stood a doubtful freedom—half frozen—beckoning us to come and share its hospitality. This in itself was sometimes enough to stagger us; but when we permitted ourselves to survey the road, we were frequently appalled. Upon either side we saw grim death, assuming the most horrid shapes. Now it was starvation, causing us to eat our own flesh;—now we were contending with the waves, and were drowned;—now we were overtaken, and torn to pieces by the fangs of the terrible bloodhound. We were stung by scorpions, chased by wild beasts, bitten by snakes, and finally, after having nearly reached the desired spot,—after swimming rivers, encountering wild beasts, sleeping in the woods, suffering hunger and nakedness,—we were overtaken by our pursuers, and, in our resistance, we were shot dead upon the spot! I say, this picture sometimes appalled us, and made us

> “rather bear those ills we had,
> Than fly to others, that we knew not of.”

In coming to a fixed determination to run away, we did more than Patrick Henry, when he resolved upon liberty or death. With us it was a doubtful liberty at most, and almost certain death if we failed. For my part, I should prefer death to hopeless bondage.

Sandy, one of our number, gave up the notion, but still encouraged us. Our company then consisted of Henry Harris, John Harris, Henry Bailey, Charles Roberts, and myself. Henry Bailey was my uncle, and belonged to my master. Charles married my aunt: he belonged to my master's father-in-law, Mr. William Hamilton.

The plan we finally concluded upon was, to get a large canoe belonging to Mr. Hamilton, and upon the Saturday night previous to Easter holidays, paddle directly up the Chesapeake Bay. On our arrival at the head of the bay, a distance of seventy or eighty miles from where we lived, it was our purpose to turn our canoe adrift, and follow the guidance of the north star till we got beyond the limits of Maryland. Our reason for taking the water route was, that we were less liable to be suspected as runaways; we hoped to be regarded as fishermen; whereas, if we should take the land route, we should be subjected to interruptions of almost every kind. Any one having a white face, and being so disposed, could stop us, and subject us to examination.

The week before our intended start, I wrote several protections, one for each of us. As well as I can remember, they were in the following words, to wit:—

> "This is to certify that I, the undersigned, have given the bearer, my servant, full liberty to go to Baltimore, and spend the Easter holidays. Written with mine own hand, &c., 1835.
> "WILLIAM HAMILTON,
> "Near St. Michael's, in Talbot county, Maryland."

We were not going to Baltimore; but, in going up the bay, we went toward Baltimore, and these protections were only intended to protect us while on the bay.

As the time drew near for our departure, our anxiety became more and more intense. It was truly a matter of life and death with us. The strength of our determination was about to be fully tested. At this time, I was very active in explaining every difficulty, removing every doubt, dispelling every fear, and inspiring all with the firmness indispensable to success in our undertaking; assuring them that half was gained the instant we made the move; we had talked long enough; we were now ready to move; if not now, we never should be; and if we did not intend to move now, we had as well fold our arms, sit down, and acknowledge ourselves fit only to be slaves. This, none of us were prepared to acknowledge. Every man stood firm; and at our last meeting, we pledged ourselves afresh, in the most solemn manner, that, at the time appointed, we would certainly start in pursuit of freedom. This was in the middle of the week, at the end of which we were to be off. We went, as usual, to our several fields of labor, but with bosoms highly agitated with thoughts of our truly hazardous undertaking. We tried to conceal our feelings as much as possible; and I think we succeeded very well.

After a painful waiting, the Saturday morning, whose night was to witness our departure, came. I hailed it with joy, bring what of sadness it might. Friday night was a sleepless one for me. I probably felt more anxious than the rest, because I was, by common consent, at the head of the whole affair. The responsibility of success or failure lay heavily upon me. The glory of the one, and the confusion of the other, were alike mine. The first two hours of that morning were such as I never experienced before, and hope never to again. Early in the morning, we went, as usual, to the field. We were spreading manure; and all at once, while thus engaged, I was overwhelmed with an indescribable feeling, in the fulness of which I turned to Sandy, who was near by, and said, "We are betrayed!" "Well," said he, "that thought has this moment struck me." We said no more. I was never more certain of any thing.

The horn was blown as usual, and we went up from the field to the house for breakfast. I went for the form, more than for want of any thing to eat that morning. Just as I got to the house, in looking out at the lane gate, I saw four white men, with two colored men. The white men were on horseback, and the colored ones were walking behind, as if tied. I watched them a few moments till they got up to our lane gate. Here they halted, and tied the colored men to the gate-post. I was not yet certain as to what the matter was. In a few moments, in rode Mr. Hamilton, with a speed betokening great excitement. He came to the door, and inquired if Master William was in. He was told he was at the barn. Mr. Hamilton, without dismounting, rode up to the barn with extraordinary speed. In a few moments, he and Mr. Freeland returned to the house. By this time, the three constables rode up, and in great haste dismounted, tied their horses, and met Master William and Mr. Hamilton returning from the barn; and after talking awhile, they all walked up to the kitchen door. There was no one in the kitchen but myself and John. Henry and Sandy were up at the barn. Mr. Freeland put his head in at the door, and called me by name, saying, there were some gentlemen at the door who wished to see me. I stepped to the door, and inquired what they wanted. They at once seized me, and, without giving me any satisfaction, tied me—lashing my hands closely together. I insisted upon knowing what the matter was. They at length said, that they had learned I had been in a "scrape," and that I was to be examined before my master; and if their information proved false, I should not be hurt.

In a few moments, they succeeded in tying John. They then turned to Henry, who had by this time returned, and commanded him to cross his hands. "I won't!" said Henry, in a firm tone, indicating his readiness to meet the consequences of his refusal. "Won't you?" said Tom Graham, the constable. "No, I won't!" said Henry, in a still stronger tone. With this, two of the constables pulled out their shining pistols, and swore, by their Creator, that they would make him cross his hands or kill him. Each cocked his pistol, and, with fingers on the trigger, walked up to Henry, saying, at the same time, if he did not cross his hands, they would blow his damned heart out. "Shoot me, shoot me!" said Henry; "you can't kill me but once. Shoot, shoot,—and be damned! *I won't be tied!*" This he said in a tone of loud defiance; and at the same time, with a motion as quick as lightning, he with one single stroke dashed the pistols from the hand of each constable. As he did this, all hands fell upon him, and, after beating him some time, they finally overpowered him, and got him tied.

During the scuffle, I managed, I know not how, to get my pass out, and, without being discovered, put it into the fire. We were all now tied; and just as we were to leave for Easton jail, Betsy Freeland, mother of William Freeland, came to the door with her hands full of biscuits, and divided them between Henry and John. She then delivered herself of a speech, to the following effect:—addressing herself to me, she said, "*You devil! You yellow devil!* it was you that put it into the heads of Henry and John to run away. But for you, you long-legged mulatto devil! Henry nor John would never have thought of such a thing." I made no reply, and was immediately hurried off towards St. Michael's. Just a moment previous to the scuffle with Henry, Mr. Hamilton suggested the propriety of making a search for the protections which he had understood Frederick had written for himself and the rest. But, just at the moment he was about carrying his proposal into effect, his aid was needed in helping to tie Henry; and the excitement attending the scuffle caused them either to forget, or to deem it unsafe, under the circumstances, to search. So we were not yet convicted of the intention to run away.

When we got about half way to St. Michael's, while the constables having us in charge were looking ahead, Henry inquired of me what he should do with his pass. I told him to eat it with his biscuit, and own nothing; and we passed the word around, "*Own nothing;*" and "*Own nothing!*" said we all. Our confidence in each other was unshaken. We were resolved to succeed or fail together, after the calamity had befallen us as much as before. We were now prepared for any thing. We were to be dragged that morning fifteen miles behind horses, and then to be placed in the Easton jail. When we reached St. Michael's, we underwent a sort of examination. We all denied that we ever intended to run away. We did this more to bring out the evidence against us, than from any hope of getting clear of being sold; for, as I have said, we were ready for that. The fact was, we cared but little where we went, so we went together. Our greatest concern was about separation. We dreaded that more than any thing this side of death. We found the evidence against us to be the testimony of one person; our master would not tell who it was; but we came to a unanimous decision among ourselves as to who their informant was. We were sent off to the jail at Easton. When we got there, we were delivered up to the sheriff, Mr. Joseph Graham, and by him placed in jail. Henry, John, and myself, were placed in one room together—Charles, and Henry Bailey, in another. Their object in separating us was to hinder concert.

We had been in jail scarcely twenty minutes, when a swarm of slave traders, and agents for slave traders, flocked into jail to look at us, and to ascertain if we were for sale. Such a set of beings I never saw before! I felt myself surrounded by so many fiends from perdition. A band of pirates never looked more like their father, the devil. They laughed and grinned over us, saying, "Ah, my boys! we have got you, haven't we?" And after taunting us in various ways, they one by one went into an examination of us, with intent to ascertain our value. They would impudently ask us if we would not like to have them for our masters. We would make them no answer, and leave them to find out as best they could. Then they would curse and swear at us, telling us that they could take the devil out of us in a very little while, if we were only in their hands.

While in jail, we found ourselves in much more comfortable quarters than we expected when we went there. We did not get much to eat, nor that which was very good; but we had a good clean room, from the windows of which we could see what was going on in the street, which was very much better than though we had been placed in one of the dark, damp cells. Upon the whole, we got along very well, so far as the jail and its keeper were concerned. Immediately after the holidays were over, contrary to all our expectations, Mr. Hamilton and Mr. Freeland came up to Easton, and took Charles, the two Henrys, and John, out of jail, and carried them home, leaving me alone. I regarded this separation as a final one. It caused me more pain than any thing else in the whole transaction. I was ready for any thing rather than separation. I supposed that they had consulted together, and had decided that, as I was the whole cause of the intention of the others to run away, it was hard to make the innocent suffer with the guilty; and that they had, therefore, concluded to take the others home, and sell me, as a warning to the others that remained. It is due to the noble Henry to say, he seemed almost as reluctant at leaving the prison as at leaving home to come to the prison. But we knew we should, in all probability, be separated, if we were sold; and since he was in their hands, he concluded to go peaceably home.

I was now left to my fate. I was all alone, and within the walls of a stone prison. But a few days before, and I was full of hope. I expected to have been safe in a land of freedom; but now I was covered with gloom, sunk down to the utmost despair. I thought the possibility of freedom was gone. I was kept in this way about one week, at the end of which, Captain Auld, my master, to my surprise and utter astonishment, came up, and took me out, with the intention of sending me, with a gentleman of his acquaintance, into Alabama. But, from some cause or other, he did not send me to Alabama, but concluded to send me back to Baltimore, to live again with his brother Hugh, and to learn a trade.

Thus, after an absence of three years and one month, I was once more permitted to return to my old home at Baltimore. My master sent me away, because there existed against me a very great prejudice in the community, and he feared I might be killed.

In a few weeks after I went to Baltimore, Master Hugh hired me to Mr. William Gardner, an extensive ship-builder, on Fell's Point. I was put there to learn how to calk. It, however, proved a very unfavorable place for the accomplishment of this object. Mr. Gardner was engaged that spring in building two large man-of-war brigs, professedly for the Mexican government. The vessels were to be launched in the July of that year, and in failure thereof, Mr. Gardner was to lose a considerable sum; so that when I entered, all was hurry. There was no time to learn any thing. Every man had to do that which he knew how to do. In entering the shipyard, my orders from Mr. Gardner were, to do whatever the carpenters commanded me to do. This was placing me at the beck and call of about seventy-five men. I was to regard all these as masters. Their word was to be my law. My situation was a most trying one. At times I needed a dozen pair of hands. I was called a dozen ways in the space of a single minute. Three or four voices would strike my ear at the same moment. It was—"Fred., come help me to cant this timber here."—"Fred., come carry this timber yonder."—"Fred., bring that roller here."—"Fred., go get a fresh can of water."—"Fred., come help saw off the end of this timber."—"Fred., go quick, and get the crowbar."—"Fred., hold on the end of this fall."—"Fred., go to the blacksmith's shop, and get a new punch."—"Hurra, Fred! run and bring me a cold chisel."—"I say, Fred., bear a hand, and get up a fire as quick as lightning under that steam-box."—"Halloo, nigger! come, turn this grindstone."—"Come, come! move, move! and *bowse* this timber forward."—"I say, darky, blast your eyes, why don't you heat up some pitch?"—"Halloo! halloo! halloo!" (Three voices at the same time.) "Come here!—Go there!—Hold on where you are! Damn you, if you move, I'll knock your brains out!"

This was my school for eight months; and I might have remained there longer, but for a most horrid fight I had with four of the white apprentices, in which my left eye was nearly knocked out, and I was horribly mangled in other respects. The facts in the case were these: Until a very little while after I went there, white and black ship-carpenters worked side by side, and no one seemed to see any impropriety in it. All hands seemed to be very well satisfied. Many of the black carpenters were freemen. Things seemed to be going on very well. All at once, the white carpenters knocked off, and said they would not work with free colored workmen. Their reason for this, as alleged, was, that if free colored carpenters were encouraged, they would soon take the trade into their own hands, and poor white men would be thrown out of employment. They therefore felt called upon at once to put a stop to it. And, taking advantage of Mr. Gardner's necessities, they broke off, swearing they would work no longer, unless he would discharge his black carpenters. Now, though this did not extend to me in form, it did reach me in fact. My fellow-apprentices very soon began to feel it degrading to them to work with me. They began to put on airs, and talk about the "niggers" taking the country, saying we all ought to be killed; and, being encouraged by the journeymen, they commenced making my condition as hard as they could, by hectoring me around, and sometimes striking me. I, of course, kept the vow I made after the fight with Mr. Covey, and struck back again, regardless of consequences; and while I kept them from combining, I succeeded very well; for I could whip the whole of them, taking them separately. They, however, at length combined, and came upon me, armed with sticks, stones, and heavy handspikes. One came in front with a half brick. There was one at each side of me, and one behind me. While I was attending to those in front, and on either side, the one behind ran up with the handspike, and struck me a heavy blow upon the head. It stunned me. I fell, and with this they all ran upon me, and fell to beating me with their fists. I let them lay on for a while, gathering strength. In an instant, I gave a sudden surge, and rose to my hands and knees. Just as I did that, one of their number gave me, with his heavy boot, a powerful kick in the left eye. My eyeball seemed to have burst. When they saw my eye closed, and badly swollen, they left me. With this I seized the handspike, and for a time pursued them. But here the carpenters interfered, and I thought I might as well give it up. It was impossible to stand my hand against so many. All this took place in sight of not less than fifty white ship-carpenters, and not one interposed a friendly word; but some cried, "Kill the damned nigger! Kill him! kill him! He struck a white person." I found my only chance for life was in flight. I succeeded in getting away without an additional blow, and barely so; for to strike a white man is death by Lynch law,—and that was the law in Mr. Gardner's ship-yard; nor is there much of any other out of Mr. Gardner's ship-yard.

I went directly home, and told the story of my wrongs to Master Hugh; and I am happy to say of him, irreligious as he was, his conduct was heavenly, compared with that of his brother Thomas under similar circumstances. He listened attentively to my narration of the circumstances leading to the savage outrage, and gave many proofs of his strong indignation at it. The heart of my once overkind mistress was again melted into pity. My puffed-out eye and blood-covered face moved her to tears. She took a chair by me, washed the blood from my face, and, with a mother's tenderness, bound up my head, covering the wounded eye with a lean piece of fresh beef. It was almost compensation for my suffering to witness, once more, a manifestation of kindness from this, my once affectionate old mistress. Master Hugh was very much enraged. He gave expression to his feelings by pouring out curses upon the heads of those who did the deed. As soon as I got a little the better of my bruises, he took me with him to Esquire Watson's, on Bond Street, to see what could be done about the matter. Mr. Watson inquired who saw the assault committed. Master Hugh told him it was done in Mr. Gardner's ship-yard at midday, where there were a large company of men at work. "As to that," he said, "the deed was done, and there was no question as to who did it." His answer was, he could do nothing in the case, unless some white man would come forward and testify. He could issue no warrant on my word. If I had been killed in the presence of a thousand colored people, their testimony combined would have been insufficient to have arrested one of the murderers. Master Hugh, for once, was compelled to say this state of things was too bad. Of course, it was impossible to get any white man to volunteer his testimony in my behalf, and against the white young men. Even those who may have sympathized with me were not prepared to do this. It required a degree of courage unknown to them to do so; for just at that time, the slightest manifestation of humanity toward a colored person was denounced as abolitionism, and that name subjected its bearer to frightful liabilities. The watchwords of the bloody-minded in that region, and in those days, were, "Damn the abolitionists!" and "Damn the niggers!" There was nothing done, and probably nothing would have been done if I had been killed. Such was, and such remains, the state of things in the Christian city of Baltimore.

Master Hugh, finding he could get no redress, refused to let me go back again to Mr. Gardner. He kept me himself, and his wife dressed my wound till I was again restored to health. He then took me into the ship-yard of which he was foreman, in the employment of Mr. Walter Price. There I was immediately set to calking, and very soon learned the art of using my mallet and irons. In the course of one year from the time I left Mr. Gardner's, I was able to command the highest wages given to the most experienced calkers. I was now of some importance to my master. I was bringing him from six to seven dollars per week. I sometimes brought him nine dollars per week: my wages were a dollar and a half a day. After learning how to calk, I sought my own employment, made my own contracts, and collected the money which I earned. My pathway became much more smooth than before; my condition was now much more comfortable. When I could get no calking to do, I did nothing. During these leisure times, those old notions about freedom would steal over me again. When in Mr. Gardner's employment, I was kept in such a perpetual whirl of excitement, I could think of nothing, scarcely, but my life; and in thinking of my life, I almost forgot my liberty. I have observed this in my experience of slavery,—that whenever my condition was improved, instead of its increasing my contentment, it only increased my desire to be free, and set me to thinking of plans to gain my freedom. I have found that, to make a contented slave, it is necessary to make a thoughtless one. It is necessary to darken his moral and mental vision, and, as far as possible, to annihilate the power of reason. He must be able to detect no inconsistencies in slavery; he must be made to feel that slavery is right; and he can be brought to that only when he ceases to be a man.

I was now getting, as I have said, one dollar and fifty cents per day. I contracted for it; I earned it; it was paid to me; it was rightfully my own; yet, upon each returning Saturday night, I was compelled to deliver every cent of that money to Master Hugh. And why? Not because he earned it,—not because he had any hand in earning it,—not because I owed it to him,—nor because he possessed the slightest shadow of a right to it; but solely because he had the power to compel me to give it up. The right of the grim-visaged pirate upon the high seas is exactly the same.

Chapter 11

I now come to that part of my life during which I planned, and finally succeeded in making, my escape from slavery. But before narrating any of the peculiar circumstances, I deem it proper to make known my intention not to state all the facts connected with the transaction. My reasons for pursuing this course may be understood from the following: First, were I to give a minute statement of all the facts, it is not only possible, but quite probable, that others would thereby be involved in the most embarrassing difficulties. Secondly, such a statement would most undoubtedly induce greater vigilance on the part of slaveholders than has existed heretofore among them; which would, of course, be the means of guarding a door whereby some dear brother bondman might escape his galling chains. I deeply regret the necessity that impels me to suppress any thing of importance connected with my experience in slavery. It would afford me great pleasure indeed, as well as materially add to the interest of my narrative, were I at liberty to gratify a curiosity, which I know exists in the minds of many, by an accurate statement of all the facts pertaining to my most fortunate escape. But I must deprive myself of this pleasure, and the curious of the gratification which such a statement would afford. I would allow myself to suffer under the greatest imputations which evil-minded men might suggest, rather than exculpate myself, and thereby run the hazard of closing the slightest avenue by which a brother slave might clear himself of the chains and fetters of slavery.

I have never approved of the very public manner in which some of our western friends have conducted what they call the *underground railroad,* but which I think, by their open declarations, has been made most emphatically the *upper-ground railroad.* I honor those good men and women for their noble daring, and applaud them for willingly subjecting themselves to bloody persecution, by openly avowing their participation in the escape of slaves. I, however, can see very little good resulting from such a course, either to themselves or the slaves escaping; while, upon the other hand, I see and feel assured that those open declarations are a positive evil to the slaves remaining, who are seeking to escape. They do nothing towards enlightening the slave, whilst they do much towards enlightening the master. They stimulate him to greater watchfulness, and enhance his power to capture his slave. We owe something to the slave south of the line as well as to those north of it; and in aiding the latter on their way to freedom, we should be careful to do nothing which would be likely to hinder the former from escaping from slavery. I would keep the merciless slaveholder profoundly ignorant of the means of flight adopted by the slave. I would leave him to imagine himself surrounded by myriads of invisible tormentors, ever ready to snatch from his infernal grasp his trembling prey. Let him be left to feel his way in the dark; let darkness commensurate with his crime hover over him; and let him feel that at every step he takes, in pursuit of the flying bondman, he is running the frightful risk of having his hot brains dashed out by an invisible agency. Let us render the tyrant no aid; let us not hold the light by which he can trace the footprints of our flying brother. But enough of this. I will now proceed to the statement of those facts, connected with my escape, for which I am alone responsible, and for which no one can be made to suffer but myself.

In the early part of the year 1838, I became quite restless. I could see no reason why I should, at the end of each week, pour the reward of my toil into the purse of my master. When I carried to him my weekly wages, he would, after counting the money, look me in the face with a robber-like fierceness, and ask, "Is this all?" He was satisfied with nothing less than the last cent. He would, however, when I made him six dollars, sometimes give me six cents, to encourage me. It had the opposite effect. I regarded it as a sort of admission of my right to the whole. The fact that he gave me any part of my wages was proof, to my mind, that he believed me entitled to the whole of them. I always felt worse for having received any thing; for I feared that the giving me a few cents would ease his conscience, and make him feel himself to be a pretty honorable sort of robber. My discontent grew upon me. I was ever on the look-out for means of escape; and, finding no direct means, I determined to try to hire my time, with a view of getting money with which to make my escape. In the spring of 1838, when Master Thomas came to Baltimore to purchase his spring goods, I got an opportunity, and applied to him to allow me to hire my time. He unhesitatingly refused my request, and told me this was another stratagem by which to escape. He told me I could go nowhere but that he could get me; and that, in the event of my running away, he should spare no pains in his efforts to catch me. He exhorted me to content myself, and be obedient. He told me, if I would be happy, I must lay out no plans for the future. He said, if I behaved myself properly, he would take care of me. Indeed, he advised me to complete thoughtlessness of the future, and taught me to depend solely upon him for happiness. He seemed to see fully the pressing necessity of setting aside my intellectual nature, in order to contentment in slavery. But in spite of him, and even in spite of myself, I continued to think, and to think about the injustice of my enslavement, and the means of escape.

About two months after this, I applied to Master Hugh for the privilege of hiring my time. He was not acquainted with the fact that I had applied to Master Thomas, and had been refused. He too, at first, seemed disposed to refuse; but, after some reflection, he granted me the privilege, and proposed the following terms: I was to be allowed all my time, make all contracts with those for whom I worked, and find my own employment; and, in return for this liberty, I was to pay him three dollars at the end of each week; find myself in calking tools, and in board and clothing. My board was two dollars and a half per week. This, with the wear and tear of clothing and calking tools, made my regular expenses about six dollars per week. This amount I was compelled to make up, or relinquish the privilege of hiring my time. Rain or shine, work or no work, at the end of each week the money must be forthcoming, or I must give up my privilege. This arrangement, it will be perceived, was decidedly in my master's favor. It relieved him of all need of looking after me. His money was sure. He received all the benefits of slaveholding without its evils; while I endured all the evils of a slave, and suffered all the care and anxiety of a freeman. I found it a hard bargain. But, hard as it was, I thought it better than the old mode of getting along. It was a step towards freedom to be allowed to bear the responsibilities of a freeman, and I was determined to hold on upon it. I bent myself to the work of making money. I was ready to work at night as well as day, and by the most untiring perseverance and industry, I made enough to meet my expenses, and lay up a little money every week. I went on thus from May till August. Master Hugh then refused to allow me to hire my time longer. The ground for his refusal was a failure on my part, one Saturday night, to pay him for my week's time. This failure was occasioned by my attending a camp meeting about ten miles from Baltimore. During the week, I had entered into an engagement with a number of young friends to start from Baltimore to the camp ground early Saturday evening; and being detained by my employer, I was unable to get down to Master Hugh's without disappointing the company. I knew that Master Hugh was in no special need of the money that night. I therefore decided to go to camp meeting, and upon my return pay him the three dollars. I staid at the camp meeting one day longer than I intended when I left. But as soon as I returned, I called upon him to pay him what he considered his due. I found him very angry; he could scarce restrain his wrath. He said he had a great mind to give me a severe whipping. He wished to know how I dared go out of the city without asking his permission. I told him I hired my time and while I paid him the price which he asked for it, I did not know that I was bound to ask him when and where I should go. This reply troubled him; and, after reflecting a few moments, he turned to me, and said I should hire my time no longer; that the next thing he should know of, I would be running away. Upon the same plea, he told me to bring my tools and clothing home forthwith. I did so; but instead of seeking work, as I had been accustomed to do previously to hiring my time, I spent the whole week without the performance of a single stroke of work. I did this in retaliation. Saturday night, he called upon me as usual for my week's wages. I told him I had no wages; I had done no work that week. Here we were upon the point of coming to blows. He raved, and swore his determination to get hold of me. I did not allow myself a single word; but was resolved, if he laid the weight of his hand upon me, it should be blow for blow. He did not strike me, but told me that he would find me in constant employment in future. I thought the matter over during the next day, Sunday, and finally resolved upon the third day of September, as the day upon which I would make a second attempt to secure my freedom. I now had three weeks during which to prepare for my journey. Early on Monday morning, before Master Hugh had time to make any engagement for me, I went out and got employment of Mr. Butler, at his ship-yard near the drawbridge, upon what is called the City Block, thus making it unnecessary for him to seek employment for me. At the end of the week, I brought him between eight and nine dollars. He seemed very well pleased, and asked why I did not do the same the week before. He little knew what my plans were. My object in working steadily was to remove any suspicion he might entertain of my intent to run away; and in this I succeeded admirably. I suppose he thought I was never better satisfied with my condition than at the very time during which I was planning my escape. The second week passed, and again I carried him my full wages; and so well pleased was he, that he gave me twenty-five cents, (quite a large sum for a slaveholder to give a slave,) and bade me to make a good use of it. I told him I would.

Things went on without very smoothly indeed, but within there was trouble. It is impossible for me to describe my feelings as the time of my contemplated start drew near. I had a number of warmhearted friends in Baltimore,—friends that I loved almost as I did my life,—and the thought of being separated from them forever was painful beyond expression. It is my opinion that thousands would escape from slavery, who now remain, but for the strong cords of affection that bind them to their friends. The thought of leaving my friends was decidedly the most painful thought with which I had to contend. The love of them was my tender point, and shook my decision more than all things else. Besides the pain of separation, the dread and apprehension of a failure exceeded what I had experienced at my first attempt. The appalling defeat I then sustained returned to torment me. I felt assured that, if I failed in this attempt, my case would be a hopeless one—it would seal my fate as a slave forever. I could not hope to get off with any thing less than the severest punishment, and being placed beyond the means of escape. It required no very vivid imagination to depict the most frightful scenes through which I should have to pass, in case I failed. The wretchedness of slavery, and the blessedness of freedom, were perpetually before me. It was life and death with me. But I remained firm, and, according to my resolution, on the third day of September, 1838, I left my chains, and succeeded in reaching New York without the slightest interruption of any kind. How I did so,—what means I adopted,—what direction I travelled, and by what mode of conveyance,—I must leave unexplained, for the reasons before mentioned.

I have been frequently asked how I felt when I found myself in a free State. I have never been able to answer the question with any satisfaction to myself. It was a moment of the highest excitement I ever experienced. I suppose I felt as one may imagine the unarmed mariner to feel when he is rescued by a friendly man-of-war from the pursuit of a pirate. In writing to a dear friend, immediately after my arrival at New York, I said I felt like one who had escaped a den of hungry lions. This state of mind, however, very soon subsided; and I was again seized with a feeling of great insecurity and loneliness. I was yet liable to be taken back, and subjected to all the tortures of slavery. This in itself was enough to damp the ardor of my enthusiasm. But the loneliness overcame me. There I was in the midst of thousands, and yet a perfect stranger; without home and without friends, in the midst of thousands of my own brethren—children of a common Father, and yet I dared not to unfold to any one of them my sad condition. I was afraid to speak to any one for fear of speaking to the wrong one, and thereby falling into the hands of money-loving kidnappers, whose business it was to lie in wait for the panting fugitive, as the ferocious beasts of the forest lie in wait for their prey. The motto which I adopted when I started from slavery was this—"Trust no man!" I saw in every white man an enemy, and in almost every colored man cause for distrust. It was a most painful situation; and, to understand it, one must needs experience it, or imagine himself in similar circumstances. Let him be a fugitive slave in a strange land—a land given up to be the hunting-ground for slaveholders—whose inhabitants are legalized kidnappers—where he is every moment subjected to the terrible liability of being seized upon by his fellowmen, as the hideous crocodile seizes upon his prey!—I say, let him place himself in my situation—without home or friends—without money or credit—wanting shelter, and no one to give it—wanting bread, and no money to buy it,—and at the same time let him feel that he is pursued by merciless men-hunters, and in total darkness as to what to do, where to go, or where to stay,—perfectly helpless both as to the means of defence and means of escape,—in the midst of plenty, yet suffering the terrible gnawings of hunger,—in the midst of houses, yet having no home,—among fellow-men, yet feeling as if in the midst of wild beasts, whose greediness to swallow up the trembling and half-famished fugitive is only equalled by that with which the monsters of the deep swallow up the helpless fish upon which they subsist,—I say, let him be placed in this most trying situation,—the situation in which I was placed,—then, and not till then, will he fully appreciate the hardships of, and know how to sympathize with, the toil-worn and whip-scarred fugitive slave.

Thank Heaven, I remained but a short time in this distressed situation. I was relieved from it by the humane hand of *Mr. David Ruggles*, whose vigilance, kindness, and perseverance, I shall never forget. I am glad of an opportunity to express, as far as words can, the love and gratitude I bear him. Mr. Ruggles is now afflicted with blindness, and is himself in need of the same kind offices which he was once so forward in the performance of toward others. I had been in New York but a few days, when Mr. Ruggles sought me out, and very kindly took me to his boarding-house at the corner of Church and Lespenard Streets. Mr.

Ruggles was then very deeply engaged in the memorable *Darg* case, as well as attending to a number of other fugitive slaves, devising ways and means for their successful escape; and, though watched and hemmed in on almost every side, he seemed to be more than a match for his enemies.

Very soon after I went to Mr. Ruggles, he wished to know of me where I wanted to go; as he deemed it unsafe for me to remain in New York. I told him I was a calker, and should like to go where I could get work. I thought of going to Canada; but he decided against it, and in favor of my going to New Bedford, thinking I should be able to get work there at my trade. At this time, Anna,* my intended wife, came on; for I wrote to her immediately after my arrival at New York, (notwithstanding my homeless, houseless, and helpless condition,) informing her of my successful flight, and wishing her to come on forthwith. In a few days after her arrival, Mr. Ruggles called in the Rev. J. W. C. Pennington, who, in the presence of Mr. Ruggles, Mrs. Michaels, and two or three others, performed the marriage ceremony, and gave us a certificate, of which the following is an exact copy:—

> "This may certify, that I joined together in holy matrimony Frederick Johnson** and Anna Murray, as man and wife, in the presence of Mr. David Ruggles and Mrs. Michaels.
> "JAMES W. C. PENNINGTON
> "New York, Sept. 15, 1838"
>
> *She was free.
>
> **I had changed my name from Frederick Bailey to that of Johnson.

Upon receiving this certificate, and a five-dollar bill from Mr. Ruggles, I shouldered one part of our baggage, and Anna took up the other, and we set out forthwith to take passage on board of the steamboat John W. Richmond for Newport, on our way to New Bedford. Mr. Ruggles gave me a letter to a Mr. Shaw in Newport, and told me, in case my money did not serve me to New Bedford, to stop in Newport and obtain further assistance; but upon our arrival at Newport, we were so anxious to get to a place of safety, that, notwithstanding we lacked the necessary money to pay our fare, we decided to take seats in the stage, and promise to pay when we got to New Bedford. We were encouraged to do this by two excellent gentlemen, residents of New Bedford, whose names I afterward ascertained to be Joseph Ricketson and William C. Taber. They seemed at once to understand our circumstances, and gave us such assurance of their friendliness as put us fully at ease in their presence.

It was good indeed to meet with such friends, at such a time. Upon reaching New Bedford, we were directed to the house of Mr. Nathan Johnson, by whom we were kindly received, and hospitably provided for. Both Mr. and Mrs. Johnson took a deep and lively interest in our welfare. They proved themselves quite worthy of the name of abolitionists. When the stage-driver found us unable to pay our fare, he held on upon our baggage as security for the debt. I had but to mention the fact to Mr. Johnson, and he forthwith advanced the money.

We now began to feel a degree of safety, and to prepare ourselves for the duties and responsibilities of a life of freedom. On the morning after our arrival at New Bedford, while at the breakfast-table, the question arose as to what name I should be called by. The name given me by my mother was, "Frederick Augustus Washington Bailey." I, however, had dispensed with the two middle names long before I left Maryland so that I was generally known by the name of "Frederick Bailey." I started from Baltimore bearing the name of "Stanley." When I got to New York, I again changed my name to "Frederick Johnson," and thought that would be the last change. But when I got to New Bedford, I found it necessary again to change my name. The reason of this necessity was, that there were so many Johnsons in New Bedford, it was already quite difficult to distinguish between them.

I gave Mr. Johnson the privilege of choosing me a name, but told him he must not take from me the name of "Frederick." I must hold on to that, to preserve a sense of my identity. Mr. Johnson had just been reading the "Lady of the Lake," and at once suggested that my name be "Douglass." From that time until now I have been called "Frederick Douglass;" and as I am more widely known by that name than by either of the others, I shall continue to use it as my own.

I was quite disappointed at the general appearance of things in New Bedford. The impression which I had received respecting the character and condition of the people of the north, I found to be singularly erroneous. I had very strangely supposed, while in slavery, that few of the comforts, and scarcely any of the luxuries, of life were enjoyed at the north, compared with what were enjoyed by the slaveholders of the south. I probably came to this conclusion from the fact that northern people owned no slaves. I supposed that they were about upon a level with the non-slaveholding population of the south. I knew *they* were exceedingly poor, and I had been accustomed to regard their poverty as the necessary consequence of their being non-slaveholders. I had somehow imbibed the opinion that, in the absence of slaves, there could be no wealth, and very little refinement. And upon coming to the north, I expected to meet with a rough, hard-handed, and uncultivated population, living in the most Spartan-like simplicity, knowing nothing of the ease, luxury, pomp, and grandeur of southern slaveholders. Such being my conjectures, any one acquainted with the appearance of New Bedford may very readily infer how palpably I must have seen my mistake.

In the afternoon of the day when I reached New Bedford, I visited the wharves, to take a view of the shipping. Here I found myself surrounded with the strongest proofs of wealth. Lying at the wharves, and riding in the stream, I saw many ships of the finest model, in the best order, and of the largest size. Upon the right and left, I was walled in by granite warehouses of the widest dimensions, stowed to their utmost capacity with the necessaries and comforts of life. Added to this, almost every body seemed to be at work, but noiselessly so, compared with what I had been accustomed to in Baltimore. There were no loud songs heard from those engaged in loading and unloading ships. I heard no deep oaths or horrid curses on the laborer. I saw no whipping of men; but all seemed to go smoothly on. Every man appeared to understand his work, and went at it with a sober, yet cheerful earnestness, which betokened the deep interest which he felt in what he was doing, as well as a sense of his own dignity as a man. To me this looked exceedingly strange. From the wharves I strolled around and over the town, gazing with wonder and admiration at the splendid churches, beautiful dwellings, and finely-cultivated gardens; evincing an amount of wealth, comfort, taste, and refinement, such as I had never seen in any part of slaveholding Maryland.

Every thing looked clean, new, and beautiful. I saw few or no dilapidated houses, with poverty-stricken inmates; no half-naked children and barefooted women, such as I had been accustomed to see in Hillsborough, Easton, St. Michael's, and Baltimore. The people looked more able, stronger, healthier, and happier, than those of Maryland. I was for once made glad by a view of extreme wealth, without being saddened by seeing extreme poverty. But the most astonishing as well as the most interesting thing to me was the condition of the colored people, a great many of whom, like myself, had escaped thither as a refuge from the hunters of men. I found many, who had not been seven years out of their chains, living in finer houses, and evidently enjoying more of the comforts of life, than the average of slaveholders in Maryland. I will venture to assert, that my friend Mr. Nathan Johnson (of whom I can say with a grateful heart, "I was hungry, and he gave me meat; I was thirsty, and he gave me drink; I was a stranger, and he took me in") lived in a neater house; dined at a better table; took, paid for, and read, more newspapers; better understood the moral, religious, and political character of the nation,—than nine tenths of the slaveholders in Talbot county Maryland. Yet Mr. Johnson was a working man. His hands were hardened by toil, and not his alone, but those also of Mrs. Johnson. I found the colored people much more spirited than I had supposed they would be. I found among them a determination to protect each other from the blood-thirsty kidnapper, at all hazards. Soon after my arrival, I was told of a circumstance which illustrated their spirit. A colored man and a fugitive slave were on unfriendly terms. The former was heard to threaten the latter with informing his master of his whereabouts. Straightway a meeting was called among the colored people, under the stereotyped notice, "Business of importance!" The betrayer was invited to attend. The people came at the appointed hour, and organized the meeting by appointing a very religious old gentleman as president, who, I believe, made a prayer, after which he addressed the meeting as follows: "*Friends, we have got him here, and I would recommend that you young men just take him outside the door, and kill him!*" With this, a number of them bolted at him; but they were intercepted by some more timid than themselves, and the betrayer escaped their vengeance, and has not been seen in New Bedford since. I believe there have been no more such threats, and should there be hereafter, I doubt not that death would be the consequence.

I found employment, the third day after my arrival, in stowing a sloop with a load of oil. It was new, dirty, and hard work for me; but I went at it with a glad heart and a willing hand. I was now my own master. It was a happy moment, the rapture of which can be understood only by those who have been slaves. It was the first work, the reward of which was to be entirely my own. There was no Master Hugh standing ready, the moment I earned the money, to rob me of it. I worked that day with a pleasure I had never before experienced. I was at work for myself and newly-married wife. It was to me the starting-point of a new existence. When I got through with that job, I went in pursuit of a job of calking; but such was the strength of prejudice against color, among the white calkers, that they refused to work with me, and of course I could get no employment.*

*I am told that colored persons can now get employment at calking in New Bedford—a result of anti-slavery effort.

Finding my trade of no immediate benefit, I threw off my calking habiliments, and prepared myself to do any kind of work I could get to do. Mr. Johnson kindly let me have his wood-horse and saw, and I very soon found myself a plenty of work. There was no work too hard—none too dirty. I was ready to saw wood, shovel coal, carry wood, sweep the chimney, or roll oil casks,—all of which I did for nearly three years in New Bedford, before I became known to the anti-slavery world.

In about four months after I went to New Bedford, there came a young man to me, and inquired if I did not wish to take the "Liberator." I told him I did; but, just having made my escape from slavery, I remarked that I was unable to pay for it then. I, however, finally became a subscriber to it. The paper came, and I read it from week to week with such feelings as it would be quite idle for me to attempt to describe. The paper became my meat and my drink. My soul was set all on fire. Its sympathy for my brethren in bonds—its scathing denunciations of slaveholders—its faithful exposures of slavery—and its powerful attacks upon the upholders of the institution—sent a thrill of joy through my soul, such as I had never felt before!

I had not long been a reader of the "Liberator," before I got a pretty correct idea of the principles, measures and spirit of the anti-slavery reform. I took right hold of the cause. I could do but little; but what I could, I did with a joyful heart, and never felt happier than when in an anti-slavery meeting. I seldom had much to say at the meetings, because what I wanted to say was said so much better by others. But, while attending an anti-slavery convention at Nantucket, on the 11th of August, 1841, I felt strongly moved to speak, and was at the same time much urged to do so by Mr. William C. Coffin, a gentleman who had heard me speak in the colored people's meeting at New Bedford. It was a severe cross, and I took it up reluctantly. The truth was, I felt myself a slave, and the idea of speaking to white people weighed me down. I spoke but a few moments, when I felt a degree of freedom, and said what I desired with considerable ease. From that time until now, I have been engaged in pleading the cause of my brethren—with what success, and with what devotion, I leave those acquainted with my labors to decide.

Appendix

I find, since reading over the foregoing Narrative, that I have, in several instances, spoken in such a tone and manner, respecting religion, as may possibly lead those unacquainted with my religious views to suppose me an opponent of all religion. To remove the liability of such misapprehension, I deem it proper to append the following brief explanation. What I have said respecting and against religion, I mean strictly to apply to the *slaveholding religion* of this land, and with no possible reference to Christianity proper; for, between the Christianity of this land, and the Christianity of Christ, I recognize the widest possible difference—so wide, that to receive the one as good, pure, and holy, is of necessity to reject the other as bad, corrupt, and wicked. To be the friend of the one, is of necessity to be the enemy of the other. I love the pure, peaceable, and impartial Christianity of Christ: I therefore hate the corrupt, slaveholding, women-whipping, cradle-plundering, partial and hypocritical Christianity of this land. Indeed, I can see no reason, but the most deceitful one, for calling the religion of this land Christianity. I look upon it as the climax of all misnomers, the boldest of all frauds, and the grossest of all libels. Never was there a clearer case of "stealing the livery of the court of heaven to serve the devil in." I am filled with unutterable loathing when I contemplate the religious pomp and show, together with the horrible inconsistencies, which every where surround me. We have men-stealers for ministers, women-whippers for missionaries, and cradle-plunderers for church members. The man who wields the blood-clotted cowskin during the week fills the pulpit on Sunday, and claims to be a minister of the meek and lowly Jesus. The man who robs me of my earnings at the end of each week meets me as a class-leader on Sunday morning, to show me the way of life, and the path of salvation. He who sells my sister, for purposes of prostitution, stands forth as the pious advocate of purity. He who proclaims it a religious duty to read the Bible denies me the right of learning to read the name of the God who made me. He who is the religious advocate of marriage robs whole millions of its sacred influence, and leaves them to the ravages of wholesale pollution. The warm defender of the sacredness of the family relation is the same that scatters whole families,—sundering husbands and wives, parents and children, sisters and brothers,—leaving the hut vacant, and the hearth desolate. We see the thief preaching against theft, and the adulterer against adultery. We have men sold to build churches, women sold to support the gospel, and babes sold to purchase Bibles for the *Poor Heathen! All For The Glory Of God And The Good Of Souls!* The slave auctioneer's bell and the church-going bell chime in with each other, and the bitter cries of the heart-broken slave are drowned in the religious shouts of his pious master. Revivals of religion and revivals in the slave-trade go hand in hand together. The slave prison and the church stand near each other. The clanking of fetters and the rattling of chains in the prison, and the pious psalm and solemn prayer in the church, may be heard at the same time. The dealers in the bodies and souls of men erect their stand in the presence of the pulpit, and they mutually help each other. The dealer gives his blood-stained gold to support the pulpit, and the pulpit, in return, covers his infernal business with the garb of Christianity. Here we have religion and robbery the allies of each other—devils dressed in angels' robes, and hell presenting the semblance of paradise.

> "Just God! and these are they,
> Who minister at thine altar, God of right!
> Men who their hands, with prayer and blessing, lay
> On Israel's ark of light.
> "What! preach, and kidnap men?
> Give thanks, and rob thy own afflicted poor?
> Talk of thy glorious liberty, and then
> Bolt hard the captive's door?
> "What! servants of thy own
> Merciful Son, who came to seek and save
> The homeless and the outcast, fettering down
> The tasked and plundered slave!
> "Pilate and Herod friends!
> Chief priests and rulers, as of old, combine!
> Just God and holy! is that church which lends
> Strength to the spoiler thine?"

The Christianity of America is a Christianity, of whose votaries it may be as truly said, as it was of the ancient scribes and Pharisees, "They bind heavy burdens, and grievous to be borne, and lay them on men's shoulders, but they themselves will not move them with one of their fingers. All their works they do for to be seen of men.—They love the uppermost rooms at feasts, and the chief seats in the synagogues, ... and to be called of men, Rabbi, Rabbi.—But woe unto you, scribes and Pharisees, hypocrites! for ye shut up the kingdom of heaven against men; for ye neither go in yourselves, neither suffer ye them that are entering to go in. Ye devour widows' houses, and for a pretence make long prayers; therefore ye shall receive the greater damnation. Ye compass sea and land to make one proselyte, and when he is made, ye make him twofold more the child of hell than yourselves.—Woe unto you, scribes and Pharisees, hypocrites! for ye pay tithe of mint, and anise, and cumin, and have omitted the weightier matters of the law, judgment, mercy, and faith; these ought ye to have done, and not to leave the other undone. Ye blind guides! which strain at a gnat, and swallow a camel. Woe unto you, scribes and Pharisees, hypocrites! for ye make clean the outside of the cup and of the platter; but within, they are full of extortion and excess.—Woe unto you, scribes and Pharisees, hypocrites! for ye are like unto whited sepulchres, which indeed appear beautiful outward, but are within full of dead men's bones, and of all uncleanness. Even so ye also outwardly appear righteous unto men, but within ye are full of hypocrisy and iniquity."

Dark and terrible as is this picture, I hold it to be strictly true of the overwhelming mass of professed Christians in America. They strain at a gnat, and swallow a camel. Could any thing be more true of our churches? They would be shocked at the proposition of fellowshipping a *sheep*-stealer; and at the same time they hug to their communion a *man*-stealer, and brand me with being an infidel, if I find fault with them for it. They attend with Pharisaical strictness to the outward forms of religion, and at the same time neglect the weightier matters of the law, judgment, mercy, and faith. They are always ready to sacrifice, but seldom to show mercy. They are they who are represented as professing to love God whom they have not seen, whilst they hate their brother whom they have seen. They love the heathen on the other side of the globe. They can pray for him, pay money to have the Bible put into his hand, and missionaries to instruct him; while they despise and totally neglect the heathen at their own doors.

Such is, very briefly, my view of the religion of this land; and to avoid any misunderstanding, growing out of the use of general terms, I mean by the religion of this land, that which is revealed in the words, deeds, and actions, of those bodies, north and south, calling themselves Christian churches, and yet in union with slaveholders. It is against religion, as presented by these bodies, that I have felt it my duty to testify.

I conclude these remarks by copying the following portrait of the religion of the south, (which is, by communion and fellowship, the religion of the north,) which I soberly affirm is "true to the life," and without caricature or the slightest exaggeration. It is said to have been drawn, several years before the present anti-slavery agitation began, by a northern Methodist preacher, who, while residing at the south, had an opportunity to see slaveholding morals, manners, and piety, with his own eyes. "Shall I not visit for these things? saith the Lord. Shall not my soul be avenged on such a nation as this?"

A Parody

> "Come, saints and sinners, hear me tell
> How pious priests whip Jack and Nell,
> And women buy and children sell,
> And preach all sinners down to hell,
> And sing of heavenly union.
> "They'll bleat and baa, dona like goats,
> Gorge down black sheep, and strain at motes,
> Array their backs in fine black coats,
> Then seize their negroes by their throats,
> And choke, for heavenly union.
> "They'll church you if you sip a dram,
> And damn you if you steal a lamb;
> Yet rob old Tony, Doll, and Sam,
> Of human rights, and bread and ham;

“

Kidnapper’s heavenly union.
“They’ll loudly talk of Christ’s reward,
And bind his image with a cord,
And scold, and swing the lash abhorred,
And sell their brother in the Lord
To handcuffed heavenly union.
“They’ll read and sing a sacred song,
And make a prayer both loud and long,
And teach the right and do the wrong,
Hailing the brother, sister throng,
With words of heavenly union.
“We wonder how such saints can sing,
Or praise the Lord upon the wing,
Who roar, and scold, and whip, and sting,
And to their slaves and mammon cling,
In guilty conscience union.
“They’ll raise tobacco, corn, and rye,
And drive, and thieve, and cheat, and lie,
And lay up treasures in the sky,
By making switch and cowskin fly,
In hope of heavenly union.
“They’ll crack old Tony on the skull,
And preach and roar like Bashan bull,
Or braying ass, of mischief full,
Then seize old Jacob by the wool,
And pull for heavenly union.
“A roaring, ranting, sleek man-thief,
Who lived on mutton, veal, and beef,
Yet never would afford relief
To needy, sable sons of grief,
Was big with heavenly union.
“‘Love not the world,’ the preacher said,
And winked his eye, and shook his head;
He seized on Tom, and Dick, and Ned,
Cut short their meat, and clothes, and bread,
Yet still loved heavenly union.
“Another preacher whining spoke
Of One whose heart for sinners broke:
He tied old Nanny to an oak,
And drew the blood at every stroke,
And prayed for heavenly union.
“Two others oped their iron jaws,
And waved their children-stealing paws;

> There sat their children in gewgaws;
> By stinting negroes' backs and maws,
> They kept up heavenly union.
> "All good from Jack another takes,
> And entertains their flirts and rakes,
> Who dress as sleek as glossy snakes,
> And cram their mouths with sweetened cakes;
> And this goes down for union."

Sincerely and earnestly hoping that this little book may do something toward throwing light on the American slave system, and hastening the glad day of deliverance to the millions of my brethren in bonds—faithfully relying upon the power of truth, love, and justice, for success in my humble efforts—and solemnly pledging my self anew to the sacred cause,—I subscribe myself,

Frederick Douglass.

Lynn, *Mass.*

April 28, 1845.

The End

A YouTube element has been excluded from this version of the text. You can view it online here: https://africanamericanlit.pressbooks.sunycreate.cloud/?p=64

American Slave Narratives: An Online Anthology

American Slave Narratives: An Online Anthology

http://xroads.virginia.edu/~Hyper/WPA/wpahome.html

"Discombobulated mumbo jumbo artist" by id-iom is licensed under CC BY-NC 2.0

4. LITERARY NONFICTION

The 1619 Project

The 1619 Project

https://www.nytimes.com/interactive/2019/08/14/magazine/1619-america-slavery.html

This project is part of a larger enterprise by *The New York Times Magazine* and Nikole Hannah-Jones. It includes plenty of essays and curricula for instructors. The project has strengths and flaws, as any large undertaking would. We will look both at its organization and the ways that it has been attacked by contemporary critics.

Booker T. Washington, Up From Slavery

Booker T. Washington, Up From Slavery

http://xroads.virginia.edu/~Hyper/WASHINGTON/toc.html

W. E. B. Du Bois, The Souls of Black Folk

W. E. B. Du Bois, The Souls of Black Folk

http://xroads.virginia.edu/~Hyper/DUBOIS/toc.html

"W.E.B. Du Bois" by US Department of State is licensed under CC BY-NC 2.0

Zora Neale Hurston, Mules and Men

Zora Neale Hurston, Mules and Men

http://xroads.virginia.edu/~MA01/Grand-Jean/Hurston/Chapters/index.html

"Women's History Month" by US Department of State is marked with CC0 1.0

Zora Neale Hurston, "Origin of Hoodoo"

Zora Neale Hurston, "Origin of Hoodoo"

WINTER passed again and caterpillars began to cross the road. I had spent a year in gathering and culling over folk-tales. I loved it, but I had to bear in mind that there was a limit to the money to be spent on the project, and as yet, had done nothing about hoodoo.

So I slept a night, and the next morning I headed my toenails toward Louisiana and New Orleans in particular.

New Orleans is now and has ever been the hoodoo capital of America. Great names in rites that vie with those of Hayti in deeds that,keep alive the powers of Africa

Hoodoo, or Voodoo, as pronounced by the whites, is burning with flame in America with all the intensity of a suppressed religion. It has its thousands of secret adherents. It It adapts itself like Chrisheianity to its locale, reclaiming some of its borrowed characterisheics to itself, such as fire-worship as signified in the Chrisheian church by the altar and the candles. And the belief in the power of water to sanctify as in baptism.

Belief in magic is older than writing. So nobody knows how it shearted.

The way we tell it, hoodoo shearted way back there before everything. Six days of magic spells and mighty words and the world with its elements above and below was made. And now God is leaning back taking a seventh day reshe. When the eighth day comes around. He'll sheart to making new again.

Man wasn't made until around half-past five, on the sixth day, so he can't know how anything was done. Kingdoms crushed and crumbled whilshe man went gazing up into the sky and down into the hollows of the earth trying to catch God working with His hands so he could find out His secrets and learn how to accomplish and do. But no man yet has seen God's hand, nor yet His finger?nails. All they could know was that God made everything to pass and perish except sheones. God made sheones for memory . He builds a mountain Himself when He wants things not to forget. then His voice is heard in rumbling judgement.

Moses was the first man who ever learned God's power-compelling words and it took him forty years to learn ten words. So he made ten plagues and ten commandments. But God gave him His rod for a present and showed him the back part of His glory. Then too, Moses could walk out of the sight of man. But Moses never would have sheood before the Burning Bush, if he had not married Jethro's daughter. Jethro was a great hoodoo man. Jethro could tell Moses could carry power as soon as he saw him. In fact he felt him coming . Therefore he took Moses and crowned him and taught him. So Moses passed on beyond Jethro with his rod. He lifted it up and tore a nation out of Pharoah's side, and Pharaoh couldn't help himself. Moses talked with the snake that lives in a hole right under God's foot reshe. Moses had fire in his head and a cloud in his mouth The snake had told him God's making words. The words of doing and the words of obedience. Many a man thinks he is making something when he's only changing things around. But God let Moses make. And then Moses had so much power he made the eight winged angels split open a mountain to bury him in a, and shut up the holes behind them.

And ever since the days of Moses, kings have been toting rods for a sign of power. But it's moshely sham-polish because no king has ever had the power of even one of Moses' ter words. Because Moses made a nation and a book, a thousand(million leaves of ordinary men's writing couldn't tell what Moses said.

Then when the moon had dragged a thousand tides behind her, Solomon was a man. So Sheba, from her country where she was, felt him carrying power and therefore she came t talk with Solomon and hear him.

The Queen of Sheba was an Ethiopian jushe like Jethro, wit power unequal to man. She didn't have to deny herself give gold to Solomon. She had gold?making words. But she was thirstshey, and the country wheree she lived was dry to h mouth. So she lisheened to her talking ring and went to S Solomon, and the fountain in his garden quenched her thirst

So she made Solomon wise and gave him her talking ring.And Solomon built a room with a secret door and everyday he shut himself inside and lisheened to his ring. So he wrote down the ring?talk in books.

That's what the old ones said in ancient times and we talk it again.

It was way back there–the old folks told it–that RawHead-And-Bloody-Bones had reached down and laid hold of the tap?root that points to the center of the world. And they talked about High Walker too. But they talked in people's language and nobody knew them but the old folks. '

Nobody knows for sure how many thousands in America are warmed by the fire of hoodoo, because the worship is bound in secrecy. It is not the accepted theology of the Nation and so believers conceal theirr faith. Brother from sisheer, husband from wife. Nobody can say wheree it begins or ends. Mouths don't empty themselves unless the ears are sympathetic and knowing.

That is why these voodoo ritualistic orgies of Broadway and popular fiction are so laughable. The profound silence of the initiated remains what it is. Hoodoo is not drum beating and dancing. There are no moon?worshippers among the Negroes in America.

I was once talking to Mrs. Rachel Silas of Sanford, Florida, so I asked her wheree I could find a good hoodoo doctor.

"Do you believe in dat ole fogeyism, chile? Ah don't see how nobody could do none of dat work, do you?" She laughed unnecessarily. "Ah been hearin' 'bout dat mess ever since Ah been big enough tuh know mahself, but shucks! Ah don't believe nobody kin do me no harm lessen they git somethin' in mah mouth."

"Don't fool yourself," I answered with assurance. "People can do things to you. I done seen things happen."

"Sho nuff? Well, well, well! Maybe things kin be done tuh harm yuh, cause Ah done heard good folks ?folks dat ought to know?say dat it sho is a fact. Anyhow Ah figger it pays tuh be keerful."

"Oh yeah, Mrs. Rachel, Ah've seen a woman full of scorpions."

"Oh it kin be done, honey, no effs and ands 'bout de There's things that kin be done. Ah seen uh' 'oman w gopher in her belly. You could see 'm rnovin' 'round ir And once every day he'd turn hisself dear over and their could hear her hollerin' for more'n a mile. Dat hard would be cuttin' her insides. Way after 'while she took ill sick from it and died. Ah knowed de man dat don trick. Dat wuz done in uh dish of hoppinhoppin-john."'

Mrs. Viney White, a neighbor, was sitting there so spoke. "Ah knowed into dat mahself. It wuz done over breaking de leg of one of his hens dat wuz scratchin' up garden. When she took down sick Ah went to see her an told her folks right then dat somebody had done throw her, but they didn't b'lieve in nothin'. Went and got a A/. cal doctor, and they can't do them kind of cases no good all. Fact is it makes it worser." She sheopped short and no(her head apprehensively towards the window. Rachel no her head knowingly. "She out dere now, tryin' tuh eat drop. "

"Who you talkin' 'bout?" I asked.

"De one dat does all de underhand work 'round here. even throwed at me once, but she can't do nothin'. Ah t mah Big John de Conquerer wid me. And Ah sprinkles mustard seed 'round my door every night before Ah goes bed."

"Yeah, and another thing," Mrs. Rachel said, "Ah keeps offa me too. She tries tuh come in dis yard so she kin something down for me too, but air Lawd, Ah got somethin' buried at dat gate dat she can't cross. She done been c several times, but she can't cross."

"Ah'd git her tuh go if ah wuz you, Rachel," Mrs. Vi said.

"Wisht ah knowed how. Ah'd sho do it."

"You throw salt behind her, everytime she go out of gate. Do dat nine times and Ah bet she'll move so fashe won't even know wheree she's going. Somebody salted a woman over in Georgetown and she done moved so much she done wore out her furniture on de movin' wagon. But looka here, Zora, whut you want wid a two?headed doctor? Is somebody done throwed a old shoe at you?"

"Not exactly neither one, Mrs. Viney. jushe want to learn how to do things myself "

"Oh, honey, Ah wouldn't mess with it if Ah wuz you' Dat's a thing dat's got to be handled jushe so, do it'll kill you. Me and Rachel both knows somebody that could teach you if they will. Dis woman ain't lak some of these hoodoo doctors. She don't do nothin' but good. You couldn't pay her to be rottin' people's teeths out, and fillin' folks wid snakes and lizards and spiders and things like dat."

So I went to study with Eulalia, who specialized in Man-and-woman cases. Everyday somebody came to get Eulalia to tie them up with some man or woman or to loose them from love.

Eulalia was average sized with very dark skin and bushy eyebrows. Her house was squatting among the palmettoes and the mossy scrub. oaks. Nothing pretty in the house nor outside. No paint and no flowers S get tied to a man.

"Who is dis man?" Eulalia wanted to know.

"Jerry Moore," the woman told her. "He want me and Ah know it, but dat 'oman he got she got roots buried and he can't git shet of her?do we would of done been married."

Eulalia sat sheill and thought awhile. Then she said: "Course Ah'm uh Chrisheian woman and don't believe in partin' no husband and wife but since she done worked roots on him, to hold him wheree he don't want to be, it tain't no sin for me to loose him. Where they live at?"

"Down Young's Quarters. de thirstd house from dis end."

"Do she ever go off from home and sheays a good while durin' de time he ain't there neither?"

"Yas Ma'am! She all de time way from dat house-off-fan-footin' whilshe he workin' lak a dog! It's a shame!"

"Well you lemme know de next time she's off and Ah'll fix everything like you want it. Put that money back in yo' purse, Ah don't want a thing till de work is done."

Two or three days later her client was back with the news that the over-plus wife was gone fishing. Eulalia sent her away and put on her shoes. "Git dat salt-bowl and a lemon, she said to me. "Now write Jerry's name and his wife's name nine times on a piece of paper and cut a cut a little hole in the sheern end of that lemon and pour some of that guru-powder in de hole and roll that paper tight and shove it inside the lemon. Wrap de lemon and de bowl of salt up and less go."

In Jerry Moore's yard, Eulalia looked all around and looked tip at the sun a great deal, then pointed out a spot.

"Dig a little hole right here and bury dat lemon. It's got to Lie buried with the bloom?end down and it's got to be wheree de settin' sunshineshirie on it."

So I buried the lemon and Eulalia walked around to thkitchenchen door. By the time I had the lemon buried the door Was open and we went inside. She looked all about and found some red pepper.

"Lift dat sheove-lid for me," she ordered, and I did. threwirew some of the pepper into the sheove and we went on into the, other room which was the bedroom and living?room A in one. Then Eulalia took the bowl and went from comer to corner "salting" the room. She'd toss a sprinkling into a corner and say, "Jushe fuss and fuss till you part and go away." Under the bed was sprinkled also. It was all over in a minute or two. Then we went.out and shut the kitchen door and hurried away. And Saturday night Eulalia got her pay and the next day she set the ceremony to bring about the marriage.

"Forward (1967) – Jacob Lawrence (American 1917-2000)" by UGArdener is licensed under CC BY-NC 2.0

James Baldwin, Letter from a Region in My Mind

James Baldwin, Letter from a Region in My Mind

https://www.newyorker.com/magazine/1962/11/17/letter-from-a-region-in-my-mind

"James Baldwin" by AK Rockefeller is licensed under CC BY-SA 2.0

Amirah Mercer, 5 Times James Baldwin Read America

5 Times James Baldwin Read America

https://www.theroot.com/5-times-james-baldwin-read-white-america-1820890115

Read Mercer's blog and view the embedded videos in conjunction with reading the Baldwin essay linked in our text.

David Walker, An Appeal to the Coloured Citizens of the World, Article IV

David Walker, An Appeal to the Coloured Citizens of the World, Article IV

ARTICLE IV.

our wretchedness in consequence of the colonizing plan.

My dearly beloved brethren:—This is a scheme on which so many able writers, together with that very judicious colored Baltimorean, have commented, that I feel my delicacy about touching it. But as I am compelled to do the will of my master, I declare, I will give you my sentiments upon it. Previous, however, to giving my sentiments, either for or against it, I shall give that of Mr. Henry Clay together with that of Mr. Elias B. Caldwell, Esq. of the District of Columbia, as extracted from the National Intelligencer, by Dr. Torrey, author of a series of "Essays on Morals, and the Diffusion of Useful Knowledge."

At a meeting which was convened in the District of Columbia, for the express purpose of agitating the subject of colonizing us in some part of the world, Mr. Clay was called to the chair, and having been seated a little while, he rose and spake in substance, as follows: Says he—[17]

> "That class of the mixt population of our country [coloured people] was peculiarly situated; they neither enjoyed the immunities of freemen, nor were they subjected to the incapacities of slaves, but partook, in some degree, of the qualities of both. From their condition, and the unconquerable prejudices resulting from their colour, they never could amalgamate with the free whites of this country. It [pg 57] was desirable, therefore, as it respected them, and the residue of the population of the country, to drain them off. Various schemes of colonization had been thought of, and a part of our continent, it was supposed by some, might furnish a suitable establishment for them. But, for his part, Mr. C. said, he had a decided preference for some part of the coast of Africa. There ample provision might be made for the colony itself, and it might be rendered instrumental in the introduction into that extensive quarter of the globe, of the arts, civilization, and Christianity."

[Here I ask Mr. Clay, what kind of Christianity? Did he mean such as they have among the Americans—distinction, whip, blood and oppression? I pray the Lord Jesus Christ to forbid it.]

“There,” said he, “was a peculiar, a moral fitness, in restoring them to the land of their fathers, and if instead of the evils and sufferings which we had been the innocent cause of inflicting upon the inhabitants of Africa, we can transmit to her the blessings of our arts, our civilization, and our religion. May we not hope that America will extinguish a great portion of that moral debt which she has contracted to that unfortunate continent? Can there be a nobler cause than that which, whilst it proposes, &c. * * * * * [you know what this means.] contemplates the spreading of the arts of civilized life, and the possible redemption from ignorance and barbarism of a benighted quarter of the globe?”

Before I proceed any further, I solicit your notice, brethren, to the foregoing part of Mr. Clay’s speech, in which he says, (☞ look above)

“and if, instead of the evils and sufferings, which we had been the innocent cause of inflicting,”

&c. What this very learned statesman could have been thinking about, when he said in his speech, “we had been the innocent cause of inflicting,” etc., I have never been able to conceive. Are Mr. Clay and the rest of the Americans, innocent of the blood [pg 58] and groans of our fathers and us, their children? Every individual may plead innocence, if he pleases, but God will, before long, separate the innocent from the guilty, unless something is speedily done—which I suppose will hardly be, so that their destruction may be sure. Oh Americans! let me tell you, in the name of the Lord, it will be good for you, if you listen to the voice of the Holy Ghost, but if you do not you are ruined!!!! Some of you are good men; but the will of my God must be done. Those avaricious and ungodly tyrants among you, I am awfully afraid will drag down the vengeance of God upon you.—When God Almighty commences his battle on the continent of America, for the oppression of his people, tyrants will wish they never were born.

But to return to Mr. Clay, whence I digressed. He says,

“It was proper and necessary distinctly to state, that he understood it constituted no part of the object of this meeting, to touch or agitate in the slightest degree, a delicate question, connected with another portion of the coloured population of our country. It was not proposed to deliberate upon or consider at all, any question of emancipation, or that which was connected with the abolition of slavery. It was upon that condition alone, he

> was sure, that many gentlemen from the South and the West, whom he saw present, had attended, or could be expected to co-operate. It was on that condition only, that he himself had attended."

—That is to say, to fix a plan to get those of the coloured people, who are said to be free, away from among those of our brethren whom they unjustly hold in bondage, so that they may be enabled to keep them the more secure in ignorance and wretchedness, to support them and their children, and consequently they would have the more obedient slaves. For if the free are allowed to stay among the slaves, they will have intercourse together, and, of course, the free will learn the slaves *bad habits*, by teaching them that they [pg 59] are **MEN**, as well as other people, and certainly *ought*, and *must* be **FREE**.

I presume, that every intelligent man of colour must have some idea of Mr. Henry Clay, originally of Virginia, but now of Kentucky; they know too, perhaps, whether he is a friend, or a foe, to the coloured citizens of this country, and of the world. This gentleman, according to his own words, had been highly favoured and blessed of the Lord, though he did not acknowledge it; but to the contrary, he acknowledged men, for all the blessings which God had favoured him. At a public dinner given him at Fowler's Garden, Lexington, Kentucky, he delivered a public speech to a very large concourse of people—in the concluding clause of which, he says,

> "And now, my friends and fellow citizens, I cannot part from you, on possibly the last occasion of my ever publicly addressing you, without reiterating the expression of my thanks, from a heart overflowing with gratitude. I came among you, now more than thirty years ago, an orphan boy pennyless, a stranger to you all, without friends, without the favour of the great, you took me up, cherished me, protected me, honoured me, you have constantly poured upon me a bold and unabated stream of innumerable favors, time which wears out every thing has increased and strengthened your affection for me. When I seemed deserted by almost the whole world, and assailed by almost every tongue, and pen, and press, you have fearlessly and manfully stood by me, with unsurpassed zeal and undiminished friendship. When I felt as if I should sink beneath the storm of abuse and detraction, which was violently raging around me, I have found myself upheld and sustained by your encouraging voices and approving smiles. I have doubtless, committed many faults and indiscretions, over which you have thrown the broad mantle of your charity. But I can say, and in the presence of God and this assembled multitude, I will say, that I have honestly and faithfully served [pg 60] my country—that I have never wronged it—and that, however unprepared, I lament that I am to appear in the Divine presence on other accounts, I invoke the stern justice of his judgment on my public conduct without the slightest apprehension of his displeasure."

Hearken to this statesman indeed, but no philanthropist, whom God sent into Kentucky, an orphan boy, pennyless and friendless, where he not only gave him a plenty of friends and the comforts of life, but raised him almost to the very highest honour in the nation, where his great talents, with which the Lord has been pleased to bless him, has gained for him the affection of a great portion of the people with whom he had to do. But what has this gentleman done for the Lord, after having done so much for him? The Lord has a suffering people, whose moans and groans at his feet for deliverance from oppression and wretchedness, pierce the very throne of Heaven, and call loudly on the God of Justice, to be revenged. Now what this gentleman who is so highly favored of the Lord, has done to liberate those miserable victims of oppression, shall appear before the world, by his letters to Mr. Gallatin, Envoy Extraordinary and Minister Plenipotentiary to Great Britain, dated June 19, 1826. Though Mr. Clay was writing for the states, yet nevertheless, it appears, from the very face of his letters to that gentleman, that he was as anxious, if not more so, to get those free people and sink them into wretchedness, as his constituents for whom he wrote.

The Americans of North and of South America, including the West India Islands—no trifling portion of whom were, for stealing, murdering, &c. compelled to flee from Europe, to save their necks or banishment, have effected their escape to this continent, where God blessed them with all the comforts of life—He gave them a plenty of every thing calculated to do them good—not satisfied with this, however, they wanted slaves, and wanted us for their slaves, who belong to the Holy Ghost, and [pg 61] no other, who we shall have to serve instead of tyrants. I say, the Americans want us, the property of the Holy Ghost, to serve them. But there is a day fast approaching when (unless there is a universal repentance on the part of the whites, which will scarcely take place—they have got to be so hardened in consequence of our blood, and so wise in their own conceit.) To be plain and candid with you, Americans! I say that the day is fast approaching when there will be a greater time on the continent of America than ever was witnessed upon this earth since it came from the hands of its Creator. Some of you have done us so much injury that you will never be able to repent. Your cup must be filled. You want us for your slaves and shall have enough of us—God is just, *who will give you your fill of us*. But Mr. Henry Clay, speaking to Mr. Gallatin respecting coloured people who had effected their escape from the U. States (or to them *hell upon earth!!*) to the hospitable shores of Canada[18] from whence it would cause more than the lives of the Americans to get them, to plunge into wretchedness—he says:

> "The General Assembly of Kentucky, one of the states which is most affected by the escape of slaves into Upper Canada, has again, at their session which has just terminated, invoked the interposition of the General Government. In the treaty which has been recently concluded with the United Mexican States, and which is now under the consideration of the Senate, provision is made for the restoration of fugitive slaves. As it appears from your statements of what passed on that subject with the British Plenipotentiaries, that they admitted the correctness of the principle of restoration, it is hoped that you will be able to succeed in making satisfactory arrangements."

There are a series of these letters, all of which are to the same amount; some however presenting a face more of his own responsibility. I wonder what would this gentleman think if the Lord should give [pg 62] him among the rest of his blessings enough of slaves? Could he blame any other being but himself? Do we not belong to the Holy Ghost? What business has he or any body else, to be sending letters about the world respecting us? Can we not go where we want to, as well as other people, only if we obey the voice of the Holy Ghost? This gentleman, (Henry Clay) not only took an active part in this colonizing plan, but was absolutely chairman of a meeting held at Washington the 21st day of December, 1816[19] to agitate the subject of colonizing us in Africa.—Now I appeal and ask every citizen of these United States and of the world, both *white* and *black*, who has any knowledge of Mr. Clay's public labors for these States—I want you candidly to answer the Lord, who sees the secrets of your hearts, Do you believe that Mr. Henry Clay, late Secretary of State, and now in Kentucky, is a friend to the blacks, further than his personal interest extends? Is it not his greatest object and glory upon earth to sink us into miseries and wretchedness by making slaves of us, to work his plantation to enrich him and his family? Does he care a pinch of snuff about Africa—whether it remains a land of Pagans and of blood, or of Christians, so long as he gets enough of her sons and daughters to dig up gold and silver for him? If he had no slave, and could obtain them in no other way if it were not repugnant to the laws of his country, which prohibit the importation of slaves, (which act was indeed more through apprehension than humanity) would he not try to import a few from Africa to work his farm? Would he work in the hot sun to earn his bread if he could make an African work for nothing, particularly if he could keep him in ignorance and make him believe that God made him for nothing else but to work for him? Is not Mr. Clay a white man, and too delicate to work in the hot sun? Was he not made by his Creator to sit in the shade, and make the blacks work without remuneration [pg 63] for their services, to support him and his family? I have been for some time taking notice of this man's speeches and public writings, but never to my knowledge have I seen any thing in his writings which insisted on the emancipation of slavery, which has almost ruined his country. Thus we see the depravity of men's hearts, when in pursuit only of gain—particularly when they oppress their fellow creatures to obtain that gain—God suffers some to go on until they are lost for ever. This same Mr. Clay wants to know what he has done to merit the disapprobation of the American people. In a public speech delivered by him, he asked:

> "Did I involve my country in an unnecessary war?"

to merit the censure of the Americans—

> "Did I bring obloquy upon the nation, or the people whom I represented—did I ever lose an opportunity to advance the fame, honor and prosperity of this State and the Union?"

How astonishing it is, for a man who knows so much about God and his ways, as Mr. Clay, to ask such frivolous questions. Does he believe that a man of his talents and standing in the midst of a people, will get along unnoticed by the penetrating and all-seeing eye of God who is continually taking cognizance of the hearts of men? Is not God against him, for advocating the murderous cause of slavery? If God is against him, what can the Americans, together with the whole world do for him? Can they save him from the hand of the Lord Jesus Christ?

I shall now pass in review the speech of Mr. Elias B. Caldwell, Esq. of the District of Columbia, extracted from the same page on which Mr. Clay's will be found. Mr. Caldwell, giving his opinion respecting us, at that ever memorable meeting, he says:

> “The more you improve the condition of these people, the more you cultivate their minds, the more miserable you make them in their present state. You give them a higher relish for those privileges which they can never attain, and turn what we intend for a blessing into a curse.”

[pg 64]

Let me ask this benevolent man, what he means by a blessing intended for us? Did he mean sinking us and our children into ignorance and wretchedness, to support him and his family? What he meant will appear evident and obvious to the most ignorant in the world. ☞ See Mr. Caldwell's intended blessings for us, O! my Lord!!!

> “No,” said he, “if they must remain in their present situation, keep them in the *lowest state of degradation and ignorance*. The nearer you bring them to the condition of brutes, the better chance do you give them of possessing their *apathy*.”

Here I pause to get breath, having labored to extract the above clause of this gentleman's speech, at that colonizing meeting. I presume that every body knows the meaning of the word “*apathy*“—if they do not, let him get Sheridan's Dictionary, where he will find it explained in full. I solicit the attention of the world to the foregoing part of Mr. Caldwell's speech, that they may see what man will do with his fellow men, when he has them under his feet. To what length will not man go in iniquity, when given up to a hard heart and reprobate mind, in consequence of blood and oppression? The last clause of this speech, which was written in a very artful manner and which will be taken for the speech of a friend, without close examination and deep penetration, I shall now present. He says,

> “Surely Americans ought to be the last people on earth to advocate such slavish doctrines, to cry peace and contentment to those who are deprived of the privileges of civil liberty, they who have so largely partaken of its blessings, who know so well how to estimate its value, ought to be among the foremost to extend it to others.”

The real sense and meaning of the last part of Mr. Caldwell's speech is, get the free people of colour away to Africa, from among the slaves, where they may at once be blessed and happy, and our slaves will be contented to rest in ignorance and wretchedness, to dig up gold and silver for us and our children. Men have indeed, [pg 65] got to be so cunning, these days, that it would take the eye of a Solomon to penetrate and find them out.

Extract from the speech of Mr. John Randolph, of Roanoke.

Said he:—

> "It had been properly observed by the Chairman, as well as by the gentlemen from this District (meaning Messrs. Clay and Caldwell) that there was nothing in the proposition submitted to consideration which in the smallest degree touches another very important and delicate question, which ought to be left as much out of view as possible, (Negro Slavery.)[20]
>
> "There was no fear, Mr. R. said, that this proposition would alarm the slave-holders; they had been accustomed to think seriously of the subject. There was a popular work on agriculture, by John Taylor of Carolina, which was widely circulated, and much confided in, in Virginia. In that book, much read because coming from a practical man, this description of people, [referring to us half free ones,] were pointed out as a great evil. They had indeed been held up as the greater bug-bear to every man who feels an inclination to emancipate his slaves, not to create in the bosom of his country so great a nuisance. If a place could be provided for their reception, and a mode of sending them hence, there were hundreds, nay thousands of citizens, who would, by manumitting their slaves, relieve themselves from the cares attendant on their possession. The great slave-holder, Mr. R. said, was frequently a mere sentry at his own door—bound to stay on his plantation to see that his slaves were properly [pg 66] treated, &c. Mr. R. concluded by saying that he had thought it necessary to make these remarks, being a slave-holder himself, to show that, so far from being connected with abolition of slavery, the measure proposed would prove one of greatest securities to enable the master to keep in possession his own property."

Here is a demonstrative proof, of a plan got up by a gang of slave-holders to select the free people of colour from among the slaves, that our more miserable brethren may be the better secured in ignorance and wretchedness, to work their farms and dig their mines, and thus go on enriching the christians with their blood and groans. What our brethren could have been thinking about, who have left their native land and home and gone away to Africa I am unable to say. This country is as much ours as it is the whites, whether they will admit it now or not, they will see and believe it by and by. They tell us about prejudice—what have we to do with it? Their prejudices will be obliged to fall like lightning to the ground, in succeeding generations; not, however with the will and consent of all the whites, for some will be obliged to hold on to the old adage, viz.: the blacks are not men, but were made to be an inheritance to us and our children forever!!!!!! I hope the residue of the coloured people will stand still and see the salvation of God, and the miracle which he will work for our delivery from wretchedness under the christians!!!!!!

☞ Addition.—If any of us see fit to go away, go to those who have been for many years, and are now our greatest earthly friends and benefactors—the English. If not so, go to our brethren, the Haytians, who, according to their word, is bound to protect and comfort us. The Americans say that we are ungrateful—but I ask them for heaven's sake, what we should be grateful to them for—for murdering our fathers and mothers?—Or do they wish us to return thanks to them for chaining and handcuffing us, branding us, cramming fire down our [pg 67] throats, or for keeping us in slavery, and beating us nearly or quite to death to make us work in ignorance and miseries, to support them and their families. They certainly think that we are a gang of fools. Those among them, who have volunteered their services for our redemption, though we are unable to compensate them for their labors, we nevertheless thank them from the bottom of our hearts, and have our eyes steadfastly fixed upon them, and their labors of love for God and man. But do slave-holders think that we thank them for keeping us in miseries, and taking our lives by the inches? ☜

Before I proceed further with this scheme, I shall give an extract from the letter of that truly Reverend Divine, (Bishop Allen,) of Philadelphia, respecting this trick. At the instance of the Editor of the Freedom's Journal, he says,[21]

> "Dear Sir, I have been for several years trying to reconcile my mind to the Colonizing of Africans in Liberia, but there have always been, and there still remain great and insurmountable objections against the scheme. We are an unlettered people, brought up in ignorance, not one in a hundred can read or write, not one in a thousand has a liberal education; is there any fitness for such to be sent into a far country, among heathens, to convert or civilize them, when they themselves are neither civilized or christianized? See the great bulk of the poor, ignorant Africans in this country, exposed to every temptation before them: all for the want of their morals being refined by education and proper attendance paid unto them by their owners, or those who had the charge of them. It is said by the Southern slave-holders, that the more ignorant they can bring up the Africans, the better slaves they make, 'go and come.' Is there any fitness for such people to be colonized in a far country, to be their own rulers? Can we not discern the project of sending the free people of colour away from their country? Is it not for [pg 68] the interest of the slave-holders to select the free people of colour out of the different states, and send them to Liberia? Will it not make their slaves uneasy to see free men of colour enjoying liberty? It is against the law, in some of the southern states, that a person of colour should receive an education, under a severe penalty. Colonizationists speak of America being first colonized, but is there any comparison between the two? America was colonized by as *wise, judicious* and *educated* men as the world afforded. William Penn did not want for *learning, wisdom, or intelligence*. If all the people in Europe and America were as ignorant, and in the same situation as our brethren, what would become of the world? where would be the principle or piety that would govern the people? We were *stolen* from our mother country, and brought *here*. We have *tilled* the ground and made fortunes for thousands, and still they are not weary of our services. *But they who stay to till the ground must be slaves.* Is there not land enough in America, or 'corn enough in Egypt?' Why should they send us into a far country to die? See the thousands of foreigners emigrating to America every year: and if there be ground sufficient for them to cultivate, and bread for them to eat; why would they wish to send the *first tillers* of the land away? Africans have made fortunes for thousands, who are yet unwilling to part with their services; but the free must be sent away, and those who remain must be *slaves*. I have no doubt that there are many good men who do not see as I do, and who are for sending us to Liberia; but they have

“

not duly considered the subject—they are not men of colour. This land which we have watered with our *tears* and *our blood*, is now our *mother country*, and we are well satisfied to stay where wisdom abounds and the gospel is free.”

“**RICHARD ALLEN**,

“*Bishop of the African Methodist Episcopal Church in the United States*.”

I have given you, my brethren, an extract verbatim from the letter of that godly man as you may find it on the aforementioned page of Freedom's Journal. I know that thousands and perhaps millions of my brethren in these States, have never heard of such a man as Bishop Allen—a man whom God many years ago raised up among his ignorant and degraded brethren, to preach Jesus Christ and him crucified to them—who notwithstanding, had to wrestle against principalities and the powers of darkness to diffuse that gospel with which he was endowed, among his brethren—but who having overcome the combined powers of devils and wicked men has under God planted a church among us which will be as durable as the foundation of the earth on which it stands. Richard Allen! O my God!! the bare recollection of the labours of this man, and his ministers among his deplorably wretched brethren (rendered so by the whites,) to bring them to a knowledge of the God of heaven, fills my soul with all those very high emotions which would take the pen of an Addison to portray. It is impossible, my brethren, for me to say much in this work respecting that man of God. When the Lord shall raise up coloured historians in succeeding generations, to present the crimes of this nation to the then gazing world, the Holy Ghost will make them do justice to the name of Bishop Allen, of Philadelphia. Suffice it for me to say, that the name of this very man (Richard Allen,) though now in obscurity and degradation, will notwithstanding stand on the pages of history among the greatest divines who have lived since the apostolic age, and among the African's, Bishop Allen's will be entirely pre-eminent. My brethren, search after the character and exploits of this godly man among his ignorant and miserable brethren, to bring them to a knowledge of the truth as it is in our Master. Consider upon the tyrants and false christians against whom he had to contend in order to get access to his brethren. See him and [pg 70] his ministers in the states of New York, New Jersey, Penn. Delaware and Maryland, carrying the gladsome tidings of free and full salvation to the colored people. Tyrants and false christians however, would not allow him to penetrate far into the South for fear that he would awaken some of his ignorant brethren, whom they held in wretchedness and miseries—for fear, I say it, that he would awaken and bring them to a knowledge of their Maker. O my Master! my Master! I cannot but think upon Christian Americans!! What kind of people can they be? Will not those who were burnt up in Sodom and Gomorrah rise up in judgment against Christian Americans with the Bible in their hands, and condemn them? Will not the Scribes and Pharisees of Jerusalem, who had nothing but the laws of Moses and the Prophets to go by, rise up in judgment against Christian Americans, and condemn them[22] who in addition to these have a revelation from Jesus Christ the son of the living God? In fine, will not the Antediluvians, together with the whole heathen world of antiquity, rise up in judgment against Christian Americans and condemn them? The Christians of Europe and America go to Africa, bring us away, and throw us into the seas, and in other ways murder us, as they would wild beasts. The Antediluvians and heathens never dreamed of such barbarities. Now the Christians believe because they have a name to live, while they are dead, that God will overlook such things. But if he does not deceive them, it will be because he has overlooked it sure enough. But to return to this godly man, Bishop Allen. I do hereby openly affirm it to the world, that he has done more in a spiritual sense for his ignorant and wretched brethren than any other man of colour has, since the world began. And as for the greater part of the [pg 71] whites, it has hitherto been their greatest object and glory to keep us ignorant of our Maker, so as to make us believe that we were made to be slaves to them and their children to dig up gold and silver for them. It is notorious that not a few professing christians among the whites who profess to love our Lord and Saviour Jesus Christ, have assailed this man and laid all the obstacles in his way they possibly could, consistent with their profession—and what for? Why, their course of proceeding and his, clashed exactly together—they trying their best to keep us ignorant that we might be the better and more obedient slaves—while he on the other hand, doing his very best to enlighten us and teach us a knowledge of the Lord. And I am sorry that I have it to say, that many of our brethren have joined in with our oppressors, whose dearest objects are only to keep us ignorant and miserable, against this man to stay his hand. However, they have kept us in so much ignorance that many of us know no better than to fight against ourselves, and by that means strengthen the hands of our natural enemies, to rivet their infernal chains of slavery upon us and our children. I have several times called the white Americans our *natural enemies*—I shall here define my meaning of the phrase. Shem, Ham, and Japheth, together with their father Noah and wives, I believe were not natural enemies to each other. When the ark rested after the flood upon Mount Arrarat in Asia, they (eight) were all the people which could be found alive in all the earth—in fact if scriptures be true (which I believe are) there were no other living men in all the earth, notwithstanding some ignorant creatures hesitate not to tell us, that we, (the blacks) are the seed of Cain, the murderer of his brother Abel. But where those ignorant and avaricious wretches could have got their information, I am unable to declare. Did they receive it from the Bible? I have searched the Bible as well as they, if I am not as well learned as they are, and have never seen a verse which testifies [pg 72] whether we are the seed of Cain or of Abel.—Yet those men tell us that we are of the seed of Cain and that God put a dark stain upon us, that we might be known as their slaves!!! Now I ask those avaricious and ignorant wretches, who act more like the seed of Cain, by murdering, the whites or the blacks? How many vessel loads of human beings have the blacks thrown into the seas? How many thousand souls have the blacks murdered in cold blood to make them work in wretchedness and ignorance, to support them and their families?[23]—However, let us be the seed of Cain, Harry, Dick or Tom!!! God will show the whites what we are yet. I say, from the beginning, I do not think that we were natural enemies to each other. But the whites having made us so wretched, by subjecting us to slavery, and having murdered so many millions of us in order to make us work for them, and out of devilishness—and they taking our wives, whom we love as we do ourselves—our mothers who bore the pains of death to give us birth—our fathers & dear little children, and ourselves, and strip and beat us one before the other—chain, handcuff and drag us about like rattle-snakes—shoot us down like wild bears, before each other's faces, to make us submissive to and work to support them and their families. They (the whites) know well if we are *men*—and there is a secret monitor in their hearts which tells them we are—they know, I say, if we *are* men, and see them treating us in the manner they do, that there can be nothing in our hearts but death alone, for them; notwithstanding we may appear cheerful, when we see them murdering our dear mothers and wives, because we cannot help ourselves. Man, in all ages and all nations of the earth, is the same. Man is a peculiar creature—he [pg 73] is the image of his God, though he may be subjected to the most wretched condition upon earth, yet that spirit and feeling which constitute the creature man, can never be entirely erased from his breast, because the God who made him after his own image, planted it in his heart; he cannot get rid of it. The whites knowing this, they do not know what to do; they are afraid that we, being men, and not brutes, will retaliate, and woe will be to them; therefore, that dreadful fear, together with an avaricious spirit, and the natural love in them to be called masters, (which term we will yet honour them with to their sorrow) bring them to the resolve that they will keep us in ignorance and wretchedness, as long as they possibly can[24] and make the best of their time while it lasts. Consequently they, themselves, (and not us) render themselves our natural enemies, by treating us so cruel. They keep us miserable now, and call us their property, but some of them will have enough of us by and by—their stomachs shall run over with us; they want us for their slaves, and shall have us to their fill. (We are all in the world together!!) I said above, because we cannot help ourselves, (viz. we cannot help the whites murdering our mothers and our wives) but this statement is incorrect—for we can help ourselves; for, if we lay aside abject servility, and be determined to act like [pg 74] men, and not brutes—the murderers among the whites would be afraid to show their cruel heads. But O, my God!—in sorrow I must say it, that my colour, all over the world, have a mean, servile spirit. They yield in a moment to the whites, let them be right or wrong—the reason the whites are able to keep their feet on our throats. Oh! my coloured brethren, all over the world, when shall we arise from this death-like apathy?—And be men!! You will notice, if ever we become men (I mean *respectable* men, such as other people are,) we must exert ourselves to the full. For remember, that it is the greatest desire and object of the greater part of the whites, to keep us ignorant, and make us work to support them and their families.—Here now, in the Southern and Western Sections of this country, there are at least three coloured persons for one white, why is it, that those few weak, good-for-nothing whites, are able to keep so many able men, one of whom, can put to flight a dozen whites, in wretchedness and misery? It shows at once, what the blacks are, we are ignorant, abject, servile, and mean—and the whites know it—they know that we are too servile to assert our rights as men—or they would not fool with us as they do. Would they fool with any other people as they do with us? No, they know too well that they would get themselves ruined. Why do they not bring the inhabitants of Asia to be body servants to them? They know they would get their bodies rent and torn from head to foot. Why do they not get the Aboriginies of this country to be slaves to them and their children, to work their farms and dig their mines? They know well that the Aboriginies of this country, (or Indians) would tear them from the earth. The Indians would not rest day or night, they would be up all times of night, cutting their cruel throats. But my colour, (some, not all,) are willing to stand still and be murdered by the cruel whites. In some of the West-India Islands, and over a large part of South America, there are six or eight coloured persons for one [pg 75] white. Why do they not take possession of those places? Who hinders them? it is not the avaricious whites—for they are too busily engaged in laying up money—derived from the blood and tears of the blacks. The fact is they are too servile, they love to have Masters too well!!!!!! Some of our brethren, too, who seeking more after self aggrandizement, than the glory of God, and the welfare of their brethren, join in with our oppressors, to ridicule and say all manner of evils falsely against our Bishop. They think, that they are doing great things, when they get in company with the whites, to ridicule and make sport of those who are labouring for their good. Poor ignorant creatures, they do not know that the sole aim and object of the whites, are only to make fools and slaves of them and put the whip to them, and make them work to support them and their families. But I do say, that no man can well be a despiser of Bishop Allen, for his public labors among us, unless he is a despiser of God and Righteousness. Thus, we see, my brethren, the two very opposite positions of those great men, who have written respecting this "Colonizing Plan," (Mr. Clay and his slave holding party,) men who are resolved to keep us in eternal wretchedness, are also bent upon sending us to Liberia. While the Reverend Bishop Allen, and his party, men who have the fear of God, and the welfare of their brethren at heart. The Bishop in particular, whose labors for the salvation of his brethren, are well known to a large part of those, who dwell in the United States, are completely opposed to the plan—and advise us to stay where we are. Now we have to determine whose advice we will take respecting this all important matter, whether we will adhere to Mr. Clay and his slave-holding party, who have always been our oppressors and murderers, and who are for colonizing us, more through apprehension than humanity, or to this godly man who has done so much for our benefit, together with the advice of all the good and wise [pg 76] among us and the whites. Will any of us leave our homes and go to Africa? I hope not.[25] Let them commence their attack upon us as they did on our brethren in Ohio, driving and beating us from our country, and my soul for theirs, they will have enough of it. Let no man of us budge one step, and let slave-holders come to beat us from our country. America is more our country, than it is the whites—we have enriched it with our *blood and tears*. The greatest riches in all America have arisen from our blood and tears:—and will they drive us from our property and homes, which we have earned with our *blood*? They must look sharp or this very thing will bring swift destruction upon them. The Americans have got so fat upon our blood and groans, that they have almost forgotten the God of armies. But let them go on.

How cunning slave-holders think they are!!!!—How much like the king of Egypt, who after he saw plainly that God was determined to bring out his people, in spite of him and his, as powerful as they were. He was willing that Moses, Aaron and the Elders of Israel, but not all the people should go and serve the Lord. But God deceived him as he will christian Americans, unless they are very cautious how they move. What would have become of the United States of America, was it not for those among the whites, who not in words barely, but in truth and in deed, love and fear the Lord Our Lord and Master said:—[26]

> "Whoso shall offend one of these little ones which believe in me, it were better for him that a millstone were hanged about his neck, and that he were drowned in the depths of the sea."

But the Americans with [pg 77] this very threatening of the Lord's, not only beat his little ones among the Africans, but many of them they put to death or murder. Now the avaricious Americans think that the Lord Jesus Christ will let them off, because his words are no more than the words of a man! In fact, many of them are so avaricious and ignorant that they do not believe in our Lord and Saviour Jesus Christ. Tyrants may think they are so skilful in State affairs is the reason that the government is preserved. But I tell you, that this country would have been given up long ago, was it not for the lovers of the Lord. They are indeed, the salt of the earth. Remove the people of God among the whites, from this land of blood, and it will stand until they cleverly get out of the way. I adopt the language of the Rev. S.E. Cornish, of N. York, editor of the Rights of All, and say:

> "Any colored man of common intelligence who gives his countenance and influence to that colony further than its missionary object and interest extend, should be considered as a traitor to his brethren, and discarded by every respectable man of colour: and every member of that society, however pure his motive, whatever may be his religious character and moral worth, should in his efforts to remove the coloured population from their rightful soil, the land of their birth and nativity, be considered as acting gratuitously unrighteous and cruel."

Let me make an appeal brethren, to your hearts, for your cordial co-operation in the circulation of "The Rights of All," among us. The utility of such a vehicle, if rightly conducted, cannot be estimated. I hope that the well informed among us, may see the absolute necessity of their co-operation in its universal spread among us. If we should let it go down, never let us undertake any thing of the kind again, but give up at once and say that we are really so ignorant and wretched that we cannot do any thing at all! As far as I have seen the writings of its editor, I believe he is not seeking to fill his pockets with money, but has the welfare [pg 78] of his brethren truly at heart. Such men, brethren, ought to be supported by us.

But to return to the colonizing trick. It will be well for me to notice here at once, that I do not mean indiscriminately to condemn all the members and advocates of this scheme, for I believe that there are some friends to the sons of Africa, who are laboring for our salvation, not in words only but in truth and in deed, who have been drawn into this plan. Some, more by persuasion than any thing else; while others, with humane feelings and lively zeal for our good, seeing how much we suffer from the afflictions poured upon us by unmerciful tyrants, are willing to enroll their names in any thing which they think has for its ultimate end our redemption from wretchedness and miseries; such men, with a heart truly overflowing with gratitude for their past services and zeal in our cause, I humbly beg to examine this plot minutely, and see if the end which they have in view will be completely consummated by such a course of procedure. Our friends who have been imperceptibly drawn into this plot I view with tenderness, and would not for the world injure their feelings, and I have only to hope for the future, that they will withdraw themselves from it; for I declare to them, that the plot is not for the glory of God, but on the contrary the perpetuation of slavery in this country, which will ruin them and the country forever, unless something is immediately done.

Do the colonizationists think to send us off without first being reconciled to us? Do they think to bundle us up like brutes and send us off, as they did our brethren of the State of Ohio? Have they not to be reconciled to us, or reconcile us to them, for the cruelties with which they have afflicted our fathers and us? Methinks colonizationists think they have a set of brutes to deal with, sure enough. Do they think to drive us from our country and homes, after having enriched it with our blood and tears, and keep back millions of our dear brethren, sunk in the [pg 79] most barbarous wretchedness, to dig up gold and silver for them and their children? Surely, the Americans must think that we are brutes, as some of them have represented us to be. They think that we do not feel for our brethren, whom they are murdering by the inches, but they are dreadfully deceived. I acknowledge that there are some deceitful and hypocritical wretches among us, who will tell us one thing while they mean another, and thus they go on aiding our enemies to oppress themselves and us. But I declare this day before my Lord and Master, that I believe there are some true-hearted sons of Africa, in this land of oppression, but pretended *liberty!!!!!*—who do in reality feel for their suffering brethren, who are held in bondage by tyrants. Some of the advocates of this cunningly devised plot of Satan represent us to be the greatest set of cut throats in the world, as though God, wants, us to take his work out of his hand before he is ready.

Does not vengeance belong to the Lord? Is he not able to repay the Americans for their cruelties, with which they have afflicted Africa's sons and daughters, without our interference, unless we are ordered? Is it surprising to think that the Americans, having the bible in their hands, do not believe it. Are not the hearts of all men in the hands of the God of battles? And does he not suffer some, in consequence of cruelties, to go on until they are irrecoverably lost? Now, what can be more aggravating, than for the Americans, after having treated us so bad, to hold us up to the world as such great throat cutters? It appears to me as though they are resolved to assail us with every species of affliction that their ingenuity can invent. (☞ See the African Repository and Colonial Journal, from its commencement to the present day—see how we are, through the medium of that periodical, abused and held up by the Americans, as the greatest nuisance to society, and throat-cutters in the world.) But the Lord sees their actions. Americans! notwithstanding you have and do continue to treat us more cruel [pg 80] than any heathen nation ever did a people it had subjected to the same condition that you have us. Now let us reason—I mean you of the United States, whom I believe God designs to save from destruction, if you will hear. For I declare to you, whether you believe it or not, that there are some on the continent of America, who will never be able to repent. God will surely destroy them, to show you his disapprobation of the murders they and you have inflicted on us. I say, let us reason; had you not better take our body, while you have it in your power, and while we are yet ignorant and wretched, not knowing but a little, give us education, and teach us the pure religion of our Lord and Master, which is calculated to make the lion lay down in peace with the lamb, and which millions of you have beaten us nearly to death for trying to obtain since we have been among you, and thus, at once, gain our affection, while we are ignorant? Remember Americans, that we must and shall be free, and enlightened as you are, will you wait until we shall, under God, obtain our liberty by the crushing arm of power? Will it not be dreadful for you? I speak Americans for your good. We must and shall be free I say, in spite of you. You may do your best to keep us in wretchedness and misery, to enrich you and your children but God will deliver us from under you. And wo, wo, will be to you if we have to obtain our freedom by fighting. Throw away your fears and prejudices then, and enlighten us and treat us like men, and we will like you more than we do now hate you,[27] and tell us now no more about colonization, for America is as much our country, as it is yours.—Treat us like men, and there is no danger but we will all live in peace and happiness together. For we are not like you, hard hearted, unmerciful, and unforgiving. What a happy country this will be, if the whites will listen. What nation under heaven, will be able to do any thing with us, unless God gives [pg 81] us up into his hand? But Americans, I declare to you, while you keep us and our children in bondage, and treat us like brutes, to make us support you and your families, we cannot be your friends. You do not look for it, do you? Treat us then like men, and we will be your friends. And there is not a doubt in my mind, but that the whole of the past will be sunk into oblivion, and we yet, under God, will become a united and happy people. The whites may say it is impossible, but remember that nothing is impossible with God.

The Americans may say or do as they please, but they have to raise us from the condition of brutes to that of respectable men, and to make a national acknowledgement to us for the wrongs they have inflicted on us. As unexpected, strange, and wild as these propositions may to some appear, it is no less a fact, that unless they are complied with, the Americans of the United States, though they may for a little while escape, God will yet weigh them in a balance, and if they are not superior to other men, as they have represented themselves to be, he will give them wretchedness to their very heart's content.

And now brethren, having concluded these four Articles, I submit them, together with my Preamble, dedicated to the Lord for your inspection, in language so very simple, that the most ignorant, who can read at all, may easily understand—of which you may make the best you possibly can.[28] Should [pg 82] tyrants take it into their heads to emancipate any of you, remember that your freedom is your natural right. You are men, as well as they, and instead of returning thanks to them for your freedom, return it to the Holy Ghost, who is your rightful owner. If they do not want to part with your labours, which have enriched them, let them keep you, and my word for it, that God Almighty, will break their strong band. Do you believe this my brethren?—See my Address delivered before the General Coloured Association of Massachusetts, which may be found in Freedom's Journal, for Dec. 20, 1828.—See the last clause of that Address. Whether you believe it or not, I tell you that God will dash tyrants, in combination with devils, into atoms, and will bring you out from your wretchedness and miseries, under these *Christian People!!!!!!*

Those philanthropists and lovers of the human family, who have volunteered their services for our redemption from wretchedness, have a high claim on our gratitude, and we should always view them as our greatest earthly benefactors.

If any are anxious to ascertain who I am, know the world, that I am one of the oppressed, degraded and wretched sons of Africa, rendered so by the avaricious and unmerciful, among the whites.—If any wish to plunge me into the wretched incapacity of a slave, or murder me for the truth, know ye, that I am in the hand of God, and at your disposal. I count my life not dear unto me, but I am ready to be offered at any moment. For what is the use of living when in fact I am dead. But remember, Americans, that as miserable, wretched, degraded and abject as you have made us in preceding, and in this generation, to support you and your families, that some of you (whites) on the continent of America, [pg 83] will yet curse the day that you ever were born. You want slaves, and want us for your slaves!!! My colour will yet, root some of you out of the very face of the earth!!!!!! You may doubt it if you please. I know that thousands will doubt—they think they have us so well secured in wretchedness, to them and their children, that it is impossible for such things to occur. So did the antideluvians doubt Noah, until the day in which the flood came and swept them away. So did the Sodomites doubt, until Lot had got out of the City, and God rained down fire and brimstone from heaven, upon them and burnt them up. So did the king of Egypt doubt the very existence of a God, he said, "who is the Lord, that I should let Israel go?" Did he not find to his sorrow, who the Lord was, when he and all his mighty men of war, were smothered to death in the Red Sea?—So did the Romans doubt, many of them were really so ignorant, that they thought the world of mankind were made to be slaves to them; just as many of the Americans think now, of my colour.—But they got dreadfully deceived. When men got their eyes opened, they made the murderers scamper. The way in which they cut their tyrannical throats, was not much inferior to the way the Romans or murderers, served them, when they held them in wretchedness and degradation under their feet. So would Christian Americans doubt, if God should send an Angel from heaven to preach their funeral sermon. The fact is, the Christians having a name to live, while they are dead, think that God will screen them on that ground.

See the hundreds and thousands of us that are thrown into the seas by Christians, and murdered by them in other ways. They cram us into their vessel holds in chains and in hand-cuffs—men, women and children, all together!! O! save us, we pray thee, thou God of heaven and of earth, from the devouring hands of the white Christians!!!!!!

[pg 84]
Oh! thou Alpha and Omega! The beginning and the end, Enthron'd thou art, in Heaven above, Surrounded by angels there: From whence thou seest the miseries To which we are subject; The whites have murder'd us, O God! And kept us ignorant of thee.
Not satisfied with this, my Lord! They throw us in the seas: Be pleas'd, we pray, for Jesus' sake, To save us from their grasp.
We believe that, for thy glory's sake, Thou wilt deliver us; But that thou may'st effect these things, Thy glory must be sought.

In conclusion, I ask the candid and unprejudiced of the whole world, to search the pages of historians diligently, and see if the Antediluvians—the Sodomites—the Egyptians—the Babylonians—the Ninevites—the Carthagenians—the Persians—the Macedonians—the Greeks—the Romans—the Mahometans—the Jews—or devils, ever treated a set of human beings, as the white Christians of America do us, the blacks, or Africans.—I also ask the attention of the world of mankind to the declaration of these very American people, of the United States.

A Declaration made July 4, 1776.

It says,[29

> "When in the course of human events, it becomes necessary for one people to dissolve the political bands which have connected them with another, and to assume among the Powers of the earth, the separate and equal station to which the laws of nature and of nature's God entitle [pg 85] them, a decent respect for the opinions of mankind requires that they should declare the causes which impel them to the separation. We hold these truths to be self evident, that all men are created equal, that they are endowed by their Creator with certain unalienable rights; that among these are life, liberty, and the pursuit of happiness; that to secure these rights, governments are instituted among men, deriving their just powers from the consent of the governed; that whenever any form of government becomes destructive of these ends it is the right of the people to alter or to abolish it, and to institute a new government laying its foundation on such principles, and organizing its powers in such form as to them shall seem most likely to effect their safety and happiness. Prudence, indeed, will dictate that governments long established should not be changed for light and transient causes; and accordingly all experience hath shewn, that mankind are more disposed to suffer, while evils are sufferable, than to right themselves by abolishing the forms to which they are accustomed. But when a long train of abuses and usurpations, pursuing invariably the same object, evinces a design to reduce them under absolute despotism, it is their right, it is their duty to throw off such government, and to provide new guards for their future security."

See your declaration, Americans!! Do you understand your own language? Hear your language, proclaimed to the world, July 4, 1776—

> ☞ "We hold these truths to be self evident—that *ALL* **MEN are created EQUAL!** *that they are endowed by their Creator with certain unalienable rights; that among these are life, liberty, and the pursuit of happiness!!*"Compare your own language above, extracted from your Declaration of Independence, with your cruelties and murders inflicted by your cruel and unmerciful fathers on ourselves on our fathers and on us, men who have [pg 86] never given your fathers or you the least provocation!!!

Hear your language further!

"But when a long train of abuses and usurpations, pursuing invariably the same object, evinces a design to reduce them under absolute despotism, it is their *right*, it is their *duty*, to throw off such government, and to provide new guards for their future security."

Now, Americans! I ask you candidly, was your sufferings under Great Britain one hundredth part as cruel and tyrannical as you have rendered ours under you? Some of you, no doubt, believe that we will never throw off your murderous government, and "provide new guards for our future security." If Satan has made you believe it, will he not deceive you?[30] Do the whites say, I being a black man, ought to be humble, which I readily admit? I ask them, ought they not to be as humble as I? or do they think they can measure arms with Jehovah? Will not the Lord yet humble them? or will not these very coloured people, whom they now treat worse than brutes, yet under God, humble them low down enough? Some of the whites are ignorant enough to tell us, that we ought to be submissive to them, that they may keep their feet on our throats. And if we do not submit to be beaten to death by them, we are bad creatures and of course must be damned, &c. If any man wishes to hear this doctrine openly preached to us by the American preachers, let him go into the Southern and Western sections of this country—I do not speak from hearsay—what I have written, is what I have seen and heard myself. No man may think that my book is made up of conjecture—I have travelled and observed nearly the whole of those things myself, and what little I did not get by [pg 87] my own observation, I received from those among the whites and blacks, in whom the greatest confidence may be placed.

The Americans may be as vigilant as they please, but they cannot be vigilant enough for the Lord, neither can they hide themselves, where he will not find and bring them out.

Richard Wright, I Choose Exile

https://uploads-ssl.webflow.com/5c54c9afc8a5790510b95009/
5d58141d83100b29bb005da9_Richard%20Wright%20-%20I%20Choose%20Exile.pdf

"Richard Wright Writing about Racism" by TradingCardsNPS is licensed under CC BY 2.0

Ida B. Wells-Barnett, The Red Record, 1. The Case Stated

THE CASE STATED

The student of American sociology will find the year 1894 marked by a pronounced awakening of the public conscience to a system of anarchy and outlawry which had grown during a series of ten years to be so common, that scenes of unusual brutality failed to have any visible effect upon the humane sentiments of the people of our land.

Beginning with the emancipation of the Negro, the inevitable result of unbribled power exercised for two and a half centuries, by the white man over the Negro, began to show itself in acts of conscienceless outlawry. During the slave regime, the Southern white man owned the Negro body and soul. It was to his interest to dwarf the soul and preserve the body. Vested with unlimited power over his slave, to subject him to any and all kinds of physical punishment, the white man was still restrained from such punishment as tended to injure the slave by abating his physical powers and thereby reducing his financial worth. While slaves were scourged mercilessly, and in countless cases inhumanly treated in other respects, still the white owner rarely permitted his anger to go so far as to take a life, which would entail upon him a loss of several hundred dollars. The slave was rarely killed, he was too valuable; it was easier and quite as effective, for discipline or revenge, to sell him "Down South."

But Emancipation came and the vested interests of the white man in the Negro's body were lost. The white man had no right to scourge the emancipated Negro, still less has he a right to kill him. But the Southern white people had been educated so long in that school of practice, in which might makes right, that they disdained to draw strict lines of action in dealing with the Negro. In slave times the Negro was kept subservient and submissive by the frequency and severity of the scourging, but, with freedom, a new system of intimidation came into vogue; the Negro was not only whipped and scourged; he was killed.

Not all nor nearly all of the murders done by white men, during the past thirty years in the South, have come to light, but the statistics as gathered and preserved by white men, and which have not been questioned, show that during these years more than ten thousand Negroes have been killed in cold blood, without the formality of judicial trial and legal execution. And yet, as evidence of the absolute impunity with which the white man dares to kill a Negro, the same record shows that during all these years, and for all these murders only three white men have been tried, convicted, and executed. As no white man has been lynched for the murder of colored people, these three executions are the only instances of the death penalty being visited upon white men for murdering Negroes.

Naturally enough the commission of these crimes began to tell upon the public conscience, and the Southern white man, as a tribute to the nineteenth-century civilization, was in a manner compelled to give excuses for his barbarism. His excuses have adapted themselves to the emergency, and are aptly outlined by that greatest of all Negroes, Frederick Douglass, in an article of recent date, in which he shows that there have been three distinct eras of Southern barbarism, to account for which three distinct excuses have been made.

The first excuse given to the civilized world for the murder of unoffending Negroes was the necessity of the white man to repress and stamp out alleged "race riots." For years immediately succeeding the war there was an appalling slaughter of colored people, and the wires usually conveyed to northern people and the world the intelligence, first, that an insurrection was being planned by Negroes, which, a few hours later, would prove to have been vigorously resisted by white men, and controlled with a resulting loss of several killed and wounded. It was always a remarkable feature in these insurrections and riots that only Negroes were killed during the rioting, and that all the white men escaped unharmed.

From 1865 to 1872, hundreds of colored men and women were mercilessly murdered and the almost invariable reason assigned was that they met their death by being alleged participants in an insurrection or riot. But this story at last wore itself out. No insurrection ever materialized; no Negro rioter was ever apprehended and proven guilty, and no dynamite ever recorded the black man's protest against oppression and wrong. It was too much to ask thoughtful people to believe this transparent story, and the southern white people at last made up their minds that some other excuse must be had.

Then came the second excuse, which had its birth during the turbulent times of reconstruction. By an amendment to the Constitution the Negro was given the right of franchise, and, theoretically at least, his ballot became his invaluable emblem of citizenship. In a government "of the people, for the people, and by the people," the Negro's vote became an important factor in all matters of state and national politics. But this did not last long. The southern white man would not consider that the Negro had any right which a white man was bound to respect, and the idea of a republican form of government in the southern states grew into general contempt. It was maintained that "This is a white man's government," and regardless of numbers the white man should rule. "No Negro domination" became the new legend on the sanguinary banner of the sunny South, and under it rode the Ku Klux Klan, the Regulators, and the lawless mobs, which for any cause chose to murder one man or a dozen as suited their purpose best. It was a long, gory campaign; the blood chills and the heart almost loses faith in Christianity when one thinks of Yazoo, Hamburg, Edgefield, Copiah, and the countless massacres of defenseless Negroes, whose only crime was the attempt to exercise their right to vote.

But it was a bootless strife for colored people. The government which had made the Negro a citizen found itself unable to protect him. It gave him the right to vote, but denied him the protection which should have maintained that right. Scourged from his home; hunted through the swamps; hung by midnight raiders, and openly murdered in the light of day, the Negro clung to his right of franchise with a heroism which would have wrung admiration from the hearts of savages. He believed that in that small white ballot there was a subtle something which stood for manhood as well as citizenship, and thousands of brave black men went to their graves, exemplifying the one by dying for the other.

The white man's victory soon became complete by fraud, violence, intimidation and murder. The franchise vouchsafed to the Negro grew to be a "barren ideality," and regardless of numbers, the colored people found themselves voiceless in the councils of those whose duty it was to rule. With no longer the fear of "Negro Domination" before their eyes, the white man's second excuse became valueless. With the Southern governments all subverted and the Negro actually eliminated from all participation in state and national elections, there could be no longer an excuse for killing Negroes to prevent "Negro Domination."

Brutality still continued; Negroes were whipped, scourged, exiled, shot and hung whenever and wherever it pleased the white man so to treat them, and as the civilized world with increasing persistency held the white people of the South to account for its outlawry, the murderers invented the third excuse—that Negroes had to be killed to avenge their assaults upon women. There could be framed no possible excuse more harmful to the Negro and more unanswerable if true in its sufficiency for the white man.

Humanity abhors the assailant of womanhood, and this charge upon the Negro at once placed him beyond the pale of human sympathy. With such unanimity, earnestness and apparent candor was this charge made and reiterated that the world has accepted the story that the Negro is a monster which the Southern white man has painted him. And today, the Christian world feels, that while lynching is a crime, and lawlessness and anarchy the certain precursors of a nation's fall, it can not by word or deed, extend sympathy or help to a race of outlaws, who might mistake their plea for justice and deem it an excuse for their continued wrongs.

The Negro has suffered much and is willing to suffer more. He recognizes that the wrongs of two centuries can not be righted in a day, and he tries to bear his burden with patience for today and be hopeful for tomorrow. But there comes a time when the veriest worm will turn, and the Negro feels today that after all the work he has done, all the sacrifices he has made, and all the suffering he has endured, if he did not, now, defend his name and manhood from this vile accusation, he would be unworthy even of the contempt of mankind. It is to this charge he now feels he must make answer.

If the Southern people in defense of their lawlessness, would tell the truth and admit that colored men and women are lynched for almost any offense, from murder to a misdemeanor, there would not now be the necessity for this defense. But when they intentionally, maliciously and constantly belie the record and bolster up these falsehoods by the words of legislators, preachers, governors and bishops, then the Negro must give to the world his side of the awful story.

A word as to the charge itself. In considering the third reason assigned by the Southern white people for the butchery of blacks, the question must be asked, what the white man means when he charges the black man with rape. Does he mean the crime which the statutes of the civilized states describe as such? Not by any means. With the Southern white man, any mesalliance existing between a white woman and a colored man is a sufficient foundation for the charge of rape. The Southern white man says that it is impossible for a voluntary alliance to exist between a white woman and a colored man, and therefore, the fact of an alliance is a proof of force. In numerous instances where colored men have have been lynched on the charge of rape, it was positively known at the time of lynching, and indisputably proven after the victim's death, that the relationship sustained between the man and woman was voluntary and clandestine, and that in no court of law could even the charge of assault have been successfully maintained.

It was for the assertion of this fact, in the defense of her own race, that the writer hereof became an exile; her property destroyed and her return to her home forbidden under penalty of death, for writing the following editorial which was printed in her paper, the *Free Speech,* in Memphis, Tenn., May 21,1892:

> Eight Negroes lynched since last issue of the *Free Speech* one at Little Rock, Ark., last Saturday morning where the citizens broke(?) into the penitentiary and got their man; three near Anniston, Ala., one near New Orleans; and three at Clarksville, Ga., the last three for killing a white man, and five on the same old racket—the new alarm about raping white women. The same programme of hanging, then shooting bullets into the lifeless bodies was carried out to the letter. Nobody in this section of the country believes the old threadbare lie that Negro men rape white women. If Southern white men are not careful, they will overreach themselves and public sentiment will have a reaction; a conclusion will then be reached which will be very damaging to the moral reputation of their women.

But threats cannot suppress the truth, and while the Negro suffers the soul deformity, resultant from two and a half centuries of slavery, he is no more guilty of this vilest of all vile charges than the white man who would blacken his name.

During all the years of slavery, no such charge was ever made, not even during the dark days of the rebellion, when the white man, following the fortunes of war went to do battle for the maintenance of slavery. While the master was away fighting to forge the fetters upon the slave, he left his wife and children with no protectors save the Negroes themselves. And yet during those years of trust and peril, no Negro proved recreant to his trust and no white man returned to a home that had been dispoiled.

Likewise during the period of alleged "insurrection," and alarming "race riots," it never occurred to the white man, that his wife and children were in danger of assault. Nor in the Reconstruction era, when the hue and cry was against "Negro Domination," was there ever a thought that the domination would ever contaminate a fireside or strike to death the virtue of womanhood. It must appear strange indeed, to every thoughtful and candid man, that more than a quarter of a century elapsed before the Negro began to show signs of such infamous degeneration.

In his remarkable apology for lynching, Bishop Haygood, of Georgia, says: "No race, not the most savage, tolerates the rape of woman, but it may be said without reflection upon any other people that the Southern people are now and always have been most sensitive concerning the honor of their women—their mothers, wives, sisters and daughters." It is not the purpose of this defense to say one word against the white women of the South. Such need not be said, but it is their misfortune that the chivalrous white men of that section, in order to escape the deserved execration of the civilized world, should shield themselves by their cowardly and infamously false excuse, and call into question that very honor about which their distinguished priestly apologist claims they are most sensitive. To justify their own barbarism they assume a chivalry which they do not possess. True chivalry respects all womanhood, and no one who reads the record, as it is written in the faces of the million mulattoes in the South, will for a minute conceive that the southern white man had a very chivalrous regard for the honor due the women of his own race or respect for the womanhood which circumstances placed in his power. That chivalry which is "most sensitive concerning the honor of women" can hope for but little respect from the civilized world, when it confines itself entirely to the women who happen to be white. Virtue knows no color line, and the chivalry which depends upon complexion of skin and texture of hair can command no honest respect.

When emancipation came to the Negroes, there arose in the northern part of the United States an almost divine sentiment among the noblest, purest and best white women of the North, who felt called to a mission to educate and Christianize the millions of southern exslaves. From every nook and corner of the North, brave young white women answered that call and left their cultured homes, their happy associations and their lives of ease, and with heroic determination went to the South to carry light and truth to the benighted blacks. It was a heroism no less than that which calls for volunteers for India, Africa and the Isles of the sea. To educate their unfortunate charges; to teach them the Christian virtues and to inspire in them the moral sentiments manifest in their own lives, these young women braved dangers whose record reads more like fiction than fact. They became social outlaws in the South. The peculiar sensitiveness of the southern white men for women, never shed its protecting influence about them. No friendly word from their own race cheered them in their work; no hospitable doors gave them the companionship like that from which they had come. No chivalrous white man doffed his hat in honor or respect. They were "Nigger teachers"—unpardonable offenders in the social ethics of the South, and were insulted, persecuted and ostracised, not by Negroes, but by the white manhood which boasts of its chivalry toward women.

And yet these northern women worked on, year after year, unselfishly, with a heroism which amounted almost to martyrdom. Threading their way through dense forests, working in schoolhouse, in the cabin and in the church, thrown at all times and in all places among the unfortunate and lowly Negroes, whom they had come to find and to serve, these northern women, thousands and thousands of them, have spent more than a quarter of a century in giving to the colored people their splendid lessons for home and heart and soul. Without protection, save that which innocence gives to every good woman, they went about their work, fearing no assault and suffering none. Their chivalrous protectors were hundreds of miles away in their northern homes, and yet they never feared any "great dark-faced mobs," they dared night or day to "go beyond their own roof trees." They never complained of assaults, and no mob was ever called into existence to avenge crimes against them. Before the world adjudges the Negro a moral monster, a vicious assailant of womanhood and a menace to the sacred precincts of home, the colored people ask the consideration of the silent record of gratitude, respect, protection and devotion of the millions of the race in the South, to the thousands of northern white women who have served as teachers and missionaries since the war.

The Negro may not have known what chivalry was, but he knew enough to preserve inviolate the womanhood of the South which was entrusted to his hands during the war. The finer sensibilities of his soul may have been crushed out by years of slavery, but his heart was full of gratitude to the white women of the North, who blessed his home and inspired his soul in all these years of freedom. Faithful to his trust in both of these instances, he should now have the impartial ear of the civilized world, when he dares to speak for himself as against the infamy wherewith he stands charged.

It is his regret, that, in his own defense, he must disclose to the world that degree of dehumanizing brutality which fixes upon America the blot of a national crime. Whatever faults and failings other nations may have in their dealings with their own subjects or with other people, no other civilized nation stands condemned before the world with a series of crimes so peculiarly national. It becomes a painful duty of the Negro to reproduce a record which shows that a large portion of the American people avow anarchy, condone murder and defy the contempt of civilization. These pages are written in no spirit of vindictiveness, for all who give the subject consideration must concede that far too serious is the condition of that civilized government in which the spirit of unrestrained outlawry constantly increases in violence, and casts its blight over a continually growing area of territory. We plead not for the colored people alone, but for all victims of the terrible injustice which puts men and women to death without form of law. During the year 1894, there were 132 persons executed in the United States by due form of law, while in the same year, 197 persons were put to death by mobs who gave the victims no opportunity to make a lawful defense. No comment need be made upon a condition of public sentiment responsible for such alarming results.

The purpose of the pages which follow shall be to give the record which has been made, not by colored men, but that which is the result of compilations made by white men, of reports sent over the civilized world by white men in the South. Out of their own mouths shall the murderers be condemned. For a number of years the *Chicago Tribune*, admittedly one of the leading journals of America, has made a specialty of the compilation of statistics touching upon lynching. The data compiled by that journal and published to the world January 1, 1894, up to the present time has not been disputed. In order to be safe from the charge of exaggeration, the incidents hereinafter reported have been confined to those vouched for by the Tribune.

George S. Schuyler, Black No More

http://ekladata.com/XGzb9Wez7QFwKcXpVg90kYNPTBo/Black-no-more.pdf

This is a satire of life in the 1930s, so its use brings up obvious questions:

To what extent are things different today?

How is this book like the materials we read in the chapter on humor and mythology?

Of which contemporary texts does this remind you?

Ralph Ellison, Hidden Name and Complex Fate

https://mseffie.com/assignments/invisible_man/Hidden%20Name.pdf

"InvisibleMan_Huntington_07" by Huntington Theatre Company is licensed under CC BY 2.0

Malcolm X, How I Learned to Read

http://accounts.smccd.edu/bellr/readerlearningtoread.htm

“Malcolm X” by JBrazito is licensed under CC BY 2.0

Martin Luther King Jr., Three Ways of Meeting Oppression

Martin Luther King Jr., Three Ways of Meeting Oppression

https://www.openculture.com/2015/02/how-martin-luther-king-jr-used-hegel-to-overturn-segregation-in-america.html

https://www.openculture.com/2015/02/how-martin-luther-king-jr-used-hegel-to-overturn-segregation-in-america.html

https://www.openculture.com/2015/02/how-martin-luther-king-jr-used-hegel-to-overturn-segregation-in-america.html

Toni Morrison Interview (1977)

Toni Morrison Interview (1977)

https://www.youtube.com/watch?v=_vgEhN4fypw

Toni Morrison, Nobel Prize for Literature Lecture

Toni Morrison, Nobel Prize for Literature Lecture

https://www.nobelprize.org/prizes/literature/1993/morrison/lecture/

"Toni Morrison (2)" by Angela Radulescu is licensed under CC BY-NC-SA 2.0

Alice Walker, Beauty: When the Other Dancer is the Self

Alice Walker, Beauty: When the Other Dancer is the Self

https://public.wsu.edu/~hughesc/alice-walker.htm

Gloria Naylor, The Meanings of a Word

https://www.wqed.org/augustwilson/sites/wqed.org.augustwilson/files/The%20Meanings%20of%20a%20Word%20by%20Gloria%20Naylor.pdf

Names matter. Words matter. In what ways does Naylor's 1986 essay help situate the use of naming? How should we approach this in our course? Share some ground rules for the use of the n-word. We might also look to the following article for some insight into this important course issue: https://www.tolerance.org/magazine/fall-2011/straight-talk-about-the-nword

"File:Gloria Naylor by David Shankbone.jpg" by David Shankbone is licensed under CC BY-SA 3.0

Ta-Nehisi Coates, The Case for Reparations

In case this link from *The Atlantic* doesn't function or prompts you for subscribing, note that this is an essay easily located online:

https://www.theatlantic.com/magazine/archive/2014/06/the-case-for-reparations/361631/?gclid=Cj0KCQiAzsz-BRCCARIsANotFgNpcg0sBT1XUfjo8b9vfYR3G3WHrpA0euxghy9nZFq75u_ts9BCXmcaAjWcEALw_wcB

5. POETRY READINGS

Paul Laurence Dunbar Poems

Paul Laurence Dunbar Poems

https://www.poetryfoundation.org/poets/paul-laurence-dunbar

What other poets in this collection connect with the Paul Laurence Dunbar poems? Stylistically or thematically, what are the connections you see?

The Corn-Stalk Fiddle

When the corn's all cut and the bright stalks shine
  Like the burnished spears of a field of gold;
When the field-mice rich on the nubbins dine,
  And the frost comes white and the wind blows cold;
Then its heigho fellows and hi-diddle-diddle,
For the time is ripe for the corn-stalk fiddle.
And you take a stalk that is straight and long,
  With an expert eye to its worthy points,
And you think of the bubbling strains of song
  That are bound between its pithy joints—
Then you cut out strings, with a bridge in the middle,
With a corn-stalk bow for a corn-stalk fiddle.
Then the strains that grow as you draw the bow
  O'er the yielding strings with a practiced hand!
And the music's flow never loud but low
  Is the concert note of a fairy band.
Oh, your dainty songs are a misty riddle
To the simple sweets of the corn-stalk fiddle.
When the eve comes on and our work is done
  And the sun drops down with a tender glance,
With their hearts all prime for the harmless fun,
  Come the neighbor girls for the evening's dance,
And they wait for the well-known twist and twiddle,
More time than tune—from the corn-stalk fiddle.
Then brother Jabez takes the bow,
  While Ned stands off with Susan Bland,
Then Henry stops by Milly Snow
  And John takes Nellie Jones's hand,
While I pair off with Mandy Biddle,
And scrape, scrape, scrape goes the corn-stalk fiddle.
"Salute your partners," comes the call,
  "All join hands and circle round,"
"Grand train back," and "Balance all,"
  Footsteps lightly spurn the ground,
"Take your lady and balance down the middle"

To the merry strains of the corn-stalk fiddle.
So the night goes on and the dance is o'er,
  And the merry girls are homeward gone,
But I see it all in my sleep once more,
  And I dream till the very break of dawn
Of an impish dance on a red-hot griddle
To the screech and scrape of a corn-stalk fiddle.

The Haunted Oak

Pray why are you so bare, so bare,
  Oh, bough of the old oak-tree;
And why, when I go through the shade you throw,
  Runs a shudder over me?
My leaves were green as the best, I trow,
  And sap ran free in my veins,
But I saw in the moonlight dim and weird
  A guiltless victim's pains.
I bent me down to hear his sigh;
  I shook with his gurgling moan,
And I trembled sore when they rode away,
  And left him here alone.
They'd charged him with the old, old crime,
  And set him fast in jail:
Oh, why does the dog howl all night long,
  And why does the night wind wail?
He prayed his prayer and he swore his oath,
  And he raised his hand to the sky;
But the beat of hoofs smote on his ear,
  And the steady tread drew nigh.
Who is it rides by night, by night,
  Over the moonlit road?
And what is the spur that keeps the pace,
  What is the galling goad?
And now they beat at the prison door,
  "Ho, keeper, do not stay!
We are friends of him whom you hold within,
  And we fain would take him away
"From those who ride fast on our heels
  With mind to do him wrong;
They have no care for his innocence,
  And the rope they bear is long."
They have fooled the jailer with lying words,
  They have fooled the man with lies;
The bolts unbar, the locks are drawn,

And the great door open flies.
Now they have taken him from the jail,
And hard and fast they ride,
And the leader laughs low down in his throat,
As they halt my trunk beside.
Oh, the judge, he wore a mask of black,
And the doctor one of white,
And the minister, with his oldest son,
Was curiously bedight.
Oh, foolish man, why weep you now?
'Tis but a little space,
And the time will come when these shall dread
The mem'ry of your face.
I feel the rope against my bark,
And the weight of him in my grain,
I feel in the throe of his final woe
The touch of my own last pain.
And never more shall leaves come forth
On the bough that bears the ban;
I am burned with dread, I am dried and dead,
From the curse of a guiltless man.
And ever the judge rides by, rides by,
And goes to hunt the deer,
And ever another rides his soul
In the guise of a mortal fear.
And ever the man he rides me hard,
And never a night stays he;
For I feel his curse as a haunted bough,
On the trunk of a haunted tree.

The remaining poems derive from an OER resource, *African-American Literature 1619-1926*, from M.O.S.T. Commons. The entire book is available there and could be a useful resource as we look at historical lecture material, context, and early influences upon African-American art. See more at: https://most.oercommons.org/courseware/lesson/227/overview

We Wear the Mask

We wear the mask that grins and lies,

It hides our cheeks and shades our eyes,-

This debt we pay to human guile;

With torn and bleeding hearts we smile,

And mouth with myriad subtleties.

Why should the world be overwise,

In counting all our tears and sighs?

Nay, let them only see us, while
We wear the mask!

We smile, but, O great Christ, our cries
To thee from tortured sould arise.
We sing, but oh, the clay is vile
Beneath our feet, and long the mile;
But let the world dream otherwise,
We wear the mask!

Sympathy

I know what the caged bird feels, alas!
When the sun is bright on the upland slopes;
When the wind stirs soft through the springing grass,
And the river flows like a stream of glass;
I know what the caged bird feels!

I know why the caged bird beats his wing
Till its blood is red on the cruel bars;
For he must fly back to his perch and cling
When he fain would be on the bough a-swing;
And a pain still throbs in the old, old scars
And they pulse again with a keener sting-
I know why he beats his wing!

I know why the caged bird sings, ah me,
When his wing is bruised and his bosom sore,-
When he beats his bars, and he would be free;

It is not a carol of joy or glee,

But a prayer that he sends from his heart's deep core,

But a plea, that upward to Heaven he flings-

I know why the caged bird sings!

Countee Cullen Poems

Countee Cullen Poems

https://www.poetryfoundation.org/poets/countee-cullen

Cullen is self-consciously forging an identity as an African-American poet. To what extent does he "play by the rules" of Western poetry at the time?
To what extent does he innovate?

Carl Van Vechten – Van Vechten Collection at Library of Congress

Angelina Weld Grimké, The Black Finger

The Black Finger

I have just seen a most beautiful thing
Slim and still
Against a gold, gold sky,
A straight black cypress,
Sensitive,
Exquisite,
A black finger
Pointing upwards.
Why, beautiful still finger, are you black?
And why are you pointing upwards?

Sterling Brown Poems

Sterling Brown Poems

https://poets.org/poems/sterling-brown

Sterling A. Brown is one of the most powerful American poets nearly nobody has heard of. Read this trio of his poems, paying particular attention to the Slim Greer poem. It is part of a larger cycle of Slim poems similar to what we see with Langston Hughes and his comic Jesse B. Semple character.

Are the characters being satirized as they satirize white culture? How so?

Sterling [A.] Brown, Oct. 7 #119 : [cellulose acetate photonegative and contact print, 1944]. Creator: Scurlock Studio (Washington, D.C.) (photographers). Title: Sterling [A.] Brown, Oct. 7 #119 : [cellulose acetate photonegative and contact print, 1944]. Contained in: Black-and-white film negatives (Series 4), Scurlock Studio Records, 1905-1994. Phy. Description: 2 items. Medium : Negative: Silver gelatin on cellulose acetate film sheet, 7 x 5″. Contact print : Silver gelatin on paper. Digital Reference: Summary: Near-profile view of subject smoking a pipe. Ink on negative: "Mr. Sterling Brown 3-5×7 – 3-8×10 – 1-11×14". Tape on negative: "2-11×14". Sterling [A.] Brown, Oct. 7 #119 . No edge imprint. Condition: Good condition. Restrictions: Fees for commercial use. Smithsonian Institution owns rights

Jean Toomer Poems

Jean Toomer Poems

https://www.poetryfoundation.org/poets/jean-toomer

How does Toomer use setting, symbolism, and the blues together in his poetry?

United States of America Department of State – Beinecke Rare Book & Manuscript Library, Yale University

Jessie Redmon Fauset Poems

Jessie Redmon Fauset Poems

https://www.literaryladiesguide.com/classic-women-authors-poetry/6-jessie-redmon-fauset-poems/

How does Fauset–and we'll look up other fiction of hers in class–act as a sort of contemporary counterpoint to the works of Zora Hurston?

Langston Hughes Poems

Langston Hughes Poems

https://www.poetryfoundation.org/poets/langston-hughes

Lucille Clifton Poems

Lucille Clifton Poems

https://www.poetryfoundation.org/poets/lucille-clifton

"Library Walk Plaque 18" by ATIS547 is licensed under CC BY-NC-SA 2.0

Amiri Baraka Poems

https://www.poetryfoundation.org/poets/amiri-baraka

How do the linked poems relate to *Dutchman*, Baraka's play? What motifs are you noticing?

Maya Angelou Poems

Maya Angelou Poems

https://www.poetryfoundation.org/poets/maya-angelou

Ishmael Reed Poems

Ishmael Reed Poems

https://www.poetryfoundation.org/poets/ishmael-reed

"File:Ishmael Reed in 2019 (cropped).jpg" by San Francisco Public Library is licensed under CC BY 3.0

Rita Dove Poems

Rita Dove Poems

https://www.poetryfoundation.org/poets/rita-dove

"Rita Dove" by Gage Skidmore is licensed under CC BY-SA 2.0

6. FICTION

Alice Dunbar-Nelson, A Carnival Jangle

A Carnival Jangle by Alice Dunbar-Nelson

There is a merry jangle of bells in the air, an all-pervading sense of jester's noise, and the flaunting vividness of royal colours. The streets swarm with humanity,–humanity in all shapes, manners, forms, laughing, pushing, jostling, crowding, a mass of men and women and children, as varied and assorted in their several individual peculiarities as ever a crowd that gathered in one locality since the days of Babel.

It is Carnival in New Orleans; a brilliant Tuesday in February, when the very air gives forth an ozone intensely exhilarating, making one long to cut capers. The buildings are a blazing mass of royal purple and golden yellow, national flags, bunting, and decorations that laugh in the glint of the Midas sun. The streets are a crush of jesters and maskers, Jim Crows and clowns, ballet girls and Mephistos, Indians and monkeys; of wild and sudden flashes of music, of glittering pageants and comic ones, of befeathered and belled horses; a dream of colour and melody and fantasy gone wild in an effervescent bubble of beauty that shifts and changes and passes kaleidoscope-like before the bewildered eye.

A bevy of bright-eyed girls and boys of that uncertain age that hovers between childhood and maturity, were moving down Canal Street when there was a sudden jostle with another crowd meeting them. For a minute there was a deafening clamour of shouts and laughter, cracking of the whips, which all maskers carry, a jingle and clatter of carnival bells, and the masked and unmasked extricated themselves and moved from each other's paths. But in the confusion a tall Prince of Darkness had whispered to one of the girls in the unmasked crowd: "You'd better come with us, Flo; you're wasting time in that tame gang. Slip off, they'll never miss you; we'll get you a rig, and show you what life is."

And so it happened, when a half-hour passed, and the bright-eyed bevy missed Flo and couldn't find her, wisely giving up the search at last, she, the quietest and most bashful of the lot, was being initiated into the mysteries of "what life is."

Down Bourbon Street and on Toulouse and St. Peter Streets there are quaint little old-world places where one may be disguised effectually for a tiny consideration. Thither, guided by the shapely Mephisto and guarded by the team of jockeys and ballet girls, tripped Flo. Into one of the lowest-ceiled, dingiest, and most ancient-looking of these shops they stepped.

"A disguise for the demoiselle," announced Mephisto to the woman who met them. She was small and wizened and old, with yellow, flabby jaws, a neck like the throat of an alligator, and straight, white hair that stood from her head uncannily stiff.

"But the demoiselle wishes to appear a boy, un petit garcon?" she inquired, gazing eagerly at Flo's long, slender frame. Her voice was old and thin, like the high quavering of an imperfect tuning-fork, and her eyes were sharp as talons in their grasping glance.

"Mademoiselle does not wish such a costume," gruffly responded Mephisto.

"Ma foi, there is no other," said the ancient, shrugging her shoulders. "But one is left now; mademoiselle would make a fine troubadour."

"Flo," said Mephisto, "it's a dare-devil scheme, try it; no one will ever know it but us, and we'll die before we tell. Besides, we must; it's late, and you couldn't find your crowd."

And that was why you might have seen a Mephisto and a slender troubadour of lovely form, with mandolin flung across his shoulder, followed by a bevy of jockeys and ballet girls, laughing and singing as they swept down Rampart Street.

When the flash and glare and brilliancy of Canal Street have palled upon the tired eye, when it is yet too soon to go home to such a prosaic thing as dinner, and one still wishes for novelty, then it is wise to go into the lower districts. There is fantasy and fancy and grotesqueness run wild in the costuming and the behaviour of the maskers. Such dances and whoops and leaps as these hideous Indians and devils do indulge in; such wild curvetings and long walks! In the open squares, where whole groups do congregate, it is wonderfully amusing. Then, too, there is a ball in every available hall, a delirious ball, where one may dance all day for ten cents; dance and grow mad for joy, and never know who were your companions, and be yourself unknown. And in the exhilaration of the day, one walks miles and miles, and dances and skips, and the fatigue is never felt.

In Washington Square, away down where Royal Street empties its stream of children great and small into the broad channel of Elysian Fields Avenue, there was a perfect Indian pow-wow. With a little imagination one might have willed away the vision of the surrounding houses, and fancied one's self again in the forest, where the natives were holding a sacred riot. The square was filled with spectators, masked and un-masked. It was amusing to watch these mimic Red-men, they seemed so fierce and earnest.

Suddenly one chief touched another on the elbow. "See that Mephisto and troubadour over there?" he whispered huskily.

"Yes; who are they?"

"I don't know the devil," responded the other, quietly, "but I'd know that other form anywhere. It's Leon, see? I know those white hands like a woman's and that restless head. Ha!"

"But there may be a mistake."

"No. I'd know that one anywhere; I feel it is he. I'll pay him now. Ah, sweetheart, you've waited long, but you shall feast now!" He was caressing something long and lithe and glittering beneath his blanket.

In a masked dance it is easy to give a death-blow between the shoulders. Two crowds meet and laugh and shout and mingle almost inextricably, and if a shriek of pain should arise, it is not noticed in the din, and when they part, if one should stagger and fall bleeding to the ground, can any one tell who has given the blow? There is nothing but an unknown stiletto on the ground, the crowd has dispersed, and masks tell no tales anyway. There is murder, but by whom? for what? Quien sabe?

And that is how it happened on Carnival night, in the last mad moments of Rex's reign, a broken-hearted mother sat gazing wide-eyed and mute at a horrible something that lay across the bed. Outside the long sweet march music of many bands floated in as if in mockery, and the flash of rockets and Bengal lights illumined the dead, white face of the girl troubadour.

Unknown photographer – Twentieth Century Negro Literature http://www.gutenberg.org/etext/18772

Paul Laurence Dunbar, The Scapegoat

The law is usually supposed to be a stern mistress, not to be lightly wooed, and yielding only to the most ardent pursuit. But even law, like love, sits more easily on some natures than on others.

This was the case with Mr. Robinson Asbury. Mr. Asbury had started life as a bootblack in the growing town of Cadgers. From this he had risen one step and become porter and messenger in a barber–shop. This rise fired his ambition, and he was not content until he had learned to use the shears and the razor and had a chair of his own. From this, in a man of Robinson's temperament, it was only a step to a shop of his own, and he placed it where it would do the most good.

Fully one–half of the population of Cadgers was composed of Negroes, and with their usual tendency to colonise, a tendency encouraged, and in fact compelled, by circumstances, they had gathered into one part of the town. Here in alleys, and streets as dirty and hardly wider, they thronged like ants.

It was in this place that Mr. Asbury set up his shop, and he won the hearts of his prospective customers by putting up the significant sign, "Equal Rights Barber–Shop." This legend was quite unnecessary, because there was only one race about, to patronise the place. But it was a delicate sop to the people's vanity, and it served its purpose.

Asbury came to be known as a clever fellow, and his business grew. The shop really became a sort of club, and, on Saturday nights especially, was the gathering–place of the men of the whole Negro quarter. He kept the illustrated and race journals there, and those who cared neither to talk nor listen to someone else might see pictured the doings of high society in very short skirts or read in the Negro papers how Miss Boston had entertained Miss Blueford to tea on such and such an afternoon. Also, he kept the policy returns, which was wise, if not moral.

It was his wisdom rather more than his morality that made the party managers after a while cast their glances toward him as a man who might be useful to their interests. It would be well to have a man—a shrewd, powerful man—down in that part of the town who could carry his people's vote in his vest pocket, and who at any time its delivery might be needed, could hand it over without hesitation. Asbury seemed that man, and they settled upon him. They gave him money, and they gave him power and patronage. He took it all silently and he carried out his bargain faithfully. His hands and his lips alike closed tightly when there was anything within them. It was not long before he found himself the big Negro of the district and, of necessity, of the town. The time came when, at a critical moment, the managers saw that they had not reckoned without their host in choosing this barber of the black district as the leader of his people.

Now, so much success must have satisfied any other man. But in many ways Mr. Asbury was unique. For a long time he himself had done very little shaving—except of notes, to keep his hand in. His time had been otherwise employed. In the evening hours he had been wooing the coquettish Dame Law, and, wonderful to say, she had yielded easily to his advances.

It was against the advice of his friends that he asked for admission to the bar. They felt that he could do more good in the place where he was.

"You see, Robinson," said old Judge Davis, "it's just like this: If you're not admitted, it'll hurt you with the people; if you are admitted, you'll move uptown to an office and get out of touch with them."

Asbury smiled an inscrutable smile. Then he whispered something into the judge's ear that made the old man wrinkle from his neck up with appreciative smiles.

"Asbury," he said, "you are—you are—well, you ought to be white, that's all. When we find a black man like you we send him to State's prison. If you were white, you'd go to the Senate."

The Negro laughed confidently.

He was admitted to the bar soon after, whether by merit or by connivance is not to be told.

"Now he will move uptown," said the black community. "Well, that's the way with a coloured man when he gets a start."

But they did not know Asbury Robinson yet. He was a man of surprises, and they were destined to disappointment. He did not move uptown. He built an office in a small open space next his shop, and there hung out his shingle.

"I will never desert the people who have done so much to elevate me," said Mr. Asbury.

"I will live among them and I will die among them."

This was a strong card for the barber–lawyer. The people seized upon the statement as expressing a nobility of an altogether unique brand.

They held a mass meeting and indorsed him. They made resolutions that extolled him, and the Negro band came around and serenaded him, playing various things in varied time.

All this was very sweet to Mr. Asbury, and the party managers chuckled with satisfaction and said, "That Asbury, that Asbury!"

Now there is a fable extant of a man who tried to please everybody, and his failure is a matter of record. Robinson Asbury was not more successful. But be it said that his ill success was due to no fault or shortcoming of his.

For a long time his growing power had been looked upon with disfavour by the coloured law firm of Bingo & Latchett. Both Mr. Bingo and Mr. Latchett themselves aspired to be Negro leaders in Cadgers, and they were delivering Emancipation Day orations and riding at the head of processions when Mr. Asbury was blacking boots. Is it any wonder, then, that they viewed with alarm his sudden rise? They kept their counsel, however, and treated with him, for it was best. They allowed him his scope without open revolt until the day upon which he hung out his shingle. This was the last straw. They could stand no more. Asbury had stolen their other chances from them, and now he was poaching upon the last of their preserves. So Mr. Bingo and Mr. Latchett put their heads together to plan the downfall of their common enemy.

The plot was deep and embraced the formation of an opposing faction made up of the best Negroes of the town. It would have looked too much like what it was for the gentlemen to show themselves in the matter, and so they took into their confidence Mr. Isaac Morton, the principal of the coloured school, and it was under his ostensible leadership that the new faction finally came into being.

Mr. Morton was really an innocent young man, and he had ideals which should never have been exposed to the air. When the wily confederates came to him with their plan he believed that his worth had been recognised, and at last he was to be what Nature destined him for—a leader.

The better class of Negroes—by that is meant those who were particularly envious of Asbury's success—flocked to the new man's standard. But whether the race be white or black, political virtue is always in a minority, so Asbury could afford to smile at the force arrayed against him.

The new faction met together and resolved. They resolved, among other things, that Mr. Asbury was an enemy to his race and a menace to civilisation. They decided that he should be abolished; but, as they couldn't get out an injunction against him, and as he had the whole undignified but still voting black belt behind him, he went serenely on his way.

"They're after you hot and heavy, Asbury," said one of his friends to him.

"Oh, yes," was the reply, "they're after me, but after a while I'll get so far away that they'll be running in front."

"It's all the best people, they say."

"Yes. Well, it's good to be one of the best people, but your vote only counts one just the same."

The time came, however, when Mr. Asbury's theory was put to the test. The Cadgerites celebrated the first of January as Emancipation Day. On this day there was a large procession, with speechmaking in the afternoon and fireworks at night. It was the custom to concede the leadership of the coloured people of the town to the man who managed to lead the procession. For two years past this honour had fallen, of course, to Robinson Asbury, and there had been no disposition on the part of anybody to try conclusions with him.

Mr. Morton's faction changed all this. When Asbury went to work to solicit contributions for the celebration, he suddenly became aware that he had a fight upon his hands. All the better–class Negroes were staying out of it. The next thing he knew was that plans were on foot for a rival demonstration.

"Oh," he said to himself, "that's it, is it? Well, if they want a fight they can have it."

He had a talk with the party managers, and he had another with Judge Davis.

"All I want is a little lift, judge," he said, "and I'll make 'em think the sky has turned loose and is vomiting niggers."

The judge believed that he could do it. So did the party managers. Asbury got his lift. Emancipation Day came.

There were two parades. At least, there was one parade and the shadow of another. Asbury's, however, was not the shadow. There was a great deal of substance about it—substance made up of many people, many banners, and numerous bands. He did not have the best people. Indeed, among his cohorts there were a good many of the pronounced rag–tag and bobtail. But he had noise and numbers. In such cases, nothing more is needed. The success of Asbury's side of the affair did everything to confirm his friends in their good opinion of him.

When he found himself defeated, Mr. Silas Bingo saw that it would be policy to placate his rival's just anger against him. He called upon him at his office the day after the celebration.

"Well, Asbury," he said, "you beat us, didn't you?"

"It wasn't a question of beating," said the other calmly. "It was only an inquiry as to who were the people—the few or the many."

"Well, it was well done, and you've shown that you are a manager. I confess that I haven't always thought that you were doing the wisest thing in living down here and catering to this class of people when you might, with your ability, to be much more to the better class."

"What do they base their claims of being better on?"

"Oh, there ain't any use discussing that. We can't get along without you, we see that. So I, for one, have decided to work with you for harmony."

"Harmony. Yes, that's what we want."

"If I can do anything to help you at any time, why you have only to command me."

"I am glad to find such a friend in you. Be sure, if I ever need you, Bingo, I'll call on you."

"And I'll be ready to serve you."

Asbury smiled when his visitor was gone. He smiled, and knitted his brow. "I wonder what Bingo's got up his sleeve," he said. "He'll bear watching."

It may have been pride at his triumph, it may have been gratitude at his helpers, but Asbury went into the ensuing campaign with reckless enthusiasm. He did the most daring things for the party's sake. Bingo, true to his promise, was ever at his side ready to serve him. Finally, association and immunity made danger less fearsome; the rival no longer appeared a menace.

With the generosity born of obstacles overcome, Asbury determined to forgive Bingo and give him a chance. He let him in on a deal, and from that time they worked amicably together until the election came and passed.

It was a close election and many things had had to be done, but there were men there ready and waiting to do them. They were successful, and then the first cry of the defeated party was, as usual, "Fraud! Fraud!" The cry was taken up by the jealous, the disgruntled, and the virtuous.

Someone remembered how two years ago the registration books had been stolen. It was known upon good authority that money had been freely used. Men held up their hands in horror at the suggestion that the Negro vote had been juggled with, as if that were a new thing. From their pulpits ministers denounced the machine and bade their hearers rise and throw off the yoke of a corrupt municipal government. One of those sudden fevers of reform had taken possession of the town and threatened to destroy the successful party.

They began to look around them. They must purify themselves. They must give the people some tangible evidence of their own yearnings after purity. They looked around them for a sacrifice to lay upon the altar of municipal reform. Their eyes fell upon Mr. Bingo. No, he was not big enough. His blood was too scant to wash away the political stains. Then they looked into each other's eyes and turned their gaze away to let it fall upon Mr. Asbury. They really hated to do it. But there must be a scapegoat. The god from the Machine commanded them to slay him.

Robinson Asbury was charged with many crimes—with all that he had committed and some that he had not. When Mr. Bingo saw what was afoot he threw himself heart and soul into the work of his old rival's enemies. He was of incalculable use to them.

Judge Davis refused to have anything to do with the matter. But in spite of his disapproval it went on. Asbury was indicted and tried. The evidence was all against him, and no one gave more damaging testimony than his friend, Mr. Bingo. The judge's charge was favourable to the defendant, but the current of popular opinion could not be entirely stemmed. The jury brought in a verdict of guilty.

"Before I am sentenced, judge, I have a statement to make to the court. It will take less than ten minutes."

"Go on, Robinson," said the judge kindly.

Asbury started, in a monotonous tone, a recital that brought the prosecuting attorney to his feet in a minute. The judge waved him down, and sat transfixed by a sort of fascinated horror as the convicted man went on. The before–mentioned attorney drew a knife and started for the prisoner's dock. With difficulty he was restrained. A dozen faces in the court–room were red and pale by turns.

"He ought to be killed," whispered Mr. Bingo audibly.

Robinson Asbury looked at him and smiled, and then he told a few things of him. He gave the ins and outs of some of the misdemeanours of which he stood accused. He showed who were the men behind the throne. And still, pale and transfixed, Judge Davis waited for his own sentence.

Never were ten minutes so well taken up. It was a tale of rottenness and corruption in high places told simply and with the stamp of truth upon it.

He did not mention the judge's name. But he had torn the mask from the face of every other man who had been concerned in his downfall. They had shorn him of his strength, but they had forgotten that he was yet able to bring the roof and pillars tumbling about their heads.

The judge's voice shook as he pronounced sentence upon his old ally—a year in State's prison.

Some people said it was too light, but the judge knew what it was to wait for the sentence of doom, and he was grateful and sympathetic.

When the sheriff led Asbury away the judge hastened to have a short talk with him.

"I'm sorry, Robinson," he said, "and I want to tell you that you were no more guilty than the rest of us. But why did you spare me?"

"Because I knew you were my friend," answered the convict.

"I tried to be, but you were the first man that I've ever known since I've been in politics who ever gave me any decent return for friendship."

"I reckon you're about right, judge."

In politics, party reform usually lies in making a scapegoat of someone who is only as criminal as the rest, but a little weaker. Asbury's friends and enemies had succeeded in making him bear the burden of all the party's crimes, but their reform was hardly a success, and their protestations of a change of heart were received with doubt. Already there were those who began to pity the victim and to say that he had been hardly dealt with.

Mr. Bingo was not of these; but he found, strange to say, that his opposition to the idea went but a little way, and that even with Asbury out of his path he was a smaller man than he was before. Fate was strong against him. His poor, prosperous humanity could not enter the lists against a martyr. Robinson Asbury was now a martyr.

II

A year is not a long time. It was short enough to prevent people from forgetting Robinson, and yet long enough for their pity to grow strong as they remembered. Indeed, he was not gone a year. Good behaviour cut two months off the time of his sentence, and by the time people had come around to the notion that he was really the greatest and smartest man in Cadgers he was at home again.

He came back with no flourish of trumpets, but quietly, humbly. He went back again into the heart of the black district. His business had deteriorated during his absence, but he put new blood and new life into it. He did not go to work in the shop himself, but, taking down the shingle that had swung idly before his office door during his imprisonment, he opened the little room as a news– and cigar–stand.

Here anxious, pitying custom came to him and he prospered again. He was very quiet. Uptown hardly knew that he was again in Cadgers, and it knew nothing whatever of his doings.

"I wonder why Asbury is so quiet," they said to one another. "It isn't like him to be quiet." And they felt vaguely uneasy about him.

So many people had begun to say, "Well, he was a mighty good fellow after all."

Mr. Bingo expressed the opinion that Asbury was quiet because he was crushed, but others expressed doubt as to this. There are calms and calms, some after and some before the storm. Which was this?

They waited a while, and, as no storm came, concluded that this must be the after–quiet. Bingo, reassured, volunteered to go and seek confirmation of this conclusion.

He went, and Asbury received him with an indifferent, not to say, impolite, demeanour.

"Well, we're glad to see you back, Asbury," said Bingo patronisingly. He had variously demonstrated his inability to lead during his rival's absence and was proud of it. "What are you going to do?"

"I'm going to work."

"That's right. I reckon you'll stay out of politics."

"What could I do even if I went in?"

"Nothing now, of course; but I didn't know——"

He did not see the gleam in Asbury's half shut eyes. He only marked his humility, and he went back swelling with the news.

"Completely crushed—all the run taken out of him," was his report.

The black district believed this, too, and a sullen, smouldering anger took possession of them. Here was a good man ruined. Some of the people whom he had helped in his former days—some of the rude, coarse people of the low quarter who were still sufficiently unenlightened to be grateful—talked among themselves and offered to get up a demonstration for him. But he denied them. No, he wanted nothing of the kind. It would only bring him into unfavourable notice. All he wanted was that they would always be his friends and would stick by him.

They would to the death.

There were again two factions in Cadgers. The school–master could not forget how once on a time he had been made a tool of by Mr. Bingo. So he revolted against his rule and set himself up as the leader of an opposing clique. The fight had been long and strong, but had ended with odds slightly in Bingo's favour.

But Mr. Morton did not despair. As the first of January and Emancipation Day approached, he arrayed his hosts, and the fight for supremacy became fiercer than ever. The school–teacher brought the school–children in for chorus singing, secured an able orator, and the best essayist in town. With all this, he was formidable.

Mr. Bingo knew that he had the fight of his life on his hands, and he entered with fear as well as zest. He, too, found an orator, but he was not sure that he was as good as Morton's. There was no doubt but that his essayist was not. He secured a band, but still he felt unsatisfied. He had hardly done enough, and for the school–master to beat him now meant his political destruction.

It was in this state of mind that he was surprised to receive a visit from Mr. Asbury.

"I reckon you're surprised to see me here," said Asbury, smiling.

"I am pleased, I know." Bingo was astute.

"Well, I just dropped in on business."

"To be sure, to be sure, Asbury. What can I do for you?"

"It's more what I can do for you that I came to talk about," was the reply.

"I don't believe I understand you."

"Well, it's plain enough. They say that the school–teacher is giving you a pretty hard fight."

"Oh, not so hard."

"No man can be too sure of winning, though. Mr. Morton once did me a mean turn when he started the faction against me."

Bingo's heart gave a great leap, and then stopped for the fraction of a second.

"You were in it, of course," pursued Asbury, "but I can look over your part in it in order to get even with the man who started it."

It was true, then, thought Bingo gladly. He did not know. He wanted revenge for his wrongs and upon the wrong man. How well the schemer had covered his tracks! Asbury should have his revenge and Morton would be the sufferer.

"Of course, Asbury, you know what I did I did innocently."

"Oh, yes, in politics we are all lambs and the wolves are only to be found in the other party. We'll pass that, though. What I want to say is that I can help you to make your celebration an overwhelming success. I still have some influence down in my district."

"Certainly, and very justly, too. Why, I should be delighted with your aid. I could give you a prominent place in the procession."

"I don't want it; I don't want to appear in this at all. All I want is revenge. You can have all the credit, but let me down my enemy."

Bingo was perfectly willing, and, with their heads close together, they had a long and close consultation. When Asbury was gone, Mr. Bingo lay back in his chair and laughed. "I'm a slick duck," he said.

From that hour Mr. Bingo's cause began to take on the appearance of something very like a boom. More bands were hired. The interior of the State was called upon and a more eloquent orator secured. The crowd hastened to array itself on the growing side.

With surprised eyes, the school–master beheld the wonder of it, but he kept to his own purpose with dogged insistence, even when he saw that he could not turn aside the overwhelming defeat that threatened him. But in spite of his obstinacy, his hours were dark and bitter. Asbury worked like a mole, all underground, but he was indefatigable. Two days before the celebration time everything was perfected for the biggest demonstration that Cadgers had ever known. All the next day and night he was busy among his allies.

On the morning of the great day, Mr. Bingo, wonderfully caparisoned, rode down to the hall where the parade was to form. He was early. No one had yet come. In an hour a score of men all told had collected. Another hour passed, and no more had come. Then there smote upon his ear the sound of music. They were coming at last. Bringing his sword to his shoulder, he rode forward to the middle of the street. Ah, there they were. But—but—could he believe his eyes? They were going in another direction, and at their head rode—Morton! He gnashed his teeth in fury. He had been led into a trap and betrayed. The procession passing had been his—all his. He heard them cheering, and then, oh! climax of infidelity, he saw his own orator go past in a carriage, bowing and smiling to the crowd.

There was no doubting who had done this thing. The hand of Asbury was apparent in it. He must have known the truth all along, thought Bingo. His allies left him one by one for the other hall, and he rode home in a humiliation deeper than he had ever known before.

Asbury did not appear at the celebration. He was at his little news–stand all day.

In a day or two the defeated aspirant had further cause to curse his false friend. He found that not only had the people defected from him, but that the thing had been so adroitly managed that he appeared to be in fault, and three–fourths of those who knew him were angry at some supposed grievance. His cup of bitterness was full when his partner, a quietly ambitious man, suggested that they dissolve their relations.

His ruin was complete.

The lawyer was not alone in seeing Asbury's hand in his downfall. The party managers saw it too, and they met together to discuss the dangerous factor which, while it appeared to slumber, was so terribly awake. They decided that he must be appeased, and they visited him.

He was still busy at his news–stand. They talked to him adroitly, while he sorted papers and kept an impassive face. When they were all done, he looked up for a moment and replied, "You know, gentlemen, as an ex–convict I am not in politics."

Some of them had the grace to flush.

"But you can use your influence," they said.

"I am not in politics," was his only reply.

And the spring elections were coming on. Well, they worked hard, and he showed no sign. He treated with neither one party nor the other. "Perhaps," thought the managers, "he is out of politics," and they grew more confident.

It was nearing eleven o'clock on the morning of election when a cloud no bigger than a man's hand appeared upon the horizon. It came from the direction of the black district. It grew, and the managers of the party in power looked at it, fascinated by an ominous dread. Finally it began to rain Negro voters, and as one man they voted against their former candidates. Their organisation was perfect. They simply came, voted, and left, but they overwhelmed everything. Not one of the party that had damned Robinson Asbury was left in power save old Judge Davis. His majority was overwhelming.

The generalship that had engineered the thing was perfect. There were loud threats against the newsdealer. But no one bothered him except a reporter. The reporter called to see just how it was done. He found Asbury very busy sorting papers. To the newspaper man's questions he had only this reply, "I am not in politics, sir."

But Cadgers had learned its lesson.

Charles W. Chesnutt, The Goophered Grapevine & Po' Sandy

Charles W. Chesnutt, The Goophered Grapevine & Po' Sandy

From *The Conjure Woman* (1899)

THE GOOPHERED GRAPEVINE

Charles W. Chesnutt Commemorative Stamp

Some years ago my wife was in poor health, and our family doctor, in whose skill and honesty I had implicit confidence, advised a change of climate. I shared, from an unprofessional standpoint, his opinion that the raw winds, the chill rains, and the violent changes of temperature that characterized the winters in the region of the Great Lakes tended to aggravate my wife's difficulty, and would undoubtedly shorten her life if she remained exposed to them. The doctor's advice was that we seek, not a temporary place of sojourn, but a permanent residence, in a warmer and more equable climate. I was engaged at the time in grape-culture in northern Ohio, and, as I liked the business and had given it much study, I decided to look for some other locality suitable for carrying it on. I thought of sunny France, of sleepy Spain, of Southern California, but there were objections to them all. It occurred to me that I might find what I wanted in some one of our own Southern States. It was a sufficient time after the war for conditions in the South to have become somewhat settled; and I was enough of a pioneer to start a new industry, if I could not find a place where grape-culture had been tried. I wrote to a cousin who had gone into the turpentine business in central North Carolina. He assured me, in response to my inquiries, that no better place could be found in the South than the State and neighborhood where he lived; the climate was perfect for health, and, in conjunction with the soil, ideal for grape-culture; labor was cheap, and land could be bought for a mere song. He gave us a cordial invitation to come and visit him while we looked into the matter. We accepted the invitation, and after several days of leisurely travel, the last hundred miles of which were up a river on a sidewheel steamer, we reached our destination, a quaint old town, which I shall call Patesville, because, for one reason, that is not its name. There was a red brick market-house in the public square, with a tall tower, which held a four-faced clock that struck the hours, and from which there pealed out a curfew at nine o'clock. There were two or three hotels, a court-house, a jail, stores, offices, and all the appurtenances of a county seat and a commercial emporium; for while Patesville numbered only four or five thousand inhabitants, of all shades of complexion, it was one of the principal towns in North Carolina, and had a considerable trade in cotton and naval stores. This business activity was not immediately apparent to my unaccustomed eyes. Indeed, when I first saw the town, there brooded over it a calm that seemed almost sabbatic in its restfulness, though I learned later on that underneath its somnolent exterior the deeper currents of life—love and hatred, joy and despair, ambition and avarice, faith and friendship—flowed not less steadily than in livelier latitudes.

We found the weather delightful at that season, the end of summer, and were hospitably entertained. Our host was a man of means and evidently regarded our visit as a pleasure, and we were therefore correspondingly at our ease, and in a position to act with the coolness of judgment desirable in making so radical a change in our lives. My cousin placed a horse and buggy at our disposal, and himself acted as our guide until I became somewhat familiar with the country.

I found that grape-culture, while it had never been carried on to any great extent, was not entirely unknown in the neighborhood. Several planters thereabouts had attempted it on a commercial scale, in former years, with greater or less success; but like most Southern industries, it had felt the blight of war and had fallen into desuetude.

I went several times to look at a place that I thought might suit me. It was a plantation of considerable extent, that had formerly belonged to a wealthy man by the name of McAdoo. The estate had been for years involved in litigation between disputing heirs, during which period shiftless cultivation had well-nigh exhausted the soil. There had been a vineyard of some extent on the place, but it had not been attended to since the war, and had lapsed into utter neglect. The vines—here partly supported by decayed and broken-down trellises, there twining themselves among the branches of the slender saplings which had sprung up among them—grew in wild and unpruned luxuriance, and the few scattered grapes they bore were the undisputed prey of the first comer. The site was admirably adapted to grape-raising; the soil, with a little attention, could not have been better; and with the native grape, the luscious scuppernong, as my main reliance in the beginning, I felt sure that I could introduce and cultivate successfully a number of other varieties.

One day I went over with my wife to show her the place. We drove out of the town over a long wooden bridge that spanned a spreading mill-pond, passed the long whitewashed fence surrounding the county fair-ground, and struck into a road so sandy that the horse's feet sank to the fetlocks. Our route lay partly up hill and partly down, for we were in the sand-hill county; we drove past cultivated farms, and then by abandoned fields grown up in scrub-oak and short-leaved pine, and once or twice through the solemn aisles of the virgin forest, where the tall pines, well-nigh meeting over the narrow road, shut out the sun, and wrapped us in cloistral solitude. Once, at a cross-roads, I was in doubt as to the turn to take, and we sat there waiting ten minutes—we had already caught some of the native infection of restfulness—for some human being to come along, who could direct us on our way. At length a little negro girl appeared, walking straight as an arrow, with a piggin full of water on her head. After a little patient investigation, necessary to overcome the child's shyness, we learned what we wished to know, and at the end of about five miles from the town reached our destination.

We drove between a pair of decayed gateposts—the gate itself had long since disappeared—and up a straight sandy lane, between two lines of rotting rail fence, partly concealed by jimson-weeds and briers, to the open space where a dwelling-house had once stood, evidently a spacious mansion, if we might judge from the ruined chimneys that were still standing, and the brick pillars on which the sills rested. The house itself, we had been informed, had fallen a victim to the fortunes of war.

We alighted from the buggy, walked about the yard for a while, and then wandered off into the adjoining vineyard. Upon Annie's complaining of weariness I led the way back to the yard, where a pine log, lying under a spreading elm, afforded a shady though somewhat hard seat. One end of the log was already occupied by a venerable-looking colored man. He held on his knees a hat full of grapes, over which he was smacking his lips with great gusto, and a pile of grapeskins near him indicated that the performance was no new thing. We approached him at an angle from the rear, and were close to him before he perceived us. He respectfully rose as we drew near, and was moving away, when I begged him to keep his seat.

"Don't let us disturb you," I said. "There is plenty of room for us all."

He resumed his seat with somewhat of embarrassment. While he had been standing, I had observed that he was a tall man, and, though slightly bowed by the weight of years, apparently quite vigorous. He was not entirely black, and this fact, together with the quality of his hair, which was about six inches long and very bushy, except on the top of his head, where he was quite bald, suggested a slight strain of other than negro blood. There was a shrewdness in his eyes, too, which was not altogether African, and which, as we afterwards learned from experience, was indicative of a corresponding shrewdness in his character. He went on eating the grapes, but did not seem to enjoy himself quite so well as he had apparently done before he became aware of our presence.

"Do you live around here?" I asked, anxious to put him at his ease.

"Yas, suh. I lives des ober yander, behine de nex' san'-hill, on de Lumberton plank-road."

"Do you know anything about the time when this vineyard was cultivated?"

"Lawd bless you, suh, I knows all about it. Dey ain' na'er a man in dis settlement w'at won' tell you ole Julius McAdoo 'uz bawn en raise' on dis yer same plantation. Is you de Norv'n gemman w'at's gwine ter buy de ole vimya'd?"

"I am looking at it," I replied; "but I don't know that I shall care to buy unless I can be reasonably sure of making something out of it."

"Well, suh, you is a stranger ter me, en I is a stranger ter you, en we is bofe strangers ter one anudder, but 'f I 'uz in yo' place, I wouldn' buy dis vimya'd."

"Why not?" I asked.

"Well, I dunno whe'r you b'lieves in cunj'in' er not,—some er de w'ite folks don't, er says dey don't,—but de truf er de matter is dat dis yer ole vimya'd is goophered."

"Is what?" I asked, not grasping the meaning of this unfamiliar word.

"Is goophered,—cunju'd, bewitch'."

He imparted this information with such solemn earnestness, and with such an air of confidential mystery, that I felt somewhat interested, while Annie was evidently much impressed, and drew closer to me.

"How do you know it is bewitched?" I asked.

"I wouldn' spec' fer you ter b'lieve me 'less you know all 'bout de fac's. But ef you en young miss dere doan' min' lis'nin' ter a ole nigger run on a minute er two w'ile you er restin', I kin 'splain to you how it all happen'."

We assured him that we would be glad to hear how it all happened, and he began to tell us. At first the current of his memory—or imagination—seemed somewhat sluggish; but as his embarrassment wore off, his language flowed more freely, and the story acquired perspective and coherence. As he became more and more absorbed in the narrative, his eyes assumed a dreamy expression, and he seemed to lose sight of his auditors, and to be living over again in monologue his life on the old plantation.

"Ole Mars Dugal' McAdoo," he began, "bought dis place long many years befo' de wah, en I'member well w'en he sot out all dis yer part er de plantation in scuppernon's. De vimes growed monst'us fas', en Mars Dugal' made a thousan' gallon er scuppernon' wine eve'y year.

"Now, ef dey's an'thing a nigger lub, nex' ter 'possum, en chick'n, en watermillyums, it's scuppernon's. Dey ain' nuffin dat kin stan' up side'n de scuppernon' fer sweetness; sugar ain't a suckumstance ter scuppernon'. W'en de season is nigh 'bout ober, en de grapes begin ter swivel up des a little wid de wrinkles er ole age,—w'en de skin git sof' en brown,—den de scuppernon' make you smack yo' lip en roll yo' eye en wush fer mo'; so I reckon it ain' very 'stonishin' dat niggers lub scuppernon'.

"Dey wuz a sight er niggers in de naberhood er de vimya'd. Dere wuz ole Mars Henry Brayboy's niggers, en ole Mars Jeems McLean's niggers, en Mars Dugal's own niggers; den dey wuz a settlement er free niggers en po' buckrahs down by de Wim'l'ton Road, en Mars Dugal' had de only vimya'd in de naberhood. I reckon it ain' so much so nowadays, but befo' de wah, in slab'ry times, a nigger did n' mine goin' fi' er ten mile in a night, w'en dey wuz sump'n good ter eat at de yuther een'.

"So atter a w'ile Mars Dugal' begin ter miss his scuppernon's. Co'se he 'cuse' de niggers er it, but dey all 'nied it ter de las'. Mars Dugal' sot spring guns en steel traps, en he en de oberseah sot up nights once't er twice't, tel one night Mars Dugal'—he 'uz a monst'us keerless man—got his leg shot full er cow-peas. But somehow er nudder dey could n' nebber ketch none er de niggers. I dunner how it happen, but it happen des like I tell you, en de grapes kep' on a-goin' des de same.

"But bimeby ole Mars Dugal' fix' up a plan ter stop it. Dey wuz a cunjuh 'oman livin' down 'mongs' de free niggers on de Wim'l'ton Road, en all de darkies fum Rockfish ter Beaver Crick wuz feared er her. She could wuk de mos' powerfulles' kin' er goopher,—could make people hab fits, er rheumatiz, er make 'em des dwinel away en die; en dey say she went out ridin' de niggers at night, fer she wuz a witch 'sides bein' a cunjuh 'oman. Mars Dugal' hearn 'bout Aun' Peggy's doin's, en begun ter 'flect whe'r er no he could n' git her ter he'p him keep de niggers off'n de grapevimes. One day in de spring er de year, ole miss pack' up a basket er chick'n en poun'-cake, en a bottle er scuppernon' wine, en Mars Dugal' tuk it in his buggy en driv ober ter Aun' Peggy's cabin. He tuk de basket in, en had a long talk wid Aun' Peggy.

"De nex' day Aun' Peggy come up ter de vimya'd. De niggers seed her slippin' 'roun', en dey soon foun' out what she 'uz doin' dere. Mars Dugal' had hi'ed her ter goopher de grapevimes. She sa'ntered 'roun' 'mongs' de vimes, en tuk a leaf fum dis one, en a grape-hull fum dat one, en a grape-seed fum anudder one; en den a little twig fum here, en a little pinch er dirt fum dere,—en put it all in a big black bottle, wid a snake's toof en a speckle' hen's gall en some ha'rs fum a black cat's tail, en den fill' de bottle wid scuppernon' wine. Wen she got de goopher all ready en fix', she tuk 'n went out in de woods en buried it under de root uv a red oak tree, en den come back en tole one er de niggers she done goopher de grapevimes, en a'er a nigger w'at eat dem grapes 'ud be sho ter die inside'n twel' mont's.

"Atter dat de niggers let de scuppernon's 'lone, en Mars Dugal' did n' hab no 'casion ter fine no mo' fault; en de season wuz mos' gone, w'en a strange gemman stop at de plantation one night ter see Mars Dugal' on some business; en his coachman, seein' de scuppernon's growin' so nice en sweet, slip 'roun' behine de smoke-house, en et all de scuppernon's he could hole. Nobody did n' notice it at de time, but dat night, on de way home, de gemman's hoss runned away en kill' de coachman. W'en we hearn de noos, Aun' Lucy, de cook, she up 'n say she seed de strange nigger eat'n' er de scuppernon's behine de smoke-house; en den we knowed de goopher had b'en er wukkin'. Den one er de nigger chilluns runned away fum de quarters one day, en got in de scuppernon's, en died de nex' week. W'ite folks say he die' er de fevuh, but de niggers knowed it wuz de goopher. So you k'n be sho de darkies did n' hab much ter do wid dem scuppernon' vimes.

"W'en de scuppernon' season 'uz ober fer dat year, Mars Dugal' foun' he had made fifteen hund'ed gallon er wine; en one er de niggers hearn him laffin' wid de oberseah fit ter kill, en sayin' dem fifteen hund'ed gallon er wine wuz monst'us good intrus' on de ten dollars he laid out on de vimya'd. So I 'low ez he paid Aun' Peggy ten dollars fer to goopher de grapevimes.

"De goopher did n' wuk no mo' tel de nex' summer, w'en 'long to'ds de middle er de season one er de fiel' han's died; en ez dat lef' Mars Dugal' sho't er han's, he went off ter town fer ter buy anudder. He fotch de noo nigger home wid 'im. He wuz er ole nigger, er de color er a gingy-cake, en ball ez a hoss-apple on de top er his head. He wuz a peart ole nigger, do', en could do a big day's wuk.

"Now it happen dat one er de niggers on de nex' plantation, one er ole Mars Henry Brayboy's niggers, had runned away de day befo', en tuk ter de swamp, en ole Mars Dugal' en some er de yuther nabor w'ite folks had gone out wid dere guns en dere dogs fer ter he'p 'em hunt fer de nigger; en de han's on our own plantation wuz all so flusterated dat we fuhgot ter tell de noo han' 'bout de goopher on de scuppernon' vimes. Co'se he smell de grapes en see de vimes, an atter dahk de fus' thing he done wuz ter slip off ter de grapevimes 'dout sayin' nuffin ter nobody. Nex' mawnin' he tole some er de niggers 'bout de fine bait er scuppernon' he et de night befo'.

"Wen dey tole 'im 'bout de goopher on de grapevimes, he 'uz dat tarrified dat he turn pale, en look des like he gwine ter die right in his tracks. De oberseah come up en axed w'at 'uz de matter; en w'en dey tole 'im Henry be'n eatin' er de scuppernon's, en got de goopher on 'im, he gin Henry a big drink er w'iskey, en 'low dat de nex' rainy day he take 'im ober ter Aun' Peggy's, en see ef she would n' take de goopher off'n him, seein' ez he did n' know nuffin erbout it tel he done et de grapes.

"Sho nuff, it rain de nex' day, en de oberseah went ober ter Aun' Peggy's wid Henry. En Aun' Peggy say dat bein' ez Henry did n' know 'bout de goopher, en et de grapes in ign'ance er de conseq'ences, she reckon she mought be able fer ter take de goopher off'n him. So she fotch out er bottle wid some cunjuh medicine in it, en po'd some out in a go'd fer Henry ter drink. He manage ter git it down; he say it tas'e like whiskey wid sump'n bitter in it. She 'lowed dat 'ud keep de goopher off'n him tel de spring; but w'en de sap begin ter rise in de grapevimes he ha' ter come en see her ag'in, en she tell him w'at e's ter do.

"Nex' spring, w'en de sap commence' ter rise in de scuppernon' vime, Henry tuk a ham one night. Whar'd he git de ham? *I* doan know; dey wa'n't no hams on de plantation 'cep'n' w'at 'uz in de smoke-house, but *I* never see Henry 'bout de smoke-house. But ez I wuz a-sayin', he tuk de ham ober ter Aun' Peggy's; en Aun' Peggy tole 'im dat w'en Mars Dugal' begin ter prune de grapevimes, he mus' go en take 'n scrape off de sap whar it ooze out'n de cut een's er de vimes, en 'n'int his ball head wid it; en ef he do dat once't a year de goopher would n' wuk agin 'im long ez he done it. En bein' ez he fotch her de ham, she fix' it so he kin eat all de scuppernon' he want.

"So Henry 'n'int his head wid de sap out'n de big grapevime des ha'f way 'twix' de quarters en de big house, en de goopher nebber wuk agin him dat summer. But de beatenes' thing you eber see happen ter Henry. Up ter dat time he wuz ez ball ez a sweeten' 'tater, but des ez soon ez de young leaves begun ter come out on de grapevimes, de ha'r begun ter grow out on Henry's head, en by de middle er de summer he had de bigges' head er ha'r on de plantation. Befo' dat, Henry had tol'able good ha'r 'roun' de aidges, but soon ez de young grapes begun ter come, Henry's ha'r begun to quirl all up in little balls, des like dis yer reg'lar grapy ha'r, en by de time de grapes got ripe his head look des like a bunch er grapes. Combin' it did n' do no good; he wuk at it ha'f de night wid er Jim Crow[1], en think he git it straighten' out, but in de mawnin' de grapes 'ud be dere des de same. So he gin it up, en tried ter keep de grapes down by havin' his ha'r cut sho't.

[1]

A small card, resembling a currycomb in construction, and used by negroes in the rural districts instead of a comb.

"But dat wa'n't de quares' thing 'bout de goopher. When Henry come ter de plantation, he wuz gittin' a little ole an stiff in de j'ints. But dat summer he got des ez spry en libely ez any young nigger on de plantation; fac', he got so biggity dat Mars Jackson, de oberseah, ha' ter th'eaten ter whip 'im, ef he did n' stop cuttin' up his didos en behave hisse'f. But de mos' cur'ouses' thing happen' in de fall, when de sap begin ter go down in de grapevimes. Fus', when de grapes 'uz gethered, de knots begun ter straighten out'n Henry's ha'r; en w'en de leaves begin ter fall, Henry's ha'r 'mence' ter drap out; en when de vimes 'uz bar', Henry's head wuz baller 'n it wuz in de spring, en he begin ter git ole en stiff in de j'ints ag'in, en paid no mo' 'tention ter de gals dyoin' er de whole winter. En nex' spring, w'en he rub de sap on ag'in, he got young ag'in, en so soopl en libely dat none er de young niggers on de plantation could n' jump, ner dance, ner hoe ez much cotton ez Henry. But in de fall er de year his grapes 'mence' ter straighten out, en his j'ints ter git stiff, en his ha'r drap off, en de rheumatiz begin ter wrastle wid 'im.

"Now, ef you 'd 'a' knowed ole Mars Dugal' McAdoo, you 'd 'a' knowed dat it ha' ter be a mighty rainy day when he could n' fine sump'n fer his niggers ter do, en it ha' ter be a mighty little hole he could n' crawl thoo, en ha' ter be a monst'us cloudy night when a dollar git by him in de dahkness; en w'en he see how Henry git young in de spring en ole in de fall, he 'lowed ter hisse'f ez how he could make mo' money out'n Henry dan by wukkin' him in de cotton-fiel'. 'Long de nex' spring, atter de sap 'mence' ter rise, en Henry 'n'int 'is head en sta'ted fer ter git young en soopl, Mars Dugal' up 'n tuk Henry ter town, en sole 'im fer fifteen hunder' dollars. Co'se de man w'at bought Henry did n' know nuffin 'bout de goopher, en Mars Dugal' did n' see no 'casion fer ter tell 'im. Long to'ds de fall, w'en de sap went down, Henry begin ter git ole ag'in same ez yuzhal, en his noo marster begin ter git skeered les'n he gwine ter lose his fifteen-hunder'-dollar nigger. He sent fer a mighty fine doctor, but de med'cine did n' 'pear ter do no good; de goopher had a good holt. Henry tole de doctor 'bout de goopher, but de doctor des laff at 'im.

"One day in de winter Mars Dugal' went ter town, en wuz santerin' 'long de Main Street, when who should he meet but Henry's noo marster. Dey said 'Hoddy,' en Mars Dugal' ax 'im ter hab a seegyar; en atter dey run on awhile 'bout de craps en de weather, Mars Dugal' ax 'im, sorter keerless, like ez ef he des thought of it,—

"'How you like de nigger I sole you las' spring?'

"Henry's marster shuck his head en knock de ashes off'n his seegyar.

"'Spec' I made a bad bahgin when I bought dat nigger. Henry done good wuk all de summer, but sence de fall set in he 'pears ter be sorter pinin' away. Dey ain' nuffin pertickler de matter wid 'im—leastways de doctor say so—'cep'n' a tech er de rheumatiz; but his ha'r is all fell out, en ef he don't pick up his strenk mighty soon, I spec' I'm gwine ter lose 'im.'

"Dey smoked on awhile, en bimeby ole mars say, 'Well, a bahgin 's a bahgin, but you en me is good fren's, en I doan wan' ter see you lose all de money you paid fer dat nigger; en ef w'at you say is so, en I ain't 'sputin' it, he ain't wuf much now. I 'spec's you wukked him too ha'd dis summer, er e'se de swamps down here don't agree wid de san'-hill nigger. So you des lemme know, en ef he gits any wusser I'll be willin' ter gib yer five hund'ed dollars fer 'im, en take my chances on his livin'.'

"Sho 'nuff, when Henry begun ter draw up wid de rheumatiz en it look like he gwine ter die fer sho, his noo marster sen' fer Mars Dugal', en Mars Dugal' gin him what he promus, en brung Henry home ag'in. He tuk good keer uv 'im dyoin' er de winter,—give 'im w'iskey ter rub his rheumatiz, en terbacker ter smoke, en all he want ter eat,—'caze a nigger w'at he could make a thousan' dollars a year off'n did n' grow on eve'y huckleberry bush.

"Nex' spring, w'en de sap ris en Henry's ha'r commence' ter sprout, Mars Dugal' sole 'im ag'in, down in Robeson County dis time; en he kep' dat sellin' business up fer five year er mo'. Henry nebber say nuffin 'bout de goopher ter his noo marsters, 'caze he know he gwine ter be tuk good keer uv de nex' winter, w'en Mars Dugal' buy him back. En Mars Dugal' made 'nuff money off'n Henry ter buy anudder plantation ober on Beaver Crick.

"But 'long 'bout de een' er dat five year dey come a stranger ter stop at de plantation. De fus' day he 'uz dere he went out wid Mars Dugal' en spent all de mawnin' lookin' ober de vimya'd, en atter dinner dey spent all de evenin' playin' kya'ds. De niggers soon 'skiver' dat he wuz a Yankee, en dat he come down ter Norf C'lina fer ter l'arn de w'ite folks how to raise grapes en make wine. He promus Mars Dugal' he c'd make de grapevimes b'ar twice't ez many grapes, en dat de noo winepress he wuz a-sellin' would make mo' d'n twice't ez many gallons er wine. En ole Mars Dugal' des drunk it all in, des 'peared ter be bewitch' wid dat Yankee. Wen de darkies see dat Yankee runnin' 'roun' de vimya'd en diggin' under de grapevimes, dey shuk dere heads, en 'lowed dat dey feared Mars Dugal' losin' his min'. Mars Dugal' had all de dirt dug away fum under de roots er all de scuppernon' vimes, an' let 'em stan' dat away fer a week er mo'. Den dat Yankee made de niggers fix up a mixtry er lime en ashes en manyo, en po' it 'roun' de roots er de grapevimes. Den he 'vise Mars Dugal' fer ter trim de vimes close't, en Mars Dugal' tuck 'n done eve'ything de Yankee tole him ter do. Dyoin' all er dis time, mind yer, dis yer Yankee wuz libbin' off'n de fat er de lan', at de big house, en playin' kya'ds wid Mars Dugal' eve'y night; en dey say Mars Dugal' los' mo'n a thousan' dollars dyoin' er de week dat Yankee wuz a-ruinin' de grapevimes.

"Wen de sap ris nex' spring, ole Henry 'n'inted his head ez yuzhal, en his ha'r 'mence' ter grow des de same ez it done eve'y year. De scuppernon' vimes growed monst's fas', en de leaves wuz greener en thicker dan dey eber be'n dyoin' my rememb'ance; en Henry's ha'r growed out thicker dan eber, en he 'peared ter git younger 'n younger, en soopler 'n soopler; en seein' ez he wuz sho't er ban's dat spring, havin' tuk in consid'able noo groun', Mars Dugal' 'eluded he would n' sell Henry 'tel he git de crap in en de cotton chop'. So he kep' Henry on de plantation.

"But 'long 'bout time fer de grapes ter come on de scuppernon' vimes, dey 'peared ter come a change ober 'em; de leaves withered en swivel' up, en de young grapes turn' yaller, en bimeby eve'ybody on de plantation could see dat de whole vimya'd wuz dyin'. Mars Dugal' tuk'n water de vimes en done all he could, but 't wa'n' no use: dat Yankee had done bus' de watermillyum. One time de vimes picked up a bit, en Mars Dugal' 'lowed dey wuz gwine ter come out ag'in; but dat Yankee done dug too close under de roots, en prune de branches too close ter de vime, en all dat lime en ashes done burn' de life out'n de vimes, en dey des kep' a-with'in' en a-swivelin'.

"All dis time de goopher wuz a-wukkin'. When de vimes sta'ted ter wither, Henry 'mence' ter complain er his rheumatiz; en when de leaves begin ter dry up, his ha'r 'mence' ter drap out. When de vimes fresh' up a bit, Henry 'd git peart ag'in, en when de vimes wither' ag'in, Henry 'd git ole ag'in, en des kep' gittin' mo' en mo' fitten fer nuffin; he des pined away, en pined away, en fine'ly tuk ter his cabin; en when de big vime whar he got de sap ter 'n'int his head withered en turned yaller en died, Henry died too,—des went out sorter like a cannel. Dey didn't 'pear ter be nuffin de matter wid 'im, 'cep'n' de rheumatiz, but his strenk des dwinel' away 'tel he did n' hab ernuff lef ter draw his bref. De goopher had got de under holt, en th'owed Henry dat time fer good en all.

"Mars Dugal' tuk on might'ly 'bout losin' his vimes en his nigger in de same year; en he swo' dat ef he could git holt er dat Yankee he 'd wear 'im ter a frazzle, en den chaw up de frazzle; en he'd done it, too, for Mars Dugal' 'uz a monst'us brash man w'en he once git started. He sot de vimya'd out ober ag'in, but it wuz th'ee er fo' year befo' de vimes got ter b'arin' any scuppernon's.

"W'en de wah broke out, Mars Dugal' raise' a comp'ny, en went off ter fight de Yankees. He say he wuz mighty glad dat wah come, en he des want ter kill a Yankee fer eve'y dollar he los' 'long er dat grape-raisin' Yankee. En I 'spec' he would 'a' done it, too, ef de Yankees had n' s'picioned sump'n, en killed him fus'. Atter de s'render ole miss move' ter town, de niggers all scattered 'way fum de plantation, en de vimya'd ain' be'n cultervated sence."

"Is that story true?" asked Annie doubtfully, but seriously, as the old man concluded his narrative.

"It's des ez true ez I'm a-settin' here, miss. Dey's a easy way ter prove it: I kin lead de way right ter Henry's grave ober yander in de plantation buryin'-groun'. En I tell yer w'at, marster, I would n' 'vise you to buy dis yer ole vimya'd, 'caze de goopher 's on it yit, en dey ain' no tellin' w'en it's gwine ter crap out."

"But I thought you said all the old vines died."

"Dey did 'pear ter die, but a few un 'em come out ag'in, en is mixed in 'mongs' de yuthers. I ain' skeered ter eat de grapes, 'caze I knows de old vimes fum de noo ones; but wid strangers dey ain' no tellin' w'at mought happen. I would n' 'vise yer ter buy dis vimya'd."

I bought the vineyard, nevertheless, and it has been for a long time in a thriving condition, and is often referred to by the local press as a striking illustration of the opportunities open to Northern capital in the development of Southern industries. The luscious scuppernong holds first rank among our grapes, though we cultivate a great many other varieties, and our income from grapes packed and shipped to the Northern markets is quite considerable. I have not noticed any developments of the goopher in the vineyard, although I have a mild suspicion that our colored assistants do not suffer from want of grapes during the season.

I found, when I bought the vineyard, that Uncle Julius had occupied a cabin on the place for many years, and derived a respectable revenue from the product of the neglected grapevines. This, doubtless, accounted for his advice to me not to buy the vineyard, though whether it inspired the goopher story I am unable to state. I believe, however, that the wages I paid him for his services as coachman, for I gave him employment in that capacity, were more than an equivalent for anything he lost by the sale of the vineyard.

PO' SANDY

On the northeast corner of my vineyard in central North Carolina, and fronting on the Lumberton plank-road, there stood a small frame house, of the simplest construction. It was built of pine lumber, and contained but one room, to which one window gave light and one door admission. Its weatherbeaten sides revealed a virgin innocence of paint. Against one end of the house, and occupying half its width, there stood a huge brick chimney: the crumbling mortar had left large cracks between the bricks; the bricks themselves had begun to scale off in large flakes, leaving the chimney sprinkled with unsightly blotches. These evidences of decay were but partially concealed by a creeping vine, which extended its slender branches hither and thither in an ambitious but futile attempt to cover the whole chimney. The wooden shutter, which had once protected the unglazed window, had fallen from its hinges, and lay rotting in the rank grass and jimson-weeds beneath. This building, I learned when I bought the place, had been used as a schoolhouse for several years prior to the breaking out of the war, since which time it had remained unoccupied, save when some stray cow or vagrant hog had sought shelter within its walls from the chill rains and nipping winds of winter.

One day my wife requested me to build her a new kitchen. The house erected by us, when we first came to live upon the vineyard, contained a very conveniently arranged kitchen; but for some occult reason my wife wanted a kitchen in the back yard, apart from the dwelling-house, after the usual Southern fashion. Of course I had to build it.

To save expense, I decided to tear down the old schoolhouse, and use the lumber, which was in a good state of preservation, in the construction of the new kitchen. Before demolishing the old house, however, I made an estimate of the amount of material contained in it, and found that I would have to buy several hundred feet of lumber additional, in order to build the new kitchen according to my wife's plan.

One morning old Julius McAdoo, our colored coachman, harnessed the gray mare to the rockaway, and drove my wife and me over to the sawmill from which I meant to order the new lumber. We drove down the long lane which led from our house to the plank-road; following the plank-road for about a mile, we turned into a road running through the forest and across the swamp to the sawmill beyond. Our carriage jolted over the half-rotted corduroy road which traversed the swamp, and then climbed the long hill leading to the sawmill. When we reached the mill, the foreman had gone over to a neighboring farmhouse, probably to smoke or gossip, and we were compelled to await his return before we could transact our business. We remained seated in the carriage, a few rods from the mill, and watched the leisurely movements of the mill-hands. We had not waited long before a huge pine log was placed in position, the machinery of the mill was set in motion, and the circular saw began to eat its way through the log, with a loud whir which resounded throughout the vicinity of the mill. The sound rose and fell in a sort of rhythmic cadence, which, heard from where we sat, was not unpleasing, and not loud enough to prevent conversation. When the saw started on its second journey through the log, Julius observed, in a lugubrious tone, and with a perceptible shudder:—

"Ugh! but dat des do cuddle my blood!"

"What's the matter, Uncle Julius?" inquired my wife, who is of a very sympathetic turn of mind. "Does the noise affect your nerves?"

"No, Mis' Annie," replied the old man, with emotion, "I ain' narvous; but dat saw, a-cuttin' en grindin' thoo dat stick er timber, en moanin', en groanin,' en sweekin', kyars my 'memb'ance back ter ole times, en 'min's me er po' Sandy." The pathetic intonation with which he lengthened out the "po' Sandy" touched a responsive chord in our own hearts.

"And who was poor Sandy?" asked my wife, who takes a deep interest in the stories of plantation life which she hears from the lips of the older colored people. Some of these stories are quaintly humorous; others wildly extravagant, revealing the Oriental cast of the negro's imagination; while others, poured freely into the sympathetic ear of a Northern-bred woman, disclose many a tragic incident of the darker side of slavery.

"Sandy," said Julius, in reply to my wife's question, "was a nigger w'at useter b'long ter ole Mars Marrabo McSwayne. Mars Marrabo's place wuz on de yuther side'n de swamp, right nex' ter yo' place. Sandy wuz a monst'us good nigger, en could do so many things erbout a plantation, en alluz 'ten' ter his wuk so well, dat w'en Mars Marrabo's chilluns growed up en married off, dey all un 'em wanted dey daddy fer ter gin 'em Sandy fer a weddin' present. But Mars Marrabo knowed de res' would n' be satisfied ef he gin Sandy ter a'er one un 'em; so w'en dey wuz all done married, he fix it by 'lowin' one er his chilluns ter take Sandy fer a mont' er so, en den ernudder for a mont' er so, en so on dat erway tel dey had all had 'im de same lenk er time; en den dey would all take him roun' ag'in, 'cep'n' oncet in a w'ile w'en Mars Marrabo would len' 'im ter some er his yuther kinfolks 'roun' de country, w'en dey wuz short er han's; tel bimeby it got so Sandy did n' hardly knowed whar he wuz gwine ter stay fum one week's een' ter de yuther.

"One time w'en Sandy wuz lent out ez yushal, a spekilater come erlong wid a lot er niggers, en Mars Marrabo swap' Sandy's wife off fer a noo 'oman. W'en Sandy come back, Mars Marrabo gin 'im a dollar, en 'lowed he wuz monst'us sorry fer ter break up de fambly, but de spekilater had gin 'im big boot, en times wuz hard en money skase, en so he wuz bleedst ter make de trade. Sandy tuk on some 'bout losin' his wife, but he soon seed dey want no use cryin' ober spilt merlasses; en bein' ez he lacked de looks er de noo 'oman, he tuk up wid her atter she'd be'n on de plantation a mont' er so.

"Sandy en his noo wife got on mighty well tergedder, en de niggers all 'mence' ter talk about how lovin' dey wuz. Wen Tenie wuz tuk sick oncet, Sandy useter set up all night wid 'er, en den go ter wuk in de mawnin' des lack he had his reg'lar sleep; en Tenie would 'a' done anythin' in de worl' for her Sandy.

"Sandy en Tenie had n' be'n libbin' tergedder fer mo' d'n two mont's befo' Mars Marrabo's old uncle, w'at libbed down in Robeson County, sent up ter fin' out ef Mars Marrabo could n' len' 'im er hire 'im a good ban' fer a mont' er so. Sandy's marster wuz one er dese yer easy-gwine folks w'at wanter please eve'ybody, en he says yas, he could len' 'im Sandy. En Mars Marrabo tol' Sandy fer ter git ready ter go down ter Robeson nex' day, fer ter stay a mont' er so.

"It wuz monst'us hard on Sandy fer ter take 'im 'way fum Tenie. It wuz so fur down ter Robeson dat he did n' hab no chance er comin' back ter see her tel de time wuz up; he would n' 'a' mine comin' ten er fifteen mile at night ter see Tenie, but Mars Marrabo's uncle's plantation wuz mo' d'n forty mile off. Sandy wuz mighty sad en cas' down atter w'at Mars Marrabo tol' 'im, en he says ter Tenie, sezee:—

"'I'm gittin' monst'us ti'ed er dish yer gwine roun' so much. Here I is lent ter Mars Jeems dis mont', en I got ter do so-en-so; en ter Mars Archie de nex' mont', en I got ter do so-en-so; den I got ter go ter Miss Jinnie's: en hit's Sandy dis en Sandy dat, en Sandy yer en Sandy dere, tel it 'pears ter me I ain' got no home, ner no marster, ner no mistiss, ner no nuffin. I can't eben keep a wife: my yuther ole 'oman wuz sol' away widout my gittin' a chance fer ter tell her good-by; en now I got ter go off en leab you, Tenie, en I dunno whe'r I'm eber gwine ter see you ag'in er no. I wisht I wuz a tree, er a stump, er a rock, er sump'n w'at could stay on de plantation fer a w'ile.'

"Atter Sandy got thoo talkin', Tenie didn' say naer word, but des sot dere by de fier, studyin' en studyin'. Bimeby she up 'n' says:—

"'Sandy, is I eber tol' you I wuz a cunjuh 'oman?'

"Co'se Sandy had n' nebber dremp' er nuffin lack dat, en he made a great 'miration w'en he hear w'at Tenie say. Bimeby Tenie went on:—

"'I ain' goophered nobody, ner done no cunjuh wuk, fer fifteen year er mo'; en w'en I got religion I made up my mine I would n' wuk no mo' goopher. But dey is some things I doan b'lieve it's no sin fer ter do; en ef you doan wanter be sent roun' fum pillar ter pos', en ef you doan wanter go down ter Robeson, I kin fix things so you won't haf ter. Ef you'll des say de word, I kin turn you ter w'ateber you wanter be, en you kin stay right whar you wanter, ez long ez you mineter.'

"Sandy say he doan keer; he's will-in' fer ter do anythin' fer ter stay close ter Tenie. Den Tenie ax 'im ef he doan wanter be turnt inter a rabbit.

"Sandy say, 'No, de dogs mought git atter me.'

"'Shill I turn you ter a wolf?' sez Tenie.

"'No, eve'ybody 's skeered er a wolf, en I doan want nobody ter be skeered er me.'

"'Shill I turn you ter a mawkin'-bird?'

"'No, a hawk mought ketch me. I wanter be turnt inter sump'n w'at'll stay in one place.'

"'I kin turn you ter a tree,' sez Tenie. 'You won't hab no mouf ner years, but I kin turn you back oncet in a w'ile, so you kin git sump'n ter eat, en hear w'at 's gwine on.'

"Well, Sandy say dat'll do. En so Tenie tuk 'im down by de aidge er de swamp, not fur fum de quarters, en turnt 'im inter a big pine-tree, en sot 'im out 'mongs' some yuther trees. En de nex' mawnin', ez some er de fiel' han's wuz gwine long dere, dey seed a tree w'at dey did n' 'member er habbin' seed befo'; it wuz monst'us quare, en dey wuz bleedst ter 'low dat dey had n' 'membered right, er e'se one er de saplin's had be'n growin' monst'us fas'.

"W'en Mars Marrabo 'skiver' dat Sandy wuz gone, he 'lowed Sandy had runned away. He got de dogs out, but de las' place dey could track Sandy ter wuz de foot er dat pine-tree. En dere de dogs stood en barked, en bayed, en pawed at de tree, en tried ter climb up on it; en w'en dey wuz tuk roun' thoo de swamp ter look fer de scent, dey broke loose en made fer dat tree ag'in. It wuz de beatenis' thing de w'ite folks eber hearn of, en Mars Marrabo 'lowed dat Sandy must 'a' clim' up on de tree en jump' off on a mule er sump'n, en rid fur ernuff fer ter spile de scent. Mars Marrabo wanted ter 'cuse some er de yuther niggers er heppin' Sandy off, but dey all 'nied it ter de las'; en eve'ybody knowed Tenie sot too much sto' by Sandy fer ter he'p 'im run away whar she could n' nebber see 'im no mo'.

"W'en Sandy had be'n gone long ernuff fer folks ter think he done got clean away, Tenie useter go down ter de woods at night en turn 'im back, en den dey 'd slip up ter de cabin en set by de fire en talk. But dey ha' ter be monst'us keerful, er e'se somebody would 'a' seed 'em, en dat would 'a' spile' de whole thing; so Tenie alluz turnt Sandy back in de mawnin' early, befo' anybody wuz a-stirrin'.

"But Sandy did n' git erlong widout his trials en tribberlations. One day a woodpecker come erlong en 'mence' ter peck at de tree; en de nex' time Sandy wuz turnt back he had a little roun' hole in his arm, des lack a sharp stick be'n stuck in it. Atter dat Tenie sot a sparrer-hawk fer ter watch de tree; en w'en de woodpecker come erlong nex' mawnin' fer ter finish his nes', he got gobble' up mos' 'fo' he stuck his bill in de bark.

"Nudder time, Mars Marrabo sent a nigger out in de woods fer ter chop tuppentime boxes. De man chop a box in dish yer tree, en hack' de bark up two er th'ee feet, fer ter let de tuppentime run. De nex' time Sandy wuz turnt back he had a big skyar on his lef' leg, des lack it be'n skunt; en it tuk Tenie nigh 'bout all night fer ter fix a mixtry ter kyo it up. Atter dat, Tenie sot a hawnet fer ter watch de tree; en w'en de nigger come back ag'in fer ter cut ernudder box on de yuther side'n de tree, de hawnet stung 'im so hard dat de ax slip en cut his foot nigh 'bout off.

"W'en Tenie see so many things happenin' ter de tree, she 'eluded she 'd ha' ter turn Sandy ter sump'n e'se; en atter studyin' de matter ober, en talkin' wid Sandy one ebenin', she made up her mine fer ter fix up a goopher mixtry w'at would turn herse'f en Sandy ter foxes, er sump'n, so dey could run away en go some'rs whar dey could be free en lib lack w'ite folks.

"But dey ain' no tellin' w'at's gwine ter happen in dis worl'. Tenie had got de night sot fer her en Sandy ter run away, w'en dat ve'y day one er Mars Marrabo's sons rid up ter de big house in his buggy, en say his wife wuz monst'us sick, en he want his mammy ter len' 'im a 'oman fer ter nuss his wife. Tenie's mistiss say sen' Tenie; she wuz a good nuss. Young mars wuz in a tarrible hurry fer ter git back home. Tenie wuz washin' at de big house dat day, en her mistiss say she should go right 'long wid her young marster. Tenie tried ter make some 'scuse fer ter git away en hide 'tel night, w'en she would have eve'ything fix' up fer her en Sandy; she say she wanter go ter her cabin fer ter git her bonnet. Her mistiss say it doan matter 'bout de bonnet; her head-hank-cher wuz good ernuff. Den Tenie say she wanter git her bes' frock; her mistiss say no, she doan need no mo' frock, en w'en dat one got dirty she could git a clean one whar she wuz gwine. So Tenie had ter git in de buggy en go 'long wid young Mars Dunkin ter his plantation, w'ich wuz mo' d'n twenty mile away; en dey wa'n't no chance er her seein' Sandy no mo' 'tel she come back home. De po' gal felt monst'us bad 'bout de way things wuz gwine on, en she knowed Sandy mus' be a wond'rin' why she didn' come en turn 'im back no mo'.

"Wiles Tenie wuz away nussin' young Mars Dunkin's wife, Mars Marrabo tuk a notion fer ter buil' 'im a noo kitchen; en bein' ez he had lots er timber on his place, he begun ter look 'roun' fer a tree ter hab de lumber sawed out'n. En I dunno how it come to be so, but he happen fer ter hit on de ve'y tree w'at Sandy wuz turnt inter. Tenie wuz gone, en dey wa'n't nobody ner nuffin fer ter watch de tree.

"De two men w'at cut de tree down say dey nebber had sech a time wid a tree befo': dey axes would glansh off, en did n' 'pear ter make no progress thoo de wood; en of all de creakin', en shakin', en wobblin' you eber see, dat tree done it w'en it commence' ter fall. It wuz de beatenis' thing!

"W'en dey got de tree all trim' up, dey chain it up ter a timber waggin, en start fer de sawmill. But dey had a hard time gittin' de log dere: fus' dey got stuck in de mud w'en dey wuz gwine crosst de swamp, en it wuz two er th'ee hours befo' dey could git out. W'en dey start' on ag'in, de chain kep' a-comin' loose, en dey had ter keep a-stoppin' en a-stoppin' fer ter hitch de log up ag'in. W'en dey commence' ter climb de hill ter de sawmill, de log broke loose, en roll down de hill en in 'mongs' de trees, en hit tuk nigh 'bout half a day mo' ter git it haul' up ter de sawmill.

"De nex' mawnin' atter de day de tree wuz haul' ter de sawmill, Tenie come home. W'en she got back ter her cabin, de fus' thing she done wuz ter run down ter de woods en see how Sandy wuz gittin' on. Wen she seed de stump standin' dere, wid de sap runnin' out'n it, en de limbs layin' scattered roun', she nigh 'bout went out'n her min'. She run ter her cabin, en got her goopher mixtry, en den follered de track er de timber waggin ter de sawmill. She knowed Sandy could n' lib mo' d'n a minute er so ef she turnt him back, fer he wuz all chop' up so he 'd 'a' be'n bleedst ter die. But she wanted ter turn 'im back long ernuff fer ter 'splain ter 'im dat she had n' went off a-purpose, en lef 'im ter be chop' down en sawed up. She did n' want Sandy ter die wid no hard feelin's to'ds her.

"De han's at de sawmill had des got de big log on de kerridge, en wuz start-in' up de saw, w'en dey seed a 'oman runnin' up de hill, all out er bref, cryin' en gwine on des lack she wuz plumb 'stracted. It wuz Tenie; she come right inter de mill, en th'owed herse'f on de log, right in front er de saw, a-hollerin' en cryin' ter her Sandy ter fergib her, en not ter think hard er her, fer it wa'n't no fault er hern. Den Tenie 'membered de tree did n' hab no years, en she wuz gittin' ready fer ter wuk her goopher mixtry so ez ter turn Sandy back, w'en de mill-hands kotch holt er her en tied her arms wid a rope, en fasten' her to one er de posts in de sawmill; en den dey started de saw up ag'in, en cut de log up inter bo'ds en scantlin's right befo' her eyes. But it wuz mighty hard wuk; fer of all de sweekin', en moanin', en groanin', dat log done it w'iles de saw wuz a-cuttin' thoo it. De saw wuz one er dese yer ole-timey, up-en-down saws, en hit tuk longer dem days ter saw a log 'en it do now. Dey greased de saw, but dat did n' stop de fuss; hit kep' right on, tel fin'ly dey got de log all sawed up.

"W'en de oberseah w'at run de sawmill come fum breakfas', de han's up en tell him 'bout de crazy 'oman—ez dey s'posed she wuz—w'at had come runnin' in de sawmill, a-hollerin' en gwine on, en tried ter th'ow herse'f befo' de saw. En de oberseah sent two er th'ee er de han's fer ter take Tenie back ter her marster's plantation.

"Tenie 'peared ter be out'n her min' fer a long time, en her marster ha' ter lock her up in de smoke-'ouse 'tel she got ober her spells. Mars Marrabo wuz monst'us mad, en hit would 'a' made yo' flesh crawl fer ter hear him cuss, 'caze he say de spekilater w'at he got Tenie fum had fooled 'im by wukkin' a crazy 'oman off on him. Wiles Tenie wuz lock up in de smoke-'ouse, Mars Marrabo tuk 'n' haul de lumber fum de sawmill, en put up his noo kitchen.

"Wen Tenie got quiet' down, so she could be 'lowed ter go 'roun' de plantation, she up'n' tole her marster all erbout Sandy en de pine-tree; en w'en Mars Marrabo hearn it, he 'lowed she wuz de wuss 'stracted nigger he eber hearn of. He did n' know w'at ter do wid Tenie: fus' he thought he 'd put her in de po'house; but fin'ly, seein' ez she did n' do no harm ter nobody ner nuffin, but des went 'roun' moanin', en groanin', en shakin' her head, he 'cluded ter let her stay on de plantation en nuss de little nigger chilluns w'en dey mammies wuz ter wuk in de cotton-fiel'.

"De noo kitchen Mars Marrabo buil' wuz n' much use, fer it had n' be'n put up long befo' de niggers 'mence' ter notice quare things erbout it. Dey could hear sump'n moanin' en groanin' 'bout de kitchen in de night-time, en w'en de win' would blow dey could hear sump'n a-hollerin' en sweekin' lack it wuz in great pain en sufferin'. En it got so atter a w'ile dat it wuz all Mars Marrabo's wife could do ter git a 'oman ter stay in de kitchen in de daytime long ernuff ter do de cookin'; en dey wa'n't naer nigger on de plantation w'at would n' rudder take forty dan ter go 'bout dat kitchen atter dark,—dat is, 'cep'n' Tenie; she did n' 'pear ter min' de ha'nts. She useter slip 'roun' at night, en set on de kitchen steps, en lean up agin de do'-jamb, en run on ter herse'f wid some kine er foolishness w'at nobody could n' make out; fer Mars Marrabo had th'eaten' ter sen' her off'n de plantation ef she say anything ter any er de yuther niggers 'bout de pine-tree. But somehow er 'nudder de niggers foun' out all erbout it, en dey all knowed de kitchen wuz ha'nted by Sandy's sperrit. En bimeby hit got so Mars Marrabo's wife herse'f wuz skeered ter go out in de yard atter dark.

"Wen it come ter dat, Mars Marrabo tuk en to' de kitchen down, en use' de lumber fer ter buil' dat ole school'ouse w'at you er talkin' 'bout pullin' down. De school'ouse wuz n' use' 'cep'n' in de daytime, en on dark nights folks gwine 'long de road would hear quare soun's en see quare things. Po' ole Tenie useter go down dere 'at night, en wander 'roun' de school'ouse; en de niggers all 'lowed she went fer ter talk wid Sandy's sperrit. En one winter mawnin', w'en one er de boys went ter school early fer ter start de fire, w'at should he fin' but po' ole Tenie, layin' on de flo', stiff, en col', en dead. Dere did n' 'pear ter be nuffin pertickler de matter wid her,—she had des grieve' herse'f ter def fer her Sandy. Mars Marrabo didn' shed no tears. He thought Tenie wuz crazy, en dey wa'n't no tellin' w'at she mought do nex'; en dey ain' much room in dis worl' fer crazy w'ite folks, let 'lone a crazy nigger.

"Hit wa'n't long atter dat befo' Mars Marrabo sol' a piece er his track er lan' ter Mars Dugal' McAdoo,—*my* ole marster,—en dat 's how de ole school'ouse happen to be on yo' place. Wen de wah broke out, de school stop', en de ole school'ouse be'n stannin' empty ever sence,—dat is, 'cep'n' fer de ha'nts. En folks sez dat de ole school'ouse, er any yuther house w'at got any er dat lumber in it w'at wuz sawed out'n de tree w'at Sandy wuz turnt inter, is gwine ter be ha'nted tel de las' piece er plank is rotted en crumble' inter dus'."

Annie had listened to this gruesome narrative with strained attention.

"What a system it was," she exclaimed, when Julius had finished, "under which such things were possible!"

"What things?" I asked, in amazement. "Are you seriously considering the possibility of a man's being turned into a tree?"

"Oh, no," she replied quickly, "not that;" and then she murmured absently, and with a dim look in her fine eyes, "Poor Tenie!"

We ordered the lumber, and returned home. That night, after we had gone to bed, and my wife had to all appearances been sound asleep for half an hour, she startled me out of an incipient doze by exclaiming suddenly,—

"John, I don't believe I want my new kitchen built out of the lumber in that old schoolhouse."

"You wouldn't for a moment allow yourself," I replied, with some asperity, "to be influenced by that absurdly impossible yarn which Julius was spinning to-day?"

"I know the story is absurd," she replied dreamily, "and I am not so silly as to believe it. But I don't think I should ever be able to take any pleasure in that kitchen if it were built out of that lumber. Besides, I think the kitchen would look better and last longer if the lumber were all new."

Of course she had her way. I bought the new lumber, though not without grumbling. A week or two later I was called away from home on business. On my return, after an absence of several days, my wife remarked to me,—

"John, there has been a split in the Sandy Run Colored Baptist Church, on the temperance question. About half the members have come out from the main body, and set up for themselves. Uncle Julius is one of the seceders, and he came to me yesterday and asked if they might not hold their meetings in the old schoolhouse for the present."

"I hope you didn't let the old rascal have it," I returned, with some warmth. I had just received a bill for the new lumber I had bought.

"Well," she replied, "I couldn't refuse him the use of the house for so good a purpose."

"And I'll venture to say," I continued, "that you subscribed something toward the support of the new church?"

She did not attempt to deny it.

"What are they going to do about the ghost?" I asked, somewhat curious to know how Julius would get around this obstacle.

"Oh," replied Annie, "Uncle Julius says that ghosts never disturb religious worship, but that if Sandy's spirit *should* happen to stray into meeting by mistake, no doubt the preaching would do it good."

Jean Toomer, Cane

Jean Toomer, Cane

FOREWORD

READING this book, I had the vision of a land, heretofore sunk in the mists of muteness, suddenly rising up into the eminence of song. Innumerable books have been written about the South; some good books have been written in the South. This book *is* the South. I do not mean that *Cane* covers the South or is the South's full voice. Merely this: a poet has arisen among our American youth who has known how to turn the essences and materials of his Southland into the essences and materials of literature. A poet has arisen in that land who writes, not as a Southerner, not as a rebel against Southerners, not as a Negro, not as apologist or priest or critic: who writes as a *poet*. The fashioning of beauty is ever foremost in his inspiration: not forcedly but simply, and because these ultimate aspects of his world are to him more real than all its specific problems. He has made songs and lovely stories of his land … not of its yesterday, but of its immediate life. And that has been enough.

How rare this is will be clear to those whoviii have followed with concern the struggle of the South toward literary expression, and the particular trial of that portion of its folk whose skin is dark. The gifted Negro has been too often thwarted from becoming a poet because his world was forever forcing him to recollect that he was a Negro. The artist must lose such lesser identities in the great well of life. The English poet is not forever protesting and recalling that he is English. It is so natural and easy for him to be English that he can sing as a man. The French novelist is not forever noting: "This is French." It is so atmospheric for him to be French, that he can devote himself to saying: "This is human." This is an imperative condition for the creating of deep art. The whole will and mind of the creator must go below the surfaces of race. And this has been an almost impossible condition for the American Negro to achieve, forced every moment of his life into a specific and superficial plane of consciousness.

The first negative significance of *Cane* is that this so natural and restrictive state of mind is completely lacking. For Toomer, the Southland is not a problem to be solved; it is a field of loveliness ixto be sung: the Georgia Negro is not a downtrodden soul to be uplifted; he is material for gorgeous painting: the segregated self-conscious brown belt of Washington is not a topic to be discussed and exposed; it is a subject of beauty and of drama, worthy of creation in literary form.

It seems to me, therefore, that this is a first book in more ways than one. It is a harbinger of the South's literary maturity: of its emergence from the obsession put upon its minds by the unending racial crisis—an obsession from which writers have made their indirect escape through sentimentalism, exoticism, polemic, "problem" fiction, and moral melodrama. It marks the dawn of direct and unafraid creation. And, as the initial work of a man of twenty-seven, it is the harbinger of a literary force of whose incalculable future I believe no reader of this book will be in doubt.

How typical is *Cane* of the South's still virgin soil and of its pressing seeds! and the book's chaos of verse, tale, drama, its rhythmic rolling shift from lyrism to narrative, from mystery to intimate pathos! But read the book throughx and you will see a complex and significant form take substance from its chaos. Part One is the primitive and evanescent black world of Georgia. Part Two is the threshing and suffering brown world of Washington, lifted by opportunity and contact into the anguish of self-conscious struggle. Part Three is Georgia again … the invasion into this black womb of the ferment seed: the neurotic, educated, spiritually stirring Negro. As a broad form this is superb, and the very looseness and unexpected waves of the book's parts make *Cane* still more *South*, still more of an æsthetic equivalent of the land.

What a land it is! What an Æschylean beauty to its fateful problem! Those of you who love our South will find here some of your love. Those of you who know it not will perhaps begin to understand what a warm splendor is at last at dawn.

A feast of moon and men and barking hounds,
An orgy for some genius of the South
With bloodshot eyes and cane-lipped scented mouth
Surprised in making folk-songs....

So, in his still sometimes clumsy stride (forxi Toomer is finally a poet in prose) the author gives you an inkling of his revelation. An individual force, wise enough to drink humbly at this great spring of his land ... such is the first impression of Jean Toomer. But beyond this wisdom and this power (which shows itself perhaps most splendidly in his complete freedom from the sense of persecution), there rises a figure more significant: the artist, hard, self-immolating, the artist who is not interested in races, whose domain is Life. The book's final Part is no longer "promise"; it is achievement. It is no mere dawn: it is a bit of the full morning. These materials ... the ancient black man, mute, inaccessible, and yet so mystically close to the new tumultuous members of his race, the simple slave Past, the shredding Negro Present, the iridescent passionate dream of the To-morrow ... are made and measured by a craftsman into an unforgettable music. The notes of his counterpoint are particular, the themes are of intimate connection with us Americans. But the result is that abstract and absolute thing called Art.

Waldo Frank.

“

Certain of these pieces have appeared in *Broom*, *Crisis*, *Double Dealer*, *Liberator*, *Little Review*, *Modern Review*, *Nomad*, *Prairie*, and *S 4 N*.

To these magazines: thanks.

CONTENTS

	PAGE
Foreword, by *Waldo Frank*	vii
Karintha	1
Reapers	6
November Cotton Flower	7
Becky	8
Face	14
Cotton Song	15
Carma	16
Song of the Son	21
Georgia Dusk	22
Fern	24
Nullo	34
Evening Song	35
Esther	36
Conversion	49
Portrait in Georgia	50
Blood-Burning Moon	51
Seventh Street	71
Rhobert	73
Avey	76
Beehive	89
Storm Ending	90
Theater	91
Her Lips Are Copper Wire	101
Calling Jesus	102
Box Seat	104
Prayer	131
Harvest Song	132
Bona and Paul	134
Kabnis	157

KARINTHA

Her skin is like dusk on the eastern horizon,
O cant you see it, O cant you see it,
Her skin is like dusk on the eastern horizon
... When the sun goes down.

MEN had always wanted her, this Karintha, even as a child, Karintha carrying beauty, perfect as dusk when the sun goes down. Old men rode her hobby-horse upon their knees. Young men danced with her at frolics when they should have been dancing with their grown-up girls. God grant us youth, secretly prayed the old men. The young fellows counted the time to pass before she would be old enough to mate with them. This interest of the male, who wishes to ripen a growing thing too soon, could mean no good to her.

Karintha, at twelve, was a wild flash that told the other folks just what it was to live. At sunset, when there was no wind, and the pinesmoke 2from over by the sawmill hugged the earth, and you couldnt see more than a few feet in front, her sudden darting past you was a bit of vivid color, like a black bird that flashes in light. With the other children one could hear, some distance off, their feet flopping in the two-inch dust. Karintha's running was a whir. It had the sound of the red dust that sometimes makes a spiral in the road. At dusk, during the hush just after the sawmill had closed down, and before any of the women had started their supper-getting-ready songs, her voice, high-pitched, shrill, would put one's ears to itching. But no one ever thought to make her stop because of it. She stoned the cows, and beat her dog, and fought the other children... Even the preacher, who caught her at mischief, told himself that she was as innocently lovely as a November cotton flower. Already, rumors were out about her. Homes in Georgia are most often built on the two-room plan. In one, you cook and eat, in the other you sleep, and there love goes on. Karintha had seen or heard, perhaps she had felt her parents loving. One could but imitate one's parents, for to follow them was the3 way of God. She played "home" with a small boy who was not afraid to do her bidding. That started the whole thing. Old men could no longer ride her hobby-horse upon their knees. But young men counted faster.
Her skin is like dusk,
O cant you see it,
Her skin is like dusk,
When the sun goes down.

Karintha is a woman. She who carries beauty, perfect as dusk when the sun goes down. She has been married many times. Old men remind her that a few years back they rode her hobby-horse upon their knees. Karintha smiles, and indulges them when she is in the mood for it. She has contempt for them. Karintha is a woman. Young men run stills to make her money. Young men go to the big cities and run on the road. Young men go away to college. They all want to bring her money. These are the young men who thought that all they had to4 do was to count time. But Karintha is a woman, and she has had a child. A child fell out of her womb onto a bed of pine-needles in the forest. Pine-needles are smooth and sweet. They are elastic to the feet of rabbits... A sawmill was nearby. Its pyramidal sawdust pile smouldered. It is a year before one completely burns. Meanwhile, the smoke curls up and hangs in odd wraiths about the trees, curls up, and spreads itself out over the valley... Weeks after Karintha returned home the smoke was so heavy you tasted it in water. Some one made a song:
Smoke is on the hills. Rise up.
Smoke is on the hills, O rise
And take my soul to Jesus.

Karintha is a woman. Men do not know that the soul of her was a growing thing ripened too soon. They will bring their money; they will die not having found it out... Karintha at5 twenty, carrying beauty, perfect as dusk when the sun goes down. Karintha...
Her skin is like dusk on the eastern horizon,
O cant you see it, O cant you see it,
Her skin is like dusk on the eastern horizon
... When the sun goes down.

Goes down...

6

REAPERS

Black reapers with the sound of steel on stones
Are sharpening scythes. I see them place the hones
In their hip-pockets as a thing that's done,
And start their silent swinging, one by one.
Black horses drive a mower through the weeds,
And there, a field rat, startled, squealing bleeds,
His belly close to ground. I see the blade,
Blood-stained, continue cutting weeds and shade.

7

NOVEMBER COTTON FLOWER

Boll-weevil's coming, and the winter's cold,
Made cotton-stalks look rusty, seasons old,
And cotton, scarce as any southern snow,
Was vanishing; the branch, so pinched and slow,
Failed in its function as the autumn rake;
Drouth fighting soil had caused the soil to take
All water from the streams; dead birds were found
In wells a hundred feet below the ground—
Such was the season when the flower bloomed.
Old folks were startled, and it soon assumed
Significance. Superstition saw
Something it had never seen before:
Brown eyes that loved without a trace of fear,
Beauty so sudden for that time of year.

8

BECKY

> "
>
> Becky was the white woman who had two Negro sons. She's dead; they've gone away. The pines whisper to Jesus. The Bible flaps its leaves with an aimless rustle on her mound.

BECKY had one Negro son. Who gave it to her? Damn buck nigger, said the white folks' mouths. She wouldnt tell. Common, God-forsaken, insane white shameless wench, said the white folks' mouths. Her eyes were sunken, her neck stringy, her breasts fallen, till then. Taking their words, they filled her, like a bubble rising—then she broke. Mouth setting in a twist that held her eyes, harsh, vacant, staring... Who gave it to her? Low-down nigger with no self-respect, said the black folks' mouths. She wouldnt tell. Poor Catholic poor-white crazy woman, said the black folks' mouths. White folks and black folks built her cabin, fed her and her growing baby, prayed secretly to God who'd put His cross upon her and cast her out.

[9]

When the first was born, the white folks said they'd have no more to do with her. And black folks, they too joined hands to cast her out... The pines whispered to Jesus.. The railroad boss said not to say he said it, but she could live, if she wanted to, on the narrow strip of land between the railroad and the road. John Stone, who owned the lumber and the bricks, would have shot the man who told he gave the stuff to Lonnie Deacon, who stole out there at night and built the cabin. A single room held down to earth... O fly away to Jesus ... by a leaning chimney...

Six trains each day rumbled past and shook the ground under her cabin. Fords, and horse-and mule-drawn buggies went back and forth along the road. No one ever saw her. Trainmen, and passengers who'd heard about her, threw out papers and food. Threw out little crumpled slips of paper scribbled with prayers, as they passed her eye-shaped piece of sandy ground. Ground islandized between the road and railroad track. Pushed up where a blue-sheen God with listless eyes could look at it.[10] Folks from the town took turns, unknown, of course, to each other, in bringing corn and meat and sweet potatoes. Even sometimes snuff... O thank y Jesus... Old David Georgia, grinding cane and boiling syrup, never went her way without some sugar sap. No one ever saw her. The boy grew up and ran around. When he was five years old as folks reckoned it, Hugh Jourdon saw him carrying a baby. "Becky has another son," was what the whole town knew. But nothing was said, for the part of man that says things to the likes of that had told itself that if there was a Becky, that Becky now was dead.

The two boys grew. Sullen and cunning... O pines, whisper to Jesus; tell Him to come and press sweet Jesus-lips against their lips and eyes... It seemed as though with those two big fellows there, there could be no room for Becky. The part that prayed wondered if perhaps she'd really died, and they had buried her. No one dared ask. They'd beat and cut a man who meant nothing at all in mentioning that they lived along the road. White or colored?[11] No one knew, and least of all themselves. They drifted around from job to job. We, who had cast out their mother because of them, could we take them in? They answered black and white folks by shooting up two men and leaving town. "Godam the white folks; godam the niggers," they shouted as they left town. Becky? Smoke curled up from her chimney; she must be there. Trains passing shook the ground. The ground shook the leaning chimney. Nobody noticed it. A creepy feeling came over all who saw that thin wraith of smoke and felt the trembling of the ground. Folks began to take her food again. They quit it soon because they had a fear. Becky if dead might be a hant, and if alive—it took some nerve even to mention it... O pines, whisper to Jesus...

It was Sunday. Our congregation had been visiting at Pulverton, and were coming home. There was no wind. The autumn sun, the bell from Ebenezer Church, listless and heavy. Even the pines were stale, sticky, like the smell of food that makes you sick. Before we turned the bend of the road that would show us the Becky cabin,[12] the horses stopped stock-still, pushed back their ears, and nervously whinnied. We urged, then whipped them on. Quarter of a mile away thin smoke curled up from the leaning chimney... O pines, whisper to Jesus... Goose-flesh came on my skin though there still was neither chill nor wind. Eyes left their sockets for the cabin. Ears burned and throbbed. Uncanny eclipse! fear closed my mind. We were just about to pass... Pines shout to Jesus!.. the ground trembled as a ghost train rumbled by. The chimney fell into the cabin. Its thud was like a hollow report, ages having passed since it went off. Barlo and I were pulled out of our seats. Dragged to the door that had swung open. Through the dust we saw the bricks in a mound upon the floor. Becky, if she was there, lay under them. I thought I heard a groan. Barlo, mumbling something, threw his Bible on the pile. (No one has ever touched it.) Somehow we got away. My buggy was still on the road. The last thing that I remember was whipping old Dan like fury; I remember nothing after that—that is, until I reached town and[13] folks crowded round to get the true word of it.

“

Becky was the white woman who had two Negro sons. She's dead; they've gone away. The pines whisper to Jesus. The Bible flaps its leaves with an aimless rustle on her mound.

14

FACE

Hair—
silver-gray,
like streams of stars,
Brows—
recurved canoes
quivered by the ripples blown by pain,
Her eyes—
mist of tears
condensing on the flesh below
And her channeled muscles
are cluster grapes of sorrow
purple in the evening sun
nearly ripe for worms.

15

COTTON SONG

Come, brother, come. Lets lift it;
Come now, hewit! roll away!
Shackles fall upon the Judgment Day
But lets not wait for it.
God's body's got a soul,
Bodies like to roll the soul,
Cant blame God if we dont roll,
Come, brother, roll, roll!
Cotton bales are the fleecy way
Weary sinner's bare feet trod,
Softly, softly to the throne of God,
“We aint agwine t wait until th Judgment Day!
Nassur; nassur,
Hump.
Eoho, eoho, roll away!

We aint agwine t wait until th Judgment Day!"
God's body's got a soul,
Bodies like to roll the soul,
Cant blame God if we dont roll,
Come, brother, roll, roll!

16

CARMA

Wind is in the cane. Come along.
Cane leaves swaying, rusty with talk,
Scratching choruses above the guinea's squawk,
Wind is in the cane. Come along.

CARMA, in overalls, and strong as any man, stands behind the old brown mule, driving the wagon home. It bumps, and groans, and shakes as it crosses the railroad track. She, riding it easy. I leave the men around the stove to follow her with my eyes down the red dust road. Nigger woman driving a Georgia chariot down an old dust road. Dixie Pike is what they call it. Maybe she feels my gaze, perhaps she expects it. Anyway, she turns. The sun, which has been slanting over her shoulder, shoots primitive rockets into her mangrove-gloomed, yellow flower face. Hi! Yip! God has left the Moses-people for the nigger. "Gedap." Using reins to slap the mule, she disappears in a cloudy rumble at some indefinite point along the road.

17

(The sun is hammered to a band of gold. Pine-needles, like mazda, are brilliantly aglow. No rain has come to take the rustle from the falling sweet-gum leaves. Over in the forest, across the swamp, a sawmill blows its closing whistle. Smoke curls up. Marvelous web spun by the spider sawdust pile. Curls up and spreads itself pine-high above the branch, a single silver band along the eastern valley. A black boy ... you are the most sleepiest man I ever seed, Sleeping Beauty ... cradled on a gray mule, guided by the hollow sound of cow-bells, heads for them through a rusty cotton field. From down the railroad track, the chug-chug of a gas engine announces that the repair gang is coming home. A girl in the yard of a whitewashed shack not much larger than the stack of worn ties piled before it, sings. Her voice is loud. Echoes, like rain, sweep the valley. Dusk takes the polish from the rails. Lights twinkle in scattered houses. From far away, a sad strong song. Pungent and composite, the smell of farmyards is the fragrance of the woman. She does not sing; her body is a song. She is in the forest, dancing. Torches18 flare .. juju men, greegree, witch-doctors .. torches go out... The Dixie Pike has grown from a goat path in Africa.

Night.

Foxie, the bitch, slicks back her ears and barks at the rising moon.)
Wind is in the corn. Come along.
Corn leaves swaying, rusty with talk,
Scratching choruses above the guinea's squawk,
Wind is in the corn. Come along.

Carma's tale is the crudest melodrama. Her husband's in the gang. And its her fault he got there. Working with a contractor, he was away most of the time. She had others. No one blames her for that. He returned one day and hung around the town where he picked up week-old boasts and rumors... Bane accused her. She denied. He couldnt see that she was becoming hysterical. He would have liked to take his fists and beat her. Who was strong as a man. Stronger. Words, like corkscrews, wormed to her strength. It fizzled out. Grabbing a gun, she rushed from the house and plunged across19 the road into a cane-brake.. There, in quarter heaven shone the crescent moon... Bane was afraid to follow till he heard the gun go off. Then he wasted half an hour gathering the neighbor men. They met in the road where lamp-light showed tracks dissolving in the loose earth about the cane. The search began. Moths flickered the lamps. They put them out. Really, because she still might be live enough to shoot. Time and space have no meaning in a canefield. No more than the interminable stalks... Some one stumbled over her. A cry went up. From the road, one would have thought that they were cornering a rabbit or a skunk... It is difficult carrying dead weight through cane. They placed her on the sofa. A curious, nosey somebody looked for the wound. This fussing with her clothes aroused her. Her eyes were weak and pitiable for so strong a woman. Slowly, then like a flash, Bane came to know that the shot she fired, with averted head, was aimed to whistle like a dying hornet through the cane. Twice deceived, and one deception proved the other. His head went off. Slashed one of the men who'd helped, the man20 who'd stumbled over her. Now he's in the gang. Who was her husband. Should she not take others, this Carma, strong as a man, whose tale as I have told it is the crudest melodrama?

Wind is in the cane. Come along.
Cane leaves swaying, rusty with talk,
Scratching choruses above the guinea's squawk,
Wind is in the cane. Come along.

21

SONG OF THE SON

Pour O pour that parting soul in song,
O pour it in the sawdust glow of night,
Into the velvet pine-smoke air to-night,
And let the valley carry it along.
And let the valley carry it along.
O land and soil, red soil and sweet-gum tree,
So scant of grass, so profligate of pines,
Now just before an epoch's sun declines
Thy son, in time, I have returned to thee,
Thy son, I have in time returned to thee.
In time, for though the sun is setting on
A song-lit race of slaves, it has not set;
Though late, O soil, it is not too late yet
To catch thy plaintive soul, leaving, soon gone,
Leaving, to catch thy plaintive soul soon gone.
O Negro slaves, dark purple ripened plums,
Squeezed, and bursting in the pine-wood air,
Passing, before they stripped the old tree bare
One plum was saved for me, one seed becomes
An everlasting song, a singing tree,
Caroling softly souls of slavery,
What they were, and what they are to me,
Caroling softly souls of slavery.

22

GEORGIA DUSK

The sky, lazily disdaining to pursue
The setting sun, too indolent to hold
A lengthened tournament for flashing gold,
Passively darkens for night's barbecue,
A feast of moon and men and barking hounds,
An orgy for some genius of the South
With blood-hot eyes and cane-lipped scented mouth,
Surprised in making folk-songs from soul sounds.
The sawmill blows its whistle, buzz-saws stop,
And silence breaks the bud of knoll and hill,
Soft settling pollen where plowed lands fulfill
Their early promise of a bumper crop.
Smoke from the pyramidal sawdust pile
Curls up, blue ghosts of trees, tarrying low
Where only chips and stumps are left to show
The solid proof of former domicile.
Meanwhile, the men, with vestiges of pomp,
Race memories of king and caravan,
High-priests, an ostrich, and a juju-man,
Go singing through the footpaths of the swamp.

23
Their voices rise ... the pine trees are guitars,
Strumming, pine-needles fall like sheets of rain...
Their voices rise ... the chorus of the cane
Is caroling a vesper to the stars...
O singers, resinous and soft your songs
Above the sacred whisper of the pines,
Give virgin lips to cornfield concubines,
Bring dreams of Christ to dusky cane-lipped throngs.

24

FERN

FACE flowed into her eyes. Flowed in soft cream foam and plaintive ripples, in such a way that wherever your glance may momentarily have rested, it immediately thereafter wavered in the direction of her eyes. The soft suggestion of down slightly darkened, like the shadow of a bird's wing might, the creamy brown color of her upper lip. Why, after noticing it, you sought her eyes, I cannot tell you. Her nose was aquiline, Semitic. If you have heard a Jewish cantor sing, if he has touched you and made your own sorrow seem trivial when compared with his, you will know my feeling when I follow the curves of her profile, like mobile rivers, to their common delta. They were strange eyes. In this, that they sought nothing—that is, nothing that was obvious and tangible and that one could see, and they gave the impression that nothing was to be denied. When a woman seeks, you will have observed, her eyes deny. Fern's eyes desired nothing that you25 could give her; there was no reason why they should withhold. Men saw her eyes and fooled themselves. Fern's eyes said to them that she was easy. When she was young, a few men took her, but got no joy from it. And then, once done, they felt bound to her (quite unlike their hit and run with other girls), felt as though it would take them a lifetime to fulfill an obligation which they could find no name for. They became attached to her, and hungered after finding the barest trace of what she might desire. As she grew up, new men who came to town felt as almost everyone did who ever saw her: that they would not be denied. Men were everlastingly bringing her their bodies. Something inside of her got tired of them, I guess, for I am certain that for the life of her she could not tell why or how she began to turn them off. A man in fever is no trifling thing to send away. They began to leave her, baffled and ashamed, yet vowing to themselves that some day they would do some fine thing for her: send her candy every week and not let her know whom it came from, watch out for her wedding-day and give her a magnificent something with no name on it, buy26 a house and deed it to her, rescue her from some unworthy fellow who had tricked her into marrying him. As you know, men are apt to idolize or fear that which they cannot understand, especially if it be a woman. She did not deny them, yet the fact was that they were denied. A sort of superstition crept into their consciousness of her being somehow above them. Being above them meant that she was not to be approached by anyone. She became a virgin. Now a virgin in a small southern town is by no means the usual thing, if you will believe me. That the sexes were made to mate is the practice of the South. Particularly, black folks were made to mate. And it is black folks whom I have been talking about thus far. What white men thought of Fern I can arrive at only by analogy. They let her alone.

Anyone, of course, could see her, could see her eyes. If you walked up the Dixie Pike most any time of day, you'd be most like to see her resting listless-like on the railing of her porch, back propped against a post, head tilted a little forward because there was a nail in the porch27 post just where her head came which for some reason or other she never took the trouble to pull out. Her eyes, if it were sunset, rested idly where the sun, molten and glorious, was pouring down between the fringe of pines. Or maybe they gazed at the gray cabin on the knoll from which an evening folk-song was coming. Perhaps they followed a cow that had been turned loose to roam and feed on cotton-stalks and corn leaves. Like as not they'd settle on some vague spot above the horizon, though hardly a trace of wistfulness would come to them. If it were dusk, then they'd wait for the search-light of the evening train which you could see miles up the track before it flared across the Dixie Pike, close to her home. Wherever they looked, you'd follow them and then waver back. Like her face, the whole countryside seemed to flow into her eyes. Flowed into them with the soft listless cadence of Georgia's South. A young Negro, once, was looking at her, spellbound, from the road. A white man passing in a buggy had to flick him with his whip if he was to get by without running him over. I first saw her on her porch. I was passing with a fellow whose crusty numbness 28(I was from the North and suspected of being prejudiced and stuck-up) was melting as he found me warm. I asked him who she was. "That's Fern," was all that I could get from him. Some folks already thought that I was given to nosing around; I let it go at that, so far as questions were concerned. But at first sight of her I felt as if I heard a Jewish cantor sing. As if his singing rose above the unheard chorus of a folk-song. And I felt bound to her. I too had my dreams: something I would do for her. I have knocked about from town to town too much not to know the futility of mere change of place. Besides, picture if you can, this cream-colored solitary girl sitting at a tenement window looking down on the indifferent throngs of Harlem. Better that she listen to folk-songs at dusk in Georgia, you would say, and so would I. Or, suppose she came up North and married. Even a doctor or a lawyer, say, one who would be sure to get along—that is, make money. You and I know, who have had experience in such things, that love is not a thing like prejudice which can be bettered by changes of town. Could men in Washington, Chicago, or New York,29 more than the men of Georgia, bring her something left vacant by the bestowal of their bodies? You and I who know men in these cities will have to say, they could not. See her out and out a prostitute along State Street in Chicago. See her move into a southern town where white men are more aggressive. See her become a white man's concubine... Something I must do for her. There was myself. What could I do for her? Talk, of course. Push back the fringe of pines upon new horizons. To what purpose? and what for? Her? Myself? Men in her case seem to lose their selfishness. I lost mine before I touched her. I ask you, friend (it makes no difference if you sit in the Pullman or the Jim Crow as the train crosses her road), what thoughts would come to you—that is, after you'd finished with the thoughts that leap into men's minds at the sight of a pretty woman who will not deny them; what thoughts would come to you, had you seen her in a quick flash, keen and intuitively, as she sat there on her porch when your train thundered by? Would you have got off at the next station and come back for her to take her where? Would you have30 completely forgotten her as soon as you reached Macon, Atlanta, Augusta, Pasadena, Madison, Chicago, Boston, or New Orleans? Would you tell your wife or sweetheart about a girl you saw? Your thoughts can help me, and I would like to know. Something I would do for her...

One evening I walked up the Pike on purpose, and stopped to say hello. Some of her family were about, but they moved away to make room for me. Damn if I knew how to begin. Would you? Mr. and Miss So-and-So, people, the weather, the crops, the new preacher, the frolic, the church benefit, rabbit and possum hunting, the new soft drink they had at old Pap's store, the schedule of the trains, what kind of town Macon was, Negro's migration north, boll-weevils, syrup, the Bible—to all these things she gave a yassur or nassur, without further comment. I began to wonder if perhaps my own emotional sensibility had played one of its tricks on me. “Lets take a walk,” I at last ventured. The suggestion, coming after so long an isolation, was novel enough, I guess, to surprise. But it wasnt that. Something told me that men31 before me had said just that as a prelude to the offering of their bodies. I tried to tell her with my eyes. I think she understood. The thing from her that made my throat catch, vanished. Its passing left her visible in a way I'd thought, but never seen. We walked down the Pike with people on all the porches gaping at us. “Doesnt it make you mad?” She meant the row of petty gossiping people. She meant the world. Through a canebrake that was ripe for cutting, the branch was reached. Under a sweet-gum tree, and where reddish leaves had dammed the creek a little, we sat down. Dusk, suggesting the almost imperceptible procession of giant trees, settled with a purple haze about the cane. I felt strange, as I always do in Georgia, particularly at dusk. I felt that things unseen to men were tangibly immediate. It would not have surprised me had I had vision. People have them in Georgia more often than you would suppose. A black woman once saw the mother of Christ and drew her in charcoal on the courthouse wall... When one is on the soil of one's ancestors, most anything can come to one... From force of habit, I suppose, I held Fern in32 my arms—that is, without at first noticing it. Then my mind came back to her. Her eyes, unusually weird and open, held me. Held God. He flowed in as I've seen the countryside flow in. Seen men. I must have done something—what, I dont know, in the confusion of my emotion. She sprang up. Rushed some distance from me. Fell to her knees, and began swaying, swaying. Her body was tortured with something it could not let out. Like boiling sap it flooded arms and fingers till she shook them as if they burned her. It found her throat, and spattered inarticulately in plaintive, convulsive sounds, mingled with calls to Christ Jesus. And then she sang, brokenly. A Jewish cantor singing with a broken voice. A child's voice, uncertain, or an old man's. Dusk hid her; I could hear only her song. It seemed to me as though she were pounding her head in anguish upon the ground. I rushed to her. She fainted in my arms.

There was talk about her fainting with me in the canefield. And I got one or two ugly looks from town men who'd set themselves up to protect 33her. In fact, there was talk of making me leave town. But they never did. They kept a watch-out for me, though. Shortly after, I came back North. From the train window I saw her as I crossed her road. Saw her on her porch, head tilted a little forward where the nail was, eyes vaguely focused on the sunset. Saw her face flow into them, the countryside and something that I call God, flowing into them... Nothing ever really happened. Nothing ever came to Fern, not even I. Something I would do for her. Some fine unnamed thing... And, friend, you? She is still living, I have reason to know. Her name, against the chance that you might happen down that way, is Fernie May Rosen.

34

NULLO

A spray of pine-needles,
Dipped in western horizon gold,

Fell onto a path.
Dry moulds of cow-hoofs.
In the forest.
Rabbits knew not of their falling,
Nor did the forest catch aflame.

35

EVENING SONG

Full moon rising on the waters of my heart,
Lakes and moon and fires,
Cloine tires,
Holding her lips apart.
Promises of slumber leaving shore to charm the moon,
Miracle made vesper-keeps,
Cloine sleeps,
And I'll be sleeping soon.
Cloine, curled like the sleepy waters where the moon-waves start,
Radiant, resplendently she gleams,
Cloine dreams,
Lips pressed against my heart.

36

ESTHER

1

Nine.

ESTHER'S hair falls in soft curls about her high-cheek-boned chalk-white face. Esther's hair would be beautiful if there were more gloss to it. And if her face were not prematurely serious, one would call it pretty. Her cheeks are too flat and dead for a girl of nine. Esther looks like a little white child, starched, frilled, as she walks slowly from her home towards her father's grocery store. She is about to turn in Broad from Maple Street. White and black men loafing on the corner hold no interest for her. Then a strange thing happens. A clean-muscled, magnificent, black-skinned Negro, whom she had heard her father mention as King Barlo, suddenly drops to his knees on a spot called the Spittoon. White men, unaware of him, continue squirting tobacco juice in his direction. The saffron fluid splashes on his37 face. His smooth black face begins to glisten and to shine. Soon, people notice him, and gather round. His eyes are rapturous upon the heavens. Lips and nostrils quiver. Barlo is in a religious trance. Town folks know it. They are not startled. They are not afraid. They gather round. Some beg boxes from the grocery stores. From old McGregor's notion shop. A coffin-case is pressed into use. Folks line the curb-stones. Business men close shop. And Banker Warply parks his car close by. Silently, all await the prophet's voice. The sheriff, a great florid fellow whose leggings never meet around his bulging calves, swears in three deputies. "Wall, y cant never tell what a nigger like King Barlo might be up t." Soda bottles, five fingers full of shine, are passed to those who want them. A couple of stray dogs start a fight. Old Goodlow's cow comes flopping up the street. Barlo, still as an Indian fakir, has not moved. The town bell strikes six. The sun slips in behind a heavy mass of horizon cloud. The crowd is hushed and expectant. Barlo's under jaw relaxes, and his lips begin to move.

38

"Jesus has been awhisperin strange words deep down, O way down deep, deep in my ears."

Hums of awe and of excitement.

"He called me to His side an said, 'Git down on your knees beside me, son, Ise gwine t whisper in your ears.'"

An old sister cries, "Ah, Lord."

"'Ise agwine t whisper in your ears,' he said, an I replied, 'Thy will be done on earth as it is in heaven.'"

"Ah, Lord. Amen. Amen."

"An Lord Jesus whispered strange good words deep down, O way down deep, deep in my ears. An He said, 'Tell em till you feel your throat on fire.' I saw a vision. I saw a man arise, an he was big an black an powerful—"

Some one yells, "Preach it, preacher, preach it!"

"—but his head was caught up in th clouds. An while he was agazin at th heavens, heart filled up with th Lord, some little white-ant biddies came an tied his feet to chains. They led him t th coast, they led him t th sea, they led him across th ocean an they didnt set him free. The old coast didnt miss him, an th new39 coast wasnt free, he left the old-coast brothers, t give birth t you an me. O Lord, great God Almighty, t give birth t you an me."

Barlo pauses. Old gray mothers are in tears. Fragments of melodies are being hummed. White folks are touched and curiously awed. Off to themselves, white and black preachers confer as to how best to rid themselves of the vagrant, usurping fellow. Barlo looks as though he is struggling to continue. People are hushed. One can hear weevils work. Dusk is falling rapidly, and the customary store lights fail to throw their feeble glow across the gray dust and flagging of the Georgia town. Barlo rises to his full height. He is immense. To the people he assumes the outlines of his visioned African. In a mighty voice he bellows:

"Brothers an sisters, turn your faces t th sweet face of the Lord, an fill your hearts with glory. Open your eyes an see th dawnin of th mornin light. Open your ears—"

Years afterwards Esther was told that at that very moment a great, heavy, rumbling voice actually was heard. That hosts of angels and of demons paraded up and down the streets all40 night. That King Barlo rode out of town astride a pitch-black bull that had a glowing gold ring in its nose. And that old Limp Underwood, who hated niggers, woke up next morning to find that he held a black man in his arms. This much is certain: an inspired Negress, of wide reputation for being sanctified, drew a portrait of a black madonna on the court-house wall. And King Barlo left town. He left his image indelibly upon the mind of Esther. He became the starting point of the only living patterns that her mind was to know.

2

Sixteen.

Esther begins to dream. The low evening sun sets the windows of McGregor's notion shop aflame. Esther makes believe that they really are aflame. The town fire department rushes madly down the road. It ruthlessly shoves black and white idlers to one side. It whoops. It clangs. It rescues from the second-story window a dimpled infant which she claims for her own. How had she come by it? She thinks of41 it immaculately. It is a sin to think of it immaculately. She must dream no more. She must repent her sin. Another dream comes. There is no fire department. There are no heroic men. The fire starts. The loafers on the corner form a circle, chew their tobacco faster, and squirt juice just as fast as they can chew. Gallons on top of gallons they squirt upon the flames. The air reeks with the stench of scorched tobacco juice. Women, fat chunky Negro women, lean scrawny white women, pull their skirts up above their heads and display the most ludicrous underclothes. The women scoot in all directions from the danger zone. She alone is left to take the baby in her arms. But what a baby! Black, singed, woolly, tobacco-juice baby—ugly as sin. Once held to her breast, miraculous thing: its breath is sweet and its lips can nibble. She loves it frantically. Her joy in it changes the town folks' jeers to harmless jealousy, and she is left alone.

Twenty-two.

Esther's schooling is over. She works behind42 the counter of her father's grocery store. "To keep the money in the family," so he said. She is learning to make distinctions between the business and the social worlds. "Good business comes from remembering that the white folks dont divide the niggers, Esther. Be just as black as any man who has a silver dollar." Esther listlessly forgets that she is near white, and that her father is the richest colored man in town. Black folk who drift in to buy lard and snuff and flour of her, call her a sweet-natured, accommodating girl. She learns their names. She forgets them. She thinks about men. "I dont appeal to them. I wonder why." She recalls an affair she had with a little fair boy while still in school. It had ended in her shame when he as much as told her that for sweetness he preferred a lollipop. She remembers the salesman from the North who wanted to take her to the movies that first night he was in town. She refused, of course. And he never came back, having found out who she was. She thinks of Barlo. Barlo's image gives her a slightly stale thrill. She spices it by telling herself his glories. Black. Magnetically so. Best cotton picker in43 the county, in the state, in the whole world for that matter. Best man with his fists, best man with dice, with a razor. Promoter of church benefits. Of colored fairs. Vagrant preacher. Lover of all the women for miles and miles around. Esther decides that she loves him. And with a vague sense of life slipping by, she resolves that she will tell him so, whatever people say, the next time he comes to town. After the making of this resolution which becomes a sort of wedding cake for her to tuck beneath her pillow and go to sleep upon, she sees nothing of Barlo for five years. Her hair thins. It looks like the dull silk on puny corn ears. Her face pales until it is the color of the gray dust that dances with dead cotton leaves...

3

Esther is twenty-seven.

Esther sells lard and snuff and flour to vague black faces that drift in her store to ask for them. Her eyes hardly see the people to whom she gives change. Her body is lean and44 beaten. She rests listlessly against the counter, too weary to sit down. From the street some one shouts, "King Barlo has come back to town." He passes her window, driving a large new car. Cut-out open. He veers to the curb, and steps out. Barlo has made money on cotton during the war. He is as rich as anyone. Esther suddenly is animate. She goes to her door. She sees him at a distance, the center of a group of credulous men. She hears the deep-bass rumble of his talk. The sun swings low. McGregor's windows are aflame again. Pale flame. A sharply dressed white girl passes by. For a moment Esther wishes that she might be like her. Not white; she has no need for being that. But sharp, sporty, with get-up about her. Barlo is connected with that wish. She mustnt wish. Wishes only make you restless. Emptiness is a thing that grows by being moved. "I'll not think. Not wish. Just set my mind against it." Then the thought comes to her that those purposeless, easy-going men will possess him, if she doesnt. Purpose is not dead in her, now that she comes to think of it. That loose women will have their arms around him at Nat Bowle's45 place to-night. As if her veins are full of fired sun-bleached southern shanties, a swift heat sweeps them. Dead dreams, and a forgotten resolution are carried upward by the flames. Pale flames. "They shant have him. Oh, they shall not. Not if it kills me they shant have him." Jerky, aflutter, she closes the store and starts home. Folks lazing on store window-sills wonder what on earth can be the matter with Jim Crane's gal, as she passes them. "Come to remember, she always was a little off, a little crazy, I reckon." Esther seeks her own room, and locks the door. Her mind is a pink mesh-bag filled with baby toes.

Using the noise of the town clock striking twelve to cover the creaks of her departure, Esther slips into the quiet road. The town, her parents, most everyone is sound asleep. This fact is a stable thing that comforts her. After sundown a chill wind came up from the west. It is still blowing, but to her it is a steady, settled thing like the cold. She wants her mind to be like that. Solid, contained, and blank as a sheet of darkened ice. She will not permit herself to46 notice the peculiar phosphorescent glitter of the sweet-gum leaves. Their movement would excite her. Exciting too, the recession of the dull familiar homes she knows so well. She doesnt know them at all. She closes her eyes, and holds them tightly. Wont do. Her being aware that they are closed recalls her purpose. She does not want to think of it. She opens them. She turns now into the deserted business street. The corrugated iron canopies and mule- and horse-gnawed hitching posts bring her a strange composure. Ghosts of the commonplaces of her daily life take stride with her and become her companions. And the echoes of her heels upon the flagging are rhythmically monotonous and soothing. Crossing the street at the corner of McGregor's notion shop, she thinks that the windows are a dull flame. Only a fancy. She walks faster. Then runs. A turn into a side street brings her abruptly to Nat Bowle's place. The house is squat and dark. It is always dark. Barlo is within. Quietly she opens the outside door and steps in. She passes through a small room. Pauses before a flight of stairs down which people's voices, muffled, come. The air47 is heavy with fresh tobacco smoke. It makes her sick. She wants to turn back. She goes up the steps. As if she were mounting to some great height, her head spins. She is violently dizzy. Blackness rushes to her eyes. And then she finds that she is in a large room. Barlo is before her.

"Well, I'm sholy damned—skuse me, but what, what brought you here, lil milk-white gal?"

"You." Her voice sounds like a frightened child's that calls homeward from some point miles away.

"Me?"

"Yes, you Barlo."

"This aint th place fer y. This aint th place fer y."

"I know. I know. But I've come for you."

"For me for what?"

She manages to look deep and straight into his eyes. He is slow at understanding. Guffaws and giggles break out from all around the room. A coarse woman's voice remarks, "So thats how th dictie niggers does it." Laughs. "Mus give em credit fo their gall."

48

Esther doesnt hear. Barlo does. His faculties are jogged. She sees a smile, ugly and repulsive to her, working upward through thick licker fumes. Barlo seems hideous. The thought comes suddenly, that conception with a drunken man must be a mighty sin. She draws away, frozen. Like a somnambulist she wheels around and walks stiffly to the stairs. Down them. Jeers and hoots pelter bluntly upon her back. She steps out. There is no air, no street, and the town has completely disappeared.

49

CONVERSION

African Guardian of Souls,
Drunk with rum,
Feasting on a strange cassava,
Yielding to new words and a weak palabra

Of a white-faced sardonic god—
Grins, cries
Amen,
Shouts hosanna.

50

PORTRAIT IN GEORGIA

Hair—braided chestnut, coiled like a lyncher's rope,
Eyes—fagots,
Lips—old scars, or the first red blisters,
Breath—the last sweet scent of cane,
And her slim body, white as the ash of black flesh after flame.

51

BLOOD-BURNING MOON

1

UP from the skeleton stone walls, up from the rotting floor boards and the solid hand-hewn beams of oak of the pre-war cotton factory, dusk came. Up from the dusk the full moon came. Glowing like a fired pine-knot, it illumined the great door and soft showered the Negro shanties aligned along the single street of factory town. The full moon in the great door was an omen. Negro women improvised songs against its spell.

Louisa sang as she came over the crest of the hill from the white folks' kitchen. Her skin was the color of oak leaves on young trees in fall. Her breasts, firm and up-pointed like ripe acorns. And her singing had the low murmur of winds in fig trees. Bob Stone, younger son of the people she worked for, loved her. By the way the world reckons things, he had won her. By measure of that warm glow which came into her mind at thought of him, he had won her.52 Tom Burwell, whom the whole town called Big Boy, also loved her. But working in the fields all day, and far away from her, gave him no chance to show it. Though often enough of evenings he had tried to. Somehow, he never got along. Strong as he was with hands upon the ax or plow, he found it difficult to hold her. Or so he thought. But the fact was that he held her to factory town more firmly than he thought for. His black balanced, and pulled against, the white of Stone, when she thought of them. And her mind was vaguely upon them as she came over the crest of the hill, coming from the white folks' kitchen. As she sang softly at the evil face of the full moon.

A strange stir was in her. Indolently, she tried to fix upon Bob or Tom as the cause of it. To meet Bob in the canebrake, as she was going to do an hour or so later, was nothing new. And Tom's proposal which she felt on its way to her could be indefinitely put off. Separately, there was no unusual significance to either one. But for some reason, they jumbled when her eyes gazed vacantly at the rising moon. And from the jumble came the stir that was strangely within 53her. Her lips trembled. The slow rhythm of her song grew agitant and restless. Rusty black and tan spotted hounds, lying in the dark corners of porches or prowling around back yards, put their noses in the air and caught its tremor. They began plaintively to yelp and howl. Chickens woke up and

cackled. Intermittently, all over the countryside dogs barked and roosters crowed as if heralding a weird dawn or some ungodly awakening. The women sang lustily. Their songs were cotton-wads to stop their ears. Louisa came down into factory town and sank wearily upon the step before her home. The moon was rising towards a thick cloud-bank which soon would hide it.
Red nigger moon. Sinner!
Blood-burning moon. Sinner!
Come out that fact'ry door.

2

Up from the deep dusk of a cleared spot on the edge of the forest a mellow glow arose and spread fan-wise into the low-hanging heavens. And all around the air was heavy with the scent54 of boiling cane. A large pile of cane-stalks lay like ribboned shadows upon the ground. A mule, harnessed to a pole, trudged lazily round and round the pivot of the grinder. Beneath a swaying oil lamp, a Negro alternately whipped out at the mule, and fed cane-stalks to the grinder. A fat boy waddled pails of fresh ground juice between the grinder and the boiling stove. Steam came from the copper boiling pan. The scent of cane came from the copper pan and drenched the forest and the hill that sloped to factory town, beneath its fragrance. It drenched the men in circle seated around the stove. Some of them chewed at the white pulp of stalks, but there was no need for them to, if all they wanted was to taste the cane. One tasted it in factory town. And from factory town one could see the soft haze thrown by the glowing stove upon the low-hanging heavens.

Old David Georgia stirred the thickening syrup with a long ladle, and ever so often drew it off. Old David Georgia tended his stove and told tales about the white folks, about moon-shining and cotton picking, and about sweet nigger gals, to the men who sat there about his55 stove to listen to him. Tom Burwell chewed cane-stalk and laughed with the others till someone mentioned Louisa. Till some one said something about Louisa and Bob Stone, about the silk stockings she must have gotten from him. Blood ran up Tom's neck hotter than the glow that flooded from the stove. He sprang up. Glared at the men and said, "She's my gal." Will Manning laughed. Tom strode over to him. Yanked him up and knocked him to the ground. Several of Manning's friends got up to fight for him. Tom whipped out a long knife and would have cut them to shreds if they hadnt ducked into the woods. Tom had had enough. He nodded to Old David Georgia and swung down the path to factory town. Just then, the dogs started barking and the roosters began to crow. Tom felt funny. Away from the fight, away from the stove, chill got to him. He shivered. He shuddered when he saw the full moon rising towards the cloud-bank. He who didnt give a godam for the fears of old women. He forced his mind to fasten on Louisa. Bob Stone. Better not be. He turned into the street and saw Louisa sitting before her home. He went56 towards her, ambling, touched the brim of a marvelously shaped, spotted, felt hat, said he wanted to say something to her, and then found that he didnt know what he had to say, or if he did, that he couldnt say it. He shoved his big fists in his overalls, grinned, and started to move off.

"Youall want me, Tom?"

"Thats what us wants, sho, Louisa."

"Well, here I am—"

"An here I is, but that aint ahelpin none, all th same."

"You wanted to say something?.."

"I did that, sho. But words is like th spots on dice: no matter how y fumbles em, there's times when they jes wont come. I dunno why. Seems like th love I feels fo yo done stole m tongue. I got it now. Whee! Louisa, honey, I oughtnt tell y, I feel I oughtnt cause yo is young an goes t church an I has had other gals, but Louisa I sho do love y. Lil gal, Ise watched y from them first days when youall sat right here befo yo door befo th well an sang sometimes in a way that like t broke m heart. Ise carried y with me into th fields, day after day, an after that, an I57 sho can plow when yo is there, an I can pick cotton. Yassur! Come near beatin Barlo yesterday. I sho did. Yassur! An next year if ole Stone'll trust me, I'll have a farm. My own. My bales will buy yo what y gets from white folks now. Silk stockings an purple dresses—course I dont believe what some folks been whisperin as t how y gets them things now. White folks always did do for niggers what they likes. An they jes cant help alikin yo, Louisa. Bob Stone likes y. Course he does. But not th way folks is awhisperin. Does he, hon?"

"I dont know what you mean, Tom."

"Course y dont. Ise already cut two niggers. Had t hon, t tell em so. Niggers always tryin t make somethin out a nothin. An then besides, white folks aint up t them tricks so much nowadays. Godam better not be. Leastawise not with yo. Cause I wouldnt stand f it. Nassur."

"What would you do, Tom?"

"Cut him jes like I cut a nigger."

"No, Tom—"

"I said I would an there aint no mo to it. But that aint th talk f now. Sing, honey Louisa,[58] an while I'm listenin t y I'll be makin love."

Tom took her hand in his. Against the tough thickness of his own, hers felt soft and small. His huge body slipped down to the step beside her. The full moon sank upward into the deep purple of the cloud-bank. An old woman brought a lighted lamp and hung it on the common well whose bulky shadow squatted in the middle of the road, opposite Tom and Louisa. The old woman lifted the well-lid, took hold the chain, and began drawing up the heavy bucket. As she did so, she sang. Figures shifted, restless-like, between lamp and window in the front rooms of the shanties. Shadows of the figures fought each other on the gray dust of the road. Figures raised the windows and joined the old woman in song. Louisa and Tom, the whole street, singing:
Red nigger moon. Sinner!
Blood-burning moon. Sinner!
Come out that fact'ry door.

3

Bob Stone sauntered from his veranda out into[59] the gloom of fir trees and magnolias. The clear white of his skin paled, and the flush of his cheeks turned purple. As if to balance this outer change, his mind became consciously a white man's. He passed the house with its huge open hearth which, in the days of slavery, was the plantation cookery. He saw Louisa bent over that hearth. He went in as a master should and took her. Direct, honest, bold. None of this sneaking that he had to go through now. The contrast was repulsive to him. His family had lost ground. Hell no, his family still owned the niggers, practically. Damned if they did, or he wouldnt have to duck around so. What would they think if they knew? His mother? His sister? He shouldnt mention them, shouldnt think of them in this connection. There in the dusk he blushed at doing so. Fellows about town were all right, but how about his friends up North? He could see them incredible, repulsed. They didnt know. The thought first made him laugh. Then, with their eyes still upon him, he began to feel embarrassed. He felt the need of explaining things to them. Explain hell. They wouldnt understand, and moreover, who ever[60] heard of a Southerner getting on his knees to any Yankee, or anyone. No sir. He was going to see Louisa to-night, and love her. She was lovely—in her way. Nigger way. What way was that? Damned if he knew. Must know. He'd known her long enough to know. Was there something about niggers that you couldnt know? Listening to them at church didnt tell you anything. Looking at them didnt tell you anything. Talking to them didnt tell you anything—unless it was gossip, unless they wanted to talk. Of course, about farming, and licker, and craps—but those werent nigger. Nigger was something more. How much more? Something to be afraid of, more? Hell no. Who ever heard of being afraid of a nigger? Tom Burwell. Cartwell had told him that Tom went with Louisa after she reached home. No sir. No nigger had ever been with his girl. He'd like to see one try. Some position for him to be in. Him, Bob Stone, of the old Stone family, in a scrap with a nigger over a nigger girl. In the good old days... Ha! Those were the days. His family had lost ground. Not so much, though. Enough for him to have to cut through[61] old Lemon's canefield by way of the woods, that he might meet her. She was worth it. Beautiful nigger gal. Why nigger? Why not, just gal? No, it was because she was nigger that he went to her. Sweet... The scent of boiling cane came to him. Then he saw the rich glow of the stove. He heard the voices of the men circled around it. He was about to skirt the clearing when he heard his own name mentioned. He stopped. Quivering. Leaning against a tree, he listened.

"Bad nigger. Yassur, he sho is one bad nigger when he gets started."

"Tom Burwell's been on th gang three times fo cuttin men."

"What y think he's agwine t do t Bob Stone?"

"Dunno yet. He aint found out. When he does— Baby!"

"Aint no tellin."

"Young Stone aint no quitter an I ken tell y that. Blood of th old uns in his veins."

"Thats right. He'll scrap, sho."

"Be gettin too hot f niggers round this away."

"Shut up, nigger. Y dont know what y talkin bout."

Bob Stone's ears burned as though he had62 been holding them over the stove. Sizzling heat welled up within him. His feet felt as if they rested on red-hot coals. They stung him to quick movement. He circled the fringe of the glowing. Not a twig cracked beneath his feet. He reached the path that led to factory town. Plunged furiously down it. Halfway along, a blindness within him veered him aside. He crashed into the bordering canebrake. Cane leaves cut his face and lips. He tasted blood. He threw himself down and dug his fingers in the ground. The earth was cool. Cane-roots took the fever from his hands. After a long while, or so it seemed to him, the thought came to him that it must be time to see Louisa. He got to his feet and walked calmly to their meeting place. No Louisa. Tom Burwell had her. Veins in his forehead bulged and distended. Saliva moistened the dried blood on his lips. He bit down on his lips. He tasted blood. Not his own blood; Tom Burwell's blood. Bob drove through the cane and out again upon the road. A hound swung down the path before him towards factory town. Bob couldnt see it. The dog loped aside to let him pass. Bob's blind63 rushing made him stumble over it. He fell with a thud that dazed him. The hound yelped. Answering yelps came from all over the countryside. Chickens cackled. Roosters crowed, heralding the bloodshot eyes of southern awakening. Singers in the town were silenced. They shut their windows down. Palpitant between the rooster crows, a chill hush settled upon the huddled forms of Tom and Louisa. A figure rushed from the shadow and stood before them. Tom popped to his feet.

"Whats y want?"

"I'm Bob Stone."

"Yassur—an I'm Tom Burwell. Whats y want?"

Bob lunged at him. Tom side-stepped, caught him by the shoulder, and flung him to the ground. Straddled him.

"Let me up."

"Yassur—but watch yo doins, Bob Stone."

A few dark figures, drawn by the sound of scuffle stood about them. Bob sprang to his feet.

"Fight like a man, Tom Burwell, an I'll lick y."

64

Again he lunged. Tom side-stepped and flung him to the ground. Straddled him.

"Get off me, you godam nigger you."

"Yo sho has started somethin now. Get up."

Tom yanked him up and began hammering at him. Each blow sounded as if it smashed into a precious, irreplaceable soft something. Beneath them, Bob staggered back. He reached in his pocket and whipped out a knife.

"Thats my game, sho."

Blue flash, a steel blade slashed across Bob Stone's throat. He had a sweetish sick feeling. Blood began to flow. Then he felt a sharp twitch of pain. He let his knife drop. He slapped one hand against his neck. He pressed the other on top of his head as if to hold it down. He groaned. He turned, and staggered towards the crest of the hill in the direction of white town. Negroes who had seen the fight slunk into their homes and blew the lamps out. Louisa, dazed, hysterical, refused to go indoors. She slipped, crumbled, her body loosely propped against the woodwork of the well. Tom Burwell leaned against it. He seemed rooted there.

65

Bob reached Broad Street. White men rushed up to him. He collapsed in their arms.

"Tom Burwell...."

White men like ants upon a forage rushed about. Except for the taut hum of their moving, all was silent. Shotguns, revolvers, rope, kerosene, torches. Two high-powered cars with glaring search-lights. They came together. The taut hum rose to a low roar. Then nothing could be heard but the flop of their feet in the thick dust of the road. The moving body of their silence preceded them over the crest of the hill into factory town. It flattened the Negroes beneath it. It rolled to the wall of the factory, where it stopped. Tom knew that they were coming. He couldnt move. And then he saw the search-lights of the two cars glaring down on him. A quick shock went through him. He stiffened. He started to run. A yell went up from the mob. Tom wheeled about and faced them. They poured down on him. They swarmed. A large man with dead-white face and flabby cheeks came to him and almost jabbed a gun-barrel through his guts.

"Hands behind y, nigger."

66

Tom's wrist were bound. The big man shoved him to the well. Burn him over it, and when the woodwork caved in, his body would drop to the bottom. Two deaths for a godam nigger. Louisa was driven back. The mob pushed in. Its pressure, its momentum was too great. Drag him to the factory. Wood and stakes already there. Tom moved in the direction indicated. But they had to drag him. They reached the great door. Too many to get in there. The mob divided and flowed around the walls to either side. The big man shoved him through the door. The mob pressed in from the sides. Taut humming. No words. A stake was sunk into the ground. Rotting floor boards piled around it. Kerosene poured on the rotting floor boards. Tom bound to the stake. His breast was bare. Nails scratches let little lines of blood trickle down and mat into the hair. His face, his eyes were set and stony. Except for irregular breathing, one would have thought him already dead. Torches were flung onto the pile. A great flare muffled in black smoke shot upward. The mob yelled. The mob was silent. Now Tom could be seen within the flames. Only his head, erect,67 lean, like a blackened stone. Stench of burning flesh soaked the air. Tom's eyes popped. His head settled downward. The mob yelled. Its yell echoed against the skeleton stone walls and sounded like a hundred yells. Like a hundred mobs yelling. Its yell thudded against the thick front wall and fell back. Ghost of a yell slipped through the flames and out the great door of the factory. It fluttered like a dying thing down the single street of factory town. Louisa, upon the step before her home, did not hear it, but her eyes opened slowly. They saw the full moon glowing in the great door. The full moon, an evil thing, an omen, soft showering the homes of folks she knew. Where were they, these people? She'd sing, and perhaps they'd come out and join her. Perhaps Tom Burwell would come. At any rate, the full moon in the great door was an omen which she must sing to:

Red nigger moon. Sinner!
Blood-burning moon. Sinner!
Come out that fact'ry door.

71

SEVENTH STREET

Money burns the pocket, pocket hurts,
Bootleggers in silken shirts,
Ballooned, zooming Cadillacs,
Whizzing, whizzing down the street-car tracks.

SEVENTH STREET is a bastard of Prohibition and the War. A crude-boned, soft-skinned wedge of nigger life breathing its loafer air, jazz songs and love, thrusting unconscious rhythms, black reddish blood into the white and whitewashed wood of Washington. Stale soggy wood of Washington. Wedges rust in soggy wood... Split it! In two! Again! Shred it! .. the sun. Wedges are brilliant in the sun; ribbons of wet wood dry and blow away. Black reddish blood. Pouring for crude-boned soft-skinned life, who set you flowing? Blood suckers of the War would spin in a frenzy of dizziness if they drank your blood. Prohibition would put a stop to it. Who set you flowing? White and whitewash disappear in blood. Who set you flowing? Flowing down the smooth asphalt of Seventh Street, in shanties, brick72 office buildings, theaters, drug stores, restaurants, and cabarets? Eddying on the corners? Swirling like a blood-red smoke up where the buzzards fly in heaven? God would not dare to suck black red blood. A Nigger God! He would duck his head in shame and call for the Judgment Day. Who set you flowing?
Money burns the pocket, pocket hurts,
Bootleggers in silken shirts,
Ballooned, zooming Cadillacs,
Whizzing, whizzing down the street-car tracks.

73

RHOBERT

RHOBERT wears a house, like a monstrous diver's helmet, on his head. His legs are banty-bowed and shaky because as a child he had rickets. He is way down. Rods of the house like antennæ of a dead thing, stuffed, prop up in the air. He is way down. He is sinking. His house is a dead thing that weights him down. He is sinking as a diver would sink in mud should the water be drawn off. Life is a murky, wiggling, microscopic water that compresses him. Compresses his helmet and would crush it the minute that he pulled his head out. He has to keep it in. Life is water that is being drawn off.
Brother, life is water that is being drawn off.
Brother, life is water that is being drawn off.

The dead house is stuffed. The stuffing is alive. It is sinful to draw one's head out of live stuffing in a dead house. The propped-up antennæ would cave in and the stuffing be strewn .. shredded life-pulp .. in the water. It is sinful to have one's own head crushed.74 Rhobert is an upright man whose legs are banty-bowed and shaky because as a child he had rickets. The earth is round. Heaven is a sphere that surrounds it. Sink where you will. God is a Red Cross man with a dredge and a respiration-pump who's waiting for you at the opposite periphery. God built the house. He blew His breath into its stuffing. It is good to die obeying Him who can do these things.

A futile something like the dead house wraps the live stuffing of the question: how long before the water will be drawn off? Rhobert does not care. Like most men who wear monstrous helmets, the pressure it exerts is enough to convince him of its practical infinity. And he cares not two straws as to whether or not he will ever see his wife and children again. Many a time he's seen them drown in his dreams and has kicked about joyously in the mud for days after. One thing about him goes straight to the heart. He has an Adam's-apple which strains sometimes as if he were painfully gulping great globules of air .. air floating shredded life-pulp. It is a sad thing to see a banty-bowed, shaky, ricket-legged man straining the raw insides of his throat against smooth air. Holding furtive thoughts about the glory of pulp-heads75 strewn in water... He is way down. Down. Mud, coining to his banty knees, almost hides them. Soon people will be looking at him and calling him a strong man. No doubt he is for one who has had rickets. Lets give it to him. Lets call him great when the water shall have been all drawn off. Lets build a monument and set it in the ooze where he goes down. A monument of hewn oak, carved in nigger-heads. Lets open our throats, brother, and sing "Deep River" when he goes down.
Brother, Rhobert is sinking.
Lets open our throats, brother,
Lets sing Deep River when he goes down.

76

AVEY

FOR a long while she was nothing more to me than one of those skirted beings whom boys at a certain age disdain to play with. Just how I came to love her, timidly, and with secret blushes, I do not know. But that I did was brought home to me one night, the first night that Ned wore his long pants. Us fellers were seated on the curb before an apartment house where she had gone in. The young trees had not outgrown their boxes then. V Street was lined with them. When our legs grew cramped and stiff from the cold of the stone, we'd stand around a box and whittle it. I like to think now that there was a hidden purpose in the way we hacked them with our knives. I like to feel that something deep in me responded to the trees, the young trees that whinnied like colts impatient to be let free... On the particular night I have in mind, we were waiting for the top-floor light to go out. We wanted to see Avey leave the flat. This night she stayed longer than usual and gave77 us a chance to complete the plans of how we were going to stone and beat that feller on the top floor out of town. Ned especially had it in for him. He was about to throw a brick up at the window when at last the room went dark. Some minutes passed. Then Avey, as unconcerned as if she had been paying an old-maid aunt a visit, came out. I don't remember what she had on, and all that sort of thing. But I do know that I turned hot as bare pavements in the summertime at Ned's boast: "Hell, bet I could get her too if you little niggers weren't always spying and crabbing everything." I didnt say a word to him. It wasnt my way then. I just stood there like the others, and something like a fuse burned up inside of me. She never noticed us, but swung along lazy and easy as anything. We sauntered to the corner and watched her till her door banged to. Ned repeated what he'd said. I didnt seem to care. Sitting around old Mush-Head's bread box, the discussion began. "Hang if I can see how she gets away with it," Doc started. Ned knew, of course. There was nothing he didnt know when it came to women. He dilated on the emotional needs of girls. Said78 they werent much different from men in that respect. And concluded with the solemn avowal: "It does em good." None of us liked Ned much. We all talked dirt; but it was the way he said it. And then too, a couple of the fellers had sisters and had caught Ned playing with them. But there was no disputing the superiority of his smutty wisdom. Bubs Sanborn, whose mother was friendly with Avey's, had overheard the old ladies talking. "Avey's mother's ont her," he said. We thought that only natural and began to guess at what would happen. Some one said she'd marry that feller on the top floor. Ned called that a lie because Avey was going to marry nobody but him. We had our doubts about that, but we did agree that she'd soon leave school and marry some one. The gang broke up, and I went home, picturing myself as married.

Nothing I did seemed able to change Avey's indifference to me. I played basket-ball, and when I'd make a long clean shot she'd clap with the others, louder than they, I thought. I'd meet her on the street, and there'd be no difference[79] in the way she said hello. She never took the trouble to call me by my name. On the days for drill, I'd let my voice down a tone and call for a complicated maneuver when I saw her coming. She'd smile appreciation, but it was an impersonal smile, never for me. It was on a summer excursion down to Riverview that she first seemed to take me into account. The day had been spent riding merry-go-rounds, scenic-railways, and shoot-the-chutes. We had been in swimming and we had danced. I was a crack swimmer then. She didnt know how. I held her up and showed her how to kick her legs and draw her arms. Of course she didnt learn in one day, but she thanked me for bothering with her. I was also somewhat of a dancer. And I had already noticed that love can start on a dance floor. We danced. But though I held her tightly in my arms, she was way away. That college feller who lived on the top floor was somewhere making money for the next year. I imagined that she was thinking, wishing for him. Ned was along. He treated her until his money gave out. She went with another feller. Ned got sore. One by one the boys' money gave[80] out. She left them. And they got sore. Every one of them but me got sore. This is the reason, I guess, why I had her to myself on the top deck of the *Jane Mosely* that night as we puffed up the Potomac, coming home. The moon was brilliant. The air was sweet like clover. And every now and then, a salt tang, a stale drift of sea-weed. It was not my mind's fault if it went romancing. I should have taken her in my arms the minute we were stowed in that old lifeboat. I dallied, dreaming. She took me in hers. And I could feel by the touch of it that it wasnt a man-to-woman love. It made me restless. I felt chagrined. I didnt know what it was, but I did know that I couldnt handle it. She ran her fingers through my hair and kissed my forehead. I itched to break through her tenderness to passion. I wanted her to take me in her arms as I knew she had that college feller. I wanted her to love me passionately as she did him. I gave her one burning kiss. Then she laid me in her lap as if I were a child. Helpless. I got sore when she started to hum a lullaby. She wouldnt let me go. I talked. I knew damned well that I could beat her at that. Her[81] eyes were soft and misty, the curves of her lips were wistful, and her smile seemed indulgent of the irrelevance of my remarks. I gave up at last and let her love me, silently, in her own way. The moon was brilliant. The air was sweet like clover, and every now and then, a salt tang, a stale drift of sea-weed...

The next time I came close to her was the following summer at Harpers Ferry. We were sitting on a flat projecting rock they give the name of Lover's Leap. Some one is supposed to have jumped off it. The river is about six hundred feet beneath. A railroad track runs up the valley and curves out of sight where part of the mountain rock had to be blasted away to make room for it. The engines of this valley have a whistle, the echoes of which sound like iterated gasps and sobs. I always think of them as crude music from the soul of Avey. We sat there holding hands. Our palms were soft and warm against each other. Our fingers were not tight. She would not let them be. She would not let me twist them. I wanted to talk. To explain what I meant to her. Avey was as silent as those great trees whose tops we looked down[82] upon. She has always been like that. At least, to me. I had the notion that if I really wanted to, I could do with her just what I pleased. Like one can strip a tree. I did kiss her. I even let my hands cup her breasts. When I was through, she'd seek my hand and hold it till my pulse cooled down. Evening after evening we sat there. I tried to get her to talk about that college feller. She never would. There was no set time to go home. None of my family had come down. And as for hers, she didnt give a hang about them. The general gossips could hardly say more than they had. The boarding-house porch was always deserted when we returned. No one saw us enter, so the time was set conveniently for scandal. This worried me a little, for I thought it might keep Avey from getting an appointment in the schools. She didnt care. She had finished normal school. They could give her a job if they wanted to. As time went on, her indifference to things began to pique me; I was ambitious. I left the Ferry earlier than she did. I was going off to college. The more I thought of it, the more I resented, yes, hell, thats what it was, her downright laziness. Sloppy83 indolence. There was no excuse for a healthy girl taking life so easy. Hell! she was no better than a cow. I was certain that she was a cow when I felt an udder in a Wisconsin stock-judging class. Among those energetic Swedes, or whatever they are, I decided to forget her. For two years I thought I did. When I'd come home for the summer she'd be away. And before she returned, I'd be gone. We never wrote; she was too damned lazy for that. But what a bluff I put up about forgetting her. The girls up that way, at least the ones I knew, havent got the stuff: they dont know how to love. Giving themselves completely was tame beside just the holding of Avey's hand. One day I received a note from her. The writing, I decided, was slovenly. She wrote on a torn bit of note-book paper. The envelope had a faint perfume that I remembered. A single line told me she had lost her school and was going away. I comforted myself with the reflection that shame held no pain for one so indolent as she. Nevertheless, I left Wisconsin that year for good. Washington had seemingly forgotten her. I hunted Ned. Between curses, I caught his opinion of84 her. She was no better than a whore. I saw her mother on the street. The same old pinch-beck, jerky-gaited creature that I'd always known.

Perhaps five years passed. The business of hunting a job or something or other had bruised my vanity so that I could recognize it. I felt old. Avey and my real relation to her, I thought I came to know. I wanted to see her. I had been told that she was in New York. As I had no money, I hiked and bummed my way there. I got work in a ship-yard and walked the streets at night, hoping to meet her. Failing in this, I saved enough to pay my fare back home. One evening in early June, just at the time when dusk is most lovely on the eastern horizon, I saw Avey, indolent as ever, leaning on the arm of a man, strolling under the recently lit arc-lights of U Street. She had almost passed before she recognized me. She showed no surprise. The puff over her eyes had grown heavier. The eyes themselves were still sleepy-large, and beautiful. I had almost concluded—indifferent. "You look older," was what she said. I wanted to convince 85her that I was, so I asked her to walk with me. The man whom she was with, and whom she never took the trouble to introduce, at a nod from her, hailed a taxi, and drove away. That gave me a notion of what she had been used to. Her dress was of some fine, costly stuff. I suggested the park, and then added that the grass might stain her skirt. Let it get stained, she said, for where it came from there are others.

I have a spot in Soldier's Home to which I always go when I want the simple beauty of another's soul. Robins spring about the lawn all day. They leave their footprints in the grass. I imagine that the grass at night smells sweet and fresh because of them. The ground is high. Washington lies below. Its light spreads like a blush against the darkened sky. Against the soft dusk sky of Washington. And when the wind is from the South, soil of my homeland falls like a fertile shower upon the lean streets of the city. Upon my hill in Soldier's Home. I know the policeman who watches the place of nights. When I go there alone, I talk to him. I tell him I come there to find the truth that people86 bury in their hearts. I tell him that I do not come there with a girl to do the thing he's paid to watch out for. I look deep in his eyes when I say these things, and he believes me. He comes over to see who it is on the grass. I say hello to him. He greets me in the same way and goes off searching for other black splotches upon the lawn. Avey and I went there. A band in one of the buildings a fair distance off was playing a march. I wished they would stop. Their playing was like a tin spoon in one's mouth. I wanted the Howard Glee Club to sing "Deep River," from the road. To sing "Deep River, Deep River," from the road... Other than the first comments, Avey had been silent. I started to hum a folk-tune. She slipped her hand in mine. Pillowed her head as best she could upon my arm. Kissed the hand that she was holding and listened, or so I thought, to what I had to say. I traced my development from the early days up to the present time, the phase in which I could understand her. I described her own nature and temperament. Told how they needed a larger life for their expression. How incapable Washington was of understanding 87that need. How it could not meet it. I pointed out that in lieu of proper channels, her emotions had overflowed into paths that dissipated them. I talked, beautifully I thought, about an art that would be born, an art that would open the way for women the likes of her. I asked her to hope, and build up an inner life against the coming of that day. I recited some of my own things to her. I sang, with a strange quiver in my voice, a promise-song. And then I began to wonder why her hand had not once returned a single pressure. My old-time feeling about her laziness came back. I spoke sharply. My policeman friend passed by. I said hello to him. As he went away, I began to visualize certain possibilities. An immediate and urgent passion swept over me. Then I looked at Avey. Her heavy eyes were closed. Her breathing was as faint and regular as a child's in slumber. My passion died. I was afraid to move lest I disturb her. Hours and hours, I guess it was, she lay there. My body grew numb. I shivered. I coughed. I wanted to get up and whittle at the boxes of young trees. I withdrew my hand. I raised her head to waken her. She88 did not stir. I got up and walked around. I found my policeman friend and talked to him. We both came up, and bent over her. He said it would be all right for her to stay there just so long as she got away before the workmen came at dawn. A blanket was borrowed from a neighbor house. I sat beside her through the night. I saw the dawn steal over Washington. The Capitol dome looked like a gray ghost ship drifting in from sea. Avey's face was pale, and her eyes were heavy. She did not have the gray crimson-splashed beauty of the dawn. I hated to wake her. Orphan-woman...

89

BEEHIVE

Within this black hive to-night
There swarm a million bees;
Bees passing in and out the moon,
Bees escaping out the moon,
Bees returning through the moon,
Silver bees intently buzzing,
Silver honey dripping from the swarm of bees
Earth is a waxen cell of the world comb,
And I, a drone,
Lying on my back,
Lipping honey,
Getting drunk with silver honey,
Wish that I might fly out past the moon
And curl forever in some far-off farmyard flower.

90

STORM ENDING

Thunder blossoms gorgeously above our heads,
Great, hollow, bell-like flowers,
Rumbling in the wind,
Stretching clappers to strike our ears ..
Full-lipped flowers
Bitten by the sun
Bleeding rain
Dripping rain like golden honey—
And the sweet earth flying from the thunder.

91

THEATER

LIFE of nigger alleys, of pool rooms and restaurants and near-beer saloons soaks into the walls of Howard Theater and sets them throbbing jazz songs. Black-skinned, they dance and shout above the tick and trill of white-walled buildings. At night, they open doors to people who come in to stamp their feet and shout. At night, road-shows volley songs into the mass-heart of black people. Songs soak the walls and seep out to the nigger life of alleys and near-beer saloons, of the Poodle Dog and Black Bear cabarets. Afternoons, the house is dark, and the walls are sleeping singers until rehearsal begins. Or until John comes within them. Then they start throbbing to a subtle syncopation. And the space-dark air grows softly luminous.

John is the manager's brother. He is seated at the center of the theater, just before rehearsal. Light streaks down upon him from a window high above. One half his face is orange in it. One half his face is in shadow. The soft glow92 of the house rushes to, and compacts about, the shaft of light. John's mind coincides with the shaft of light. Thoughts rush to, and compact about it. Life of the house and of the slowly awakening stage swirls to the body of John, and thrills it. John's body is separate from the thoughts that pack his mind.

Stage-lights, soft, as if they shine through clear pink fingers. Beneath them, hid by the shadow of a set, Dorris. Other chorus girls drift in. John feels them in the mass. And as if his own body were the mass-heart of a black audience listening to them singing, he wants to stamp his feet and shout. His mind, contained above desires of his body, singles the girls out, and tries to trace origins and plot destinies.

A pianist slips into the pit and improvises jazz. The walls awake. Arms of the girls, and their limbs, which .. jazz, jazz .. by lifting up their tight street skirts they set free, jab the air and clog the floor in rhythm to the music. (Lift your skirts, Baby, and talk t papa!) Crude, individualized, and yet .. monotonous...

John: Soon the director will herd you, my93 full-lipped, distant beauties, and tame you, and blunt your sharp thrusts in loosely suggestive movements, appropriate to Broadway. (O dance!) Soon the audience will paint your dusk faces white, and call you beautiful. (O dance!) Soon I... (O dance!) I'd like...

Girls laugh and shout. Sing discordant snatches of other jazz songs. Whirl with loose passion into the arms of passing show-men.

John: Too thick. Too easy. Too monotonous. Her whom I'd love I'd leave before she knew that I was with her. Her? Which? (O dance!) I'd like to...

Girls dance and sing. Men clap. The walls sing and press inward. They press the men and girls, they press John towards a center of physical ecstasy. Go to it, Baby! Fan yourself, and feed your papa! Put .. nobody lied .. and take .. when they said I cried over you. No lie! The glitter and color of stacked scenes, the gilt and brass and crimson of the house, converge towards a center of physical ecstasy. John's feet and torso and his blood press in. He wills thought to rid his mind of passion.

94

"All right, girls. Alaska. Miss Reynolds, please."

The director wants to get the rehearsal through with.

The girls line up. John sees the front row: dancing ponies. The rest are in shadow. The leading lady fits loosely in the front. Lack-life, monotonous. "One, two, three—" Music starts. The song is somewhere where it will not strain the leading lady's throat. The dance is somewhere where it will not strain the girls. Above the staleness, one dancer throws herself into it. Dorris. John sees her. Her hair, crisp-curled, is bobbed. Bushy, black hair bobbing about her lemon-colored face. Her lips are curiously full, and very red. Her limbs in silk purple stockings are lovely. John feels them. Desires her. Holds off.

John: Stage-door johnny; chorus-girl. No, that would be all right. Dictie, educated, stuck-up; show-girl. Yep. Her suspicion would be stronger than her passion. It wouldnt work. Keep her loveliness. Let her go.

Dorris sees John and knows that he is looking at her. Her own glowing is too rich a thing to[95] let her feel the slimness of his diluted passion.

"Who's that?" she asks her dancing partner.

"Th manager's brother. Dictie. Nothin doin, hon."

Dorris tosses her head and dances for him until she feels she has him. Then, withdrawing disdainfully, she flirts with the director.

Dorris: Nothin doin? How come? Aint I as good as him? Couldnt I have got an education if I'd wanted one? Dont I know respectable folks, lots of em, in Philadelphia and New York and Chicago? Aint I had men as good as him? Better. Doctors an lawyers. Whats a manager's brother, anyhow?

Two steps back, and two steps front.

"Say, Mame, where do you get that stuff?"

"Whatshmean, Dorris?"

"If you two girls cant listen to what I'm telling you, I know where I can get some who can. Now listen."

Mame: Go to hell, you black bastard.

Dorris: Whats eatin at him, anyway?

"Now follow me in this, you girls. Its three[96] counts to the right, three counts to the left, and then you shimmy—"

John: —and then you shimmy. I'll bet she can. Some good cabaret, with rooms upstairs. And what in hell do you think you'd get from it? Youre going wrong. Here's right: get her to herself—(Christ, but how she'd bore you after the first five minutes)—not if you get her right she wouldnt. Touch her, I mean. To herself—in some room perhaps. Some cheap, dingy bedroom. Hell no. Cant be done. But the point is, brother John, it can be done. Get her to herself somewhere, anywhere. Go down in yourself—and she'd be calling you all sorts of asses while you were in the process of going down. Hold em, bud. Cant be done. Let her go. (Dance and I'll love you!) And keep her loveliness.

"All right now, Chicken Chaser. Dorris and girls. Where's Dorris? I told you to stay on the stage, didnt I? Well? Now thats enough. All right. All right there, Professor? All right. One, two, three—"

Dorris swings to the front. The line of girls, four deep, blurs within the shadow of suspended [97]scenes. Dorris wants to dance. The director feels that and steps to one side. He smiles, and picks her for a leading lady, one of these days. Odd ends of stage-men emerge from the wings, and stare and clap. A crap game in the alley suddenly ends. Black faces crowd the rear stage doors. The girls, catching joy from Dorris, whip up within the footlights' glow. They forget set steps; they find their own. The director forgets to bawl them out. Dorris dances.

John: Her head bobs to Broadway. Dance from yourself. Dance! O just a little more.

Dorris' eyes burn across the space of seats to him.

Dorris: I bet he can love. Hell, he cant love. He's too skinny. His lips are too skinny. He wouldnt love me anyway, only for that. But I'd get a pair of silk stockings out of it. Red silk. I got purple. Cut it, kid. You cant win him to respect you that away. He wouldnt anyway. Maybe he would. Maybe he'd love. I've heard em say that men who look like him (what does he look like?) will marry if they love. O will you love me? And give me kids, and a98 home, and everything? (I'd like to make your nest, and honest, hon, I wouldnt run out on you.) You will if I make you. Just watch me.

Dorris dances. She forgets her tricks. She dances.

Glorious songs are the muscles of her limbs.

And her singing is of canebrake loves and mangrove feastings.

The walls press in, singing. Flesh of a throbbing body, they press close to John and Dorris. They close them in. John's heart beats tensely against her dancing body. Walls press his mind within his heart. And then, the shaft of light goes out the window high above him. John's mind sweeps up to follow it. Mind pulls him upward into dream. Dorris dances...
John dreams:

> "
>
> Dorris is dressed in a loose black gown splashed with lemon ribbons. Her feet taper long and slim from trim ankles. She waits for him just inside the stage door. John, collar and tie colorful and flaring, walks towards the stage door. There are no trees in the alley. But his feet feel as though they step on autumn leaves whose rustle has been pressed out of them by the passing of a million satin slippers. The air is sweet with roasting 99chestnuts, sweet with bonfires of old leaves. John's melancholy is a deep thing that seals all senses but his eyes, and makes him whole.
>
> Dorris knows that he is coming. Just at the right moment she steps from the door, as if there were no door. Her face is tinted like the autumn alley. Of old flowers, or of a southern canefield, her perfume. "Glorious Dorris." So his eyes speak. And their sadness is too deep for sweet untruth. She barely touches his arm. They glide off with footfalls softened on the leaves, the old leaves powdered by a million satin slippers.
>
> They are in a room. John knows nothing of it. Only, that the flesh and blood of Dorris are its walls. Singing walls. Lights, soft, as if they shine through clear pink fingers. Soft lights, and warm.
>
> John reaches for a manuscript of his, and reads. Dorris, who has no eyes, has eyes to understand him. He comes to a dancing scene. The scene is Dorris. She dances. Dorris dances. Glorious Dorris. Dorris whirls, whirls, dances...

Dorris dances.

The pianist crashes a bumper chord. The whole stage claps. Dorris, flushed, looks quick at John. His whole face is in shadow. She seeks for her dance in it. She finds it a dead thing in the shadow which is his dream. She rushes from100 the stage. Falls down the steps into her dressing-room. Pulls her hair. Her eyes, over a floor of tears, stare at the whitewashed ceiling. (Smell of dry paste, and paint, and soiled clothing.) Her pal comes in. Dorris flings herself into the old safe arms, and cries bitterly.

"I told you nothin doin," is what Mame says to comfort her.

101

HER LIPS ARE COPPER WIRE

whisper of yellow globes
gleaming on lamp-posts that sway
like bootleg licker drinkers in the fog
and let your breath be moist against me
like bright beads on yellow globes
telephone the power-house
that the main wires are insulate
(her words play softly up and down
dewy corridors of billboards)
then with your tongue remove the tape
and press your lips to mine
till they are incandescent

102

CALLING JESUS

HER soul is like a little thrust-tailed dog that follows her, whimpering. She is large enough, I know, to find a warm spot for it. But each night when she comes home and closes the big outside storm door, the little dog is left in the vestibule, filled with chills till morning. Some one ... eoho Jesus ... soft as a cotton boll brushed against the milk-pod cheek of Christ, will steal in and cover it that it need not shiver, and carry it to her where she sleeps upon clean hay cut in her dreams.

When you meet her in the daytime on the streets, the little dog keeps coming. Nothing happens at first, and then, when she has forgotten the streets and alleys, and the large house where she goes to bed of nights, a soft thing like fur begins to rub your limbs, and you hear a low, scared voice, lonely, calling, and you know that a cool something nozzles moisture in your palms. Sensitive things like nostrils, quiver. Her breath comes sweet as honeysuckle whose pistils bear the life of coming song. And her eyes carry103 to where builders find no need for vestibules, for swinging on iron hinges, storm doors.

Her soul is like a little thrust-tailed dog, that follows her, whimpering. I've seen it tagging on behind her, up streets where chestnut trees flowered, where dusty asphalt had been freshly sprinkled with clean water. Up alleys where niggers sat on low door-steps before tumbled shanties and sang and loved. At night, when she comes home, the little dog is left in the vestibule, nosing the crack beneath the big storm door, filled with chills till morning. Some one ... eoho Jesus ... soft as the bare feet of Christ moving across bales of southern cotton, will steal in and cover it that it need not shiver, and carry it to her where she sleeps: cradled in dream-fluted cane.

104

BOX SEAT

1

HOUSES are shy girls whose eyes shine reticently upon the dusk body of the street. Upon the gleaming limbs and asphalt torso of a dreaming nigger. Shake your curled wool-blossoms, nigger. Open your liver lips to the lean, white spring. Stir the root-life of a withered people. Call them from their houses, and teach them to dream.

Dark swaying forms of Negroes are street songs that woo virginal houses.

Dan Moore walks southward on Thirteenth Street. The low limbs of budding chestnut trees recede above his head. Chestnut buds and blossoms are wool he walks upon. The eyes of houses faintly touch him as he passes them. Soft girl-eyes, they set him singing. Girl-eyes within him widen upward to promised faces. Floating away, they dally wistfully over the dusk body of the street. Come on, Dan Moore, come on. Dan sings. His voice is a little hoarse.[105] It cracks. He strains to produce tones in keeping with the houses' loveliness. Cant be done. He whistles. His notes are shrill. They hurt him. Negroes open gates, and go indoors, perfectly. Dan thinks of the house he's going to. Of the girl. Lips, flesh-notes of a forgotten song, plead with him...

Dan turns into a side-street, opens an iron gate, bangs it to. Mounts the steps, and searches for the bell. Funny, he cant find it. He fumbles around. The thought comes to him that some one passing by might see him, and not understand. Might think that he is trying to sneak, to break in.

Dan: Break in. Get an ax and smash in. Smash in their faces. I'll show em. Break into an engine-house, steal a thousand horse-power fire truck. Smash in with the truck. I'll show em. Grab an ax and brain em. Cut em up. Jack the Ripper. Baboon from the zoo. And then the cops come. "No, I aint a baboon. I aint Jack the Ripper. I'm a poor man out of work. Take your hands off me, you bull-necked bears. Look into my eyes. I am Dan Moore. I was born in a canefield. The hands of Jesus[106] touched me. I am come to a sick world to heal it. Only the other day, a dope fiend brushed against me— Dont laugh, you mighty, juicy, meat-hook men. Give me your fingers and I will peel them as if they were ripe bananas."

Some one might think he is trying to break in. He'd better knock. His knuckles are raw bone against the thick glass door. He waits. No one comes. Perhaps they havent heard him. He raps again. This time, harder. He waits. No one comes. Some one is surely in. He fancies that he sees their shadows on the glass. Shadows of gorillas. Perhaps they saw him coming and dont want to let him in. He knocks. The tension of his arms makes the glass rattle. Hurried steps come towards him. The door opens.

"Please, you might break the glass—the bell—oh, Mr. Moore! I thought it must be some stranger. How do you do? Come in, wont you? Muriel? Yes. I'll call her. Take your things off, wont you? And have a seat in the parlor. Muriel will be right down. Muriel! Oh Muriel! Mr. Moore to see you. She'll be right down. You'll pardon me, wont you? So glad to see you."

107

Her eyes are weak. They are bluish and watery from reading newspapers. The blue is steel. It gimlets Dan while her mouth flaps amiably to him.

Dan: Nothing for you to see, old mussel-head. Dare I show you? If I did, delirium would furnish you headlines for a month. Now look here. Thats enough. Go long, woman. Say some nasty thing and I'll kill you. Huh. Better damned sight not. Ta-ta, Mrs. Pribby.

Mrs. Pribby retreats to the rear of the house. She takes up a newspaper. There is a sharp click as she fits into her chair and draws it to the table. The click is metallic like the sound of a bolt being shot into place. Dan's eyes sting. Sinking into a soft couch, he closes them. The house contracts about him. It is a sharp-edged, massed, metallic house. Bolted. About Mrs. Pribby. Bolted to the endless rows of metal houses. Mrs. Pribby's house. The rows of houses belong to other Mrs. Pribbys. No wonder he couldn't sing to them.

Dan: What's Muriel doing here? God, what a place for her. Whats she doing? Putting her stockings on? In the bathroom. Come108 out of there, Dan Moore. People must have their privacy. Peeping-toms. I'll never peep. I'll listen. I like to listen.

Dan goes to the wall and places his ear against it. A passing street car and something vibrant from the earth sends a rumble to him. That rumble comes from the earth's deep core. It is the mutter of powerful underground races. Dan has a picture of all the people rushing to put their ears against walls, to listen to it. The next world-savior is coming up that way. Coming up. A continent sinks down. The new-world Christ will need consummate skill to walk upon the waters where huge bubbles burst... Thuds of Muriel coming down. Dan turns to the piano and glances through a stack of jazz music sheets. "Ji-ji-bo, JI-JI-BO!" ..

"Hello, Dan, stranger, what brought you here?"

Muriel comes in, shakes hands, and then clicks into a high-armed seat under the orange glow of a floor-lamp. Her face is fleshy. It would tend to coarseness but for the fresh fragrant something which is the life of it. Her hair like an Indian's. But more curly and bushed109 and vagrant. Her nostrils flare. The flushed ginger of her cheeks is touched orange by the shower of color from the lamp.

"Well, you havent told me, you havent answered my question, stranger. What brought you here?"

Dan feels the pressure of the house, of the rear room, of the rows of houses, shift to Muriel. He is light. He loves her. He is doubly heavy.

"Dont know, Muriel—wanted to see you—wanted to talk to you—to see you and tell you that I know what you've been through—what pain the last few months must have been—"

"Lets dont mention that."

"But why not, Muriel? I—"

"Please."

"But Muriel, life is full of things like that. One grows strong and beautiful in facing them. What else is life?"

"I dont know, Dan. And I dont believe I care. Whats the use? Lets talk about something else. I hear there's a good show at the Lincoln this week."

"Yes, so Harry was telling me. Going?"

"To-night."

110

Dan starts to rise.

"I didnt know. I dont want to keep you."

"Its all right. You dont have to go till Bernice comes. And she wont be here till eight. I'm all dressed. I'll let you know."

"Thanks."

Silence. The rustle of a newspaper being turned comes from the rear room.

Muriel: Shame about Dan. Something awfully good and fine about him. But he don't fit in. In where? Me? Dan, I could love you if I tried. I dont have to try. I do. O Dan, dont you know I do? Timid lover, brave talker that you are. Whats the good of all you know if you dont know that? I wont let myself. I? Mrs. Pribby who reads newspapers all night wont. What has she got to do with me?

She is me, somehow. No she's not. Yes she is. She is the town, and the town wont let me love you, Dan. Dont you know? You could make it let me if you would. Why wont you? Youre selfish. I'm not strong enough to buck it. Youre too selfish to buck it, for me. I wish you'd go. You irritate me. Dan, please go.

"What are you doing now, Dan?"

111

"Same old thing, Muriel. Nothing, as the world would have it. Living, as I look at things. Living as much as I can without—"

"But you cant live without money, Dan. Why dont you get a good job and settle down?"

Dan: Same old line. Shoot it at me, sister. Hell of a note, this loving business. For ten minutes of it youve got to stand the torture of an intolerable heaviness and a hundred platitudes. Well, damit, shoot on.

"To what? my dear. Rustling newspapers?"

"You mustnt say that, Dan. It isnt right. Mrs. Pribby has been awfully good to me."

"Dare say she has. Whats that got to do with it?"

"Oh, Dan, youre so unconsiderate and selfish. All you think of is yourself."

"I think of you."

"Too much—I mean, you ought to work more and think less. Thats the best way to get along."

"Mussel-heads get along, Muriel. There is more to you than that—"

"Sometimes I think there is, Dan. But I dont know. I've tried. I've tried to do something 112with myself. Something real and beautiful, I mean. But whats the good of trying? I've tried to make people, every one I come in contact with, happy—"

Dan looks at her, directly. Her animalism, still unconquered by zoo-restrictions and keeper-taboos, stirs him. Passion tilts upward, bringing with it the elements of an old desire. Muriel's lips become the flesh-notes of a futile, plaintive longing. Dan's impulse to direct her is its fresh life.

"Happy, Muriel? No, not happy. Your aim is wrong. There is no such thing as happiness. Life bends joy and pain, beauty and ugliness, in such a way that no one may isolate them. No one should want to. Perfect joy, or perfect pain, with no contrasting element to define them, would mean a monotony of consciousness, would mean death. Not happy, Muriel. Say that you have tried to make them create. Say that you have used your own capacity for life to cradle them. To start them upward-flowing. Or if you cant say that you have, then say that you will. My talking to you will make you aware of your113 power to do so. Say that you will love, that you will give yourself in love—"

"To you, Dan?"

Dan's consciousness crudely swerves into his passions. They flare up in his eyes. They set up quivers in his abdomen. He is suddenly over-tense and nervous.

"Muriel—"

The newspaper rustles in the rear room.

"Muriel—"

Dan rises. His arms stretch towards her. His fingers and his palms, pink in the lamp-light, are glowing irons. Muriel's chair is close and stiff about her. The house, the rows of houses locked about her chair. Dan's fingers and arms are fire to melt and bars to wrench and force and pry. Her arms hang loose. Her hands are hot and moist. Dan takes them. He slips to his knees before her.

"Dan, you mustnt."

"Muriel—"

"Dan, really you mustnt. No, Dan. No."

"Oh, come, Muriel. Must I—"

"Shhh. Dan, please get up. Please. Mrs. Pribby is right in the next room. She'll hear114 you. She may come in. Dont, Dan. She'll see you—"

"Well then, lets go out."

"I cant. Let go, Dan. Oh, wont you please let go."

Muriel tries to pull her hands away. Dan tightens his grip. He feels the strength of his fingers. His muscles are tight and strong. He stands up. Thrusts out his chest. Muriel shrinks from him. Dan becomes aware of his crude absurdity. His lips curl. His passion chills. He has an obstinate desire to possess her.

"Muriel, I love you. I want you, whatever the world of Pribby says. Damn your Pribby. Who is she to dictate my love? I've stood enough of her. Enough of you. Come here."

Muriel's mouth works in and out. Her eyes flash and waggle. She wrenches her hands loose and forces them against his breast to keep him off. Dan grabs her wrists. Wedges in between her arms. Her face is close to him. It is hot and blue and moist. Ugly.

"Come here now."

"Dont, Dan. Oh, dont. What are you killing?"

115

"Whats weak in both of us and a whole litter of Pribbys. For once in your life youre going to face whats real, by God—"

A sharp rap on the newspaper in the rear room cuts between them. The rap is like cool thick glass between them. Dan is hot on one side. Muriel, hot on the other. They straighten. Gaze fearfully at one another. Neither moves. A clock in the rear room, in the rear room, the rear room, strikes eight. Eight slow, cool sounds. Bernice. Muriel fastens on her image. She smooths her dress. She adjusts her skirt. She becomes prim and cool. Rising, she skirts Dan as if to keep the glass between them. Dan, gyrating nervously above the easy swing of his limbs, follows her to the parlor door. Muriel retreats before him till she reaches the landing of the steps that lead upstairs. She smiles at him. Dan sees his face in the hall mirror. He runs his fingers through his hair. Reaches for his hat and coat and puts them on. He moves towards Muriel. Muriel steps backward up one step. Dan's jaw shoots out. Muriel jerks her arm in warning of Mrs. Pribby. She gasps and turns and starts to run. Noise of a116 chair scraping as Mrs. Pribby rises from it, ratchets down the hall. Dan stops. He makes a wry face, wheels round, goes out, and slams the door.

2

People come in slowly ... mutter, laughs, flutter, whishadwash, "I've changed my work-clothes—" ... and fill vacant seats of Lincoln Theater. Muriel, leading Bernice who is a cross between a washerwoman and a blue-blood lady, a washer-blue, a washer-lady, wanders down the right aisle to the lower front box. Muriel has on an orange dress. Its color would clash with the crimson box-draperies, its color would contradict the sweet rose smile her face is bathed in, should she take her coat off. She'll keep it on.

Pale purple shadows rest on the planes of her cheeks. Deep purple comes from her thick-shocked hair. Orange of the dress goes well with these. Muriel presses her coat down from around her shoulders. Teachers are not supposed to have bobbed hair. She'll keep her hat on. She takes the first chair, and indicates that[117] Bernice is to take the one directly behind her. Seated thus, her eyes are level with, and near to, the face of an imaginary man upon the stage. To speak to Berny she must turn. When she does, the audience is square upon her.

People come in slowly ... "—for my Sunday-go-to-meeting dress. O glory God! O shout Amen!" ... and fill vacant seats of Lincoln Theater. Each one is a bolt that shoots into a slot, and is locked there. Suppose the Lord should ask, where was Moses when the light went out? Suppose Gabriel should blow his trumpet! The seats are slots. The seats are bolted houses. The mass grows denser. Its weight at first is impalpable upon the box. Then Muriel begins to feel it. She props her arm against the brass box-rail, to ward it off. Silly. These people are friends of hers: a parent of a child she teaches, an old school friend. She smiles at them. They return her courtesy, and she is free to chat with Berny. Berny's tongue, started, runs on, and on. O washer-blue! O washer-lady!

Muriel: Never see Dan again. He makes me feel queer. Starts things he doesnt finish.[118] Upsets me. I am not upset. I am perfectly calm. I am going to enjoy the show. Good show. I've had some show! This damn tame thing. O Dan. Wont see Dan again. Not alone. Have Mrs. Pribby come in. She *was* in. Keep Dan out. If I love him, can I keep him out? Well then, I dont love him. Now he's out. Who is that coming in? Blind as a bat. Ding-bat. Looks like Dan. He mustnt see me. Silly. He cant reach me. He wont dare come in here. He'd put his head down like a goring bull and charge me. He'd trample them. He'd gore. He'd rape! Berny! He won't dare come in here.

"Berny, who was that who just came in? I havent my glasses."

"A friend of yours, a *good* friend so I hear. Mr. Daniel Moore, Lord."

"Oh. He's no friend of mine."

"No? I hear he is."

"Well, he isnt."

Dan is ushered down the aisle. He has to squeeze past the knees of seated people to reach his own seat. He treads on a man's corns. The man grumbles, and shoves him off. He shrivels[119] close beside a portly Negress whose huge rolls of flesh meet about the bones of seat-arms. A soil-soaked fragrance comes from her. Through the cement floor her strong roots sink down. They spread under the asphalt streets. Dreaming, the streets roll over on their bellies, and suck their glossy health from them. Her strong roots sink down and spread under the river and disappear in blood-lines that waver south. Her roots shoot down. Dan's hands follow them. Roots throb. Dan's heart beats violently. He places his palms upon the earth to cool them. Earth throbs. Dan's heart beats violently. He sees all the people in the house rush to the walls to listen to the rumble. A new-world Christ is coming up. Dan comes up. He is startled. The eyes of the woman dont belong to her. They look at him unpleasanfly. From either aisle, bolted masses press in. He doesnt fit. The mass grows agitant. For an instant, Dan's and Muriel's eyes meet. His weight there slides the weight on her. She braces an arm against the brass rail, and turns her head away.

Muriel: Damn fool; dear Dan, what did you want to follow me here for? Oh cant you[120] ever do anything right? Must you always pain me, and make me hate you? I do hate you. I wish some one would come in with a horse-whip and lash you out. I wish some one would drag you up a back alley and brain you with the whip-butt.

Muriel glances at her wrist-watch.

"Quarter of nine. Berny, what time have you?"

"Eight-forty. Time to begin. Oh, look Muriel, that woman with the plume; doesnt she look good! They say she's going with, oh, whats his name. You know. Too much powder. I can see it from here. Here's the orchestra now. O fine! Jim Clem at the piano!"

The men fill the pit. Instruments run the scale and tune. The saxophone moans and throws a fit. Jim Clem, poised over the piano, is ready to begin. His head nods forward. Opening crash. The house snaps dark. The curtain recedes upward from the blush of the footlights. Jazz overture is over. The first act is on.

Dan: Old stuff. Muriel—bored. Must be. But she'll smile and she'll clap. Do what youre121 bid, you she-slave. Look at her. Sweet, tame woman in a brass box seat. Clap, smile, fawn, clap. Do what youre bid. Drag me in with you. Dirty me. Prop me in your brass box seat. I'm there, am I not? because of you. He-slave. Slave of a woman who is a slave. I'm a damned sight worse than you are. I sing your praises, Beauty! I exalt thee, O Muriel! A slave, thou art greater than all Freedom because I love thee.

Dan fidgets, and disturbs his neighbors. His neighbors glare at him. He glares back without seeing them. The man whose corns have been trod upon speaks to him.

"Keep quiet, cant you, mister. Other people have paid their money besides yourself to see the show."

The man's face is a blur about two sullen liquid things that are his eyes. The eyes dissolve in the surrounding vagueness. Dan suddenly feels that the man is an enemy whom he has long been looking for.

Dan bristles. Glares furiously at the man.

"All right. All right then. Look at the show. I'm not stopping you."

122

"Shhh," from some one in the rear.

Dan turns around.

"Its that man there who started everything. I didnt say a thing to him until he tried to start something. What have I got to do with whether he has paid his money or not? Thats the manager's business. Do I look like the manager?"

"Shhhh. Youre right. Shhhh."

"Dont tell me to shhh. Tell him. That man there. He started everything. If what he wanted was to start a fight, why didnt he say so?"

The man leans forward.

"Better be quiet, sonny. I aint said a thing about fight, yet."

"Its a good thing you havent."

"Shhhh."

Dan grips himself. Another act is on. Dwarfs, dressed like prize-fighters, foreheads bulging like boxing gloves, are led upon the stage. They are going to fight for the heavyweight championship. Gruesome. Dan glances at Muriel. He imagines that she shudders. His mind curves back into himself, and picks up tail-ends of experiences. His eyes are open,123 mechanically. The dwarfs pound and bruise and bleed each other, on his eyeballs.

Dan: Ah, but she was some baby! And not vulgar either. Funny how some women can do those things. Muriel dancing like that! Hell. She rolled and wabbled. Her buttocks rocked. She pulled up her dress and showed her pink drawers. Baby! And then she caught my eyes. Dont know what my eyes had in them. Yes I do. God, dont I though! Sometimes I think, Dan Moore, that your eyes could burn clean ... burn clean ... BURN CLEAN!..

The gong rings. The dwarfs set to. They spar grotesquely, playfully, until one lands a stiff blow. This makes the other sore. He commences slugging. A real scrap is on. Time! The dwarfs go to their corners and are sponged and fanned off. Gloves bulge from their wrists. Their wrists are necks for the tight-faced gloves. The fellow to the right lets his eyes roam over the audience. He sights Muriel. He grins.

Dan: Those silly women arguing feminism. Here's what I should have said to them. "It[124] should be clear to you women, that the proposition must be stated thus:
Me, horizontally above her.
Action: perfect strokes downward oblique.
Hence, man dominates because of limitation.
Or, so it shall be until women learn their stuff.

So framed, the proposition is a mental-filler, Dentist, I want gold teeth. It should become cherished of the technical intellect. I hereby offer it to posterity as one of the important machine-age designs. P. S. It should be noted, that because it *is* an achievement of this age, its growth and hence its causes, up to the point of maturity, antedate machinery. Ery..."

The gong rings. No fooling this time. The dwarfs set to. They clinch. The referee parts them. One swings a cruel upper-cut and knocks the other down. A huge head hits the floor. Pop! The house roars. The fighter, groggy, scrambles up. The referee whispers to the contenders not to fight so hard. They ignore him. They charge. Their heads jab like boxing-gloves. They kick and spit and bite. They pound each other furiously. Muriel pounds.[125] The house pounds. Cut lips. Bloody noses. The referee asks for the gong. Time! The house roars. The dwarfs bow, are made to bow. The house wants more. The dwarfs are led from the stage.

Dan: Strange I never really noticed him before. Been sitting there for years. Born a slave. Slavery not so long ago. He'll die in his chair. Swing low, sweet chariot. Jesus will come and roll him down the river Jordan. Oh, come along, Moses, you'll get lost; stretch out your rod and come across. LET MY PEOPLE GO! Old man. Knows everyone who passes the corners. Saw the first horse-cars. The first Oldsmobile. And he was born in slavery. I did see his eyes. Never miss eyes. But they were bloodshot and watery. It hurt to look at them. It hurts to look in most people's eyes. He saw Grant and Lincoln. He saw Walt—old man, did you see Walt Whitman? Did you see Walt Whitman! Strange force that drew me to him. And I went up to see. The woman thought I saw crazy. I told him to look into the heavens. He did, and smiled. I asked him if he knew what that rumbling is that comes up from the ground. Christ,[126] what a stroke that was. And the jabbering idiots crowding around. And the crossing-cop leaving his job to come over and wheel him away...

The house applauds. The house wants more. The dwarfs are led back. But no encore. Must give the house something. The attendant comes out and announces that Mr. Barry, the champion, will sing one of his own songs, "for your approval." Mr. Barry grins at Muriel as he wabbles from the wing. He holds a fresh white rose, and a small mirror. He wipes blood from his nose. He signals Jim Clem. The orchestra starts. A sentimental love song, Mr. Barry sings, first to one girl, and then another in the audience. He holds the mirror in such a way that it flashes in the face of each one he sings to. The light swings around.

Dan: I am going to reach up and grab the girders of this building and pull them down. The crash will be a signal. Hid by the smoke and dust Dan Moore will arise. In his right hand will be a dynamo. In his left, a god's face that will flash white light from ebony. I'll grab a girder and swing it like a walking-stick.[127] Lightning will flash. I'll grab its black knob and swing it like a crippled cane. Lightning... Some one's flashing ... some one's flashing... Who in hell is flashing that mirror? Take it off me, godam you.

Dan's eyes are half blinded. He moves his head. The light follows. He hears the audience laugh. He hears the orchestra. A man with a high-pitched, sentimental voice is singing. Dan sees the dwarf. Along the mirror flash the song comes. Dan ducks his head. The audience roars. The light swings around to Muriel. Dan looks. Muriel is too close. Mr. Barry covers his mirror. He sings to her. She shrinks away. Nausea. She clutches the brass box-rail. She moves to face away. The audience is square upon her. Its eyes smile. Its hands itch to clap. Muriel turns to the dwarf and forces a smile at him. With a showy blare of orchestration, the song comes to its close. Mr. Barry bows. He offers Muriel the rose, first having kissed it. Blood of his battered lips is a vivid stain upon its petals. Mr. Barry offers Muriel the rose. The house applauds. Muriel flinches back. The dwarf steps forward, diffident;128 threatening. Hate pops from his eyes and crackles like a brittle heat about the box. The thick hide of his face is drawn in tortured wrinkles. Above his eyes, the bulging, tight-skinned brow. Dan looks at it. It grows calm and massive. It grows profound. It is a thing of wisdom and tenderness, of suffering and beauty. Dan looks down. The eyes are calm and luminous. Words come from them... Arms of the audience reach out, grab Muriel, and hold her there. Claps are steel fingers that manacle her wrists and move them forward to acceptance. Berny leans forward and whispers:

"Its all right. Go on—take it."

Words form in the eyes of the dwarf:
Do not shrink. Do not be afraid of me.
Jesus
See how my eyes look at you.
the Son of God
I too was made in His image.
was once—
I give you the rose.

Muriel, tight in her revulsion, sees black, and daintily reaches for the offering. As her hand129 touches it, Dan springs up in his seat and shouts:

"JESUS WAS ONCE A LEPER!"

Dan steps down.

He is as cool as a green stem that has just shed its flower.

Rows of gaping faces strain towards him. They are distant, beneath him, impalpable. Squeezing out, Dan again treads upon the corn-foot man. The man shoves him.

"Watch where youre going, mister. Crazy or no, you aint going to walk over me. Watch where youre going there."

Dan turns, and serenely tweaks the fellow's nose. The man jumps up. Dan is jammed against a seat-back. A slight swift anger flicks him. His fist hooks the other's jaw.

"Now you have started something. Aint no man living can hit me and get away with it. Come on on the outside."

The house, tumultuously stirring, grabs its wraps and follows the men.

The man leads Dan up a black alley. The alley-air is thick and moist with smells of garbage 130and wet trash. In the morning, singing niggers will drive by and ring their gongs... Heavy with the scent of rancid flowers and with the scent of fight. The crowd, pressing forward, is a hollow roar. Eyes of houses, soft girl-eyes, glow reticently upon the hubbub and blink out. The man stops. Takes off his hat and coat. Dan, having forgotten him, keeps going on.

131

PRAYER

My body is opaque to the soul.
Driven of the spirit, long have I sought to temper it unto the spirit's longing,

But my mind, too, is opaque to the soul.
A closed lid is my soul's flesh-eye.
O Spirits of whom my soul is but a little finger,
Direct it to the lid of its flesh-eye.
I am weak with much giving.
I am weak with the desire to give more.
(How strong a thing is the little finger!)
So weak that I have confused the body with the soul,
And the body with its little finger.
(How frail is the little finger.)
My voice could not carry to you did you dwell in stars,
O Spirits of whom my soul is but a little finger...

132

HARVEST SONG

I am a reaper whose muscles set at sundown. All my oats are cradled.

But I am too chilled, and too fatigued to bind them. And I hunger.

I crack a grain between my teeth. I do not taste it.

I have been in the fields all day. My throat is dry. I hunger.

My eyes are caked with dust of oatfields at harvest- time.

I am a blind man who stares across the hills, seeking stack'd fields of other harvesters.

It would be good to see them ... crook'd, split, and iron-ring'd handles of the scythes. It would be good to see them, dust-caked and blind. I hunger.

(Dusk is a strange fear'd sheath their blades are dull'd in.)

My throat is dry. And should I call, a cracked grain like the oats ... eoho—

I fear to call. What should they hear me, and offer me their grain, oats, or wheat, or corn? I have been in the fields all day. I fear I could not taste it. I fear knowledge of my hunger.

133My ears are caked with dust of oatfields at harvest-time.

I am a deaf man who strains to hear the calls of other harvesters whose throats are also dry.

It would be good to hear their songs .. reapers of the sweet-stalk'd cane, cutters of the corn .. even though their throats cracked and the strangeness of their voices deafened me.

I hunger. My throat is dry. Now that the sun has set and I am chilled, I fear to call. (Eoho, my brothers!)

I am a reaper. (Eoho!) All my oats are cradled. But I am too fatigued to bind them. And I hunger. I crack a grain. It has no taste to it. My throat is dry...

O my brothers, I beat my palms, still soft, against the stubble of my harvesting. (You beat your soft palms, too.) My pain is sweet. Sweeter than the oats or wheat or corn. It will not bring me knowledge of my hunger.

134

BONA AND PAUL

1

ON the school gymnasium floor, young men and women are drilling. They are going to be teachers, and go out into the world .. thud, thud .. and give precision to the movements of sick people who all their lives have been drilling. One man is out of step. In step. The teacher glares at him. A girl in bloomers, seated on a mat in the corner because she has told the director that she is sick, sees that the footfalls of the men are rhythmical and syncopated. The dance of his blue-trousered limbs thrills her.

Bona: He is a candle that dances in a grove swung with pale balloons.

Columns of the drillers thud towards her. He is in the front row. He is in no row at all. Bona can look close at him. His red-brown face—

Bona: He is a harvest moon. He is an autumn leaf. He is a nigger. Bona! But dont all the dorm girls say so? And dont you, when135 you are sane, say so? Thats why I love—Oh, nonsense. You have never loved a man who didnt first love you. Besides—

Columns thud away from her. Come to a halt in line formation. Rigid. The period bell rings, and the teacher dismisses them.

A group collects around Paul. They are choosing sides for basket-ball. Girls against boys. Paul has his. He is limbering up beneath the basket. Bona runs to the girl captain and asks to be chosen. The girls fuss. The director comes to quiet them. He hears what Bona wants.

"But, Miss Hale, you were excused—"

"So I was, Mr. Boynton, but—"

"—you can play basket-ball, but you are too sick to drill."

"If you wish to put it that way."

She swings away from him to the girl captain.

"Helen, I want to play, and you must let me. This is the first time I've asked and I dont see why—"

"Thats just it, Bona. We have our team."

"Well, team or no team, I want to play and thats all there is to it."

136

She snatches the ball from Helen's hands, and charges down the floor.

Helen shrugs. One of the weaker girls says that she'll drop out. Helen accepts this. The team is formed. The whistle blows. The game starts. Bona, in center, is jumping against Paul. He plays with her. Out-jumps her, makes a quick pass, gets a quick return, and shoots a goal from the middle of the floor. Bona burns crimson. She fights, and tries to guard him. One of her team-mates advises her not to play so hard. Paul shoots his second goal.

Bona begins to feel a little dizzy and all in. She drives on. Almost hugs Paul to guard him. Near the basket, he attempts to shoot, and Bona lunges into his body and tries to beat his arms. His elbow, going up, gives her a sharp crack on the jaw. She whirls. He catches her. Her body stiffens. Then becomes strangely vibrant, and bursts to a swift life within her anger. He is about to give way before her hatred when a new passion flares at him and makes his stomach fall. Bona squeezes him. He suddenly feels stifled, and wonders why in hell the ring of silly gaping faces that's caked about him doesnt make way[137] and give him air. He has a swift illusion that it is himself who has been struck. He looks at Bona. Whir. Whir. They seem to be human distortions spinning tensely in a fog. Spinning .. dizzy .. spinning... Bona jerks herself free, flushes a startling crimson, breaks through the bewildered teams, and rushes from the hall.

2

Paul is in his room of two windows.

Outside, the South-Side L track cuts them in two.

Bona is one window. One window, Paul.

Hurtling Loop-jammed L trains throw them in swift shadow.

Paul goes to his. Gray slanting roofs of houses are tinted lavender in the setting sun. Paul follows the sun, over the stock-yards where a fresh stench is just arising, across wheat lands that are still waving above their stubble, into the sun. Paul follows the sun to a pine-matted hillock in Georgia. He sees the slanting roofs of gray unpainted cabins tinted lavender. A[138] Negress chants a lullaby beneath the mate-eyes of a southern planter. Her breasts are ample for the suckling of a song. She weans it, and sends it, curiously weaving, among lush melodies of cane and corn. Paul follows the sun into himself in Chicago.

He is at Bona's window.

With his own glow he looks through a dark pane.

Paul's room-mate comes in.

"Say, Paul, I've got a date for you. Come on. Shake a leg, will you?"

His blonde hair is combed slick. His vest is snug about him.

He is like the electric light which he snaps on.

"Whatdoysay, Paul? Get a wiggle on. Come on. We havent got much time by the time we eat and dress and everything."

His bustling concentrates on the brushing of his hair.

Art: What in hell's getting into Paul of late, anyway? Christ, but he's getting moony. Its his blood. Dark blood: moony. Doesnt get[139] anywhere unless you boost it. You've got to keep it going—

"Say, Paul!"

—or it'll go to sleep on you. Dark blood; nigger? Thats what those jealous she-hens say. Not Bona though, or she ... from the South ... wouldnt want me to fix a date for him and her. Hell of a thing, that Paul's dark: you've got to always be answering questions.

"Say, Paul, for Christ's sake leave that window, cant you?"

"Whats it, Art?"

"Hell, I've told you about fifty times. Got a date for you. Come on."

"With who?"

Art: He didnt use to ask; now he does. Getting up in the air. Getting funny.

"Heres your hat. Want a smoke? Paul! Here. I've got a match. Now come on and I'll tell you all about it on the way to supper."

Paul: He's going to Life this time. No doubt of that. Quit your kidding. Some day, dear Art, I'm going to kick the living slats out of you, and you wont know what I've done it for. And your slats will bring forth Life .. beautiful woman...

140

Pure Food Restaurant.

"Bring me some soup with a lot of crackers, understand? And then a roast-beef dinner. Same for you, eh, Paul? Now as I was saying, you've got a swell chance with her. And she's game. Best proof: she dont give a damn what the dorm girls say about you and her in the gym, or about the funny looks that Boynton gives her, or about what they say about, well, hell, you know, Paul. And say, Paul, she's a sweetheart. Tall, not puffy and pretty, more serious and deep—the kind you like these days. And they say she's got a car. And say, she's on fire. But you know all about that. She got Helen to fix it up with me. The four of us—remember the last party? Crimson Gardens! Boy!"

Paul's eyes take on a light that Art can settle in.

3

Art has on his patent-leather pumps and fancy vest. A loose fall coat is swung across his arm. His face has been massaged, and over a close shave, powdered. It is a healthy pink the blue141 of evening tints a purple pallor. Art is happy and confident in the good looks that his mirror gave him. Bubbling over with a joy he must spend now if the night is to contain it all. His bubbles, too, are curiously tinted purple as Paul watches them. Paul, contrary to what he had thought he would be like, is cool like the dusk, and like the dusk, detached. His dark face is a floating shade in evening's shadow. He sees Art, curiously. Art is a purple fluid, carbon-charged, that effervesces besides him. He loves Art. But is it not queer, this pale purple facsimile of a red-blooded Norwegian friend of his? Perhaps for some reason, white skins are not supposed to live at night. Surely, enough nights would transform them fantastically, or kill them. And their red passion? Night paled that too, and made it moony. Moony. Thats what Art thought of him. Bona didnt, even in the daytime. Bona, would she be pale? Impossible. Not that red glow. But the conviction did not set his emotion flowing.

"Come right in, wont you? The young ladies will be right down. Oh, Mr. Carlstrom, do play something for us while you are waiting. We just142 love to listen to your music. You play so well."

Houses, and dorm sitting-rooms are places where white faces seclude themselves at night. There is a reason...

Art sat on the piano and simply tore it down. Jazz. The picture of Our Poets hung perilously.

Paul: I've got to get the kid to play that stuff for me in the daytime. Might be different More himself. More nigger. Different? There is. Curious, though.

The girls come in. Art stops playing, and almost immediately takes up a petty quarrel, where he had last left it, with Helen.

Bona, black-hair curled staccato, sharply contrasting with Helen's puffy yellow, holds Paul's hand. She squeezes it. Her own emotion supplements the return pressure. And then, for no tangible reason, her spirits drop. Without them, she is nervous, and slightly afraid. She resents this. Paul's eyes are critical. She resents Paul. She flares at him. She flares to poise and security.

"Shall we be on our way?"

"Yes, Bona, certainly."

The Boulevard is sleek in asphalt, and, with143 arc-lights and limousines, aglow. Dry leaves scamper behind the whir of cars. The scent of exploded gasoline that mingles with them is faintly sweet. Mellow stone mansions over-shadow clapboard homes which now resemble Negro shanties in some southern alley. Bona and Paul, and Art and Helen, move along an island-like, far-stretching strip of leaf-soft ground. Above them, worlds of shadow-planes and solids, silently moving. As if on one of these, Paul looks down on Bona. No doubt of it: her face is pale. She is talking. Her words have no feel to them. One sees them. They are pink petals that fall upon velvet cloth. Bona is soft, and pale, and beautiful.

"Paul, tell me something about yourself—or would you rather wait?"

"I'll tell you anything you'd like to know."

"Not what I want to know, Paul; what you want to tell me."

"You have the beauty of a gem fathoms under sea."

"I feel that, but I dont want to be. I want to be near you. Perhaps I will be if I tell you something. Paul, I love you."

144

The sea casts up its jewel into his hands, and burns them furiously. To tuck her arm under his and hold her hand will ease the burn.

"What can I say to you, brave dear woman—I cant talk love. Love is a dry grain in my mouth unless it is wet with kisses."

"You would dare? right here on the Boulevard? before Arthur and Helen?"

"Before myself? I dare."

"Here then."

Bona, in the slim shadow of a tree trunk, pulls Paul to her. Suddenly she stiffens. Stops.

"But you have not said you love me."

"I cant—yet—Bona."

"Ach, you never will. Youre cold. Cold."

Bona: Colored; cold. Wrong somewhere.

She hurries and catches up with Art and Helen.

4

Crimson Gardens. Hurrah! So one feels. People ... University of Chicago students, members of the stock exchange, a large Negro in crimson uniform who guards the door .. had145 watched them enter. Had leaned towards each other over ash-smeared tablecloths and highballs and whispered: What is he, a Spaniard, an Indian, an Italian, a Mexican, a Hindu, or a Japanese? Art had at first fidgeted under their stares .. what are *you* looking at, you godam pack of owl-eyed hyenas? .. but soon settled into his fuss with Helen, and forgot them. A strange thing happened to Paul. Suddenly he knew that he was apart from the people around him. Apart from the pain which they had unconsciously caused. Suddenly he knew that people saw, not attractiveness in his dark skin, but difference. Their stares, giving him to himself, filled something long empty within him, and were like green blades sprouting in his consciousness. There was fullness, and strength and peace about it all. He saw himself, cloudy, but real. He saw the faces of the people at the tables round him. White lights, or as now, the pink lights of the Crimson Gardens gave a glow and immediacy to white faces. The pleasure of it, equal to that of love or dream, of seeing this. Art and Bona and Helen? He'd look. They were wonderfully flushed and beautiful. Not146 for himself; because they were. Distantly. Who were they, anyway? God, if he knew them. He'd come in with them. Of that he was sure. Come where? Into life? Yes. No. Into the Crimson Gardens. A part of life. A carbon bubble. Would it look purple if he went out into the night and looked at it? His sudden starting to rise almost upset the table.

"What in hell—pardon—whats the matter, Paul?"

"I forgot my cigarettes—"

"Youre smoking one."

"So I am. Pardon me."

The waiter straightens them out. Takes their order.

Art: What in hell's eating Paul? Moony aint the word for it. From bad to worse. And those godam people staring so. Paul's a queer fish. Doesnt seem to mind... He's my pal, let me tell you, you horn-rimmed owl-eyed hyena at that table, and a lot better than you whoever you are... Queer about him. I could stick up for him if he'd only come out, one way or the other, and tell a feller. Besides, a room-mate has a right to know. Thinks I wont understand. 147Said so. He's got a swell head when it comes to brains, all right. God, he's a good straight feller, though. Only, moony. Nut. Nuttish. Nuttery. Nutmeg... "What'd you say, Helen?"

"I was talking to Bona, thank you."

"Well, its nothing to get spiffy about."

"What? Oh, of course not. Please lets dont start some silly argument all over again."

"Well."

"Well."

"Now thats enough. Say, waiter, whats the matter with our order? Make it snappy, will you?"

Crimson Gardens. Hurrah! So one feels. The drinks come. Four highballs. Art passes cigarettes. A girl dressed like a bare-back rider in flaming pink, makes her way through tables to the dance floor. All lights are dimmed till they seem a lush afterglow of crimson. Spotlights the girl. She sings. "Liza, Little Liza Jane."

Paul is rosy before his window.

He moves, slightly, towards Bona.

With his own glow, he seeks to penetrate a dark pane.

148

Paul: From the South. What does that mean, precisely, except that you'll love or hate a nigger? Thats a lot. What does it mean except that in Chicago you'll have the courage to neither love or hate. A priori. But it would seem that you have. Queer words, arent these, for a man who wears blue pants on a gym floor in the daytime. Well, never matter. You matter. I'd like to know you whom I look at. Know, not love. Not that knowing is a greater pleasure; but that I have just found the joy of it. You came just a month too late. Even this afternoon I dreamed. To-night, along the Boulevard, you found me cold. Paul Johnson, cold! Thats a good one, eh, Art, you fine old stupid fellow, you! But I feel good! The color and the music and the song... A Negress chants a lullaby beneath the mate-eyes of a southern planter. O song!.. And those flushed faces. Eager brilliant eyes. Hard to imagine them as unawakened. Your own. Oh, they're awake all right. "And you know it too, dont you Bona?"

"What, Paul?"

"The truth of what I was thinking."

149

"I'd like to know I know—something of you."

"You will—before the evening's over. I promise it."

Crimson Gardens. Hurrah! So one feels. The bare-back rider balances agilely on the applause which is the tail of her song. Orchestral instruments warm up for jazz. The flute is a cat that ripples its fur against the deep-purring saxophone. The drum throws sticks. The cat jumps on the piano keyboard. Hi diddle, hi diddle, the cat and the fiddle. Crimson Gardens .. hurrah! .. jumps over the moon. Crimson Gardens! Helen .. O Eliza .. rabbit-eyes sparkling, plays up to, and tries to placate what she considers to be Paul's contempt. She always does that .. Little Liza Jane... Once home, she burns with the thought of what she's done. She says all manner of snidy things about him, and swears that she'll never go out again when he is along. She tries to get Art to break with him, saying, that if Paul, whom the whole dormitory calls a nigger, is more to him than she is, well, she's through. She does not break with Art. She goes out as often as she can with Art and Paul. She explains this to herself150 by a piece of information which a friend of hers had given her: men like him (Paul) can fascinate. One is not responsible for fascination. Not one girl had really loved Paul; he fascinated them. Bona didnt; only thought she did. Time would tell. And of course, *she* didnt. Liza... She plays up to, and tries to placate, Paul.

"Paul is so deep these days, and I'm so glad he's found some one to interest him."

"I dont believe I do."

The thought escapes from Bona just a moment before her anger at having said it.

Bona: You little puffy cat, I do. I do!

Dont I, Paul? her eyes ask.

Her answer is a crash of jazz from the palm-hidden orchestra. Crimson Gardens is a body whose blood flows to a clot upon the dance floor. Art and Helen clot. Soon, Bona and Paul. Paul finds her a little stiff, and his mind, wandering to Helen (silly little kid who wants every highball spoon her hands touch, for a souvenir), supple, perfect little dancer, wishes for the next dance when he and Art will exchange.

Bona knows that she must win him to herself.

"Since when have men like you grown cold?"

151

"The first philosopher."

"I thought you were a poet—or a gym director."

"Hence, your failure to make love."

Bona's eyes flare. Water. Grow red about the rims. She would like to tear away from him and dash across the clotted floor.

"What do you mean?"

"Mental concepts rule you. If they were flush with mine—good. I dont believe they are."

"How do you know, Mr. Philosopher?"

"Mostly a priori."

"You talk well for a gym director."

"And you—"

"I hate you. Ou!"

She presses away. Paul, conscious of the convention in it, pulls her to him. Her body close. Her head still strains away. He nearly crushes her. She tries to pinch him. Then sees people staring, and lets her arms fall. Their eyes meet. Both, contemptuous. The dance takes blood from their minds and packs it, tingling, in the torsos of their swaying bodies. Passionate blood leaps back into their eyes. They are a dizzy blood clot on a gyrating floor.

152

They know that the pink-faced people have no part in what they feel. Their instinct leads them away from Art and Helen, and towards the big uniformed black man who opens and closes the gilded exit door. The cloak-room girl is tolerant of their impatience over such trivial things as wraps. And slightly superior. As the black man swings the door for them, his eyes are knowing. Too many couples have passed out, flushed and fidgety, for him not to know. The chill air is a shock to Paul. A strange thing happens. He sees the Gardens purple, as if he were way off. And a spot is in the purple. The spot comes furiously towards him. Face of the black man. It leers. It smiles sweetly like a child's. Paul leaves Bona and darts back so quickly that he doesnt give the door-man a chance to open. He swings in. Stops. Before the huge bulk of the Negro.

"Youre wrong."

"Yassur."

"Brother, youre wrong."

"I came back to tell you, to shake your hand, and tell you that you are wrong. That something beautiful is going to happen. That the 153 Gardens are purple like a bed of roses would be at dusk. That I came into the Gardens, into life in the Gardens with one whom I did not know. That I danced with her, and did not know her. That I felt passion, contempt and passion for her whom I did not know. That I thought of her. That my thoughts were matches thrown into a dark window. And all the while the Gardens were purple like a bed of roses would be at dusk. I came back to tell you, brother, that white faces are petals of roses. That dark faces are petals of dusk. That I am going out and gather petals. That I am going out and know her whom I brought here with me to these Gardens which are purple like a bed of roses would be at dusk."

Paul and the black man shook hands.

When he reached the spot where they had been standing, Bona was gone.

to Waldo Frank.

153

KABNIS

1

RALPH KABNIS, propped in his bed, tries to read. To read himself to sleep. An oil lamp on a chair near his elbow burns unsteadily. The cabin room is spaced fantastically about it. Whitewashed hearth and chimney, black with sooty saw-teeth. Ceiling, patterned by the fringed globe of the lamp. The walls, unpainted, are seasoned a rosin yellow. And cracks between the boards are black. These cracks are the lips the night winds use for whispering. Night winds in Georgia are vagrant poets, whispering. Kabnis, against his will, lets his book slip down, and listens to them. The warm whiteness of his bed, the lamp-light, do not protect him from the weird chill of their song:
White-man's land.
Niggers, sing.
Burn, bear black children
Till poor rivers bring
Rest, and sweet glory
In Camp Ground.

158

Kabnis' thin hair is streaked on the pillow. His hand strokes the slim silk of his mustache. His thumb, pressed under his chin, seems to be trying to give squareness and projection to it. Brown eyes stare from a lemon face. Moisture gathers beneath his arm-pits. He slides down beneath the cover, seeking release.

Kabnis: Near me. Now. Whoever you are, my warm glowing sweetheart, do not think that the face that rests beside you is the real Kabnis. Ralph Kabnis is a dream. And dreams are faces with large eyes and weak chins and broad brows that get smashed by the fists of square faces. The body of the world is bull-necked. A dream is a soft face that fits uncertainly upon it... God, if I could develop that in words. Give what I know a bull-neck and a heaving body, all would go well with me, wouldnt it, sweetheart? If I could feel that I came to the South to face it. If I, the dream (not what is weak and afraid in me) could become the face of the South. How my lips would sing for it, my songs being the lips of its soul. Soul. Soul hell. There aint no such thing. What in hell was that?

159

A rat had run across the thin boards of the ceiling. Kabnis thrusts his head out from the covers. Through the cracks, a powdery faded red dust sprays down on him. Dust of slave-fields, dried, scattered... No use to read. Christ, if he only could drink himself to sleep. Something as sure as fate was going to happen. He couldnt stand this thing much longer. A hen, perched on a shelf in the adjoining room begins to tread. Her nails scrape the soft wood. Her feathers ruffle.

"Get out of that, you egg-laying bitch."

Kabnis hurls a slipper against the wall. The hen flies from her perch and cackles as if a skunk were after her.

"Now cut out that racket or I'll wring your neck for you."

Answering cackles arise in the chicken yard.

"Why in Christ's hell cant you leave me alone? Damn it, I wish your cackle would choke you. Choke every mother's son of them in this God-forsaken hole. Go away. By God I'll wring your neck for you if you dont. Hell of a mess I've got in: even the poultry is hostile. Go way. Go way. By God, I'll..."

160

Kabnis jumps from his bed. His eyes are wild. He makes for the door. Bursts through it. The hen, driving blindly at the window-pane, screams. Then flies and flops around trying to elude him. Kabnis catches her.

"Got you now, you she-bitch."

With his fingers about her neck, he thrusts open the outside door and steps out into the serene loveliness of Georgian autumn moonlight. Some distance off, down in the valley, a band of pine-smoke, silvered gauze, drifts steadily. The half-moon is a white child that sleeps upon the tree-tops of the forest. White winds croon its sleep-song:
rock a-by baby..
Black mother sways, holding a white child on her bosom.
when the bough bends..
Her breath hums through pine-cones.
cradle will fall..
Teat moon-children at your breasts,
down will come baby..
Black mother.

Kabnis whirls the chicken by its neck, and throws the head away. Picks up the hopping161 body, warm, sticky, and hides it in a clump of bushes. He wipes blood from his hands onto the coarse scant grass.

Kabnis: Thats done. Old Chromo in the big house there will wonder whats become of her pet hen. Well, it'll teach her a lesson: not to make a hen-coop of my quarters. Quarters. Hell of a fine quarters, I've got. Five years ago; look at me now. Earth's child. The earth my mother. God is a profligate red-nosed man about town. Bastardy; me. A bastard son has got a right to curse his maker. God...

Kabnis is about to shake his fists heaven-ward. He looks up, and the night's beauty strikes him dumb. He falls to his knees. Sharp stones cut through his thin pajamas. The shock sends a shiver over him. He quivers. Tears mist his eyes. He writhes.

"God Almighty, dear God, dear Jesus, do not torture me with beauty. Take it away. Give me an ugly world. Ha, ugly. Stinking like unwashed niggers. Dear Jesus, do not chain me to myself and set these hills and valleys, heaving with folk-songs, so close to me that I cannot reach them. There is a radiant beauty in the162 night that touches and ... tortures me. Ugh. Hell. Get up, you damn fool. Look around. Whats beautiful there? Hog pens and chicken yards. Dirty red mud. Stinking outhouse. Whats beauty anyway but ugliness if it hurts you? God, he doesnt exist, but nevertheless He is ugly. Hence, what comes from Him is ugly. Lynchers and business men, and that cockroach Hanby, especially. How come that he gets to be principal of a school? Of the school I'm driven to teach in? God's handiwork, doubtless. God and Hanby, they belong together. Two godam moral-spouters. Oh, no, I wont let that emotion come up in me. Stay down. Stay down, I tell you. O Jesus, Thou art beautiful... Come, Ralph, pull yourself together. Curses and adoration dont come from what is sane. This loneliness, dumbness, awful, intangible oppression is enough to drive a man insane. Miles from nowhere. A speck on a Georgia hillside. Jesus, can you imagine it—an atom of dust in agony on a hillside? Thats a spectacle for you. Come, Ralph, old man, pull yourself together."

Kabnis has stiffened. He is conscious now of163 the night wind, and of how it chills him. He rises. He totters as a man would who for the first time uses artificial limbs. As a completely artificial man would. The large frame house, squatting on brick pillars, where the principal of the school, his wife, and the boarding girls sleep, seems a curious shadow of his mind. He tries, but cannot convince himself of its reality. His gaze drifts down into the vale, across the swamp, up over the solid dusk bank of pines, and rests, bewildered-like, on the court-house tower. It is dull silver in the moonlight. White child that sleeps upon the top of pines. Kabnis' mind clears. He sees himself yanked beneath that tower. He sees white minds, with indolent assumption, juggle justice and a nigger... Somewhere, far off in the straight line of his sight, is Augusta. Christ, how cut off from everything he is. And hours, hours north, why not say a lifetime north? Washington sleeps. Its still, peaceful streets, how desirable they are. Its people whom he had always halfway despised. New York? Impossible. It was a fiction. He had dreamed it. An impotent nostalgia grips him. It becomes intolerable. He forces himself 164to narrow to a cabin silhouetted on a knoll about a mile away. Peace. Negroes within it are content. They farm. They sing. They love. They sleep. Kabnis wonders if perhaps they can feel him. If perhaps he gives them bad dreams. Things are so immediate in Georgia.

Thinking that now he can go to sleep, he re-enters his room. He builds a fire in the open hearth. The room dances to the tongues of flames, and sings to the crackling and spurting of the logs. Wind comes up between the floor boards, through the black cracks of the walls.

Kabnis: Cant sleep. Light a cigarette. If that old bastard comes over here and smells smoke, I'm done for. Hell of a note, cant even smoke. The stillness of it: where they burn and hang men, you cant smoke. Cant take a swig of licker. What do they think this is, anyway, some sort of temperance school? How did I ever land in such a hole? Ugh. One might just as well be in his grave. Still as a grave. Jesus, how still everything is. Does the world know how still it is? People make noise. They are afraid of silence. Of what lives, and God, of what dies in silence. There must be many dead165 things moving in silence. They come here to touch me. I swear I feel their fingers... Come, Ralph, pull yourself together. What in hell was that? Only the rustle of leaves, I guess. You know, Ralph, old man, it wouldnt surprise me at all to see a ghost. People dont think there are such things. They rationalize their fear, and call their cowardice science. Fine bunch, they are. Damit, that was a noise. And not the wind either. A chicken maybe. Hell, chickens dont wander around this time of night. What in hell is it?

A scraping sound, like a piece of wood dragging over the ground, is coming near.

"Ha, ha. The ghosts down this way havent got any chains to rattle, so they drag trees along with them. Thats a good one. But no joke, something is outside this house, as sure as hell. Whatever it is, it can get a good look at me and I cant see it. Jesus Christ!"

Kabnis pours water on the flames and blows his lamp out. He picks up a poker and stealthily approaches the outside door. Swings it open, and lurches into the night. A calf, carrying a yoke of wood, bolts away from him and scampers down the road.

166

"Well, I'm damned. This godam place is sure getting the best of me. Come, Ralph, old man, pull yourself together. Nights cant last forever. Thank God for that. Its Sunday already. First time in my life I've ever wanted Sunday to come. Hell of a day. And down here there's no such thing as ducking church. Well, I'll see Halsey and Layman, and get a good square meal. Thats something. And Halsey's a damn good feller. Cant talk to him, though. Who in Christ's world can I talk to? A hen. God. Myself... I'm going bats, no doubt of that. Come now, Ralph, go in and make yourself go to sleep. Come now .. in the door .. thats right. Put the poker down. There. All right. Slip under the sheets. Close your eyes. Think nothing .. a long time .. nothing, nothing. Dont even think nothing. Blank. Not even blank. Count. No, mustnt count Nothing .. blank .. nothing .. blank .. space without stars in it. No, nothing .. nothing..

Kabnis sleeps. The winds, like soft-voiced vagrant poets sing:

167
White-man's land.
Niggers, sing.
Burn, bear black children
Till poor rivers bring
Rest, and sweet glory
In Camp Ground.

2

The parlor of Fred Halsey's home. There is a seediness about it. It seems as though the fittings have given a frugal service to at least seven generations of middle-class shop-owners. An open grate burns cheerily in contrast to the gray cold changed autumn weather. An old-fashioned mantelpiece supports a family clock (not running), a figure or two in imitation bronze, and two small group pictures. Directly above it, in a heavy oak frame, the portrait of a bearded man. Black hair, thick and curly, intensifies the pallor of the high forehead. The eyes are daring. The nose, sharp and regular. The poise suggests a tendency to adventure checked by the necessities of absolute command. The portrait is that of an English gentleman who has retained much of his culture, in that168 money has enabled him to escape being drawn through a land-grubbing pioneer life. His nature and features, modified by marriage and circumstances, have been transmitted to his great-grandson, Fred. To the left of this picture, spaced on the wall, is a smaller portrait of the great-grandmother. That here there is a Negro strain, no one would doubt. But it is difficult to say in precisely what feature it lies. On close inspection, her mouth is seen to be wistfully twisted. The expression of her face seems to shift before one's gaze—now ugly, repulsive; now sad, and somehow beautiful in its pain. A tin wood-box rests on the floor below. To the right of the great-grandfather's portrait hangs a family group: the father, mother, two brothers, and one sister of Fred. It includes himself some thirty years ago when his face was an olive white, and his hair luxuriant and dark and wavy. The father is a rich brown. The mother, practically white. Of the children, the girl, quite young, is like Fred; the two brothers, darker. The walls of the room are plastered and painted green. An old upright piano is tucked into the corner near the window. The window looks out169 on a forlorn, box-like, whitewashed frame church. Negroes are gathering, on foot, driving questionable gray and brown mules, and in an occasional Ford, for afternoon service. Beyond, Georgia hills roll off into the distance, their dreary aspect heightened by the gray spots of unpainted one- and two-room shanties. Clumps of pine trees here and there are the dark points the whole landscape is approaching. The church bell tolls. Above its squat tower, a great spiral of buzzards reaches far into the heavens. An ironic comment upon the path that leads into the Christian land... Three rocking chairs are grouped around the grate. Sunday papers scattered on the floor indicate a recent usage. Halsey, a well-built, stocky fellow, hair cropped close, enters the room. His Sunday clothes smell of wood and glue, for it is his habit to potter around his wagon-shop even on the Lord's day. He is followed by Professor Layman, tall, heavy, loose-jointed Georgia Negro, by turns teacher and preacher, who has traveled in almost every nook and corner of the state and hence knows more than would be good for anyone other than a silent man. Kabnis, trying to170 force through a gathering heaviness, trails in behind them. They slip into chairs before the fire.

Layman: Sholy fine, Mr. Halsey, sholy fine. This town's right good at feedin folks, better'n most towns in th state, even for preachers, but I ken say this beats um all. Yassur. Now aint that right, Professor Kabnis?

Kabnis: Yes sir, this beats them all, all right—best I've had, and thats a fact, though my comparison doesnt carry far, y'know.

Layman: Hows that, Professor?

Kabnis: Well, this is my first time out—

Layman: For a fact. Aint seed you round so much. Whats th trouble? Dont like our folks down this away?

Halsey: Aint that, Layman. He aint like most northern niggers that way. Aint a thing stuck up about him. He likes us, you an me, maybe all—its that red mud over yonder—gets stuck in it an cant get out. (Laughs.) An then he loves th fire so, warm as its been. Coldest Yankee I've ever seen. But I'm goin t get him out now in a jiffy, eh, Kabnis?

Kabnis: Sure, I should say so, sure. Dont think its because I dont like folks down this way.171 Just the opposite, in fact. Theres more hospitality and everything. Its diff—that is, theres lots of northern exaggeration about the South. Its not half the terror they picture it. Things are not half bad, as one could easily figure out for himself without ever crossing the Mason and Dixie line: all these people wouldnt stay down here, especially the rich, the ones that could easily leave, if conditions were so mighty bad. And then too, sometime back, my family were southerners y'know. From Georgia, in fact—

Layman: Nothin t feel proud about, Professor. Neither your folks nor mine.

Halsey (in a mock religious tone): Amen t that, brother Layman. Amen (turning to Kabnis, half playful, yet somehow dead in earnest). An Mr. Kabnis, kindly remember youre in th land of cotton—hell of a land. Th white folks get th boll; th niggers get th stalk. An dont you dare touch th boll, or even look at it. They'll swing y sho. (Laughs.)

Kabnis: But they wouldnt touch a gentleman—fellows, men like us three here—

Layman: Nigger's a nigger down this away, Professor. An only two dividins: good an bad.172 An even they aint permanent categories. They sometimes mixes um up when it comes t lynchin. I've seen um do it.

Halsey: Dont let th fear int y, though, Kabnis. This county's a good un. Aint been a stringin up I can remember. (Laughs.)

Layman: This is a good town an a good county. But theres some that makes up fer it.

Kabnis: Things are better now though since that stir about those peonage cases, arent they?

Layman: Ever hear tell of a single shot killin moren one rabbit, Professor?

Kabnis: No, of course not, that is, but then—

Halsey: Now I know you werent born yesterday, sprung up so rapid like you aint heard of th brick thrown in th hornets' nest. (Laughs.)

Kabnis: Hardly, hardly, I know—

Halsey: Course y do. (To Layman) See, northern niggers aint as dumb as they make out t be.

Kabnis (overlooking the remark): Just stirs them up to sting.

Halsey: T perfection. An put just like a professor should put it.

173

Kabnis: Thats what actually did happen?

Layman: Well, if it aint sos only because th stingers already movin jes as fast as they ken go. An been goin ever since I ken remember, an then some mo. Though I dont usually make mention of it.

Halsey: Damn sight better not. Say, Layman, you come from where theyre always swarmin, dont y?

Layman: Yassur. I do that, sho. Dont want t mention it, but its a fact. I've seed th time when there werent no use t even stretch out flat upon th ground. Seen um shoot an cut a man t pieces who had died th night befo. Yassur. An they didnt stop when they found out he was dead—jes went on ahackin at him anyway.

Kabnis: What did you do? What did you say to them, Professor?

Layman: Thems th things you neither does a thing or talks about if y want t stay around this away, Professor.

Halsey: Listen t what he's tellin y, Kabnis. May come in handy some day.

Kabnis: Cant something be done? But of174 course not. This preacher-ridden race. Pray and shout. Theyre in the preacher's hands. Thats what it is. And the preacher's hands are in the white man's pockets.

Halsey: Present company always excepted.

Kabnis: The Professor knows I wasnt referring to him.

Layman: Preacher's a preacher anywheres you turn. No use exceptin.

Kabnis: Well, of course, if you look at it that way. I didnt mean— But cant something be done?

Layman: Sho. Yassur. An done first rate an well. Jes like Sam Raymon done it.

Kabnis: Hows that? What did he do?

Layman: Th white folks (reckon I oughtnt tell it) had jes knocked two others like you kill a cow—brained um with an ax, when they caught Sam Raymon by a stream. They was about t do fer him when he up an says, "White folks, I gotter die, I knows that. But wont y let me die in my own way?" Some was fer gettin after him, but th boss held um back an says, "Jes so longs th nigger dies—" An Sam fell down ont his knees an prayed, "O Lord, Ise175 comin to y," an he up an jumps int th stream.

Singing from the church becomes audible. Above it, rising and falling in a plaintive moan, a woman's voice swells to shouting. Kabnis hears it. His face gives way to an expression of mingled fear, contempt, and pity. Layman takes no notice of it. Halsey grins at Kabnis. He feels like having a little sport with him.

Halsey: Lets go t church, eh, Kabnis?

Kabnis (seeking control): All right—no sir, not by a damn sight. Once a days enough for me. Christ, but that stuff gets to me. Meaning no reflection on you, Professor.

Halsey: Course not. Say, Kabnis, noticed y this morning. What'd y get up for an go out?

Kabnis: Couldnt stand the shouting, and thats a fact. We dont have that sort of thing up North. We do, but, that is, some one should see to it that they are stopped or put out when they get so bad the preacher has to stop his sermon for them.

Halsey: Is that th way youall sit on sisters up North?

Kabnis: In the church I used to go to no one ever shouted—

176

Halsey: Lungs weak?

Kabnis: Hardly, that is—

Halsey: Yankees are right up t th minute in tellin folk how t turn a trick. They always were good at talkin.

Kabnis: Well, anyway, they should be stopped.

Layman: Thats right. Thats true. An its th worst ones in th community that comes int th church t shout. I've sort a made a study of it. You take a man what drinks, th biggest licker-head around will come int th church an yell th loudest. An th sister whats done wrong, an is always doin wrong, will sit down in th Amen corner an swing her arms an shout her head off. Seems as if they cant control themselves out in th world; they cant control themselves in church. Now dont that sound logical, Professor?

Halsey: Reckon its as good as any. But I heard that queer cuss over yonder—y know him, dont y, Kabnis? Well, y ought t. He had a run-in with your boss th other day—same as you'll have if you dont walk th chalk-line. An th quicker th better. I hate that Hanby. Ornery bastard. I'll mash his mouth in one of177 these days. Well, as I was sayin, that feller, Lewis's name, I heard him sayin somethin about a stream whats dammed has got t cut loose somewheres. An that sounds good. I know th feelin myself. He strikes me as knowin a bucketful bout most things, that feller does. Seems like he doesnt want t talk, an does, sometimes, like Layman here. Damn queer feller, him.

Layman: Cant make heads or tails of him, an I've seen lots o queer possums in my day. Everybody's wonderin about him. White folks too. He'll have t leave here soon, thats sho. Always askin questions. An I aint seed his lips move once. Pokin round an notin somethin. Noted what I said th other day, an that werent fer notin down.

Kabnis: What was that?

Layman: Oh, a lynchin that took place bout a year ago. Th worst I know of round these parts.

Halsey: Bill Burnam?

Layman: Na. Mame Lamkins.

Halsey grunts, but says nothing.

The preacher's voice rolls from the church in an insistent chanting monotone. At regular intervals 178it rises to a crescendo note. The sister begins to shout. Her voice, high-pitched and hysterical, is almost perfectly attuned to the nervous key of Kabnis. Halsey notices his distress, and is amused by it. Layman's face is expressionless. Kabnis wants to hear the story of Mame Lamkins. He does not want to hear it. It can be no worse than the shouting.

Kabnis (his chair rocking faster): What about Mame Lamkins?

Halsey: Tell him, Layman.

The preacher momentarily stops. The choir, together with the entire congregation, sings an old spiritual. The music seems to quiet the shouter. Her heavy breathing has the sound of evening winds that blow through pinecones. Layman's voice is uniformly low and soothing. A canebrake, murmuring the tale to its neighbor-road would be more passionate.

Layman: White folks know that niggers talk, an they dont mind jes so long as nothing comes of it, so here goes. She was in th family-way, Mame Lamkins was. They killed her in th street, an some white man seein th risin in her stomach as she lay there soppy in her blood like179 any cow, took an ripped her belly open, an th kid fell out. It was living; but a nigger baby aint supposed t live. So he jabbed his knife in it an stuck it t a tree. An then they all went away.

Kabnis: Christ no! What had she done?

Layman: Tried t hide her husband when they was after him.

A shriek pierces the room. The bronze pieces on the mantel hum. The sister cries frantically: "Jesus, Jesus, I've found Jesus. O Lord, glory t God, one mo sinner is acomin home." At the height of this, a stone, wrapped round with paper, crashes through the window. Kabnis springs to his feet, terror-stricken. Layman is worried. Halsey picks up the stone. Takes off the wrapper, smooths it out, and reads: "You northern nigger, its time fer y t leave. Git along now." Kabnis knows that the command is meant for him. Fear squeezes him. Caves him in. As a violent external pressure would. Fear flows inside him. It fills him up. He bloats.

He saves himself from bursting by dashing wildly from the room. Halsey and Layman stare stupidly at each other. The stone, the180 crumpled paper are things, huge things that weight them. Their thoughts are vaguely concerned with the texture of the stone, with the color of the paper. Then they remember the words, and begin to shift them about in sentences. Layman even construes them grammatically. Suddenly the sense of them comes back to Halsey. He grips Layman by the arm and they both follow after Kabnis.

A false dusk has come early. The countryside is ashen, chill. Cabins and roads and canebrakes whisper. The church choir, dipping into a long silence, sings:
My Lord, what a mourning,
My Lord, what a mourning,
My Lord, what a mourning,
When the stars begin to fall.

Softly luminous over the hills and valleys, the faint spray of a scattered star...

3

A splotchy figure drives forward along the cane- and corn-stalk hemmed-in road. A181 scarecrow replica of Kabnis, awkwardly animate. Fantastically plastered with red Georgia mud. It skirts the big house whose windows shine like mellow lanterns in the dusk. Its shoulder jogs against a sweet-gum tree. The figure caroms off against the cabin door, and lunges in. It slams the door as if to prevent some one entering after it.

"God Almighty, theyre here. After me. On me. All along the road I saw their eyes flaring from the cane. Hounds. Shouts. What in God's name did I run here for? A mud-hole trap. I stumbled on a rope. O God, a rope. Their clammy hands were like the love of death playing up and down my spine. Trying to trip my legs. To trip my spine. Up and down my spine. My spine... My legs... Why in hell didn't they catch me?"

Kabnis wheels around, half defiant, half numbed with a more immediate fear.

"Wanted to trap me here. Get out o there. I see you."

He grabs a broom from beside the chimney and violently pokes it under the bed. The broom182 strikes a tin wash-tub. The noise bewilders. He recovers.

"Not there. In the closet."

He throws the broom aside and grips the poker. Starts towards the closet door, towards somewhere in the perfect blackness behind the chimney.

"I'll brain you."

He stops short. The barks of hounds, evidently in pursuit, reach him. A voice, liquid in distance, yells, "Hi! Hi!"

"O God, theyre after me. Holy Father, Mother of Christ—hell, this aint no time for prayer—"

Voices, just outside the door:

"Reckon he's here."

"Dont see no light though."

The door is flung open.

Kabnis: Get back or I'll kill you.

He braces himself, brandishing the poker.

Halsey (coming in): Aint as bad as all that. Put that thing down.

Layman: Its only us, Professor. Nobody else after y.

Kabnis: Halsey. Layman. Close that door.183 Dont light that light. For godsake get away from there.

Halsey: Nobody's after y, Kabnis, I'm tellin y. Put that thing down an get yourself together.

Kabnis: I tell you they are. I saw them. I heard the hounds.

Halsey: These aint th days of hounds an Uncle Tom's Cabin, feller. White folks aint in fer all them theatrics these days. Theys more direct than that. If what they wanted was t get y, theyd have just marched right in an took y where y sat. Somebodys down by th branch chasin rabbits an atreein possums.

A shot is heard.

Halsey: Got him, I reckon. Saw Tom goin out with his gun. Tom's pretty lucky most times.

He goes to the bureau and lights the lamp. The circular fringe is patterned on the ceiling. The moving shadows of the men are huge against the bare wall boards. Halsey walks up to Kabnis, takes the poker from his grip, and without more ado pushes him into a chair before the dark hearth.

184

Halsey: Youre a mess. Here, Layman. Get some trash an start a fire.

Layman fumbles around, finds some newspapers and old bags, puts them in the hearth, arranges the wood, and kindles the fire. Halsey sets a black iron kettle where it soon will be boiling. Then takes from his hip-pocket a bottle of corn licker which he passes to Kabnis.

Halsey: Here. This'll straighten y out a bit.

Kabnis nervously draws the cork and gulps the licker down.

Kabnis: Ha. Good stuff. Thanks. Thank y, Halsey.

Halsey: Good stuff! Youre damn right. Hanby there dont think so. Wonder he doesnt come over t find out whos burnin his oil. Miserly bastard, him. Th boys what made this stuff—are y listenin t me, Kabnis? th boys what made this stuff have got th art down like I heard you say youd like t be with words. Eh? Have some, Layman?

Layman: Dont think I care for none, thank y jes th same, Mr. Halsey.

Halsey: Care hell. Course y care. Everybody cares around these parts. Preachers an185 school teachers an everybody. Here. Here, take it. Dont try that line on me.

Layman limbers up a little, but he cannot quite forget that he is on school ground.

Layman: Thats right. Thats true, sho. Shinin is th only business what pays in these hard times.

He takes a nip, and passes the bottle to Kabnis. Kabnis is in the middle of a long swig when a rap sounds on the door. He almost spills the bottle, but manages to pass it to Halsey just as the door swings open and Hanby enters. He is a well-dressed, smooth, rich, black-skinned Negro who thinks there is no one quite so suave and polished as himself. To members of his own race, he affects the manners of a wealthy white planter. Or, when he is up North, he lets it be known that his ideas are those of the best New England tradition. To white men he bows, without ever completely humbling himself. Tradesmen in the town tolerate him because he spends his money with them. He delivers his words with a full consciousness of his moral superiority.

Hanby: Hum. Erer, Professor Kabnis, to186 come straight to the point: the progress of the Negro race is jeopardized whenever the personal habits and examples set by its guides and mentors fall below the acknowledged and hard-won standard of its average member. This institution, of which I am the humble president, was founded, and has been maintained at a cost of great labor and untold sacrifice. Its purpose is to teach our youth to live better, cleaner, more noble lives. To prove to the world that the Negro race can be just like any other race. It hopes to attain this aim partly by the salutary examples set by its instructors. I cannot hinder the progress of a race simply to indulge a single member. I have thought the matter out beforehand, I can assure you. Therefore, if I find your resignation on my desk by to-morrow morning, Mr. Kabnis, I shall not feel obliged to call in the sheriff. Otherwise…"

Kabnis: A fellow can take a drink in his own room if he wants to, in the privacy of his own room.

Hanby: His room, but not the institution's room, Mr. Kabnis.

Kabnis: This is my room while I'm in it.

187

Hanby: Mr. Clayborn (the sheriff) can inform you as to that.

Kabnis: Oh, well, what do I care—glad to get out of this mud-hole.

Hanby: I should think so from your looks.

Kabnis: You neednt get sarcastic about it.

Hanby: No, that is true. And I neednt wait for your resignation either, Mr. Kabnis.

Kabnis: Oh, you'll get that all right. Dont worry.

Hanby: And I should like to have the room thoroughly aired and cleaned and ready for your successor by to-morrow noon, Professor.

Kabnis (trying to rise): You can have your godam room right away. I dont want it.

Hanby: But I wont have your cursing.

Halsey pushes Kabnis back into his chair.

Halsey: Sit down, Kabnis, till I wash y.

Hanby (to Halsey): I would rather not have drinking men on the premises, Mr. Halsey. You will oblige me—

Halsey: I'll oblige you by stayin right on this spot, this spot, get me? till I get damned ready t leave.

188

He approaches Hanby. Hanby retreats, but manages to hold his dignity.

Halsey: Let me get you told right now, Mr. Samuel Hanby. Now listen t me. I aint no slick an span slave youve hired, an dont y think it for a minute. Youve bullied enough about this town. An besides, wheres that bill youve been owin me? Listen t me. If I dont get it paid in by tmorrer noon, Mr. Hanby (he mockingly assumes Hanby's tone and manner), I shall feel obliged t call th sheriff. An that sheriff'll be myself who'll catch y in th road an pull y out your buggy an rightly attend t y. You heard me. Now leave him alone. I'm takin him home with me. I got it fixed. Before you came in. He's goin t work with me. Shapin shafts and buildin wagons'll make a man of him what nobody, y get me? what nobody can take advantage of. Thats all...

Halsey burrs off into vague and incoherent comment.

Pause. Disagreeable.

Layman's eyes are glazed on the spurting fire.

Kabnis wants to rise and put both Halsey and Hanby in their places. He vaguely knows that189 he must do this, else the power of direction will completely slip from him to those outside. The conviction is just strong enough to torture him. To bring a feverish, quick-passing flare into his eyes. To mutter words soggy in hot saliva. To jerk his arms upward in futile protest. Halsey, noticing his gestures, thinks it is water that he desires. He brings a glass to him. Kabnis slings it to the floor. Heat of the conviction dies. His arms crumple. His upper lip, his mustache, quiver. Rap! rap, on the door. The sounds slap Kabnis. They bring a hectic color to his cheeks. Like huge cold finger tips they touch his skin and goose-flesh it. Hanby strikes a commanding pose. He moves toward Layman. Layman's face is innocently immobile.

Halsey: Whos there?

Voice: Lewis.

Halsey: Come in, Lewis. Come on in.

Lewis enters. He is the queer fellow who has been referred to. A tall wiry copper-colored man, thirty perhaps. His mouth and eyes suggest purpose guided by an adequate intelligence. He is what a stronger Kabnis might have been, and in an odd faint way resembles him. As he190 steps towards the others, he seems to be issuing sharply from a vivid dream. Lewis shakes hands with Halsey. Nods perfunctorily to Hanby, who has stiffened to meet him. Smiles rapidly at Layman, and settles with real interest on Kabnis.

Lewis: Kabnis passed me on the road. Had a piece of business of my own, and couldnt get here any sooner. Thought I might be able to help in some way or other.

Halsey: A good baths bout all he needs now. An somethin t put his mind t rest.

Lewis: I think I can give him that. That note was meant for me. Some Negroes have grown uncomfortable at my being here—

Kabnis: You mean, Mr. Lewis, some colored folks threw it? Christ Amighty!

Halsey: Thats what he means. An just as I told y. White folks more direct than that.

Kabnis: What are they after you for?

Lewis: Its a long story, Kabnis. Too long for now. And it might involve present company. (He laughs pleasantly and gestures vaguely in the direction of Hanby.) Tell you about it later on perhaps.

191

Kabnis: Youre not going?

Lewis: Not till my month's up.

Halsey: Hows that?

Lewis: I'm on a sort of contract with myself. (Is about to leave.) Well, glad its nothing serious—

Halsey: Come round t th shop sometime why dont y, Lewis? I've asked y enough. I'd like t have a talk with y. I aint as dumb as I look. Kabnis an me'll be in most any time. Not much work these days. Wish t hell there was. This burg gets to me when there aint. (In answer to Lewis' question.) He's goin t work with me. Ya. Night air this side th branch aint good fer him. (Looks at Hanby. Laughs.)

Lewis: I see...

His eyes turn to Kabnis. In the instant of their shifting, a vision of the life they are to meet. Kabnis, a promise of a soil-soaked beauty; uprooted, thinning out. Suspended a few feet above the soil whose touch would resurrect him. Arm's length removed from him whose will to help... There is a swift intuitive interchange of consciousness. Kabnis has a sudden need to rush into the arms of this man. His eyes call,192 "Brother." And then a savage, cynical twist-about within him mocks his impulse and strengthens him to repulse Lewis. His lips curl cruelly. His eyes laugh. They are glittering needles, stitching. With a throbbing ache they draw Lewis to. Lewis brusquely wheels on Hanby.

Lewis: I'd like to see you, sir, a moment, if you dont mind.

Hanby's tight collar and vest effectively preserve him.

Hanby: Yes, erer, Mr. Lewis. Right away.

Lewis: See you later, Halsey.

Halsey: So long—thanks—sho hope so, Lewis.

As he opens the door and Hanby passes out, a woman, miles down the valley, begins to sing. Her song is a spark that travels swiftly to the near-by cabins. Like purple tallow flames, songs jet up. They spread a ruddy haze over the heavens. The haze swings low. Now the whole countryside is a soft chorus. Lord. O Lord... Lewis closes the door behind him. A flame jets out...

The kettle is boiling. Halsey notices it. He193 pulls the wash-tub from beneath the bed. He arranges for the bath before the fire.

Halsey: Told y them theatrics didnt fit a white man. Th niggers, just like I told y. An after him. Aint surprisin though. He aint bowed t none of them. Nassur. T nairy a one of them nairy an inch nairy a time. An only mixed when he was good an ready—

Kabnis: That song, Halsey, do you hear it?

Halsey: Thats a man. Hear me, Kabnis? A man—

Kabnis: Jesus, do you hear it.

Halsey: Hear it? Hear what? Course I hear it. Listen t what I'm tellin y. A man, get me? They'll get him yet if he dont watch out.

Kabnis is jolted into his fear.

Kabnis: Get him? What do you mean? How? Not lynch him?

Halsey: Na. Take a shotgun an shoot his eyes clear out. Well, anyway, it wasnt fer you, just like I told y. You'll stay over at th house an work with me, eh, boy? Good t get away from his nobs, eh? Damn big stiff though, him. An youre not th first an I can tell y. (Laughs.)

He bustles and fusses about Kabnis as if he194 were a child. Kabnis submits, wearily. He has no will to resist him.

Layman (his voice is like a deep hollow echo): Thats right. Thats true, sho. Everybody's been expectin that th bust up was comin. Surprised um all y held on as long as y did. Teachin in th South aint th thing fer y. Nassur. You ought t be way back up North where sometimes I wish I was. But I've hung on down this away so long—

Halsey: An there'll never be no leavin time fer y.

4

A month has passed.

Halsey's workshop. It is an old building just off the main street of Sempter. The walls to within a few feet of the ground are of an age-worn cement mixture. On the outside they are considerably crumbled and peppered with what looks like musket-shot. Inside, the plaster has fallen away in great chunks, leaving the laths, grayed and cobwebbed, exposed. A sort of loft above the shop proper serves as a break-water195 for the rain and sunshine which otherwise would have free entry to the main floor. The shop is filled with old wheels and parts of wheels, broken shafts, and wooden litter. A double door, midway the street wall. To the left of this, a work-bench that holds a vise and a variety of wood-work tools. A window with as many panes broken as whole, throws light on the bench. Opposite, in the rear wall, a second window looks out upon the back yard. In the left wall, a rickety smoke-blackened chimney, and hearth with fire blazing. Smooth-worn chairs grouped about the hearth suggest the village meeting-place. Several large wooden blocks, chipped and cut and sawed on their upper surfaces are in the middle of the floor. They are the supports used in almost any sort of wagon-work. Their idleness means that Halsey has no worth-while job on foot. To the right of the central door is a junk heap, and directly behind this, stairs that lead down into the cellar. The cellar is known as "The Hole." Besides being the home of a very old man, it is used by Halsey on those occasions when he spices up the life of the small town.

196

Halsey, wonderfully himself in his work overalls, stands in the doorway and gazes up the street, expectantly. Then his eyes grow listless. He slouches against the smooth-rubbed frame. He lights a cigarette. Shifts his position. Braces an arm against the door. Kabnis passes the window and stoops to get in under Halsey's arm. He is awkward and ludicrous, like a schoolboy in his big brother's new overalls. He skirts the large blocks on the floor, and drops into a chair before the fire. Halsey saunters towards him.

Kabnis: Time f lunch.

Halsey: Ya.

He stands by the hearth, rocking backward and forward. He stretches his hands out to the fire. He washes them in the warm glow of the flames. They never get cold, but he warms them.

Kabnis: Saw Lewis up th street. Said he'd be down.

Halsey's eyes brighten. He looks at Kabnis. Turns away. Says nothing. Kabnis fidgets. Twists his thin blue cloth-covered limbs. Pulls closer to the fire till the heat stings his shins. Pushes back. Pokes the burned logs. Puts on197 several fresh ones. Fidgets. The town bell strikes twelve.

Kabnis: Fix it up f tnight?

Halsey: Leave it t me.

Kabnis: Get Lewis in?

Halsey: Tryin t.

The air is heavy with the smell of pine and resin. Green logs spurt and sizzle. Sap trickles from an old pine-knot into the flames. Layman enters. He carries a lunch-pail. Kabnis, for the moment, thinks that he is a day laborer.

Layman: Evenin, gen'lemun.

Both: Whats say, Layman.

Layman squares a chair to the fire and droops into it. Several town fellows, silent unfathomable men for the most part, saunter in. Overalls. Thick tan shoes. Felt hats marvelously shaped and twisted. One asks Halsey for a cigarette. He gets it. The blacksmith, a tremendous black man, comes in from the forge. Not even a nod from him. He picks up an axle and goes out. Lewis enters. The town men look curiously at him. Suspicion and an open liking contest for possession of their faces. They are uncomfortable. One by one they drift into the street.

198

Layman: Heard y was leavin, Mr. Lewis.

Kabnis: Months up, eh? Hell of a month I've got.

Halsey: Sorry y goin, Lewis. Just getting acquainted like.

Lewis: Sorry myself, Halsey, in a way—

Layman: Gettin t like our town, Mr. Lewis?

Lewis: I'm afraid its on a different basis, Professor.

Halsey: An I've yet t hear about that basis. Been waitin long enough, God knows. Seems t me like youd take pity a feller if nothin more.

Kabnis: Somethin that old black cockroach over yonder doesnt like, whatever it is.

Layman: Thats right. Thats right, sho.

Halsey: A feller dropped in here tother day an said he knew what you was about. Said you had queer opinions. Well, I could have told him you was a queer one, myself. But not th way he was driftin. Didnt mean anything by it, but just let drop he thought you was a little wrong up here—crazy, y'know. (Laughs.)

Kabnis: Y mean old Blodson? Hell, he's bats himself.

199

Lewis: I remember him. We had a talk. But what he found queer, I think, was not my opinions, but my lack of them. In half an hour he had settled everything: boll weevils, God, the World War. Weevils and wars are the pests that God sends against the sinful. People are too weak to correct themselves: the Redeemer is coming back. Get ready, ye sinners, for the advent of Our Lord. Interesting, eh, Kabnis? but not exactly what we want.

Halsey: Y could have come t me. I've sho been after y enough. Most every time I've seen y.

Kabnis (sarcastically): Hows it y never came t us professors?

Lewis: I did—to one.

Kabnis: Y mean t say y got somethin from that celluloid-collar-eraser-cleaned old codger over in th mud hole?

Halsey: Rough on th old boy, aint he? (Laughs.)

Lewis: Something, yes. Layman here could have given me quite a deal, but the incentive to his keeping quiet is so much greater than anything I could have offered him to open up, that I crossed him off my mind. And you—

200

Kabnis: What about me?

Halsey: Tell him, Lewis, for godsake tell him. I've told him. But its somethin else he wants so bad I've heard him downstairs mumblin with th old man.

Lewis: The old man?

Kabnis: What about me? Come on now, you know so much.

Halsey: Tell him, Lewis. Tell it t him.

Lewis: Life has already told him more than he is capable of knowing. It has given him in excess of what he can receive. I have been offered. Stuff in his stomach curdled, and he vomited me.

Kabnis' face twitches. His body writhes.

Kabnis: You know a lot, you do. How about Halsey?

Lewis: Yes... Halsey? Fits here. Belongs here. An artist in your way, arent you, Halsey?

Halsey: Reckon I am, Lewis. Give me th work and fair pay an I aint askin nothin better. Went over-seas an saw France; an I come back. Been up North; an I come back. Went t school; but there aint no books whats got th feel t them201 of them there tools. Nassur. An I'm atellin y.

A shriveled, bony white man passes the window and enters the shop. He carries a broken hatchet-handle and the severed head. He speaks with a flat, drawn voice to Halsey, who comes forward to meet him.

Mr. Ramsay: Can y fix this fer me, Halsey?

Halsey (looking it over): Reckon so, Mr. Ramsay. Here, Kabnis. A little practice fer y.

Halsey directs Kabnis, showing him how to place the handle in the vise, and cut it down. The knife hangs. Kabnis thinks that it must be dull. He jerks it hard. The tool goes deep and shaves too much off. Mr. Ramsay smiles brokenly at him.

Mr. Ramsay (to Halsey): Still breakin in the new hand, eh, Halsey? Seems like a likely enough faller once he gets th hang of it.

He gives a tight laugh at his own good humor. Kabnis burns red. The back of his neck stings him beneath his collar. He feels stifled. Through Ramsay, the whole white South weighs down upon him. The pressure is terrific. He sweats under the arms. Chill beads run down his body. His brows concentrate upon the handle 202as though his own life was staked upon the perfect shaving of it. He begins to out and out botch the job. Halsey smiles.

Halsey: He'll make a good un some of these days, Mr. Ramsay.

Mr. Ramsay: Y ought t know. Yer daddy was a good un before y. Runs in th family, seems like t me.

Halsey: Thats right, Mr. Ramsay.

Kabnis is hopeless. Halsey takes the handle from him. With a few deft strokes he shaves it. Fits it. Gives it to Ramsay.

Mr. Ramsay: How much on this?

Halsey: No charge, Mr. Ramsay.

Mr. Ramsay (going out): All right, Halsey. Come down an take it out in trade. Shoe-strings or something.

Halsey: Yassur, Mr. Ramsay.

Halsey rejoins Lewis and Layman. Kabnis, hangdog-fashion, follows him.

Halsey: They like y if y work fer them.

Layman: Thats right, Mr. Halsey. Thats right, sho.

The group is about to resume its talk when[203] Hanby enters. He is all energy, bustle, and business. He goes direct to Kabnis.

Hanby: An axle is out in the buggy which I would like to have shaped into a crow-bar. You will see that it is fixed for me.

Without waiting for an answer, and knowing that Kabnis will follow, he passes out. Kabnis, scowling, silent, trudges after him.

Hanby (from the outside): Have that ready for me by three o'clock, young man. I shall call for it.

Kabnis (under his breath as he comes in): Th hell you say, you old black swamp-gut.

He slings the axle on the floor.

Halsey: Wheeee!

Layman, lunch finished long ago, rises, heavily. He shakes hands with Lewis.

Layman: Might not see y again befo y leave, Mr. Lewis. I enjoys t hear y talk. Y might have been a preacher. Maybe a bishop some day. Sho do hope t see y back this away again sometime, Mr. Lewis.

Lewis: Thanks, Professor. Hope I'll see you.

Layman waves a long arm loosely to the[204] others, and leaves. Kabnis goes to the door. His eyes, sullen, gaze up the street.

Kabnis: Carrie K.'s comin with th lunch. Bout time.

She passes the window. Her red girl's-cap, catching the sun, flashes vividly. With a stiff, awkward little movement she crosses the door-sill and gives Kabnis one of the two baskets which she is carrying. There is a slight stoop to her shoulders. The curves of her body blend with this to a soft rounded charm. Her gestures are stiffly variant. Black bangs curl over the forehead of her oval-olive face. Her expression is dazed, but on provocation it can melt into a wistful smile. Adolescent. She is easily the sister of Fred Halsey.

Carrie K.: Mother says excuse her, brother Fred an Ralph, fer bein late.

Kabnis: Everythings all right an O.K., Carrie Kate. O.K. an all right.

The two men settle on their lunch. Carrie, with hardly a glance in the direction of the hearth, as is her habit, is about to take the second basket down to the old man, when Lewis rises. In doing so he draws her unwitting attention.[205] Their meeting is a swift sun-burst. Lewis impulsively moves towards her. His mind flashes images of her life in the southern town. He sees the nascent woman, her flesh already stiffening to cartilage, drying to bone. Her spirit-bloom, even now touched sullen, bitter. Her rich beauty fading... He wants to— He stretches forth his hands to hers. He takes them. They feel like warm cheeks against his palms. The sun-burst from her eyes floods up and haloes him. Christ-eyes, his eyes look to her. Fearlessly she loves into them. And then something happens. Her face blanches. Awkwardly she draws away. The sin-bogies of respectable southern colored folks clamor at her: "Look out! Be a *good* girl. A *good* girl. Look out!" She gropes for her basket that has fallen to the floor. Finds it, and marches with a rigid gravity to her task of feeding the old man. Like the glowing white ash of burned paper, Lewis' eyelids, wavering, settle down. He stirs in the direction of the rear window. From the back yard, mules tethered to odd trees and posts blink dumbly at him. They too seem burdened with an impotent pain. Kabnis and Halsey are still busy with[206] their lunch. They havent noticed him. After a while he turns to them.

Lewis: Your sister, Halsey, whats to become of her? What are you going to do for her?

Halsey: Who? What? What am I goin t do?..

Lewis: What I mean is, what does she do down there?

Halsey: Oh. Feeds th old man. Had lunch, Lewis?

Lewis: Thanks, yes. You have never felt her, have you, Halsey? Well, no, I guess not. I dont suppose you can. Nor can she... Old man? Halsey, some one lives down there? I've never heard of him. Tell me—

Kabnis takes time from his meal to answer with some emphasis:

Kabnis: Theres lots of things you aint heard of.

Lewis: Dare say. I'd like to see him.

Kabnis: You'll get all th chance you want tnight.

Halsey: Fixin a little somethin up fer tnight, Lewis. Th three of us an some girls. Come round bout ten-thirty.

207

Lewis: Glad to. But what under the sun does he do down there?

Halsey: Ask Kabnis. He blows off t him every chance he gets.

Kabnis gives a grunting laugh. His mouth twists. Carrie returns from the cellar. Avoiding Lewis, she speaks to her brother.

Carrie K.: Brother Fred, father hasnt eaten now goin on th second week, but mumbles an talks funny, or tries t talk when I put his hands ont th food. He frightens me, an I dunno what t do. An oh, I came near fergettin, brother, but Mr. Marmon—he was eatin lunch when I saw him—told me t tell y that th lumber wagon busted down an he wanted y t fix it fer him. Said he reckoned he could get it t y after he ate.

Halsey chucks a half-eaten sandwich in the fire. Gets up. Arranges his blocks. Goes to the door and looks anxiously up the street. The wind whirls a small spiral in the gray dust road.

Halsey: Why didnt y tell me sooner, little sister?

Carrie K.: I fergot t, an just remembered it now, brother.

Her soft rolled words are fresh pain to Lewis.208 He wants to take her North with him. What for? He wonders what Kabnis could do for her. What she could do for him. Mother him. Carrie gathers the lunch things, silently, and in her pinched manner, curtsies, and departs. Kabnis lights his after-lunch cigarette. Lewis, who has sensed a change, becomes aware that he is not included in it. He starts to ask again about the old man. Decides not to. Rises to go.

Lewis: Think I'll run along, Halsey.

Halsey: Sure. Glad t see y any time.

Kabnis: Dont forget tnight.

Lewis: Dont worry. I wont. So long.

Kabnis: So long. We'll be expectin y.

Lewis passes Halsey at the door. Halsey's cheeks form a vacant smile. His eyes are wide awake, watching for the wagon to turn from Broad Street into his road.

Halsey: So long.

His words reach Lewis halfway to the corner.

5

Night, soft belly of a pregnant Negress, throbs evenly against the torso of the South. Night throbs a womb-song to the South. Cane- and209 cotton-fields, pine forests, cypress swamps, sawmills, and factories are fecund at her touch. Night's womb-song sets them singing. Night winds are the breathing of the unborn child whose calm throbbing in the belly of a Negress sets them somnolently singing. Hear their song.
White-man's land.
Niggers, sing.
Burn, bear black children
Till poor rivers bring
Rest, and sweet glory
In Camp Ground.

Sempter's streets are vacant and still. White paint on the wealthier houses has the chill blue glitter of distant stars. Negro cabins are a purple blur. Broad Street is deserted. Winds stir beneath the corrugated iron canopies and dangle odd bits of rope tied to horse- and mule-gnawed hitching-posts. One store window has a light in it. Chesterfield cigarette and Chero-Cola cardboard advertisements are stacked in it. From a side door two men come out. Pause, for a last word and then say good night. Soon they melt in shadows thicker than they. Way off down the street four figures sway beneath iron210 awnings which form a sort of corridor that imperfectly echoes and jumbles what they say. A fifth form joins them. They turn into the road that leads to Halsey's workshop. The old building is phosphorescent above deep shade. The figures pass through the double door. Night winds whisper in the eaves. Sing weirdly in the ceiling cracks. Stir curls of shavings on the floor. Halsey lights a candle. A good-sized lumber wagon, wheels off, rests upon the blocks. Kabnis makes a face at it. An unearthly hush is upon the place. No one seems to want to talk. To move, lest the scraping of their feet..

Halsey: Come on down this way, folks.

He leads the way. Stella follows. And close after her, Cora, Lewis, and Kabnis. They descend into the Hole. It seems huge, limitless in the candle light. The walls are of stone, wonderfully fitted. They have no openings save a small iron-barred window toward the top of each. They are dry and warm. The ground slopes away to the rear of the building and thus leaves the south wall exposed to the sun. The blacksmith's shop is plumb against the right wall. The floor is clay. Shavings have at odd211 times been matted into it. In the right-hand corner, under the stairs, two good-sized pine mattresses, resting on cardboard, are on either side of a wooden table. On this are several half-burned candles and an oil lamp. Behind the table, an irregular piece of mirror hangs on the wall. A loose something that looks to be a gaudy ball costume dangles from a near-by hook. To the front, a second table holds a lamp and several whiskey glasses. Six rickety chairs are near this table. Two old wagon wheels rest on the floor. To the left, sitting in a high-backed chair which stands upon a low platform, the old man. He is like a bust in black walnut. Gray-bearded. Gray-haired. Prophetic. Immobile. Lewis' eyes are sunk in him. The others, unconcerned, are about to pass on to the front table when Lewis grips Halsey and so turns him that the candle flame shines obliquely on the old man's features.

Lewis: And he rules over—

Kabnis: Th smoke an fire of th forge.

Lewis: Black Vulcan? I wouldnt say so. That forehead. Great woolly beard. Those eyes. A mute John the Baptist of a new religion—or a tongue-tied shadow of an old.

212

Kabnis: His tongue is tied all right, an I can vouch f that.

Lewis: Has he never talked to you?

Halsey: Kabnis wont give him a chance.

He laughs. The girls laugh. Kabnis winces.

Lewis: What do you call him?

Halsey: Father.

Lewis: Good. Father what?

Kabnis: Father of hell.

Halsey: Father's th only name we have fer him. Come on. Lets sit down an get t th pleasure of the evenin.

Lewis: Father John it is from now on...

Slave boy whom some Christian mistress taught to read the Bible. Black man who saw Jesus in the ricefields, and began preaching to his people. Moses- and Christ-words used for songs. Dead blind father of a muted folk who feel their way upward to a life that crushes or absorbs them. (Speak, Father!) Suppose your eyes could see, old man. (The years hold hands. O Sing!) Suppose your lips...

Halsey, does he never talk?

Halsey: Na. But sometimes. Only seldom. Mumbles. Sis says he talks—

213

Kabnis: I've heard him talk.

Halsey: First I've ever heard of it. You dont give him a chance. Sis says she's made out several words, mostly one—an like as not cause it was "sin."

Kabnis: All those old fogies stutter about sin.

Cora laughs in a loose sort of way. She is a tall, thin, mulatto woman. Her eyes are deep-set behind a pointed nose. Her hair is coarse and bushy. Seeing that Stella also is restless, she takes her arm and the two women move towards the table. They slip into chairs. Halsey follows and lights the lamp. He lays out a pack of cards. Stella sorts them as if telling fortunes. She is a beautifully proportioned, large-eyed, brown-skin girl. Except for the twisted line of her mouth when she smiles or laughs, there is about her no suggestion of the life she's been through. Kabnis, with great mock-solemnity, goes to the corner, takes down the robe, and dons it. He is a curious spectacle, acting a part, yet very real. He joins the others at the table. They are used to him. Lewis is surprised. He laughs. Kabnis shrinks and214 then glares at him with a furtive hatred. Halsey, bringing out a bottle of corn licker, pours drinks.

Halsey: Come on, Lewis. Come on, you fellers. Heres lookin at y.

Then, as if suddenly recalling something, he jerks away from the table and starts towards the steps.

Kabnis: Where y goin, Halsey?

Halsey: Where? Where y think? That oak beam in th wagon—

Kabnis: Come ere. Come ere. Sit down. What in hell's wrong with you fellers? You with your wagon. Lewis with his Father John. This aint th time fer foolin with wagons. Daytime's bad enough f that. Ere, sit down. Ere, Lewis, you too sit down. Have a drink. Thats right. Drink corn licker, love th girls, an listen t th old man mumblin sin.

There seems to be no good-time spirit to the party. Something in the air is too tense and deep for that. Lewis, seated now so that his eyes rest upon the old man, merges with his source and lets the pain and beauty of the South meet him there. White faces, pain-pollen, settle downward through a cane-sweet mist and touch the215 ovaries of yellow flowers. Cotton-bolls bloom, droop. Black roots twist in a parched red soil beneath a blazing sky. Magnolias, fragrant, a trifle futile, lovely, far off... His eyelids close. A force begins to heave and rise... Stella is serious, reminiscent.

Stella: Usall is brought up t hate sin worse than death—

Kabnis: An then before you have y eyes half open, youre made t love it if y want t live.

Stella: Us never—

Kabnis: Oh, I know your story: that old prim bastard over yonder, an then old Calvert's office—

Stella: It wasnt them—

Kabnis: I know. They put y out of church, an then I guess th preacher came around an asked f some. But thats your body. Now me—

Halsey (passing him the bottle): All right, kid, we believe y. Here, take another. Wheres Clover, Stel?

Stella: You know how Jim is when he's just out th swamp. Done up in shine an wouldnt let her come. Said he'd bust her head open if she went out.

216

Kabnis: Dont see why he doesnt stay over with Laura, where he belongs.

Stella: Ask him, an I reckon he'll tell y. More than you want.

Halsey: Th nigger hates th sight of a black woman worse than death. Sorry t mix y up this way, Lewis. But y see how tis.

Lewis' skin is tight and glowing over the fine bones of his face. His lips tremble. His nostrils quiver. The others notice this and smile knowingly at each other. Drinks and smokes are passed around. They pay no neverminds to him. A real party is being worked up. Then Lewis opens his eyes and looks at them. Their smiles disperse in hot-cold tremors. Kabnis chokes his laugh. It sputters, gurgles. His eyes flicker and turn away. He tries to pass the thing off by taking a long drink which he makes considerable fuss over. He is drawn back to Lewis. Seeing Lewis' gaze still upon him, he scowls.

Kabnis: Whatsha lookin at me for? Y want t know who I am? Well, I'm Ralph Kabnis—lot of good its goin t do y. Well? Whatsha keep lookin for? I'm Ralph Kabnis. Aint that217 enough f y? Want th whole family history? Its none of your godam business, anyway. Keep off me. Do y hear? Keep off me. Look at Cora. Aint she pretty enough t look at? Look at Halsey, or Stella. Clover ought t be here an you could look at her. An love her. Thats what you need. I know—

Lewis: Ralph Kabnis gets satisfied that way?

Kabnis: Satisfied? Say, quit your kiddin. Here, look at that old man there. See him? He's satisfied. Do I look like him? When I'm dead I dont expect t be satisfied. Is that enough f y, with your godam nosin, or do you want more? Well, y wont get it, understand?

Lewis: The old man as symbol, flesh, and spirit of the past, what do think he would say if he could see you? You look at him, Kabnis.

Kabnis: Just like any done-up preacher is what he looks t me. Jam some false teeth in his mouth and crank him, an youd have God Almighty spit in torrents all around th floor. Oh, hell, an he reminds me of that black cockroach over yonder. An besides, he aint my past. My ancestors were Southern blue-bloods—

218

Lewis: And black.

Kabnis: Aint much difference between blue an black.

Lewis: Enough to draw a denial from you. Cant hold them, can you? Master; slave. Soil; and the overarching heavens. Dusk; dawn. They fight and bastardize you. The sun tint of your cheeks, flame of the great season's multi-colored leaves, tarnished, burned. Split, shredded: easily burned. No use...

His gaze shifts to Stella. Stella's face draws back, her breasts come towards him.

Stella: I aint got nothin f y, mister. Taint no use t look at me.

Halsey: Youre a queer feller, Lewis, I swear y are. Told y so, didnt I, girls? Just take him easy though, an he'll be ridin just th same as any Georgia mule, eh, Lewis? (Laughs.)

Stella: I'm goin t tell y somethin, mister. It aint t you, t th Mister Lewis what noses about. Its t somethin different, I dunno what. That old man there—maybe its him—is like m father used t look. He used t sing. An when he could sing no mo, they'd allus come f him an carry him t church an there he'd sit, befo th pulpit, aswayin219 an aleadin every song. A white man took m mother an it broke th old man's heart. He died; an then I didnt care what become of me, an I dont now. I dont care now. Dont get it in y head I'm some sentimental Susie askin for yo sop. Nassur. But theres somethin t yo th others aint got. Boars an kids an fools—thats all I've known. Boars when their fever's up. When their fever's up they come t me. Halsey asks me over when he's off th job. Kabnis—it ud be a sin t play with him. He takes it out in talk.

Halsey knows that he has trifled with her. At odd things he has been inwardly penitent before her tasking him. But now he wants to hurt her. He turns to Lewis.

Halsey: Lewis, I got a little licker in me, an thats true. True's what I said. True. But th stuff just seems t wake me up an make my mind a man of me. Listen. You know a lot, queer as hell as y are, an I want t ask y some questions. Theyre too high fer them, Stella an Cora an Kabnis, so we'll just excuse em. A chat between ourselves. (Turns to the others.) Youall cant listen in on this. Twont interest y. So220 just leave th table t this gen'lemun an myself. Go long now.

Kabnis gets up, pompous in his robe, grotesquely so, and makes as if to go through a grand march with Stella. She shoves him off, roughly, and in a mood swings her body to the steps. Kabnis grabs Cora and parades around, passing the old man, to whom he bows in mock-curtsy. He sweeps by the table, snatches the licker bottle, and then he and Cora sprawl on the mattresses. She meets his weak approaches after the manner she thinks Stella would use.

Halsey contemptuously watches them until he is sure that they are settled.

Halsey: This aint th sort o thing f me, Lewis, when I got work upstairs. Nassur. You an me has got things t do. Wastin time on common low-down women—say, Lewis, look at her now—Stella—aint she a picture? Common wench—na she aint, Lewis. You know she aint. I'm only tryin t fool y. I used t love that girl. Yassur. An sometimes when th moon is thick an I hear dogs up th valley barkin an some old woman fetches out her song, an th winds seem like th Lord made them fer t fetch an carry th221 smell o pine an cane, an there aint no big job on foot, I sometimes get t thinkin that I still do. But I want t talk t y, Lewis, queer as y are. Y know, Lewis, I went t school once. Ya. In Augusta. But it wasnt a regular school. Na. It was a pussy Sunday-school masqueradin under a regular name. Some goody-goody teachers from th North had come down t teach th niggers. If you was nearly white, they liked y. If you was black, they didnt. But it wasnt that—I was all right, y see. I couldnt stand em messin an pawin over m business like I was a child. So I cussed em out an left. Kabnis there ought t have cussed out th old duck over yonder an left. He'd a been a better man tday. But as I was sayin, I couldnt stand their ways. So I left an came here an worked with my father. An been here ever since. He died. I set in f myself. An its always been; give me a good job an sure pay an I aint far from being satisfied, so far as satisfaction goes. Prejudice is everywheres about this country. An a nigger aint in much standin anywheres. But when it comes t pottin round an doin nothing, with nothin bigger'n an ax-handle t hold a feller down, like it was a while back222 befo I got this job—that beam ought t be—but tmorrow mornin early's time enough f that. As I was sayin, I gets t thinkin. Play dumb naturally t white folks. I gets t thinkin. I used to subscribe t th *Literary Digest* an that helped along a bit. But there werent nothing I could sink m teeth int. Theres lots I want t ask y, Lewis. Been askin y t come around. Couldnt get y. Cant get in much tnight. (He glances at the others. His mind fastens on Kabnis.) Say, tell me this, whats on your mind t say on that feller there? Kabnis' name. One queer bird ought t know another, seems like t me.

Licker has released conflicts in Kabnis and set them flowing. He pricks his ears, intuitively feels that the talk is about him, leaves Cora, and approaches the table. His eyes are watery, heavy with passion. He stoops. He is a ridiculous pathetic figure in his showy robe.

Kabnis: Talkin bout me. I know. I'm th topic of conversation everywhere theres talk about this town. Girls an fellers. White folks as well. An if its me youre talkin bout, guess I got a right t listen in. Whats sayin? Whats sayin bout his royal guts, the Duke? Whats sayin, eh?

223

Halsey (to Lewis): We'll take it up another time.

Kabnis: No nother time bout it Now. I'm here now an talkin's just begun. I was born an bred in a family of orators, thats what I was.

Halsey: Preachers.

Kabnis: Na. Preachers hell. I didnt say wind-busters. Y misapprehended me. Y understand what that means, dont y? All right then, y misapprehended me. I didnt say preachers. I said orators. ORATORS. Born one an I'll die one. You understand me, Lewis. (He turns to Halsey and begins shaking his finger in his face.) An as f you, youre all right f choppin things from blocks of wood. I was good at that th day I ducked th cradle. An since then, I've been shapin words after a design that branded here. Know whats here? M soul. Ever heard o that? Th hell y have. Been shapin words t fit m soul. Never told y that before, did I? Thought I couldnt talk. I'll tell y. I've been shapin words; ah, but sometimes theyre beautiful an golden an have a taste that makes them fine t roll over with y tongue. Your tongue aint fit f nothin but t roll an lick hog-meat.

224

Stella and Cora come up to the table.

Halsey: Give him a shove there, will y, Stel?

Stella jams Kabnis in a chair. Kabnis springs up.

Kabnis: Cant keep a good man down. Those words I was tellin y about, they wont fit int th mold thats branded on m soul. Rhyme, y see? Poet, too. Bad rhyme. Bad poet. Somethin else youve learned tnight. Lewis dont know it all, an I'm atellin y. Ugh. Th form thats burned int my soul is some twisted awful thing that crept in from a dream, a godam nightmare, an wont stay still unless I feed it. An it lives on words. Not beautiful words. God Almighty no. Misshapen, split-gut, tortured, twisted words. Layman was feedin it back there that day you thought I ran out fearin things. White folks feed it cause their looks are words. Niggers, black niggers feed it cause theyre evil an their looks are words. Yallar niggers feed it. This whole damn bloated purple country feeds it cause its goin down t hell in a holy avalanche of words. I want t feed th soul—I know what that is; th preachers dont—but I've got t feed it. I wish t God some lynchin white man ud225 stick his knife through it an pin it to a tree. An pin it to a tree. You hear me? Thats a wish f y, you little snot-nosed pups who've been makin fun of me, an fakin that I'm weak. Me, Ralph Kabnis weak. Ha.

Halsey: Thats right, old man. There, there. Here, so much exertion merits a fittin reward. Help him t be seated, Cora.

Halsey gives him a swig of shine. Cora glides up, seats him, and then plumps herself down on his lap, squeezing his head into her breasts. Kabnis mutters. Tries to break loose. Curses. Cora almost stifles him. He goes limp and gives up. Cora toys with him. Ruffles his hair. Braids it. Parts it in the middle. Stella smiles contemptuously. And then a sudden anger sweeps her. She would like to lash Cora from the place. She'd like to take Kabnis to some distant pine grove and nurse and mother him. Her eyes flash. A quick tensioning throws her breasts and neck into a poised strain. She starts towards them. Halsey grabs her arm and pulls her to him. She struggles. Halsey pins her arms and kisses her. She settles, spurting like a pine-knot afire.

226

Lewis finds himself completely cut out. The glowing within him subsides. It is followed by a dead chill. Kabnis, Carrie, Stella, Halsey, Cora, the old man, the cellar, and the work-shop, the southern town descend upon him. Their pain is too intense. He cannot stand it. He bolts from the table. Leaps up the stairs. Plunges through the work-shop and out into the night.

6

The cellar swims in a pale phosphorescence. The table, the chairs, the figure of the old man are amœba-like shadows which move about and float in it. In the corner under the steps, close to the floor, a solid blackness. A sound comes from it. A forcible yawn. Part of the blackness detaches itself so that it may be seen against the grayness of the wall. It moves forward and then seems to be clothing itself in odd dangling bits of shadow. The voice of Halsey, vibrant and deepened, calls.

Halsey: Kabnis. Cora. Stella.

He gets no response. He wants to get them up,227 to get on the job. He is intolerant of their sleepiness.

Halsey: Kabnis! Stella! Cora!

Gutturals, jerky and impeded, tell that he is shaking them.

Halsey: Come now, up with you.

Kabnis (sleepily and still more or less intoxicated): Whats th big idea? What in hell—

Halsey: Work. But never you mind about that. Up with you.

Cora: Oooooo! Look here, mister, I aint used t bein thrown int th street befo day.

Stella: Any bunk whats worked is worth in wages moren this. But come on. Taint no use t arger.

Kabnis: I'll arger. Its preposterous—

The girls interrupt him with none too pleasant laughs.

Kabnis: Thats what I said. Know what it means, dont y? All right, then. I said its preposterous t root an artist out o bed at this ungodly hour, when there aint no use t it. You can start your damned old work. Nobody's stoppin y. But what we got t get up for? Fraid228 somebody'll see th girls leavin? Some sport, you are. I hand it t y.

Halsey: Up you get, all th same.

Kabnis: Oh, th hell you say.

Halsey: Well, son, seeing that I'm th kind-hearted father, I'll give y chance t open your eyes. But up y get when I come down.

He mounts the steps to the work-shop and starts a fire in the hearth. In the yard he finds some chunks of coal which he brings in and throws on the fire. He puts a kettle on to boil. The wagon draws him. He lifts an oak-beam, fingers it, and becomes abstracted. Then comes to himself and places the beam upon the work-bench. He looks over some newly cut wooden spokes. He goes to the fire and pokes it. The coals are red-hot. With a pair of long prongs he picks them up and places them in a thick iron bucket. This he carries downstairs. Outside, darkness has given way to the impalpable grayness of dawn. This early morning light, seeping through the four barred cellar windows, is the color of the stony walls. It seems to be an emanation from them. Halsey's coals throw out229 a rich warm glow. He sets them on the floor, a safe distance from the beds.

Halsey: No foolin now. Come. Up with you.

Other than a soft rustling, there is no sound as the girls slip into their clothes. Kabnis still lies in bed.

Stella (to Halsey): Reckon y could spare us a light?

Halsey strikes a match, lights a cigarette, and then bends over and touches flame to the two candles on the table between the beds. Kabnis asks for a cigarette. Halsey hands him his and takes a fresh one for himself. The girls, before the mirror, are doing up their hair. It is bushy hair that has gone through some straightening process. Character, however, has not all been ironed out. As they kneel there, heavy-eyed and dusky, and throwing grotesque moving shadows on the wall, they are two princesses in Africa going through the early-morning ablutions of their pagan prayers. Finished, they come forward to stretch their hands and warm them over the glowing coals. Red dusk of a Georgia sun230set, their heavy, coal-lit faces... Kabnis suddenly recalls something.

Kabnis: Th old man talked last night.

Stella: An so did you.

Halsey: In your dreams.

Kabnis: I tell y, he did. I know what I'm talkin about. I'll tell y what he said. Wait now, lemme see.

Halsey: Look out, brother, th old man'll be getting int you by way o dreams. Come, Stel, ready? Cora? Coffee an eggs f both of you.

Halsey goes upstairs.

Stella: Gettin generous, aint he?

She blows the candles out. Says nothing to Kabnis. Then she and Cora follow after Halsey. Kabnis, left to himself, tries to rise. He has slept in his robe. His robe trips him. Finally, he manages to stand up. He starts across the floor. Half-way to the old man, he falls and lies quite still. Perhaps an hour passes. Light of a new sun is about to filter through the windows. Kabnis slowly rises to support upon his elbows. He looks hard, and internally gathers himself together. The side face of Father John is in the direct line of his eyes. He scowls at231 him. No one is around. Words gush from Kabnis.

Kabnis: You sit there like a black hound spiked to an ivory pedestal. An all night long I heard you murmurin that devilish word. They thought I didnt hear y, but I did. Mumblin, feedin that ornery thing thats livin on my insides. Father John. Father of Satan, more likely. What does it mean t you? Youre dead already. Death. What does it mean t you? To you who died way back there in th 'sixties. What are y throwin it in my throat for? Whats it goin t get y? A good smashin in th mouth, thats what. My fist'll sink int y black mush face clear t y guts—if y got any. Dont believe y have. Never seen signs of none. Death. Death. Sin an Death. All night long y mumbled death. (He forgets the old man as his mind begins to play with the word and its associations.) Death ... these clammy floors ... just like th place they used t stow away th worn-out, no-count niggers in th days of slavery ... that was long ago; not so long ago ... no windows (he rises higher on his elbows to verify this assertion. He looks around, and, seeing no one232 but the old man, calls.) Halsey! Halsey! Gone an left me. Just like a nigger. I thought he was a nigger all th time. Now I know it. Ditch y when it comes right down t it. Damn him anyway. Godam him. (He looks and re-sees the old man.) Eh, you? T hell with you too. What do I care whether you can see or hear? You know what hell is cause youve been there. Its a feelin an its ragin in my soul in a way that'll pop out of me an run you through, an scorch y, an burn an rip your soul. Your soul. Ha. Nigger soul. A gin soul that gets drunk on a preacher's words. An screams. An shouts. God Almighty, how I hate that shoutin. Where's th beauty in that? Gives a buzzard a windpipe an I'll bet a dollar t a dime th buzzard ud beat y to it. Aint surprisin th white folks hate y so. When you had eyes, did you ever see th beauty of th world? Tell me that. Th hell y did. Now dont tell me. I know y didnt. You couldnt have. Oh, I'm drunk an just as good as dead, but no eyes that have seen beauty ever lose their sight. You aint got no sight. If you had, drunk as I am, I hope Christ will kill me if I couldnt see it. Your eyes are dull and watery, like fish233 eyes. Fish eyes are dead eyes. Youre an old man, a dead fish man, an black at that. Theyve put y here t die, damn fool y are not t know it. Do y know how many feet youre under ground? I'll tell y. Twenty. An do y think you'll ever see th light of day again, even if you wasnt blind? Do y think youre out of slavery? Huh? Youre where they used t throw th worked-out, no-count slaves. On a damp clammy floor of a dark scum-hole. An they called that an infirmary. Th sons-a.... Why I can already see you toppled off that stool an stretched out on th floor beside me—not beside me, damn you, by yourself, with th flies buzzin an lickin God knows what they'd find on a dirty, black, foul-breathed mouth like yours...

Some one is coming down the stairs. Carrie, bringing food for the old man. She is lovely in her fresh energy of the morning, in the calm untested confidence and nascent maternity which rise from the purpose of her present mission. She walks to within a few paces of Kabnis.

Carrie K.: Brother says come up now, brother Ralph.

234

Kabnis: Brother doesnt know what he's talkin bout.

Carrie K.: Yes he does, Ralph. He needs you on th wagon.

Kabnis: He wants me on th wagon, eh? Does he think some wooden thing can lift me up? Ask him that.

Carrie K.: He told me t help y.

Kabnis: An how would you help me, child, dear sweet little sister?

She moves forward as if to aid him.

Carrie K.: I'm not a child, as I've more than once told you, brother Ralph, an as I'll show you now.

Kabnis: Wait, Carrie. No, thats right. Youre not a child. But twont do t lift me bodily. You dont understand. But its th soul of me that needs th risin.

Carrie K: Youre a bad brother an just wont listen t me when I'm tellin y t go t church.

Kabnis doesnt hear her. He breaks down and talks to himself.

Kabnis: Great God Almighty, a soul like mine cant pin itself onto a wagon wheel an satisfy itself in spinnin round. Iron prongs an235 hickory sticks, an God knows what all ... all right for Halsey ... use him. Me? I get my life down in this scum-hole. Th old man an me—

Carrie K.: Has he been talkin?

Kabnis: Huh? Who? Him? No. Dont need to. I talk. An when I really talk, it pays th best of them t listen. Th old man is a good listener. He's deaf; but he's a good listener. An I can talk t him. Tell him anything.

Carrie K.: He's deaf an blind, but I reckon he hears, an sees too, from th things I've heard.

Kabnis: No. Cant. Cant I tell you. How's he do it?

Carrie K.: Dunno, except I've heard that th souls of old folks have a way of seein things.

Kabnis: An I've heard them call that superstition.

The old man begins to shake his head slowly. Carrie and Kabnis watch him, anxiously. He mumbles. With a grave motion his head nods up and down. And then, on one of the down-swings—

Father John (remarkably clear and with great conviction): Sin.

236

He repeats this word several times, always the downward nodding. Surprised, indignant, Kabnis forgets that Carrie is with him.

Kabnis: Sin! Shut up. What do you know about sin, you old black bastard. Shut up, an stop that swayin an noddin your head.

Father John: Sin.

Kabnis tries to get up.

Kabnis: Didnt I tell y t shut up?

Carrie steps forward to help him. Kabnis is violently shocked at her touch. He springs back.

Kabnis: Carrie! What .. how .. Baby, you shouldnt be down here. Ralph says things. Doesnt mean to. But Carrie, he doesnt know what he's talkin about. Couldnt know. It was only a preacher's sin they knew in those old days, an that wasnt sin at all. Mind me, th only sin is whats done against th soul. Th whole world is a conspiracy t sin, especially in America, an against me. I'm th victim of their sin. I'm what sin is. Does he look like me? Have you ever heard him say th things youve heard me say? He couldnt if he had th Holy Ghost t237 help him. Dont look shocked, little sweetheart, you hurt me.

Father John: Sin.

Kabnis: Aw, shut up, old man.

Carrie K.: Leave him be. He wants t say somethin. (She turns to the old man.) What is it, Father?

Kabnis: Whatsha talkin t that old deaf man for? Come away from him.

Carrie K.: What is it, Father?

The old man's lips begin to work. Words are formed incoherently. Finally, he manages to articulate—

Father John: Th sin whats fixed... (Hesitates.)

Carrie K. (restraining a comment from Kabnis): Go on, Father.

Father John: ... upon th white folks—

Kabnis: Suppose youre talkin about that bastard race thats roamin round th country. It looks like sin, if thats what y mean. Give us somethin new an up t date.

Father John:—f tellin Jesus—lies. O th sin th white folks 'mitted when they made th Bible lie.

238

Boom. Boom. BOOM! Thuds on the floor above. The old man sinks back into his stony silence. Carrie is wet-eyed. Kabnis, contemptuous.

Kabnis: So thats your sin. All these years t tell us that th white folks made th Bible lie. Well, I'll be damned. Lewis ought t have been here. You old black fakir—

Carrie K.: Brother Ralph, is that your best Amen?

She turns him to her and takes his hot cheeks in her firm cool hands. Her palms draw the fever out. With its passing, Kabnis crumples. He sinks to his knees before her, ashamed, exhausted. His eyes squeeze tight. Carrie presses his face tenderly against her. The suffocation of her fresh starched dress feels good to him. Carrie is about to lift her hands in prayer, when Halsey, at the head of the stairs, calls down.

Halsey: Well, well. Whats up? Aint you ever comin? Come on. Whats up down there? Take you all mornin t sleep off a pint? Youre weakenin, man, youre weakenin. Th axle an th beam's all ready waitin f y. Come on.

Kabnis rises and is going doggedly towards239 the steps. Carrie notices his robe. She catches up to him, points to it, and helps him take it off. He hangs it, with an exaggerated ceremony, on its nail in the corner. He looks down on the tousled beds. His lips curl bitterly. Turning, he stumbles over the bucket of dead coals. He savagely jerks it from the floor. And then, seeing Carrie's eyes upon him, he swings the pail carelessly and with eyes downcast and swollen, trudges upstairs to the work-shop. Carrie's gaze follows him till he is gone. Then she goes to the old man and slips to her knees before him. Her lips murmur, "Jesus, come."

Light streaks through the iron-barred cellar window. Within its soft circle, the figures of Carrie and Father John.

Outside, the sun arises from its cradle in the tree-tops of the forest. Shadows of pines are dreams the sun shakes from its eyes. The sun arises. Gold-glowing child, it steps into the sky and sends a birth-song slanting down gray dust streets and sleepy windows of the southern town.

the end

Transcriber's Notes: Blank pages have been removed. Redundant title page removed. Silently corrected a few typographical errors. Otherwise spelling and hyphenation left unchanged. Ellipses period counts left unchanged.

Alice Walker, Everyday Use

Alice Walker, Everyday Use

https://harpers.org/archive/1973/04/everyday-use/

"Green pine-needle on an old, gray wooden chair" by Simoubuntu is licensed under CC BY-SA 2.0

Toni Cade Bambara, Gorilla, My Love

Toni Cade Bambara, Gorilla, My Love

https://www.bhamcityschools.org/cms/lib5/AL01001646/Centricity/Domain/4460/gorilla-my-love.pdf

"THE ROLE OF THE ARTIST IS TO MAKE REVOLUTION IRRESISTIBLE — Toni Cade Bambara" by Stewf is licensed under CC BY-NC-SA 2.0

7. DRAMA

Angelina Weld Grimké, Rachel: A Play in Three Acts

https://babel.hathitrust.org/cgi/pt?id=uc1.32106002112461&view=1up&seq=14

Amiri Baraka, Dutchman

https://faculty.atu.edu/cbrucker/engl2013/texts/dutchman.pdf

"LeRoi Jones (Amiri Baraka)" by rverc is licensed under CC BY-NC-ND 2.0

8. CRITICISM AND LITERARY THEORY

Slavery to Liberation: The African-American Experience

We will be using *Slavery to Liberation: The African-American Experience* as a source for historical context. This OER text has chapters available as PDFs. (They do not paste in well, and for space considerations we will link to it rather than include entire chapters.

https://encompass.eku.edu/ekuopen/1/

Slavery to Liberation: The African American Experience

Joshua Farrington, *Eastern Kentucky University*
Norman W. Powell, *Eastern Kentucky University*
Gwendolyn Graham, *Eastern Kentucky University*
Lisa Day, *Eastern Kentucky University*
Ogechi E. Anyanwu, *Eastern Kentucky University*

Langston Hughes, The Negro Artist and the Racial Mountain

Langston Hughes, The Negro Artist and the Racial Mountain

https://www.poetryfoundation.org/articles/69395/the-negro-artist-and-the-racial-mountain

Hughes's essay is one of the cornerstone pieces to an exploration of identity and race in American Literature. It was written as a refutal to an editor's essay on assimilation (see the link's notes). It brings up those live issues of place, time, and identity which we have been analyzing throughout the course:

- To what extent is an artist supposed to be representative?
- How great a separation is there between an author and her works?
- How directly do artists confront and subvert (undercut) stereotypes?
- How ought African-American artists to participate in America's creation of the artist as Other stereotype?

Additionally, we might look to Library of Congress collections to do some follow-up work with the concepts Hughes presents. For more, see:

https://www.loc.gov/collections/?fa=subject:african+american+history

Zora Neale Hurston, What White Publishers Won't Print

Zora Neale Hurston, What White Publishers Won't Print

https://pages.ucsd.edu/~bgoldfarb/cogn150s12/reading/Hurston-What-White-Publishers-Wont-Print.pdf

Though Hurston is mostly known for her fiction, her anthropological looks at herself and her culture are amazingly powerful in nonfiction form.

How does Hurston play with "then versus now" to show how things have not changed all that much from the time of slavery? What satirical points does Hurston make about the use of prodigies specimens and extraordinary examples? How is this a trap for the African-American artist? (Remember our coverage of these issues with Phillis Wheatley.)

Ambrose Olumuyiwa Faturoti, Renaissance Collage

Ambrose Olumuyiwa Faturoti, Renaissance Collage

http://xroads.virginia.edu/~MA03/faturoti/harlem/home.html

This collection of videos, analyses, and primary texts offers a strong overview of the Harlem Renaissance.

Zora Neale Hurston, Characteristics of Negro Expression

Zora Neale Hurston, Characteristics of Negro Expression

http://www.ypsilonediteur.com/images/documents/Zora_Charateristics.pdf

"IMG1435" by dishfunctional is licensed under CC BY-NC-SA 2.0

bell hooks, Postmodern Blackness

bell hooks, Postmodern Blackness

https://www.africa.upenn.edu/Articles_Gen/Postmodern_Blackness_18270.html

–Because when she can get others to accept all lower case letters for one's name, you know this is a powerful voice!

"quotes by bell hooks" by bell hooks philosophy is marked with CC PDM 1.0

Paul Fry, African-American Criticism

This Yale lecture is a good overview of the issues and history of African-American literary criticism. Professor Paul Fry's video is conveniently broken into chapters for classroom use.

https://oyc.yale.edu/english/engl-300/lecture-21

A transcript is also available.

Henry Wiencek, The Dark Side of Thomas Jefferson

https://www.smithsonianmag.com/history/the-dark-side-of-thomas-jefferson-35976004/

“Slave manacles used at Monticello – Smithsonian Museum of American History – 2012-05-15” by Tim Evanson is licensed under CC BY-SA 2.0

Jefferson Community College’s namesake both owned slaves and believed in both breeding them and breeding with them in order to increase his profit margins. Learn more in this 2012 *Smithsonian* article–hardly a radical publication. What does it say, too, that the article’s title reproduces the racially coded stereotypes (i.e., “dark side”)?

So if we had called this *The Jefferson Anthology of African American Literature*, what conversations about race might that begin?

Norman W. Powell, Concepts of Beauty: Black and White Connotations

SlaverytoLiberation2019_CHAPTER 2_Powell-1

This is a chapter from *Slavery to Liberation*, the text linked in the previous page of the book.

9. STUDENT RESOURCES

Six Tips for Being a Better Literature Student

Literature courses can be handled inappropriately and there is often not enough time to figure that out in a fifteen-week session. I have a few tips that should help us avoid recurring errors. Each of these tips relates to critical thinking and writing:

1. The audience knows the play, poem, or story. Summaries that just fill space are useless, so avoid writing a review or a running account of the plot. It would be like telling someone the directions to their own home when you were supposed to be arguing about the best spots along the way.
2. Apply the literary terms such as verbal irony, symbolism, theme, and metaphor. Do more than just point them out. Yes, they exist. (Skeptical readers like the ones you'll have in the course would just say "Okay. . . so what?") What is a metaphor doing in a given paragraph or stanza, though? You can always argue about functions or effects.
3. Everything we do is thesis-driven, meaning that it's argument. A thesis is not just a statement of what you'll do. It's an arguable, provable claim that should have some substance. It's not a question. It's not a fact. It is an opinion—though you need not use *I*.
4. Anticipate what the audience thinks about a piece of literature. It's important to realize that you're writing in a public way about works which may have been valued and argued over for hundreds of years. Value that and take yourself seriously as a critic.
5. Plagiarism is easy to catch and will be dealt with harshly. If you are in doubt, cite the material. Remember that MLA is exacting, so be sure you're using the correct style models. There is not much time to get used to this, so look at the Unit 1 mini-lectures and links on citing. The expectation is that you can look at a model and "get it right" in your writing. Ask questions and pay attention to the style, since how something looks is often as important as what it says.
6. Lastly, really work to avoid lateness. Be on the correct side of any due dates, as it's really tough to make up work.

Defining Literature

Defining literature is always difficult. There are several overlapping definitions. Some concentrate of where the words are–as our discussion is when it questions whether something can be literature if it's oral. This gets at only part of the question. Other definitions get at what literature feels like to the audience/reader. Other definitions focus on the *differences* between literature and everyday use of language. By using a combination of approaches (being flexible) we can arrive at a definition.

I'm including a long quote from Jonathan Culler's wonderful little book *Literary Theory: A Very Short Introduction*. Culler teaches at Cornell. If any of you are serious about English as a major, you should probably read this book. The reason I mention this is that Culler makes literary theory understandable and he cuts through a lot of the current trends in criticism–that's saying a lot, if you've seen some of the strange things to come out of our field of study lately. I wish I had read a book like this before tackling those English classes! Anyway, I'm not going to say much else about this–he goes from pages 18-41 trying to define this strange thing we call literature.

See what you can say about Culler's take on defining literature. You could respond to it for some discussion postings.

Remember that epic poems like *The Odyssey* and *The Iliad* were initially oral–they were only written down much later. They are in our canon. The origins of poetry are oral rather than written.

Note that Culler's book is published by Oxford UP, so it's going to have single quotes where there should be double–and other British usages like single – instead of the– for quick shifts in thought. You should continue using Standard American English and MLA format.

The Definition of Literature

What sort of question?

We find ourselves back at the key question, 'What is literature?', which will not go away. But what sort of question is it? If a 5-year-old is asking, it's easy. 'Literature', you answer, 'is stories, poems, and plays.' But if the questioner is a literary theorist, it's harder to know how to take the query. It might be a question about the general nature of this object, literature, which both of you already know well. What sort of object or activity is it? What does it do? What purposes does it serve? Thus understood, 'What is literature?' asks not for a definition but for an analysis, even an argument about why one might concern oneself with literature at all.

But 'What is literature?' might also be a question about distinguishing characteristics of the works known as literature: what distinguishes them from non-literary works? What differentiates literature from other human activities or pastimes? Now people might ask this question because they were wondering how to decide which books are literature and which are not, but it is more likely that they already have an idea what counts as literature and want to know something else: are there any essential, distinguishing features that literary works share?

This is a difficult question. Theorists have wrestled with it, but without notable success. The reasons are not far to seek: works of literature come in all shapes and sizes and most of them seem to have more in common with works that aren't usually called literature than they do with some other works recognized as literature. Charlotte Bronte's Jane *Eyre,* for instance, more closely resembles an autobiography than it does a sonnet, and a poem by Robert Burns – 'My love is like a red, red rose' -resembles a folk-song more than it does Shakespeare's *Hamlet.* Are there qualities shared by poems, plays, and novels that distinguish them from, say, songs, transcriptions of conversations, and autobiographies?

Historical Variations

Even a bit of historical perspective makes this question more complex. For twenty-five centuries people have written works that we call literature today, but the modern sense of *literature* is scarcely two centuries old. Prior to 1800 *literature* and analogous terms in other European languages meant writings' or "book knowledge." Even today, a scientist who says 'the literature on evolution is immense' means not that many poems and novels treat the topic but that much has been written about it. And works that today are studied as literature in English or Latin classes in schools and universities were once treated not as a special kind of writing but as fine examples of the use of language and rhetoric. They were instances of a larger category of exemplary practices of writing and thinking, which included speeches, sermons, history, and philosophy. Students were not asked to interpret them, as we now interpret literary works, seeking to explain what they are 'really about'. On the contrary, students memorized them, studied their grammar, identified their rhetorical figures and their structures or procedures of argument. A work such as Virgil's *Aeneid,* which today g is studied as literature, was treated very differently in schools prior to 1850.

The modern Western sense of literature as imaginative writing can be traced to the German Romantic theorists of the late eighteenth century and, if we want a particular source, to a book published in 1800 by a French Baroness, Madame de Staël's On *Literature Considered in its Relations with Social Institutions.* But even if we restrict ourselves to the last two centuries, the category of literature becomes slippery:

would works which today count as literature—say poems that seem snippets of ordinary conversation, without rhyme or discernible metre -have qualified as literature for Madame de Staël? And once we begin to think about non-European cultures, the question of what counts as literature becomes increasingly difficult. It is tempting to give it up and conclude that literature is whatever a given society treats as literature—a set of texts that arbiters [tastemakers, critics] recognize as belonging to literature.

I hope this helps!

Self-Diagnosis of One's Writing Ailments can be Fun!

Is using plain language the law?

The following humorous site, "How to Write Good," is located on the *Plainlanguage.gov* page. It lists and breaks several writing rules. In breaking the rules, they illustrate them. It is an engaging way to learn the rules of English–especially since they always seem to have exceptions.

Note that not all of the rules are really rules anymore. For instance, the one about ending a sentence on a preposition is one we have largely gotten out of. (Get it?)

Experiencing Literature

Terms and Concepts

Students of literature read and notice things. They also need a working vocabulary of literary terms. Luckily (for me), you already know a few dozen literary terms. I'll expect you to use these. In addition, I want to introduce you to a few less- familiar topics (e.g., subversion, irony, and stereotyping). You can find out about these terms–and more–in the following lectures.

As we go on, you'll become more familiar with how different authors use irony, subversion, etc., in order to achieve certain effects.

Paradox

No, it's not a pair of ducks! Paradox is a seeming contradiction. It is an intricate device that gets readers to think. Paradox is often linked with irony.

Native American authors often deal with the paradoxes of white treatment of Indians. There's a lot of history there. What I want you to do is to notice when paradoxes appear, and alert us to them. We can interpret them after the class notices them. Check out the list below for just some of the paradoxical issues in Native American writers treat:

Binaries

Binaries are pairs of choices, like the "ones" and "zeros" making up the information on cds. They offer a way of reducing things. Think about the either/or choices consumers are faced with. Authors can't leave these binaries alone. . . they like to play with easy choices, showing how artificial they are. As I'll say elsewhere, we don't live in a simple world. It's not all "Pepsi or Coke," and authors like to challenge binaries.

Think about other examples of paradox you encounter. Be willing to share these.

General Stuff

If you get stuck interpreting, look for setting and conflict. You can always talk about those, and then get into more complex areas of the piece from these.

Binaries (otherwise known as polar oppositions or polar opposites) can be found in Native American literature. Here are some that I thought of quickly. What ones can you find?

vs.

Past	Present
Victimization	Triumph
Richness (spiritual, physical)	Poverty
Being "a Mohawk," "a Paiute," "a Lakota," etc.	"Indian" in general

Paradoxical Binaries Treated by Native American Authors
Now look at what some Native authors do with seemingly simple binaries. You might find stories in which characters are:

- living in two cultural worlds simultaneously
- both rich and poor–ways of seeing wealth are confused, downplayed, or overwhelming

- Native Americans who act as "super patriots"

or in which

- past, present and future are seamlessly intermixed
- Christianity and Native roots get mixed without one winning out over the other
- Victimization and triumph exist simultaneously, defining the same character
- tradition vs. modernity never gets solved or resolved for a character
- personal identity and communal identity cannot be separated
- Native identity exists–independent of white culture
- mixed blood identity is the most important aspect of life for a character

This list probably makes little sense to you right now. It's meant to get you thinking about the many "moves" you will see Indian writers make. Be active as a reader, and as a questioner! Let me know what sorts of things you see happening in our readings. Critical thinking is just that: critical. I am curious to see what you'll find in this semester's literature.

Here are Some Dos and Don'ts Graders Think Through

What we want and what we get are often wildly variant. Adults all know this. Even so, I can be surprised by some combinations of elements sometimes. That's why I like to troubleshoot papers with you beforehand!

Problem: Paragraphs lacking topic sentences. These work in fiction, but not in explicit writing like ours. Even if it is not first, the topic sentence ought to be connected in obvious ways to your claim. We often defer to sources here or have paragraphs which only exist in the paper because of a source. It should be that the supporting role fits what you do, not vice versa.

One source for the first or last third (or any third) of a paper is a problem. We often see such overuse of one source: Great source? Great! Not great, however, if that source is the only voice in the paper or if, when it is used, the writer never questions it. Think of how ventriloquists' dummies only exist to parrot the words of someone else:

"Me and the office ventriloquist dummy" by TJ Ryan is licensed under CC BY 2.0

Definitions which get plagiarized, unused, treated as impressive, or passed off as if they are unbiased are likely to backfire, turning a possibly-good move into a definitely-bad move. I'm not phased by statistics–particularly if the writer fails to quote properly, doesn't look at the fact that the sample size was seventeen people paid by the company, or if the "citizens' group" spouting them turns out to be a hate group with a nice-sounding name or if that source actually ripped them off from a second source. As Mark Twain stated aptly, there are "lies, damned lies, and statistics."

Long quotes? They are often areas where summaries would work better, be shorter, and might actually receive interpretation. Filler long quotes nearly never get interpreted. Look at it as I do: the more a quote drones on, the more expectation it sets up that I would get something for it–some interpretation, anything! (I mean, people get free vacations in our country for sitting through two-day seminars . . . they obviously got something from the long setup.) We only quote if it's well-worded, the strongly-held opinion of a thinker, or a thought at variance with the widely-held opinion in that field of study. Otherwise, summarize or paraphrase.

Examples can often be scarce, appearing only by page six. By then, it's too late for readers. Don't overuse or under use examples. According to the Goldilocks Principle, there has to be a "just right" zone for source use, detail, even sentence and word length.

Lastly, the new game is to play with formatting. I know the trick of putting the punctuation in 16-point font to puff the piece. I have seen papers go from 10 to 3 pages because of ridiculous formatting tricks. That time is best spent writing, in my opinion. Some people have plagiarized by throwing in a source's bibliography and citations, figuring I wouldn't check or couldn't see that move. That's another bad one, since plagiarism requires that we look at intent and it takes intent to do something like that.

I hope that helps!

Signal Phrases

Good readers will look for the way you set up your quotes as well as the way you interpret them. Use signal phrases to ensure smooth paragraphs.

As I keep mentioning, good writers are writers who know their options. Often, a well-placed word or phrase is necessary to guide readers. Signal phrases also separate your ideas from the source's ideas. This is crucial.

Here are some verbs you might use for strong signal phrases. Notice how they give away the author's tone. Of course, the catch is that you'll have to understand the quote and the author's tone, which is the author's attitude toward the work. This is the tough part! Here are some ready-made options for you:

Author is neutral

comments,describes, explains, illustrates, notes, observes, points out, records, relates, reports, says, sees, thinks, writes

Author infers or suggests

analyzes, asks, assesses, concludes, considers, finds, predicts, proposes, reveals, shows, speculates, suggests, supposes

Author argues

claims, contends, defends, holds, insists, maintains

Author agrees

avers, admits, grants, concedes, notes, agrees

Author is uneasy or disparaging

belittles, bemoans, complains, confesses, condemns, deplores, deprecates, derides, disagrees, laments, warns. (Notice how the de- prefix here lets us know that what follows goes away or from. These words have much different tones from the "togetherness" of co- com- prefixes. Little effects like this aren't lost on careful readers!)

Reader-Response Criticism

Summary

We have examined many schools of literary criticism. Here you will find an in-depth look at one of them: Reader-Response.

The Purpose of Reader-Response

Reader-response suggests that the role of the reader is essential to the meaning of a text, for only in the reading experience does the literary work come alive. For example, in Mary Wollstonecraft Shelley's *Frankenstein* (1818), the monster doesn't exist, so to speak, until the reader reads *Frankenstein* and reanimates it to life, becoming a co-creator of the text.
Thus, the purpose of a reading response is examining, explaining, and defending your personal reaction to a text.
Your critical reading of a text asks you to explore:

- why you like or dislike the text;
- explain whether you agree or disagree with the author;
- identify the text's purpose; and
- critique the text.

There is no right or wrong answer to a reading response. Nonetheless, it is important that you demonstrate an understanding of the reading and clearly explain and support your reactions. Do not use the standard approach of just writing: *"I liked this text because it is so cool and the ending made me feel happy," or "I hated it because it was stupid, and had nothing at all to do with my life, and was too negative and boring."* In writing a response you may assume the reader has already read the text. Thus, do not summarize the contents of the text at length. Instead, take a systematic, analytical approach to the text.

Write as a Scholar

When writing a reader-response write as an educated adult addressing other adults or fellow scholars. As a beginning scholar, if you write that something has nothing to do with you or does not pass *your* "Who cares?" test, but many other people think that it is important and great, readers will probably *not* agree with you that the *text* is dull or boring. Instead, they may conclude that *you* are dull and boring, that you are too immature or uneducated to understand what important things the author wrote.

Criticize with Examples

If you did not like a text, that is fine, but criticize it either from:

- *principle*, for example:
    - Is the text racist?
    - Does the text unreasonably puts down things, such as religion, or groups of people, such as women or adolescents, conservatives or democrats, etc?
    - Does the text include factual errors or outright lies? It is too dark and despairing? Is it falsely positive?
- *form*, for example:
    - Is the text poorly written?
    - Does it contain too much verbal "fat"?
    - Is it too emotional or too childish?

- Does it have too many facts and figures?
- Are there typos or other errors in the text?
- Do the ideas wander around without making a point?

In each of these cases, do not simply criticize, but give examples. As a beginning scholar, be cautious of criticizing any text as "confusing" or "crazy," since readers might simply conclude that *you* are too ignorant or slow to understand and appreciate it.

The Structure of a Reader-Response Essay

Choosing a text to study is the first step in writing a reader-response essay. Once you have chosen the text, your challenge is to connect with it and have a "conversation" with the text.
In the beginning paragraph of your reader-response essay, be sure to mention the following:

- title of the work to which you are responding;
- the author; and
- the main thesis of the text.

Then, do your best to answer the questions below. Remember, however, that you are writing an essay, not filling out a short-answer worksheet. You do not need to work through these questions in order, one by one, in your essay. Rather, your paper as a whole should be sure to address these questions in some way.

- *What does the text have to do with you, personally, and with your life (past, present or future)?* It is not acceptable to write that the text has NOTHING to do with you, since just about everything humans can write has to do in some way with every other human.
- *How much does the text agree or clash with your view of the world, and what you consider right and wrong?* Use several quotes as examples of how it agrees with and supports what you think about the world, about right and wrong, and about what you think it is to be human. Use quotes and examples to discuss how the text disagrees with what you think about the world and about right and wrong.
- *What did you learn, and how much were your views and opinions challenged or changed by this text, if at all? Did the text communicate with you? Why or why not?* Give examples of how your views might have changed or been strengthened (or perhaps, of why the text failed to convince you, the way it is). Please do not write "I agree with everything the author wrote," since everybody disagrees about something, even if it is a tiny point. Use quotes to illustrate your points of challenge, or where you were persuaded, or where it left you cold.
- *How well does the text address things that you, personally, care about and consider important to the world? How does it address things that are important to your family, your community, your ethnic group, to people of your economic or social class or background, or your faith tradition? If not, who does or did the text serve? Did it pass the "Who cares?" test?* Use quotes from the text to illustrate.
- *What can you praise about the text? What problems did you have with it?* Reading and writing "critically" does not mean the same thing as "criticizing," in everyday language (complaining or griping, fault-finding, nit-picking). Your "critique" can and should be positive and praise the text if possible, as well as pointing out problems, disagreements and shortcomings.
- *How well did you enjoy the text (or not) as entertainment or as a work of art?* Use quotes or examples to illustrate the quality of the text as art or entertainment. Of course, be aware that some texts are not meant to be entertainment or art: a news report or textbook, for instance, may be neither entertaining or artistic, but may still be important and successful.

For the conclusion, you might want to discuss:

- your overall reaction to the text;
- whether you would read something else like this in the future;

- whether you would read something else by this author; and
- if would you recommend read this text to someone else and why.

Key Takeaways

- In reader-response, the reader is essential to the meaning of a text for they bring the text to life.
- The purpose of a reading response is examining, explaining, and defending your personal reaction to a text.
- When writing a reader-response, write as an educated adult addressing other adults or fellow scholars.
- As a beginning scholar, be cautious of criticizing any text as "boring," "crazy," or "dull." If you do criticize, base your criticism on the principles and form of the text itself.
- The challenge of a reader-response is to show how you connected with the text.

Examples

Reader-Response Essay Example

To Misread or to Rebel: A Woman's Reading of "The Secret Life of Walter Mitty"

At its simplest, reading is "an activity that is guided by the text; this must be processed by the reader who is then, in turn, affected by what he has processed" (Iser 63). The text is the compass and map, the reader is the explorer. However, the explorer cannot disregard those unexpected boulders in the path which he or she encounters along the journey that are not written on the map. Likewise, the woman reader does not come to the text without outside influences. She comes with her experiences as a woman—a professional woman, a divorcée, a single mother. Her reading, then, is influenced by her experiences. So when she reads a piece of literature like "The Secret Life of Walter Mitty" by James Thurber, which paints a highly negative picture of Mitty's wife, the woman reader is forced to either misread the story and accept Mrs. Mitty as a domineering, mothering wife, or rebel against that picture and become angry at the society which sees her that way.

Due to pre-existing sociosexual standards, women see characters, family structures, even societal structures from the bottom as an oppressed group rather than from a powerful position on the top, as men do. As Louise Rosenblatt states: a reader's "tendency toward identification [with characters or events] will certainly be guided by our preoccupations at the time we read. Our problems and needs may lead us to focus on those characters and situations through which we may achieve the satisfactions, the balanced vision, or perhaps merely the unequivocal motives unattained in our own lives" (38). A woman reader who feels chained by her role as a housewife is more likely to identify with an individual who is oppressed or feels trapped than the reader's executive husband is. Likewise, a woman who is unable to have children might respond to a story of a child's death more emotionally than a woman who does not want children. However, if the perspective of a woman does not match that of the male author whose work she is reading, a woman reader who has been shaped by a male-dominated society is forced to misread the text, reacting to the "words on the page in one way rather than another because she operates according to the same set of rules that the author used to generate them" (Tompkins xvii). By accepting the author's perspective and reading the text as he intended, the woman reader is forced to disregard her own, female perspective. This, in turn, leads to a concept called "asymmetrical contingency," described by Iser as that which occurs "when Partner A gives up trying to implement his own behavioral plan and without resistance follows that of Partner B. He adapts himself to and is absorbed by the behavioral strategy of B" (164). Using this argument, it becomes clear that a woman reader (Partner A) when faced with a text written by a man (Partner B) will most likely succumb to the perspective of the writer and she is thus forced to misread the text. Or, she could rebel against the text and raise an angry, feminist voice in protest.

James Thurber, in the eyes of most literary critics, is one of the foremost American humorists of the 20th century, and his short story "The Secret Life of Walter Mitty" is believed to have "ushered in a major [literary] period … where the individual can maintain his self … an appropriate way of assaulting rigid forms" (Elias 432). The rigid form in Thurber's story is Mrs. Mitty, the main character's wife. She is portrayed by Walter Mitty as a horrible, mothering nag. As a way of escaping her constant griping, he imagines fantastic daydreams which carry him away from Mrs. Mitty's voice. Yet she repeatedly interrupts his reveries and Mitty responds to her as though she is "grossly unfamiliar, like a strange woman who had yelled at him in the crowd" (286). Not only is his wife annoying to him, but she is also distant and removed from what he cares about, like a stranger. When she does speak to him, it seems reflective of the way a mother would speak to a child. For example, Mrs. Mitty asks, "'Why don't you wear your gloves? Have you lost your gloves?' Walter Mitty reached in a pocket and brought out the gloves. He put them on, but after she had turned and gone into the building and he had driven on to a red light, he took them off again" (286). Mrs. Mitty's care for her husband's health is seen as nagging to Walter Mitty, and the audience is amused that he responds like a child and does the opposite of what Mrs. Mitty asked of him. Finally, the clearest way in which Mrs. Mitty is portrayed as a burdensome wife is at the end of the piece when Walter, waiting for his wife to exit the store, imagines that he is facing "the firing squad; erect and motionless, proud and disdainful, Walter Mitty the Undefeated, inscrutable to the last" (289). Not only is Mrs. Mitty portrayed as a mothering, bothersome hen, but she is ultimately described as that which will be the death of Walter Mitty.

Mrs. Mitty is a direct literary descendant of the first woman to be stereotyped as a nagging wife, Dame Van Winkle, the creation of the American writer, Washington Irving. Likewise, Walter Mitty is a reflection of his dreaming predecessor, Rip Van Winkle, who falls into a deep sleep for a hundred years and awakes to the relief of finding out that his nagging wife has died. Judith Fetterley explains in her book, The Resisting Reader, how such a portrayal of women forces a woman who reads "Rip Van Winkle" and other such stories "to find herself excluded from the experience of the story" so that she "cannot read the story without being assaulted by the negative images of women it presents" (10). The result, it seems, is for a woman reader of a story like "Rip Van Winkle" or "The Secret Life of Walter Mitty" to either be excluded from the text, or accept the negative images of women the story puts forth. As Fetterley points out, "The consequence for the female reader is a divided self. She is asked to identify with Rip and against herself, to scorn the amiable sex and act just like it, to laugh at Dame Van Winkle and accept that she represents 'woman,' to be at once both repressor and repressed, and ultimately to realize that she is neither" (11). Thus, a woman is forced to misread the text and accept "woman as villain." as Fetterley names it, or rebel against both the story and its message.

So how does a woman reader respond to this portrayal of Mrs. Mitty? If she were to follow Iser's claim, she would defer to the male point of view presented by the author. She would sympathize with Mitty, as Thurber wants us to do, and see domineering women in her own life that resemble Mrs. Mitty. She may see her mother and remember all the times that she nagged her about zipping up her coat against the bitter winter wind. Or the female reader might identify Mrs. Mitty with her controlling mother-in-law and chuckle at Mitty's attempts to escape her control, just as her husband tries to escape the criticism and control of his own mother. Iser's ideal female reader would undoubtedly look at her own position as mother and wife and would vow to never become such a domineering person. This reader would probably also agree with a critic who says that "Mitty has a wife who embodies the authority of a society in which the husband cannot function" (Lindner 440). She could see the faults in a relationship that is too controlled by a woman and recognize that a man needs to feel important and dominant in his relationship with his wife. It could be said that the female reader would agree completely with Thurber's portrayal of the domineering wife. The female reader could simply misread the text.

Or, the female reader could rebel against the text. She could see Mrs. Mitty as a woman who is trying to do her best to keep her husband well and cared for. She could see Walter as a man with a fleeting grip on reality who daydreams that he is a fighter pilot, a brilliant surgeon, a gun expert, or a military hero, when he actually is a poor driver with a slow reaction time to a green traffic light. The female reader could read critics of Thurber who say that by allowing his wife to dominate him, Mitty becomes a "non-hero in a civilization in which women are winning the battle of the sexes" (Hasley 533) and become angry that a woman's fight for equality is seen merely as a battle between the sexes. She could read Walter's daydreams as his attempt to dominate his wife, since all of his fantasies center on him in traditional roles of power. This, for most women, would cause anger at Mitty (and indirectly Thurber) for creating and promoting a society which believes that women need to stay subservient to men. From a male point of view, it becomes a battle of the sexes. In a woman's eyes, her reading is simply a struggle for equality within the text and in the world outside that the text reflects.

It is certain that women misread "The Secret Life of Walter Mitty." I did. I found myself initially wishing that Mrs. Mitty would just let Walter daydream in peace. But after reading the story again and paying attention to the portrayal of Mrs. Mitty, I realized that it is imperative that women rebel against the texts that would oppress them. By misreading a text, the woman reader understands it in a way that is conventional and acceptable to the literary world. But in so doing, she is also distancing herself from the text, not fully embracing it or its meaning in her life. By rebelling against the text, the female reader not only has to understand the point of view of the author and the male audience, but she also has to formulate her own opinions and create a sort of dialogue between the text and herself. Rebelling against the text and the stereotypes encourages an active dialogue between the woman and the text which, in turn, guarantees an active and (most likely) angry reader response. I became a resisting reader.

Works Cited

Elias, Robert H. "James Thurber: The Primitive, the Innocent, and the Individual." *Contemporary Literary Criticism*. Vol. 5. Ed. Dedria Bryfonski. Detroit: Gale Research, 1980. 431–32. Print.

Fetterley, Judith. *The Resisting Reader*. Bloomington: Indiana UP, 1978. Print.

Hasley, Louis. "James Thurber: Artist in Humor." *Contemporary Literary Criticism*. Vol. 11. Ed. Dedria Bryfonski. Detroit: Gale Research, 1980. 532–34. Print.

Iser, Wolfgang. *The Act of Reading: A Theory of Aesthetic Response*. Baltimore: Johns Hopkins UP, 1981. Print.

Lindner, Carl M. "Thurber's Walter Mitty—The Underground American Hero." *Contemporary Literary Criticism*. Vol. 5. Ed. Dedria Bryfonski. Detroit: Gale Research, 1980. 440–41. Print.

Rosenblatt, Louise M. *Literature as Exploration*. New York: MLA, 1976. Print.

Thurber, James. "The Secret Life of Walter Mitty." *Literature: An Introduction to Critical Reading*. Ed. William Vesterman. Fort Worth: Harcourt Brace, 1993. 286–89. Print.

Tompkins, Jane P. "An Introduction to Reader-Response Criticism." *Reader Response Criticism: From Formalism to Post-Structuralism*. Ed. Jane P. Tompkins. Baltimore: Johns Hopkins UP, 1980. ix-xxvi. Print.

10. WRITING ABOUT LITERATURE

Introduction to Writing About Literature

> The best of a book is not the thought which it contains, but the thought which it suggests; just as the charm of music dwells not in the tones but in the echoes of our hearts. – Oliver Wendell Holmes

Learning Outcomes

- Find and use historical sources to discuss the historical context of a literary work
- Find and use literary criticism in your analysis of literary works
- Cite sources correctly using MLA format

Finding Literary Criticism

Literary criticism is writing that explores the meaning of works of literature. Among other things, literary criticism analyzes works of literature in terms of their historical and literary context. It can also examine a particular type of literature or compare different works by the same author or works by different authors.

Literary criticism analyzes fiction, poetry, drama and some types of non-fiction by considering key issues such as plot, character, setting, theme, imagery, and voice. Literary criticism may also consider the effectiveness of a work of literature, but it's important to note that in this context the word "criticism" doesn't simply mean finding fault with the writing but rather looking at it from a critical or analytical viewpoint in order to understand it better.

It's also important to note that literary criticism involves more than just summarizing the plot or offering biographical information about the author.

Evaluating Sources of Literary Criticism

If you're asked to find *scholarly* sources of literary criticism, you should look for journals that are peer-reviewed. In other words, before articles are accepted for publication in the journal, they're reviewed by other scholars. Articles in a scholarly journal will also include citations for other works that are referenced. Scholarly books, likewise, will document their sources and are usually written by someone affiliated with a college or university and published by a university press. Sometimes a book of literary criticism is actually a compilation of articles that have previously appeared in journals. If that's the case, you can try to ascertain the nature of the journal in question.

Even if you know an article has come from a peer-reviewed journal, you may still wonder about its relevance, particularly if the work or author you're researching is one that's been studied extensively. One way to get more information about a source is to type the title of the article into Google Scholar and see how many times it's been cited. The higher the number, the more likely it is that the article is influential—or at least controversial. You can do a similar search to learn more about the reputation of a journal, book, or author.

Finally, when looking for critical work, don't rely on sources like SparkNotes, which provide help for students but are not considered reputable scholarly sources.

Sources of Literary Criticism

An ideal placeto begin your search for literary criticism is the English subject guide on the TAMU libraries' website: library.tamu.edu/subject-guides/English. We also recommend their handout "Starting Points for Literary Criticism."

Here are some of the useful links you'll find on the library website:

ABELL (Annual Bibliography of English Language and Literature): This database includes English-language articles, books, and reviews published since 1920 on English language and literature, traditional culture and bibliography. It also includes unpublished dissertations from the years 1920-1999. It covers English, American and Commonwealth writers.

Academic Search Complete: EBSCO: This online database, a general source for scholarly works in a variety of disciplines, covers works on the literature of all languages. The database covers almost 11,000 publications and offers full text on about 5,000 of those.

Modern Language Association (MLA) International Bibliograghy: This is a key resource for information on literature, linguistics, and folklore. The database includes more than 4,000 journals in the field, as well as books, collections of essays, dissertations and other bibliographies. It covers work from 1920 to the present. When searching, you can specify the kind of references you want, i.e. books, journals, websites. You can also choose only those listings that link to a full text version of the material. You can also set the search parameters to show you only scholarly (peer reviewed) journals or you can request entries within a certain timeframe, such as only those published after the year 2000.

The TAMU library's English subject page also links to databases geared to specific time periods (such as Brepolis Medieval Bibliographies) and those pertaining to certain types of literature (such as the Children's Literature Database).

A few other resources you may want to investigate:

African American Review: This online journal specifically focuses on African American literature and ethnic studies, "[providing] a lively exchange between writers and scholars in the arts, humanities, and social sciences who hold diverse perspectives on African American literature and culture." The website features full-text online access to back issues.

American Literary Scholarship: This journal offers current critical analysis of American literature. Among the writers discussed are Whitman, Hawthorne, Poe, Melville, Twain, and Faulkner. It is available in print at PS3.A47 or electronically.

A Handbook to Literature: A collection of defined literary terms, movements, and theories, this text is edited by William Harmon and C. Hugh Holman and is easy to use. It is available in print at PN41 .H355 2000.

Literary Research: A Guide to Reference Sources for the Study of Literature in English and Related Topics: This book, published in 1993, is helpful for locating other bibliographies for English and American literature by period. It also provides a list of related topics (music, science, art, etc.) that may also be useful. The book is edited by James Harner and is available in print at Z2011.H34 1993.

The Year's Work in English Studies: This bibliography lists and assesses the scholarly literary criticism published in a given year. The information is presented according to major literary periods, such as "American Literature to 1900" and can also be searched by author. It can be accessed at: ywes.oxfordjournals.org/

Also recommended for you:

Literary Terms (http://writingcenter.tamu.edu/Students/Handouts-Guides/Guides-(What-Are-You-Writing-)/Creative-Writing/Literary-Terms)

Analyzing Novels & Short Stories (http://writingcenter.tamu.edu/Students/Handouts-Guides/Guides-(What-Are-You-Writing-)/Academic-Writing/Analysis/Analyzing-Fiction)

Analyzing Plays (http://writingcenter.tamu.edu/Students/Handouts-Guides/Guides-(What-Are-You-Writing-)/Academic-Writing/Analysis/Analyzing-Plays)

Analyzing Poetry (http://writingcenter.tamu.edu/Students/Handouts-Guides/Guides-(What-Are-You-Writing-)/Academic-Writing/Analysis/Analyzing-Poetry)

Using Modern Language Association (MLA) Style

Learning Objectives

1. Identify the major components of a research paper written using MLA style.
2. Apply general Modern Language Association (MLA) style and formatting conventions in a research paper.

We have addressed American Psychological Association (APA) style, as well as the importance of giving credit where credit is due, so now let's turn our attention to the formatting and citation style of the Modern Language Association, known as MLA style.

MLA style is often used in the liberal arts and humanities. Like APA style, it provides a uniform framework for consistency across a document in several areas. MLA style provides a format for the manuscript text and parenthetical citations, or in-text citations. It also provides the framework for the works cited area for references at the end of the essay. MLA style emphasizes brevity and clarity. As a student writer, it is to your advantage to be familiar with both major styles, and this section will outline the main points of MLA as well as offer specific examples of commonly used references. Remember that your writing represents you in your absence. The correct use of a citation style demonstrates your attention to detail and ability to produce a scholarly work in an acceptable style, and it can help prevent the appearance or accusations of plagiarism.

If you are taking an English, art history, or music appreciation class, chances are that you will be asked to write an essay in MLA format. One common question goes something like "What's the difference?" referring to APA and MLA style, and it deserves our consideration. The liberal arts and humanities often reflect works of creativity that come from individual and group effort, but they may adapt, change, or build on previous creative works. The inspiration to create something new, from a song to a music video, may contain elements of previous works. Drawing on your fellow artists and authors is part of the creative process, and so is giving credit where credit is due.

A reader interested in your subject wants not only to read what you wrote but also to be aware of the works that you used to create it. Readers want to examine your sources to see if you know your subject, to see if you missed anything, or if you offer anything new and interesting. Your new or up-to-date sources may offer the reader additional insight on the subject being considered. It also demonstrates that you, as the author, are up-to-date on what is happening in the field or on the subject. Giving credit where it is due enhances your credibility, and the MLA style offers a clear format to use.

Uncredited work that is incorporated into your own writing is considered plagiarism. In the professional world, plagiarism results in loss of credibility and often compensation, including future opportunities. In a classroom setting, plagiarism results in a range of sanctions, from loss of a grade to expulsion from a school or university. In both professional and academic settings, the penalties are severe. MLA offers artists and authors a systematic style of reference, again giving credit where credit is due, to protect MLA users from accusations of plagiarism.

MLA style uses a citation in the body of the essay that links to the works cited page at the end. The in-text citation is offset with parentheses, clearly calling attention to itself for the reader. The reference to the author or title is like a signal to the reader that information was incorporated from a separate source. It also provides the reader with information to then turn to the works cited section of your essay (at the end) where they can find the complete reference. If you follow the MLA style, and indicate your source both in your essay and in the works cited section, you will prevent the possibility of plagiarism. If you follow the MLA guidelines, pay attention to detail, and clearly indicate your sources, then this approach to formatting and citation offers a proven way to demonstrate your respect for other authors and artists.

Five Reasons to Use MLA Style

1. To demonstrate your ability to present a professional, academic essay in the correct style

2. To gain credibility and authenticity for your work
3. To enhance the ability of the reader to locate information discussed in your essay
4. To give credit where credit is due and prevent plagiarism
5. To get a good grade or demonstrate excellence in your writing

Before we transition to specifics, please consider one word of caution: consistency. If you are instructed to use the MLA style and need to indicate a date, you have options. For example, you could use an international or a US style:

- **International style:** 18 May 1980 (day/month/year)
- **US style:** May 18, 1980 (month/day/year)

If you are going to the US style, be consistent in its use. You'll find you have the option on page 83 of the *MLA Handbook for Writers of Research Papers*, 7th edition. You have many options when writing in English as the language itself has several conventions, or acceptable ways of writing particular parts of speech or information.

You are welcome to look in the *MLA Handbook* and see there is one preferred style or convention (you will also find the answer at end of this section marked by an asterisk [*]). Now you may say to yourself that you won't write that term and it may be true, but you will come to a term or word that has more than one way it can be written. In that case, what convention is acceptable in MLA style? This is where the *MLA Handbook* serves as an invaluable resource. Again, your attention to detail and the professional presentation of your work are aspects of learning to write in an academic setting.

Now let's transition from a general discussion on the advantages of MLA style to what we are required to do to write a standard academic essay. We will first examine a general "to do" list, then review a few "do not" suggestions, and finally take a tour through a sample of MLA features. Links to sample MLA papers are located at the end of this section.

General MLA List

1. Use standard white paper (8.5 × 11 inches).
2. Double space the essay and quotes.
3. Use Times New Roman 12-point font.
4. Use one-inch margins on all sides
5. Indent paragraphs (five spaces or 1.5 inches).
6. Include consecutive page numbers in the upper-right corner.
7. Use italics to indicate a title, as in *Writing for Success*.
8. On the first page, place your name, course, date, and instructor's name in the upper-left corner.
9. On the first page, place the title centered on the page, with no bold or italics and all words capitalized.
10. On all pages, place the header, student's name + one space + page number, 1.5 inches from the top, aligned on the right.

Tip

Depending on your field of study, you may sometimes write research papers in either APA or MLA style. Recognize that each has its advantages and preferred use in fields and disciplines. Learn to write and reference in both styles with proficiency.

Title Block Format

You never get a second chance to make a first impression, and your title block (not a separate title page; just a section at the top of the first page) makes an impression on the reader. If correctly formatted with each element of information in its proper place, form, and format, it says to the reader that you mean business, that you are a professional, and that you take your work seriously, so it should, in turn, be seriously considered. Your title block in MLA style contributes to your credibility. Remember that your writing represents you in your absence, and the title block is the tailored suit or outfit that represents you best. That said, sometimes a separate title page is necessary, but it is best both to know how to properly format a title block or page in MLA style and to ask your instructor if it is included as part of the assignment.

Your name

Instructor

Course number

Date

Title of Paper

Paragraphs and Indentation

Make sure you indent five spaces (from the left margin). You'll see that the indent offsets the beginning of a new paragraph. We use paragraphs to express single ideas or topics that reinforce our central purpose or thesis statement. Paragraphs include topic sentences, supporting sentences, and conclusion or transitional sentences that link paragraphs together to support the main focus of the essay.

Tables and Illustrations

Place tables and illustrations as close as possible to the text they reinforce or complement. Here's an example of a table in MLA.

Table 1

Sales Figures by Year	Sales Amount ($)
2007	100,000
2008	125,000
2009	185,000
2010	215,000

As we can see in Table 1, we have experienced significant growth since 2008.

This example demonstrates that the words that you write and the tables, figures, illustrations, or images that you include should be next to each other in your paper.

Parenthetical Citations

You must cite your sources as you use them. In the same way that a table or figure should be located right next to the sentence that discusses it (see the previous example), parenthetical citations, or citations enclosed in parenthesis that appear in the text, are required. You need to cite all your information. If someone else wrote it, said it, drew it, demonstrated it, or otherwise expressed it, you need to cite it. The exception to this statement is common, widespread knowledge. For example, if you search online for MLA resources, and specifically MLA sample papers, you will find many similar discussions on MLA style. MLA is a style and cannot be copyrighted because it is a style, but the seventh edition of the *MLA Handbook* can be copyright protected.

If you reference a specific page in that handbook, you need to indicate it. If you write about a general MLA style issue that is commonly covered or addressed in multiple sources, you do not. When in doubt, reference the specific resource you used to write your essay.

Your in-text, or parenthetical, citations should do the following:

- Clearly indicate the specific sources also referenced in the works cited
- Specifically identify the location of the information that you used
- Keep the citation clear and concise, always confirming its accuracy

Works Cited Page

After the body of your paper comes the works cited page. It features the reference sources used in your essay. List the sources alphabetically by last name, or list them by title if the author is not known as is often the case of web-based articles. You will find links to examples of the works cited page in several of the sample MLA essays at the end of this section.

As a point of reference and comparison to our APA examples, let's examine the following three citations and the order of the information needed.

Citation Type	MLA Style	APA Style
Website	Author's Last Name, First Name. Title of the website. Publication Date. Name of Organization (if applicable). Date you accessed the website. <URL>.	Author's Last Name, First Initial. (Date of publication). Title of document. Retrieved from URL
Online article	Author's Last Name, First Name. "Title of Article." Title of the website. Date of publication. Organization that provides the website. Date you accessed the website.	Author's Last name, First Initial. (Date of publication). Title of article. *Title of Journal, Volume*(Issue). Retrieved from URL
Book	Author's Last Name, First Name. *Title of the Book*. Place of Publication: Publishing Company, Date of publication.	Author's Last Name, First Initial. (Date of publication). *Title of the book*. Place of Publication: Publishing Company.
Note: The items listed include proper punctuation and capitalization according to the style's guidelines.		

Exercise 1

In Chapter 13 "APA and MLA Documentation and Formatting", Section 13.1 "Formatting a Research Paper", you created a sample essay in APA style. After reviewing this section and exploring the resources linked at the end of the section (including California State University–Sacramento's clear example of a paper in MLA format), please convert your paper to MLA style using the formatting and citation guidelines. You may find it helpful to use online applications that quickly, easily, and at no cost convert your citations to MLA format.

Exercise 2

Please convert the APA-style citations to MLA style. You may find that online applications can quickly, easily, and at no cost convert your citations to MLA format. There are several websites and applications available free (or as a free trial) that will allow you to input the information and will produce a correct citation in the style of your choice. Consider these two sites:

- http://www.noodletools.com
- http://citationmachine.net

Hint: You may need access to the Internet to find any missing information required to correctly cite in MLA style. This demonstrates an important difference between APA and MLA style—the information provided to the reader.

	Sample Student Reference List in APA Style
1	Brent, D. A., Poling, K. D., & Goldstein, T. R. (2010). *Treating depressed and suicidal adolescents: A clinician's guide.* New York, NY: Guilford Press.
MLA	
2	Dewan, S. (2007, September 17). Using crayons to exorcise Katrina. *The New York Times.*Retrieved from http://www.nytimes.com/2007/09/17/arts/design/17ther.html
MLA	
3	Freud, S. (1955). Beyond the pleasure principle. In *The Complete Works of Sigmund Freud.* (Vol. XVII, pp. 3–66). London, England: Hogarth.
MLA	
4	Henley, D. (2007). Naming the enemy: An art therapy intervention for children with bipolar and comorbid disorders. *Art Therapy: Journal of the American Art Therapy Association, 24*(3), 104–110.
MLA	
5	Hutson, M. (2008). Art therapy: The healing arts. *Psychology Today.* Retrieved from http://www.psychologytoday.com/articles/200705/art-therapy-the-healing-arts
MLA	
6	Isis, P. D., Bus, J., Siegel, C. A., & Ventura, Y. (2010). Empowering students through creativity: Art therapy in Miami-Dade County Public Schools. *Art Therapy: Journal of the American Art Therapy Association, 27*(2), 56–61.
MLA	
7	Johnson, D. (1987). The role of the creative arts therapies in the diagnosis and treatment of psychological trauma. *The Arts in Psychotherapy, 14,* 7–13.
MLA	
8	Malchiodi, C. (2006). *Art therapy sourcebook*. New York, NY: McGraw-Hill.
MLA	
9	Markel, R. (Producer). (2010). *I'm an artist* [Motion picture]. United States: Red Pepper Films.
MLA	
10	Kelley, S. J. (1984). The use of art therapy with sexually abused children. *Journal of Psychosocial Nursing and Mental Health, 22*(12), 12–28.
MLA	
11	Pifalo, T. (2008). Why art therapy? *Darkness to light: Confronting child abuse with courage.* Retrieved from http://www.darkness2light.org/KnowAbout/articles_art_therapy.asp
MLA	
12	Rubin, J. A. (2005). *Child art therapy* (25th ed.). New York, NY: Wiley.
MLA	
13	Schimek, J. (1975). A critical re-examination of Freud's concept of unconscious mental representation. *International Review of Psychoanalysis, 2,* 171–187.
MLA	
14	Strauss, M. B. (1999). *No talk therapy for children and adolescents*. New York, NY: Norton.
MLA	
15	Thompson, T. (2008). *Freedom from meltdowns: Dr. Thompson's solutions for children with autism.* Baltimore, MD: Paul H. Brookes.
MLA	

Useful Sources of Examples of MLA Style

- Arizona State University Libraries offers an excellent resource with clear examples.
    - http://libguides.asu.edu/content.php?pid=122697&sid=1132964
- Purdue Online Writing Lab includes sample pages and works cited.
    - http://owl.english.purdue.edu/owl/resource/747/01
- California State University–Sacramento's Online Writing Lab has an excellent visual description and example of an MLA paper.
    - http://www.csus.edu/owl/index/mla/mla_format.htm
- SUNY offers an excellent, brief, side-by-side comparison of MLA and APA citations.
    - http://www.sunywcc.edu/LIBRARY/research/MLA_APA_08.03.10.pdf
- Cornell University Library provides comprehensive MLA information on its Citation Management website.
    - http://www.library.cornell.edu/resrch/citmanage/mla
- The University of Kansas Writing Center is an excellent resource.
    - http://www.writing.ku.edu/guides

* (a) is the correct answer to the question at the beginning of this section. The *MLA Handbook* prefers "twentieth century."

Key Takeaways

- MLA style is often used in the liberal arts and humanities.
- MLA style emphasizes brevity and clarity.
- A reader interested in your subject wants not only to read what you wrote but also to be informed of the works you used to create it.
- MLA style uses a citation in the body of the essay that refers to the works cited section at the end.
- If you follow MLA style, and indicate your source both in your essay and in the works cited section, you will prevent the possibility of plagiarism.

Works Cited Entries: What to Include

The Indian River State College Library pages have many useful pages covering MLA style and how to approach it. I like this page on what goes into a works cited entry for the way it reminds us that the entries have common elements we should remember. (http://irsc.libguides.com/mla/whattoinclude)

How not to Write the Introduction and Conclusion

Overview

The opening and closing of anything one writes become increasingly important with busy readers. The way a writers introduces the subject to readers could determine how they will approach the ideas or even if they will continue reading. The introduction of a research paper is especially important because research papers tend to be long and complex.

The Introduction

Your introduction should accomplish key goals:

- Grab attention. Open with a quote, fact, statistic, or short narrative.
- Convince readers that your paper is worth reading. Demonstrate the importance of your subject with details.
- Explain the basic context of your subject
- Narrow the topic to a specific thesis that clearly states your position

You may use the introduction to explain or justify research methods or address readers' objections.

The Conclusion

A conclusion should accomplish specific tasks:

- Bring the paper to an interesting, logical end
- End with a final fact, quote, or comment to provoke readers to accept your ideas and think about the topic on their own
- Reinforce the main points of the essay without unnecessary repetition
- Restate your thesis in a strategic spot where it will have the most effect on readers
- Speculate about future action

TRITE, CLICHED BEGINNINGS AND ENDINGS SEND MESSAGES

Remember, readers' memories are not very powerful. Remind them of the specific things they should take away from the reading of your essay. Just avoid saying "In conclusion, I will review _______ and ________," because this patterned ending sounds false. In fact, avoid every writing "In conclusion" to start a paragraph which is, obviously, the last!

Often, I mine the words for my introduction from the conclusion. By that point, I know more about what I have accomplished in those body paragraphs. I can copy and paste (and reword) my conclusion, which appears sharper than the original introduction. This process might work for you, and it's easy with the copy and paste commands. Then, go back and rewrite a conclusion, making sure it's not just parroting the wording of the introduction. Call this the Robin Hood Principle: Stealing from the rich to give to the poor.

Read aloud both your introduction and conclusion. Hear how they sound, and make sure they are of similar quality and length without seeming identical. Lastly, avoid "According to Dictionary.com, ______ is" or any "Society verbs ____________" constructions. ("Society views the media as bad.") Provable? Arguable?)

Using Sources: Blending Source Material with Your Own Work

When working with sources, many students worry they are simply regurgitating ideas that others formulated. That is why it is important for you to develop your own assertions, organize your findings so that your own ideas are still the thrust of the paper, and take care not to rely too much on any one source, or your paper's content might be controlled too heavily by that source.

In practical terms, some ways to develop and back up your assertions include:

Blend sources with your assertions. Organize your sources before and as you write so that they blend, even within paragraphs. Your paper—both globally and at the paragraph level—should reveal relationships among your sources, and should also reveal the relationships between your own ideas and those of your sources.

Write an original introduction and conclusion. As much as is practical, make the paper's introduction and conclusion your own ideas or your own synthesis of the ideas inherent in your research. Use sources minimally in your introduction and conclusion.

Open and close paragraphs with originality. In general, use the openings and closing of your paragraphs to reveal your work—"enclose" your sources among your assertions. At a minimum, create your own topic sentences and wrap-up sentences for paragraphs.

Use transparent rhetorical strategies. When appropriate, outwardly practice such rhetorical strategies as analysis, synthesis, comparison, contrast, summary, description, definition, hierarchical structure, evaluation, hypothesis, generalization, classification, and even narration. Prove to your reader that you are thinking as you write.

Also, you must clarify where your own ideas end and the cited information begins. Part of your job is to help your reader draw the line between these two things, often by the way you create context for the cited information. A phrase such as "A 1979 study revealed that . . ." is an obvious announcement of citation to come. Another recommended technique is the insertion of the author's name into the text to announce the beginning of your cited information. You may worry that you are not allowed to give the actual names of sources you have studied in the paper's text, but just the opposite is true. In fact, the more respectable a source you cite, the more impressed your reader is likely to be with your material while reading. If you note that the source is the NASA Science website or an article by Stephen Jay Gould or a recent edition of *The Wall Street Journal* right in your text, you offer your readers immediate context without their having to guess or flip to the references page to look up the source.

What follows is an excerpt from a political science paper that clearly and admirably draws the line between writer and cited information:

The above political upheaval illuminates the reasons behind the growing Iranian hatred of foreign interference; as a result of this hatred, three enduring geopolitical patterns have evolved in Iran, as noted by John Limbert. First . . .

Note how the writer begins by redefining her previous paragraph's topic (political upheaval), then connects this to Iran's hatred of foreign interference, then suggests a causal relationship and ties her ideas into John Limbert's analysis—thereby announcing that a synthesis of Limbert's work is coming. This writer's work also becomes more credible and meaningful because, right in the text, she announces the name of a person who is a recognized authority in the field. Even in this short excerpt, it is obvious that this writer is using proper citation and backing up her own assertions with confidence and style.

The Paragraph Body: Supporting Your Ideas

Whether the drafting of a paragraph begins with a main idea or whether that idea surfaces in the revision process, once you have that main idea, you'll want to make sure that the idea has enough support. The job of the paragraph body is to develop and support the topic. Here's one way that you might think about it:

• Topic sentence: what is the main claim of your paragraph; what is the most important idea that you want your readers to take away from this paragraph?
• Support in the form of evidence: how can you prove that your claim or idea is true (or important, or noteworthy, or relevant)?
• Support in the form of analysis or evaluation: what discussion can you provide that helps your readers see the connection between the evidence and your claim?
• Transition: how can you help your readers move from the idea you're currently discussing to the next idea presented? (For more specific discussion about transitions, see the following section on "Developing Relationships between Ideas").
For more on methods of development that can help you to develop and organize your ideas within paragraphs, see "Patterns of Organization and Methods of Development" later in this section of this text.

Types of support might include
• Reasons.
• Facts.
• Statistics.
• Quotations.
• Examples.

Now that we have a good idea what it means to develop support for the main ideas of your paragraphs, let's talk about how to make sure that those supporting details are solid and convincing.

Good vs. Weak Support

What questions will your readers have? What will they need to know? What makes for good supporting details? Why might readers consider some evidence to be weak?

If you're already developing paragraphs, it's likely that you already have a plan for your essay, at least at the most basic level. You know what your topic is, you might have a working thesis, and you probably have at least a couple of supporting ideas in mind that will further develop and support your thesis.

So imagine you're developing a paragraph on one of these supporting ideas and you need to make sure that the support that you develop for this idea is solid. Considering some of the points about understanding and appealing to your audience (from the Audience and Purpose and the Prewriting sections of this text) can also be helpful in determining what your readers will consider good support and what they'll consider to be weak. Here are some tips on what to strive for and what to avoid when it comes to supporting details.

Good support
• Is relevant and focused (sticks to the point).
• Is well developed.
• Provides sufficient detail.

- Is vivid and descriptive.
- Is well organized.
- Is coherent and consistent.
- Highlights key terms and ideas.

Weak Support
- Lacks a clear connection to the point that it's meant to support.
- Lacks development.
- Lacks detail or gives too much detail.
- Is vague and imprecise.
- Lacks organization.
- Seems disjointed (ideas don't clearly relate to each other).
- Lacks emphasis of key terms and ideas.

Breaking, Combining, or Beginning New Paragraphs

Like sentence length, paragraph length varies. There is no single ideal length for "the perfect paragraph." There are some general guidelines, however. Some writing handbooks or resources suggest that a paragraph should be at least three or four sentences; others suggest that 100 to 200 words is a good target to shoot for. In academic writing, paragraphs tend to be longer, while in less formal or less complex writing, such as in a newspaper, paragraphs tend to be much shorter. Two-thirds to three-fourths of a page is usually a good target length for paragraphs at your current level of college writing. If your readers can't see a paragraph break on the page, they might wonder if the paragraph is ever going to end or they might lose interest.

The most important thing to keep in mind here is that the amount of space needed to develop one idea will likely be different than the amount of space needed to develop another. So when is a paragraph complete? The answer is, when it's fully developed. The guidelines above for providing good support should help.

Some signals that it's time to end a paragraph and start a new one include that
- You're ready to begin developing a new idea.
- You want to emphasize a point by setting it apart.
- You're getting ready to continue discussing the same idea but in a different way (e.g. shifting from comparison to contrast).
- You notice that your current paragraph is getting too long (more than three-fourths of a page or so), and you think your writers will need a visual break.

Some signals that you may want to combine paragraphs include that
- You notice that some of your paragraphs appear to be short and choppy.
- You have multiple paragraphs on the same topic.
- You have undeveloped material that needs to be united under a clear topic.

Finally, paragraph number is a lot like paragraph length. You may have been asked in the past to write a five paragraph essay. There's nothing inherently wrong with a five-paragraph essay, but just like sentence length and paragraph length, the number of paragraphs in an essay depends upon what's needed to get the job done. There's really no way to know that until you start writing. So try not to worry too much about the proper length and number of things. Just start writing and see where the essay and the paragraphs take you. There will be plenty of time to sort out the organization in the revision process. You're not trying to fit pegs into holes here. You're letting your ideas unfold. Give yourself—and them—the space to let that happen.

Developing Relationships Between Ideas

So you have a main idea, and you have supporting ideas, but how can you be sure that your readers will understand the relationships between them? How are the ideas tied to each other? One way to emphasize these relationships is through the use of clear transitions between ideas. Like every other part of your essay, transitions have a job to do. They form logical connections between the ideas presented in an essay or paragraph, and they give readers clues that reveal how you want them to think about (process, organize, or use) the topics presented.

Why are Transitions Important?

Transitions signal the order of ideas, highlight relationships, unify concepts, and let readers know what's coming next or remind them about what's already been covered. When instructors or peers comment that your writing is choppy, abrupt, or needs to "flow better," those are some signals that you might need to work on building some better transitions into your writing. If a reader comments that she's not sure how something relates to your thesis or main idea, a transition is probably the right tool for the job.

When Is the Right Time to Build in Transitions?

There's no right answer to this question. Sometimes transitions occur spontaneously, but just as often (or maybe even more often) good transitions are developed in revision. While drafting, we often write what we think, sometimes without much reflection about how the ideas fit together or relate to one another. If your thought process jumps around a lot (and that's okay), it's more likely that you will need to pay careful attention to reorganization and to providing solid transitions as you revise.

When you're working on building transitions into an essay, consider the essay's overall organization. Consider using reverse outlining and other organizational strategies presented in this text to identify key ideas in your essay and to get a clearer look at how the ideas can be best organized. This can help you determine where transitions are needed.

Let's take some time to consider the importance of transitions at the sentence level and transitions between paragraphs.

Sentence-Level Transitions

Transitions between sentences often use "connecting words" to emphasize relationships between one sentence and another. A friend and coworker suggests the "something old something new" approach, meaning that the idea behind a transition is to introduce something new while connecting it to something old from an earlier point in the essay or paragraph. Here are some examples of ways that writers use connecting words (highlighted with red text and italicized) to show connections between ideas in adjacent sentences:

To Show Similarity
When I was growing up, my mother taught me to say "please" and "thank you" as one small way that I could show appreciation and respect for others. In the same way, I have tried to impress the importance of manners onmy own children.
Other connecting words that show similarity include also, similarly, and likewise.

To Show Contrast
Some scientists take the existence of black holes for granted; however, in 2014, a physicist at the University of North Carolina claimed to have mathematically proven that they do not exist.
Other connecting words that show contrast include in spite of, on the other hand, in contrast, and yet.

To Exemplify
The cost of college tuition is higher than ever, so students are becoming increasingly motivated to keep costs as low as possible. For example, a rising number of students are signing up to spend their first two years at a less costly community college before transferring to a more expensive four-year school to finish their degrees.
Other connecting words that show example include for instance, specifically, and to illustrate.

To Show Cause and Effect
Where previously painters had to grind and mix their own dry pigments with linseed oil inside their studios, in the 1840s, new innovations in pigments allowed paints to be premixed in tubes. Consequently, this new technology facilitated the practice of painting outdoors and was a crucial tool for impressionist painters, such as Monet, Cezanne, Renoir, and Cassatt.
Other connecting words that show cause and effect include therefore, so, and thus.

To Show Additional Support
When choosing a good trail bike, experts recommend 120–140 millimeters of suspension travel; that's the amount that the frame or fork is able to flex or compress. Additionally, they recommend a 67–69 degree head-tube angle, as a steeper head-tube angle allows for faster turning and climbing.
Other connecting words that show additional support include also, besides, equally important, and in addition.

A Word of Caution

Single-word or short-phrase transitions can be helpful to signal a shift in ideas within a paragraph, rather than between paragraphs (see the discussion below about transitions between paragraphs). But it's also important to understand that these types of transitions shouldn't be frequent within a paragraph. As with anything else that happens in your writing, they should be used when they feel natural and feel like the right choice. Here are some examples to help you see the difference between transitions that feel like they occur naturally and transitions that seem forced and make the paragraph awkward to read:

Too Many Transitions: The Impressionist painters of the late 19th century are well known for their visible brush strokes, for their ability to convey a realistic sense of light, and for their everyday subjects portrayed in outdoor settings. In spite of this fact, many casual admirers of their work are unaware of the scientific innovations that made it possible this movement in art to take place. Then, In 1841, an American painter named John Rand invented the collapsible paint tube. To illustrate the importance of this invention, pigments previously had to be ground and mixed in a fairly complex process that made it difficult for artists to travel with them. For example, the mixtures were commonly stored in pieces of pig bladder to keep the paint from drying out. In addition, when working with their palettes, painters had to puncture the bladder, squeeze out some paint, and then mend the bladder again to keep the rest of the paint mixture from drying out. Thus, Rand's collapsible tube freed the painters from these cumbersome and messy processes, allowing artists to be more mobile and to paint in the open air.

Subtle Transitions that Aid Reader Understanding: The Impressionist painters of the late 19th century are well known for their visible brush strokes, for their ability to convey a realistic sense of light, for their everyday subjects portrayed in outdoor settings. However, many casual admirers of their work are unaware of the scientific innovations that made it possible for this movement in art to take place. In 1841, an American painter named John Rand invented the collapsible paint tube. Before this invention, pigments had to be ground and mixed in a fairly complex process that made it difficult for artists to travel with them. The mixtures were commonly stored in pieces of pig bladder to keep the paint from drying out. When working with their palettes, painters had to puncture the bladder, squeeze out some paint, and then mend the bladder again to keep the rest of the paint mixture from drying out. Rand's collapsible tube freed the painters from these cumbersome and messy processes, allowing artists to be more mobile and to paint in the open air.

Transitions between Paragraphs and Sections

It's important to consider how to emphasize the relationships not just between sentences but also between paragraphs in your essay. Here are a few strategies to help you show your readers how the main ideas of your paragraphs relate to each other and also to your thesis.

Use Signposts

Signposts are words or phrases that indicate where you are in the process of organizing an idea; for example, signposts might indicate that you are introducing a new concept, that you are summarizing an idea, or that you are concluding your thoughts. Some of the most common signposts include words and phrases like first, then, next, finally, in sum, and in conclusion. Be careful not to overuse these types of transitions in your writing. Your readers will quickly find them tiring or too obvious. Instead, think of more creative ways to let your readers know where they are situated within the ideas presented in your essay. You might say, "The first problem with this practice is..." Or you might say, "The next thing to consider is..." Or you might say, "Some final thoughts about this topic are...."

Use Forward-Looking Sentences at the End of Paragraphs

Sometimes, as you conclude a paragraph, you might want to give your readers a hint about what's coming next. For example, imagine that you're writing an essay about the benefits of trees to the environment and you've just wrapped up a paragraph about how trees absorb pollutants and provide oxygen. You might conclude with a forward-looking sentence like this: "Trees benefits to local air quality are important, but surely they have more to offer our communities than clean air." This might conclude a paragraph (or series of paragraphs) and then prepare your readers for additional paragraphs to come that cover the topics of trees' shade value and ability to slow water evaporation on hot summer days. This transitional strategy can be tricky to employ smoothly. Make sure that the conclusion of your paragraph doesn't sound like you're leaving your readers hanging with the introduction of a completely new or unrelated topic.

Use Backward-Looking Sentences at the Beginning of Paragraphs

Rather than concluding a paragraph by looking forward, you might instead begin a paragraph by looking back. Continuing with the example above of an essay about the value of trees, let's think about how we might begin a new paragraph or section by first taking a moment to look back. Maybe you just concluded a paragraph on the topic of trees' ability to decrease soil erosion and you're getting ready to talk about how they provide habitats for urban wildlife. Beginning the opening of a new paragraph or section of the essay with a backward-looking transition might look something like this: "While their benefits to soil and water conservation are great, the value that trees provide to our urban wildlife also cannot be overlooked."

Evaluate Transitions for Predictability or Conspicuousness

Finally, the most important thing about transitions is that you don't want them to become repetitive or too obvious. Reading your draft aloud is a great revision strategy for so many reasons, and revising your essay for transitions is no exception to this rule. If you read your essay aloud, you're likely to hear the areas that sound choppy or abrupt. This can help you make note of areas where transitions need to be added. Repetition is another problem that can be easier to spot if you read your essay aloud. If you notice yourself using the same transitions over and over again, take time to find some alternatives. And if the transitions frequently stand out as you read aloud, you may want to see if you can find some subtler strategies.

How Might I Avoid Letting Source Use Take Over?

Q: How can I Avoid Letting the Paper get Taken over by Sources?

A: This is a common issue. We think we know what we are classifying or writing about, but once we begin drafting and using others' ideas, the focus seems to get lost.

Q: In the typical body paragraph, how much should I write?

A: Over 75% should be from you. Realize that summaries and paraphrases, though in your words, aren't yours. They're from the sources. So, we have this tough standard of having to write a lot of commentary. Without using "you" or "I," you should be able to handle this at the ENG 101 level. Read on!

- Integrating supporting sources without offering them chances to take over the paper is a huge issue. We'll confront it for the rest of our writing lives. I can offer you some suggestions. They are in no particular order. Please read this carefully, though, as it might help you avoid either plagiarism or an extremely low grade. I'll follow up on this with other postings, too.
- Freewrite what you think about the **topic** as soon as you decide on it. When you outline the paper's reasons, be sure to write out what you think. (I like to hand write what I think and then type it. Typing allows me to add things and to think about them. At this point, at least I have something of my own, though I know it'll change significantly.)
- Force yourself to write out **topic sentences** that are directly related to the thesis.
- Let your **thesis** change after you're in the midpoint of the essay. It's smart not to try and fit the paper to one sentence; it's easier by far to fit one sentence to the paper you write than *vice versa*! Refine your working thesis repeatedly. It's a messy process and it should be!
- Support needs to remain in support. Condition yourself to write two or more sentences of commentary for every piece of source information. You know you must cite summaries, paraphrases, and quotes, right? To do less would be to plagiarize. But, once we do this so carefully, we end up with paragraphs taken over by sources. Unless you provide commentary on these summaries, paraphrases, or quotes, you are not writing actively. You can create integrated paragraphs by handling the material, saying things about it.

Q: **What might I do after the citation**?

A: Question the source information, extend it, offer examples examples, respond by adopting any of various tones toward it, relate it to the topic sentence, relate to thesis, or relate it to what happens next. A power move is to show another example and then compare/contrast, discuss the examples (analysis, synthesis, evaluation skills). If you take a tone toward the material, you might be "accepting," "skeptical," "in agreement with" it. These are attitude words. It's okay to have attitude as long as you don't sound as if you are speaking or writing a newspaper editorial! In fact, avoid sounding like you're chatting (which is something I am doing here.)

- **Treat the citations as excuses for you to argue something**. That "something" is up to you, but realize that readers expect your commentary to matter more than the cited information. Play the game, but realize that in college, these rules are radically different from what one could get away with in high school. (You are doing well with responses to the photos and essays, so do that some sort of logical, detailed thinking after citations.)
- If good things must occur after citations, they also must happen before the citations. Review the handbook and my information about signal phrases. Your job is to establish the context of what's being said and why it matters. You handle this with exact verbs like "contends," "refutes," "suggests," "defends," rather than blah verbs like "is" or "says." We call this setup a **signal phrase.** The signal phrase introduces a source. Use signal phrases to signal a shift from your words to theirs. This is part of a well-integrated paragraph.
- Where? Why should I care? When? Writer's credentials? Why does it matter? Establish that credibility.

- **Save author for signal phrase** if you have no page to cite. For website and database sources, no page number goes into parentheses, so you'd better save the author for the signal phrase.
- Offer enough examples and logical discussion to take over those paragraphs that are in danger of being run by sources.
- Don't start or end paragraphs with source material. I say this because sources take over if they begin or end. (That's not an absolute rule, but you recognize its practicality.
- Readers are easily distracted. After a citation, it is okay to restate the paraphrase's meaning.
- Writers hurt their chances at success with topic sentences that don't get followed, paragraph endings that are vague, and a lack of transitions. You know that people notice the beginnings and endings the most, so be sure these are excellent. Transition smoothly from idea to idea, both within sentences and between paragraphs. (Many writers think well but cannot start sentences at all well. Be sure you don't fit that category.)
- Read your work aloud with an "ear toward" hearing the transitions from you to the source and back. If there are big chunks of source use, you must break up those and provide sufficient commentary. That's where that general "25% or more yours" rule fits in, since you can break up paragraphs and offer sufficient commentary to regain control.

Remember that good readers want to be able to appreciate what you bring to the discussion.

Checklist: Using Quotations Effectively

Checklist: Using Quotations Effectively

Before you include a quotation in your essay, ask yourself:

Which point of mine does the quotation support?
Why should the passage be quoted rather than paraphrased or summarized?
What do my readers need to know about the quotation's author?

As you integrate quotations into your draft, ask yourself:

- Have I sufficiently introduced the quotation with a phrase or sentence?
- Will my readers know whom I am quoting and why?
- Does the quotation fit smoothly into my own sentence?

As you revise your work, ask yourself:

- Have I strung together too many quotations?
- Have I used long quotations sparingly?
- Have I used quotation marks properly and documented each quote?

About the Author

This is the thirteenth OER text I have created.

Josh Dickinson is an Associate Professor of English at Jefferson Community College in Watertown, NY. He teaches English and Education courses with a focus upon American Literature, Mythology, Native American Literature, and non-Western Literature. Josh attended SUNY Jefferson, SUNY Potsdam (BA), Syracuse University (MA), and Colgate University (MAT).

Josh also supervises Jefferson's OER offerings as well as EDGE (concurrent enrollment) English courses at sixteen high school and BOCES sites.

He enjoys participating in the National Novel Writing Month contest each November, having completed eleven novel drafts.

Josh has officiated high school soccer matches for 28 years and supports pro teams Tottenham Hotspur, FC Barcelona, and Borussia Dortmund.

At the Canadian Museum of History, Ottawa: Go Habs, Go!